Labour, Employment and Economic Growth in India

T0304790

Edited by
K. V. Ramaswamy

CAMBRIDGE
UNIVERSITY PRESS

Shaftesbury Road, Cambridge CB2 8EA, United Kingdom

One Liberty Plaza, 20th Floor, New York, NY 10006, USA

477 Williamstown Road, Port Melbourne, VIC 3207, Australia

314–321, 3rd Floor, Plot 3, Splendor Forum, Jasola District Centre, New Delhi – 110025, India

103 Penang Road, #05–06/07, Visioncrest Commercial, Singapore 238467

Cambridge University Press in part of Cambridge University Press & Assessment,
a department of the University of Cambridge.

We share the University's mission to contribute to society through the pursuit of
education, learning and research at the highest international levels of excellence.

www.cambridge.org
Information on this title: www.cambridge.org/9781107096806

First published 2015

A catalogue record for this publication is available from the British Library

Library of Congress Cataloging-in-Publication data
Labour, employment and economic growth : the Indian experience / edited by
K.V.Ramaswamy.
pages cm
Includes bibliographical references and index.
Summary: "Discusses some key aspects in the interrelated areas of
economic development, employment and structural change"– Provided by
publisher.
ISBN 978-1-107-09680-6 (hardback)
1. Labor supply–India. 2. Labor market–India. 3. Economic
development–India. I. Ramaswamy, K. V., editor.
HD5819.L295 2015
331.10954–dc23
2014045888

ISBN   978-1-107-09680-6   Hardback

For

Professor K. L. Krishna

and

In memory of

Professor D. U. Sastry

Contents

List of Tables and Figures

Tables

Boxes

Appendix Tables and Figures

Preface

This volume presents an analysis of India's development experience in the sphere of labour, employment and economic growth in the recent past. Labour and employment issues have been central to India's growth and development debate in the 1980s through the 2000s. The economic policy debate in this area has been rather narrow, often confined to issues of jobless growth in the formal manufacturing sector, constraint of specific labour laws, informalization of employment relationships and information technology services sector growth. Authors in this volume have extended the boundaries of this debate in a variety of ways by undertaking a fairly detailed analysis of selected issues. Each author has approached the selected topic differently but consistent with the broad theme of the volume. They have used reliable data sets over time to uncover many quantitative dimensions of employment growth, structural change, population ageing, worker status (job quality), intensity of labour-use, gender discrimination and impact of labour laws and regulation. Some authors have pursued qualitative analysis like re-examining the legal definition of industrial worker through the lens of economic theory; how judiciary (Supreme Court of India) has interpreted labour laws and workers' protection in the years of economic liberalization. Their separate contributions read together I believe make a positive contribution to the existing empirical literature on growth and employment in India. The issues investigated are highly contemporary, live and are expected to challenge the evolution of economic policy in the immediate future.

I sincerely hope this volume will appeal to those in the area of academic research and as well as non-academic community of readers interested in the deep issue of growth and employment. Selected papers from this volume can be used as supplementary readings in any graduate course in Indian economy, development economics and policy and labour markets in developing countries.

Papers in this volume were first presented at a seminar held at Indira Gandhi Institute of Development Research (IGIDR) in Mumbai on 6–7 September 2013 on the occasion of Silver Jubilee Year of IGIDR. I am indebted to my colleagues at IGIDR, Dr R. Nagaraj and Dr Rupayan Pal, for their initial support in organizing this seminar. I owe special thanks to Professor T. S. Papola, Professor K. P. Kannan, Dr Sandip Sarkar and Dr G. Manjunath (Joint Labour Commissioner, Government of Karnataka) among others who participated and shared their views. I am thankful to Vikash Vaibhav, PhD student at IGIDR for his assistance in my editorial tasks. My gratitude is due to anonymous external referees commissioned by Cambridge University Press of all the papers for their valuable inputs and encouraging comments. I am grateful to all the contributors of different chapters for their prompt responses to my queries and repeated emails that made the task of editing this book hassle free and a learning process.

I am grateful to IGIDR Director Dr S. Mahendra Dev for his academic support and encouragement in bringing out this edited volume.

I sincerely thank Dhiraj Pandey, economics commissioning editor at Cambridge University Press (CUP), for his assistance. His readiness to answer all my queries and doubts was a big relief and reduced possible editorial delays. I wish to thank Ranjini Majumdar, production editor at CUP, for her editorial efforts that ensured excellent production of this book that involved the difficult task of handling manuscripts of different styles and formats.

Part 1

Economic Growth
and
Employment

1

Introduction and Review of Issues

K. V. Ramaswamy

India's transition to an economy capable of high growth in the years since 1980 has been of global interest, discussion and research. The metaphor of an elephant to describe Indian economy muddling through gave way to that of a tiger uncaged in the 1990s.[1] The Gross Domestic Product (GDP) per capita grew annually by an average of 1.2 per cent in the 1960s and 1970s but this growth rate changed to an average of 3.5 per cent in the 1980s, 3.7 per cent in the 1990s and 5.5 per cent in the 2000s.[2] India has transformed itself to be counted among the fastest growing economies in the world with an average GDP per capita growth rate of 3.7 per cent in the years 1980 to 2004.[3] In terms of GDP growth performance alone one finds that Indian economy's average annual growth rate was 3.5 per cent during 1951–82 (euphemistically called the Hindu Rate of Growth) that increased to 5.4 per cent in the next two decades (1983–99) followed by a growth rate of above 7 per cent in the 2000s. The causes and outcomes of this economic transformation have been the subject of research and analysis in recent years.[4] A perceptive analytical assessment of the evidence and factors driving change is available in Kotwal, Ramaswami and Wadhwa (2011). The economic policy reform of 1991 has played an important role in driving this growth but other pre-existing factors have also influenced the pattern of development (Kochhar, *et al.*, 2006). First and perhaps the foremost feature of India's growth experience is that it is led by services sector unlike in other countries of East Asia and China. In the broader context of economic development and structural change, the observed sequence was that manufacturing followed agriculture while the service sector became prominent only at later stage. India's experience appeared to be different with the share of services sector in GDP sharply going up in the 1990s, beginning with a share of 43 per cent in 1990–91, to reach a high share of 57 per cent in 2009–10. This rapid rise in the share of services has taken place at lower levels of per capita income when compared to presently advanced countries and other Asian economies. In 1895, the share of services in the UK was about 53 per cent comparable to India in 2004 but the level of GDP per capita was 4,100 international dollars (at 1990 prices)[5] compared to 2,278 dollars in India in 2004. Similarly, in Germany the share of services was 53 per cent during 1890–99 with an average per capita GDP of 6000 dollars and came down to 38 per cent by the end of the period. In the case of Japan, services accounted for 48 per cent during 1933–37 and declined to 42 per cent by 1942. The GDP per capita of Japan increased to 2,700 dollars in 1942 from 2,200 dollars in 1937. The upshot is that at similar stages of development India had a larger share of services in GDP. If one takes another fast growing comparable developing country like Malaysia it may be found that the share of services was 49 per cent in 2005 with a per capita GDP level of 9,000 dollars. By 2005, India's per capita GDP was about 2,400 dollars but with a services share of 54 per cent.[6] The flip side of this structural development is that of premature deindustrialization (to borrow the term used by Dani Rodrik). In developed countries like the US (in 1953), Britain (in 1961), Germany (1970) and Sweden (in 1961) manufacturing's share of employment peaked (more than 30 per cent) when their per capita GDP levels were $9,000–$11,000 and then deindustrialization began with the decline of manufacturing sector. The developing countries like Brazil, China and India seem to exhibit a contrasting experience. Their employment shares have been observed to shrink while per capita GDP levels have been in the range $2000–$5000 (at 1990 prices, Rodrik, 2013a).

In this background, the emphasis of chapters in this volume is on the challenge of structural transformation and employment growth that India faces today. The challenge is how to ensure movement of labour resources in the economy to sectors and activities of higher productivity. Employment outcomes of economic growth are crucial for poverty reduction and inclusive growth as growth effects are transmitted through the labour market.[7] A look at some aggregate statistics will reveal the importance of the issue and the severity of India's employment problem. India has a population of 1.227 billion of which 472 million are employed.[8] A redeeming development is that population growth rate shows a significant slowdown from 1.97 per cent per annum in the decade of 1991–2001 to 1.64 per cent per annum in the decade of 2001–11. The reduction in the population growth rate is expected to shift the population away from children in the 0–14 age group towards the prime working age group

(15–59) raising the rate of growth of labour force above the population growth rate.[9] If India could provide productive employment to this larger labour force then this will raise the GDP growth rate resulting in demographic dividend. Population and work force projections by the World Bank, based on United Nations data, indicate that India needs to create 10 million new jobs annually for the next 10 years to absorb the additions to the working age population. This estimate is true even if one argues that not everyone entering the working age will be seeking jobs as many of them would be in educational institutions. The severity of the problem can be underlined by noting that the Indian economy has created only 2.5 million jobs per year during the last seven years (2005–12).[10]

What are the distinctive features of Indian growth experience particularly in the sphere of labour and employment during recent years of growth? A major issue has been that of labour market outcomes. The high share of agriculture in employment (47.5 per cent in 2012 compared to 68.2 per cent in 1982–83) has been the dominant structural characteristic of Indian economy and it has not changed much over the last three decades. Why has India's growth process not resulted in substantial labour absorption in the non-agricultural sector comparable to East Asian countries and China that have experienced similar high growth? What hinders manufacturing sector growth and employment in particular? This is a recurring question in the Indian development policy debate on employment and growth in recent years.[11]

What has been the impact of this growth transition on labour and employment conditions in the Indian economy? Has it involved or changed the structure of employment distribution among agriculture, industry and services? Has growth drawn labour out of agriculture â la Lewis? What are the challenges of demographic change in the Indian context? Will growth create equal opportunities for men and women or does gender discrimination work against expected benefits of growth? Do labour laws and regulations adversely impact size expansion of firms and job creation? How does one view the legal definition of workers through the lens of economic theory of the firm? Has there been a perspective change in the labour jurisprudence of the Supreme Court of India in recent years? This volume explores these key questions in the interrelated areas of economic growth, structural change, and employment and labour laws. Some of these issues are often not well understood or discussed only with respect to specific sectors like registered manufacturing or explored in insufficient detail in the existing literature on growth and employment in India. Few illustrative examples may be instructive. In recent years, a popular perception is that economic growth in India has been jobless with no growth in formal manufacturing employment (widespread informalization and unorganized sector growth); services-led growth is a recent phenomenon, services revolution is driven by software services (information technology [IT] and IT-enabled services) only, little employment opportunities are available for rural women in India and withdrawal of rural females from labour market is due to lack of job opportunities, wage inequality among men and women is the dominant form of discrimination against women workers, employment conditions have worsened and *de facto* flexibility is sufficiently high to accommodate market-oriented growth, and the judiciary and courts have become 'anti workers' among others. All these are important empirical propositions that require careful scrutiny and analysis with consistent data. The objective of studies in this volume is to contribute and extend our understanding of these issues.

The volume is organized in two parts. In part one there are six chapters, excluding this introduction, that discuss issues related to economic growth, structural change and employment in India. They lay out in fair detail the different dimensions of the labour market and employment in the context of economic transformation in India. They cover issues related to growth and composition of workforce, services sector growth, inter-sector differences in labour productivity and its impact on poverty, age structure transition and demographic dividend, and labour intensity in Indian manufacturing. It ends with a chapter on gender discrimination in Indian manufacturing. In part two the issues related to employment and labour law are investigated. The four chapters in part two are a mix of analytical, econometric and descriptive analysis of labour regulations, legal definitions and India's Supreme Court judgements.

In chapter 2, Jayan Jose Thomas presents an overview of recent developments in the labour market and employment growth in India mainly during the 2000s. He uses the results of the quinquennial surveys of employment and unemployment (EUS or Employment and Unemployment Survey) conducted by the National Sample Survey Organization (NSSO) and his data covers the latest NSS large-scale survey results (68th Round in 2011–12). A popular perception is that of jobless growth in India during the second half of 2000s. This perception is driven by the NSSO survey results that showed that employment increased by 4.7 million (less than 1 million per year) between 2004–05 and 2009–10 in contrast to a gain of 59.4 million between 1999–2000 and 2004–

05. A closer look revealed that generation of non-agricultural employment in India was at the rate of 8.4 million a year between 1999–2000 and 2004–05, which slowed down to 5 million a year between 2004–05 and 2009–10, but accelerated again to 11.5 million a year between 2009–10 and 2011–12. In this sense, there is no justification to characterize Indian growth since mid-2000s as jobless. However, Thomas argues that the slowdown of employment in the second half of 2000s is due to structural change in the economy. Two elements of this structural change are: (1) fall in agricultural workforce; and (2) sharp rise in the student population ratio (SPR). He finds that the SPR among rural males and females (age group 15–19) increased by 20 percentage points and by 13 percentage points among urban males and females between 2004–05 and 2011–12. The future labour force in India will be more educated and productive. Equal and perhaps of more significance is the first element.[12] For the first time the total agricultural workforce in India is found to have declined in absolute terms by 20.4 million between 2004–05 and 2009–10. This is in contrast to an increase of 17.4 million between 1999–2000 and 2004–05. He points out that a majority of those who joined the workforce in the first half of 2000s were self-employed rural women who perhaps moved back to their household when income earning opportunities improved for male members of the family in rural areas in the second half of the 2000s. Thomas adduces to evidence of better rural economic conditions in terms of real wages of rural males and consumption expenditure in the second half of 2000s. Notice that agricultural GDP was increasing at 3.9 per cent per annum during the same period. It is pertinent in this context to note that the sharp decline in female workforce (close to 21 million) during 2004–05 to 2009–10 is responsible for the meagre increase in total workforce during the same period. This largely reflects, as observed in another important study, a withdrawal of unpaid helpers (self-employed rural females) and among them those who were in the workforce only in a subsidiary status (Sundaram, 2013). In his analysis of non-agricultural employment, Thomas brings out a striking fact that, during 2004–05 and 2011–12, the construction sector accounted for half of the incremental non-agricultural employment generated in India and all of the employment in rural areas. The contribution of construction sector to GDP did not increase much compared to first half of the 2000s. The obvious conclusion is that the construction sector created only low productivity jobs. Thomas argues that employment opportunities for women in India are inadequate and India's record has been dismal with respect to participation of women in labour force. He finds that the proportion of rural and urban females attending to

'domestic duties only' has increased in 2000s and rightly observes that this is the other side of the low female labour participation rates in India. It may be noted that there is a U-shaped relationship between female labour participation rate and economic development and it is well supported by econometric evidence (Mammen and Paxson, 2000). Economic development initially moves women out of the labour force because labour market opportunities for men increase and because of social barriers or norms against women taking up paid work. India is no exception. This situation changes as education levels of women rise with economic development and women move back into labour force.[13] This overview of labour market changes in 2000s by Thomas sets the stage for other chapters in the volume.

In chapter 3, Ajit Ghose presents an empirical analysis of India's experience of services-led growth and the associated employment and labour market developments. He conducts the analysis by comparing performance in two sub-periods: 1981–2000 and 2000–10. The analysis brings in experiences of three selected comparator countries namely, China, Indonesia and Thailand to improve one's understanding of the issues. First, Ghose shows that growth in India has always been services-led except during 1951–82 when services grew at a slower rate than industry. Economic reforms initiated since 1991 merely strengthened the pre-existing tendency and did not cause new services-led economy. A simple regression analysis based on data for a selected sample of developing countries shows that the share of services in GDP in India is on average in line with international experience.[14] What is different about India is the exceptionally low share of industry in GDP. In other words, industry and manufacturing in particular has been marginalized in the growth process by the rise of services. At the same time, the employment share of services turns out to be far lower than that predicted by the average international experience. In short, the employment intensity of services in India is exceptionally low. Second, Ghose makes a contribution to the literature by his disaggregated analysis in terms of organized and unorganized segments within the three types of services: traditional, modern and social services. He finds that the services sector had become dominant in both organized and unorganized parts of the economy by 2010. Social services (read largely government services) were the most important contributor to services growth in the organized sector during 1981–2000, but the modern services replaced it in 2000s. The acceleration in the modern services was driven by business services dominated by software services in the organized segment and communication services (read mobile phone services) in the unorganized segment. Ghose's analysis establishes that growth was driven largely by non–traded services and by domestic demand in both periods. Export of software services constituted less than 6 per cent of services output in 2010. The upshot of the analysis is that the role of software services that earned India its sobriquet 'back-office' of the world was rather small in the making of 'services revolution' of India. Third, Ghose finds rather surprisingly that employment intensity of services growth was actually higher than that of manufacturing in both periods. He measures employment intensity by the ratio of employment growth to output growth (often wrongly called employment elasticity of output[15]) and measures employment by the number of persons in the age group 15–59 who reported being gainfully employed for a major part of the reference year (majority time criterion) in the Indian surveys. This idea enables him to focus on core workers in the economy and develop a better understanding of the employment effects of services-led growth in India. Contrary to the widely held belief that services sector growth has been 'jobless', Ghose shows that services sector contribution to employment growth in India is higher than manufacturing in 2000s relative to 1983–2000. However, services created more jobs for high-skilled workers and less number of jobs for low-skilled workers relative to manufacturing in 2000s. Fourth, he draws attention to the often overlooked fact that India's past policies have led to a strange situation wherein the organized sector has comparative advantage in capital and skill-intensive activities in contrast to the economy-wide factor endowments. India's premature services-led growth has been essentially an outcome of its economic and educational (read tertiary education) policies in the past. Ghose further argues that employment conditions in the Indian economy have improved over the years because employment in the organized sector as well as regular-formal employment grew at a faster rate during 2000s.[16] Finally he concludes by emphasizing the importance of the manufacturing sector for generating demand for low-skilled labour and advocates removal of policy biases against manufacturing. My summary does not do justice to this highly perceptive paper by Ajit Ghose.

How to make growth more pro-poor in labour abundant economies like India is a challenge. In chapter 4, Hasan, Lamba and Sengupta (HLS hereafter) present a study that examines the channels through which aggregate productivity impacts poverty rates in India. Their empirical work draws upon the idea of productivity decomposition recently suggested by McMillan and Rodrik (2011).[17] Economic growth can impact the poor in different sectors through higher labour productivity that in turns improves the earnings of the poor leading to poverty reduction. How do economies achieve higher labour productivity? Broadly in either of the following two ways – the first way is to raise labour productivity in individual sectors (regarded as *within* sector growth neoclassical perspective à la Solow). The second way is by moving labour from low productivity to high productivity sectors (structural change perspective à la Lewis). HLS use data on poverty, employment, and productivity for 15 states to decompose states' aggregate productivity growth into two components: *within* sector productivity growth and the growth that happens due to structural change or re-allocation of labour. The importance of this channel is found to vary across Indian states. States with the best performance in poverty reduction over 1987-2009 (such as Tamil Nadu, Karnataka and Andhra Pradesh) are found to have high degree of structural change in contrast to states with weak performance in poverty reduction (like Bihar, Madhya Pradesh and Assam) who were found to have a low degree of structural change. Their chapter reveals some interesting insights about combination of outcomes (within sector growth and structural change) in individual states like Bihar (low productivity agriculture to low productivity construction), Karnataka (relatively weak *within* sector growth but high structural change) and Punjab (good *within* sector productivity growth but weak structural change). The takeaway from this interesting exercise is that growth enhancing structural change is intimately connected with poverty reduction. They also examine other possible determinants of structural change like indicators of financial development, ease of doing business and labour market flexibility. They underline the importance of investment climate for pro-poor growth in a labour abundant economy. HLS analysis is interesting in its own right and opens up further avenues for more research, and replication using future NSSO surveys. The impact of growth enhancing structural change on quality of employment in terms of worker composition (like regular-formal, regular-informal, casual worker etc.) in different states would be useful. Absolute measures of poverty are not distribution sensitive and future work can attempt to experiment with alternative measures.

In chapter 5 Narayana presents an informative analysis of the question of population ageing and provision of social security in India. This is a topic frequently neglected in the labour market discussions and growth in India. Often the cost of financing old age pension schemes is assumed to be entirely financed by taxing the working adults. Narayana presents a framework based on the National Transfer Accounts (NTA) that recognizes that all elderly individuals are *not* out of labour force and they do contribute to government tax revenues. This new framework of NTA enables the estimation of growth effects of age structure transition through First Demographic Dividend (FDD) with special reference to population ageing effects. In this framework, Narayana estimates the public cost of financing a universal old age pension scheme and its effects on financing lifecycle deficit (LCD) for the elderly population in India. India's age structure transition is marked by a higher share of working age population. This transition is considered to have positive growth effects through demographic dividends. At the same time, population ageing is presumed to have negative impact on economic growth as it increases old age dependency ratio, and impose additional burden on tax paying working population. The burden of public financing of consumption of goods and services by the old age population falls on the working adults. He estimates the aggregate LCD for elderly based on projected population from 2005 to 2050. Narayana's analysis offers new evidence and implications for public policy. First, the growth effect of age structure transition is positive from 2005 to 2045, due to FDD and largely contributed by productivity growth. He finds that the growth rate of national income per effective worker is higher than the labour productivity growth rate, a measure of FDD. FDD growth begins to decline after 2040. Second, due to the presence of informal sector with no formal age of retirement, elderly persons can continue to work beyond the age of 60 and earn labour income. Third, labour and retirement incomes (including asset income) of elderly persons are important sources of direct and indirect (or consumption-based) taxes for general government. This is a partial source of public financing the old age support systems, such as, a publicly-funded universal old age pension scheme (UOAPS). In addition, a publicly-funded UOAPS is found to be supportable to finance the entire LCD of elderly people. Analysis of population ageing recognizes the importance of informal sector as a source of income in general and for the elderly, in particular. Narayana's instructive use of NTA shows significant scope for future researchers in the area of social security finance to incorporate many other omitted variables like gender differences in demographic transition.

Why India has failed to foster labour-intensive manufacturing has long been debated. Employment generation is aided by faster growth of labour-intensive industries and if their share in manufacturing employment is higher. In chapter 6, Das, Sen and Das (DSD here after) analyse the patterns and determinants of labour intensity in the organized sector of Indian manufacturing. First they measure labour intensity by the ratio of number of workers to real fixed capital.

The estimated average of labour-intensity ratio for all the three–digit industries turns out to be 0.84 for the period from 1980–81 to 2009–10. Labour-intensive industries are those with average ratio greater than 0.84. They found 13 such industries and labeled the group as labour-intensive industries/sectors (LI, here after) within organized manufacturing. Labour intensity is found to have declined in LI much steeply compared to all organized manufacturing. However, the share of LI in manufacturing value added remained constant at around 12 per cent on average since the 1980s; but the employment share increased from 26 per cent in 1980s to 29 per cent in 1990s and further to 31 per cent in 2000s. Expectedly, labour productivity growth in LI was found to be very moderate. On the contrary there was a sharp increase in labour productivity growth in organized manufacturing. The absence of medium-sized firms in Indian manufacturing in general and in labour intensive industries in particular has argued to have been a source of weakness. DSD do not find substantial change in the average number of workers per factory in LI industries in 2000s. Industry-mix of states in India exhibit large differences. DSD have attempted to take advantage of inter-state differences in LI industries and apply the concept of Revealed Comparative Advantage (RCA) used in the international trade literature to measure RCA in LI industries among major states in India during 1980–81 to 2009–10. They have calculated the advantage or disadvantage of a state in LI industries relative to the total manufacturing sector. The idea behind RCA is a comparison of each state's performance relative to that of reference group of states that is India in this context. They carry out econometric regressions to find out the determinants of inter-state differences in RCA indices. They use several potentially important indicators to measure inter-state differences in labour regulation, transport infrastructure, trade openness, access to credit and literacy rate. However none of them turn out to be significant except literacy rate. It is known that the index of RCA of a state in LI is affected by many factors like relative size of the state (size bias), inherited industrial structure etc. It is not surprising that no statistically significant factor emerges from the preliminary regression analysis. Their approach can be refined, for instance, by including the unorganized sector, to improve our understanding of determinants of LI industries in India. The RCA approach and its determinants bring value to the discussion of labour intensity in Indian manufacturing.

In chapter 7, Goldar and Aggrawal investigate the problem of gender discrimination in Indian manufacturing in a nuanced way. The problem of gender discrimination and wage employment opportunities for females has been an important labour market issue in India and other developing countries. Many studies have discussed gender wage gaps, wage inequality and their determinants in manufacturing and other industries post trade liberalization in India. These studies find that after controlling for endowments and certain other factors, the wages received by women are relatively lower than those received by men. In this study, a different aspect of discrimination is examined, namely discrimination in job tenure (regular jobs versus casual jobs). Their data reveals that the proportion of casual workers out of paid workers is 33 per cent among male workers and 61 per cent among female workers in the total manufacturing sector. The main hypothesis tested econometrically is that after controlling for endowments and industry affiliation, women tend to get discriminated in the matter of getting regular jobs. This has implication for the wages received by women because the wage rates for casual workers are considerably lower than those for regular workers. The econometric analysis is undertaken using unit level data of NSS employment-unemployment surveys for 1999–2000, 2004–05 and 2009–10. They find that there is significant gender discrimination in manufacturing employment in India and the extent of gender discrimination has not declined in the 2000s. Also there is significant inter-state variation in the extent of gender discrimination. Interestingly, they find that the extent of gender discrimination bears an inverse relationship with labour market flexibility. Thus, gender discrimination is relatively less in those states which have a more flexible industrial labour market. In line with expectation, the extent of gender discrimination in manufacturing employment is relatively less in the states that have better social status of women and greater women empowerment. Their analysis raises several questions. Why has greater product competition in Indian markets not reduced gender discrimination? What drives entrepreneurs to discriminate against women for regular jobs? What explains their preference for male regular workers? Is it because women (if given regular jobs) have higher rate of quitting than men (higher quit rate could raise expected cost of hiring) or because women have less bargaining power and are not unionized? What drives a wedge between male and female regular workers? These are questions with no easy answers but with potential scope for both theoretical and empirical research. At a more general economy-wide level they report that casualization has gone up among women despite improved education levels since 1999.

The second part contains four chapters that take up different aspects related to labour market rigidity and labour laws in India. India is well known for its employment protection laws and labour regulations applied to firms in the formal sector. The issue related to their possible reform has been the most contentious in the discourse on economic reform process in India. In short, labour law reform has been a vexed issue (Pranab Bardhan in a Business Standard column on 28 September 2009, 'The vexed issue of labour laws'). In chapter 8 Bibhas Saha looks at some theoretical issues surrounding labour market rigidity and provides an overview of current research for India and implications for policy. He notes that rigidity has not disappeared in the sense of labour law restrictions but the practice has allowed flexibility. Large firms in India are legally restricted to restructure their labour force by employment protection laws. Firms are reported to have responded by hiring more temporary or contract workers and outsourcing production to firms in the informal sector (outside the purview of labour regulations) resulting in de facto flexibility. Saha calls this outcome imperfect flexibility. It may be regarded as employers' attempts to bypass rigid labour legislations and militant trade unions. Saha points out that flexible practice does not fully offset the absence of flexible labour laws for two reasons. First, practice is unlikely to constitute transparent and transferable knowledge, and requires investment in network relationships and disputes are harder to resolve. Second, lack of transparency in inter-state differences in labour laws could deter entry of foreign firms. Arguably, the existence of de facto flexibility is not a justification for stringent labour laws if the social outcome is greater number of low quality jobs. This dimension of labour law outcome is pursued further by Ramaswamy in chapter 9. One of the studies that Saha mentioned showed that industrial employment is more sensitive to shocks (say demand fluctuations) in areas where labour regulations are less restrictive or more pro-employer. Saha argues that available empirical evidence suggests that labour market rigidity is causing significant negative effects in terms of employment. He underlines the importance of three types of dualism in the Indian industry: regulation (formal and informal), technology (modern and backward) and worker's skills (skilled and unskilled labour) that analysts take into account. Saha has explained how in a dualistic economy the incentive for contract hiring could get accentuated with import liberalization and increased unionization. However, he agrees that more research is needed to understand the rationale of labour laws. If one believes that their objective is to correct economic inefficiencies either with markets or property rights, then the source of these inefficiencies needs to be identified. In this context, it is instructive to refer to the discourse on labour law in advanced countries (Hyde, 2006). After asking the question what is labour law? Hyde points out that the concept of employment as a foundation for legal regulation is simultaneously under-inclusive and over-inclusive. Hyde observes that labour law leaves out those (neediest) who require legal protection and includes many who do not need its attention. This observation is equally applicable to the situation in Indian labour markets in a sense and it is elaborately discussed in chapter 10 by Jaivir Singh.

In chapter 9, Ramaswamy takes an entirely empirical approach to study the impact of employment protection legislation on workforce composition within firms in Indian manufacturing. Labour regulations like employment protection legislation in India are size-dependent and therefore constitute a basis for threshold effects. The analytical idea of threshold effect is that if labour legislation (or any other economic policy like tax rates) changes discontinuously at the threshold employment size (or it could be asset size or output level) then it should result in discontinuous change in firms' behaviour. The higher the costs of compliance above the threshold, the greater the change in behaviour of firms. The discontinuous regulation can have two effects. First, it could influence the propensity of the firm to expand employment above the threshold size impacting firm size distribution. Second, it could change the employment policy of firms that cross the threshold size in favour of fixed-term or short-term contracts in order to circumvent costs of regulation. In short, firms could use non-permanent workers to stay below the legal establishment size threshold of hundred workers. This outcome can be measured by contract-worker intensity. It is the ratio of contract workers to total workers. Ramaswamy's study is based on a large nationally representative unbalanced panel of manufacturing plants in the formal sector covering 25 states and 5 union territories of India spanning the period 1998–2008. His results are consistent with the theoretical expectation. Contract-worker intensity is found to be higher in size class 50–99 relative to others. The average contract-worker intensity of factories in size group 50–99 is found to be higher in labour-intensive industries located in states categorized as inflexible. In other words, employment protection legislation (EPL) changes the workforce composition and hiring practices of Indian manufacturing firms. His results have two implications. First, the presence of significant threshold effect suggest loss of potential output gains. Size-dependent labour regulations perhaps restrict the emergence of large firms in labour intensive industries in Indian manufacturing. Second, they do not necessarily improve access to good jobs. Contrary to the job security enhancing intension of EPL the employment status of average workers in establishments close to or just above the employment size of hundred workers appears to be worse and more vulnerable because of stricter size-dependent regulations. This chapter can be extended in several directions for further verification and analysis. First, one would like to know what proportion of new entrants in manufacturing belongs to employment size below the legal threshold and what proportion graduates into larger size. Second, one may examine the relationship between initial employment size and employment growth of firms over time in flexible states relative to inflexible states. The idea of threshold effects of regulations is important and is applicable in other areas of industrial policy in India and other developing countries. For example, defining tax and other fiscal incentives based on asset size of firms could encourage firms to stay below the specified size and discourage firm growth overtime.

In chapter 10, Jaivir Singh argues for a more nuanced understanding of the role of labour market reforms in India. Toward this objective he surveys theoretical perspectives, both economic and legal, on the relationship between the firm, workers and the boundaries of the firm. The subtle difference in perspectives matters because reform is apparently centred on the contractual employment relationship between the employer and the employee. He first establishes that the benefits workers enjoy are contingent on their legal status/recognition as workmen and this requires a clear understanding of employment relationships. The complexity of the employment relationships in the Indian labour law and courts context is crucial. It is important to note that labour laws in India cover a small proportion of the total workforce. Labour laws do not cover the agriculture and informal sector. Labour laws are operational only for a worker who is employed in a legally recognized category of establishment and where the person is legally recognized as workman. In this context, the interpretation of courts have played an important role in defining the conditions necessary for a person to be declared as 'workman' employed to do the work in the industry under consideration. The analysis of important court cases revealed that courts have essentially conceived the employment contract in the framework of the orthodox 'master and servant' model. Jaivir Singh argues that one needs to go beyond this traditional view based on a master-servant model to appreciate the intricacies of employment relationships in a modern industrial firm. Standard microeconomic theory takes the size of the firm or the firm boundary as a given parameter. What determines the boundaries of the firm (one integrated plant or two separate plants to manufacture automobiles and their components)? He draws together insights from property rights theory, property in work concept and legal concepts of firms to enrich the legal understanding of labour. He points out that the conceptualization of the firm by Ronald Coase that vastly improved our understanding of the boundaries of the firm in economic theory, essentially uses the rather narrow concept of master-servant (direction and control) as an important factor in setting the economic boundary of the firm. Later advances recognize that workers make firm specific relational investments (for example training or firm-specific human capital investments) and their employment security affects their ex ante incentives to make these investments and that in turn affects productivity. The basic idea is that firms cannot own workers (humans) but only non-human assets; if workers with firm-specific skills (assets) are important for productivity then it is important to understand the impact of labour laws on incentives to make relation specific investments. This has obvious implications for human capital accumulation and growth. If workers are a part of the firm with strong job security rights (have property in work) then that firm is viewed as more integrated (organizational assimilation). This perspective calls for 'organization test' in place of a 'control' test as currently followed in judicial practice. In brief one might have to go beyond 'control test' and move towards an 'organization-integration test' to determine employer-worker relationships. Jaivir Singh has attempted to deepen the discourse on labour market reforms in India. These analytical perspectives demand more creative responses from the stakeholders and policymakers involved in the challenging task of labour market reform in India. The labour law reform issue perhaps provides the starkest instance of regulatory dilemmas facing India today.

India follows the common law tradition with court judgements having a substantive role in the making and unmaking of labour laws through their interpretation and judgements in cases involving labour disputes. In the background of India's economic transition and liberalization policies that demand institutional change the approach of the Supreme Court of India towards labour rights assumes critical importance. In chapter 11, Ramapriya Gopalakrishnan (hereafter RG) examines the approach of the Court over the last decade and a half to collective as well as individual labour rights issues of workers in the formal as well as informal sectors. She asks upfront, as argued by some critics, whether the Court in the last decade has inclined towards adopting an 'anti-worker stance' and overly sympathetic to market orientation of economic policies that favours employers. RG compares and contrasts the Supreme Court rulings related to entitlement of contract workers permanent absorption, wage parity for contract workers with permanent workers, entitlement of temporary workers to regularization and wrongful termination of casual workers among other things. RG based on some of the land mark cases in 2000s argues that there has been a significant change in the manner in which the Court has interpreted and applied labour legislation. The Court has changed its earlier viewpoint that emphasized protection of workers interests to a more balanced approach that recognized the importance of fast industrial growth. Economic considerations like financial burden on the state, viability and growth of private industrial enterprises have been given due consideration. This apparent shift has attracted criticism that the Court has been biased towards employers. On the contrary, RG notes that there are several cases where the Court ruled to uphold the rights of workers during the same period. In other words the evidence in favour of the view that the Court has become 'anti-worker' is rather weak. It is perhaps arguably more of a course correction of its earlier viewpoint that had become inimical to private enterprise and entrepreneurship without losing sight of constitutional principles of social justice. The careful discussion of Supreme Court's judgements by RG complements some of the issues raised in the earlier chapters. This last chapter brings to a close part two of the volume on labour, employment and growth in India.

Conclusion

The objective of different chapters in this volume has been to shed light on important selected aspects of the problem of labour and employment in recent years of economic growth and policy change in India. Authors of different chapters have discussed in detail the selected issues and raised relevant questions that contribute to our understanding of the overall problems of structural transformation. It is hoped the set of chapters in this volume will make a positive contribution to the literature on labour market issues and encourages more research, and informed contemporary discussion on policies related to growth and employment in India.

Endnotes

1   The Economist magazine in May 1991 titled its special report 'India: Uncaged Tiger'. In 2008, another special report on India was titled 'India: Elephant not a Tiger' (11 December 2008). At the same time analysts and scholars began describing India as awakening giant, emerging giant etc., and see Panagariya (2008) as an example among others.

2   This is in terms of five-year moving average of annual growth rates. See Hasan, Lamba and Sengupta (Chapter 4 in this volume).

3   See Table 4.1 in Hasan, Lamba and Sengupta (Chapter 4) based on Bosworth, Collins and Virmani (2008).

4   See J. Bhagwati and A. Panagariya (2012), eds. *Reforms and Economic Transformation in India,* (Delhi: Oxford University Press), for the most recent addition to this literature.

5   These figures are taken from Verma (2011) and measured in terms of 1990 Geary-Khemis (GK) dollars. Refer to the original for more comparisons with other countries.

6   This has raised the expectation in development policy discussions of the possibility of India skipping the traditional sequence and the services sector assuming the role of the lead sector in India's growth path. See Eichengreen and Gupta (2011) among others.

7   In view of the slow growth of employment the Planning Commission of India had set up a task force on employment opportunities in 1999 which submitted its report in 2001.See GOI (2001).

8   The estimates are as on 1 January 2012

9   See Sundaram (2013) for a discussion of this point and actual shift in the age distribution of the population and the worker-population ratio between 2005–10.

10 This estimate is based on a comparison of EUS estimates of total employment based on usual principal status (UPS) of workers in 2004–04 and 2011–12, respectively. See Shaw (2013) for details

11 See Papola (2006) among others. GOI (2013) devotes a special chapter (Chapter 2) to highlight the policy concerns. Rubina Verma (2011) discusses the structural transformation in India's GDP using economy-wide aggregate three-sector general equilibrium model and her growth accounting exercises show services sector has the highest total factor productivity growth during the period 1970 to 2007. In her model, the differential productivity growth accounts for the dominance of the services sector in India. The inter-sector differences in employment shares are not discussed much. Also see *India: Labour and Employment Report 2014* (IHD, 2014).

12 Also see Rangarajan, Kaul and Seema (2011) for a similar discussion in the context of reduction of labour force between 2004–05 and 2009–10.

13 Thomas also argues that the increasing number of women attending domestic duties implies massive withdrawal of women from the labour force. This is a debatable point because the notion of withdrawal implies involuntary withdrawal of previously employed women from the labour force. Obviously this is hard to estimate and the implied discouragement effect due to unavailability of employment opportunities in rural areas is a difficult empirical issue. This aspect needs more research.

14 Also see in this context Gordon and Gupta (2004) and Eishengreen and Gupta (2011)

15 Srinivasan (2010) has been severely critical of employment elasticity as used in policy discussions.

16 It is important to note that higher regular-formal employment need not imply higher job quality as it may just involve higher employment of contract workers (See Chapter 10 in this volume). See Ramaswamy and Agrawal (2012) for another discussion of quality of employment in services relative to manufacturing in urban India.

17 Also see the excellent discussion in Rodrik (2013b)

References

Bosworth, B., S. M. Collins and A. Virmani. 2007. 'Sources of Growth in the Indian Economy', *NBER Working Paper 12901.* Cambridge, MA: National Bureau of Economic Research.

Eichengreen, B. and P. Gupta. 2011. 'The Service Sector as India's Road to Economic Growth in India'. *India Policy Forum: 2010–11*, Vol. 7. New Delhi: Sage Publications.

Gordon, J. and P. Gupta. 2004. 'Understanding India's Services Revolution'. *Working Paper No. 04/171*. Washington DC: International Monetary Fund.

Government of India. 2013. *Economic Survey 2012–13*. New Delhi: Ministry of Finance.

_____. 2001. *Report of the Task Force on Employment Opportunities*. New Delhi: Planning Commission.

Hyde, A. 2006. 'What is Labour Law?' In *Boundaries and Frontiers of Labour Law: Goals and Means in the Regulation of Work*, edited by G. Davidov and B. Langille. Oxford and Portland: Hart Publishing.

Institute of Human Development. 2014. *Labour and Employment Report 2014*. New Delhi: Academic Foundation and IHD.

Kochhar, K., U. Kumar, R. Rajan, A. Subramanian and I. Tokatlidis. 2006. 'India's Pattern of Development: What Happened, What Follows?' *Journal of Monetary Economics* 53(5): 981–1019.

Kotwal, Ashok, B. Ramaswami and W. Wadhwa. 2011. 'Economic Liberalization and Indian Economic Growth: What's the Evidence?' *Journal of Economic Literature* 49(4): 1152–99.

McMillan, Margaret S. and Dani Rodrik. 2011. 'Globalization, Structural Change and Productivity Growth'. *NBER Working Papers 17143*. Cambridge, Massachusetts, USA: National Bureau of Economic Research.

Mammen, Kristin and Christina Paxson. 2000. 'Women's Work and Economic Development', *Journal of Economic Perspectives* 14(4): 141–64.

Panagariya, Arvind. 2008. *India: The Emerging Giant*. Oxford and New York: Oxford University Press.

Papola, T. S. 2006. 'Emerging Structure of Indian Economy: Implications of Growing Intersectoral Imbalances', *The Indian Economic Journal* 54(1): 5–25

Rangarajan, C., Padma Iyer Kaul and Seema. 2011. 'Where Is the Missing Labour Force?' *Economic and Political Weekly* 46(39): 68–72

Ramaswamy, K. V. and T. Agrawal. 2012. 'Services-led Growth, Employment, and Skill and Job Quality: A study of Manufacturing and Service Sectors in Urban India'. In *India Development Report 2012–13*, edited by S. Mahendra Dev. New Delhi: Oxford University Press.

Rodrick, Dani. 2013a. *Perils of Premature Deindustrialization*. Available at: http://www.project-syndicate.org/commentary/dani-rodrikdeveloping-economies--missing-manufacturing#K9k ffEZoSPSVT3xT.99. Accessed on 18 June 2014.

_____. 2013b. *Structural Change, Fundamentals, and Growth: An Overview*. Available at: http://www.sss.ias.edu/files/pdfs/Rodrik/Research/Structural-Change-Fundamentals-and-Growth-An-Overview_revised.pdf. Accessed on 25 June 2014.

Shaw, Abhishek. 2013. 'Employment Trends in India: An Overview of NSSO's 68th Round', *Economic and Political Weekly* 48(42): 23–25

Srinivasan, T. N. 2010. 'Employment and India's Development and Reforms', *Journal of Comparative Economics* 38(1): 82–106

Sundaram, K. 2013. 'Some Recent Trends in Population, Employment and Poverty in India: An Analysis', *Indian Economic Review* 48(1): 83–128

Verma, Rubina. 2012. 'Structural Transformation and Jobless Growth in the Indian Economy'. In *The Oxford Handbook of the Indian Economy*, edited by C. Ghate, 276–310. New York: Oxford University Press.

2

India's Labour Market during the 2000s
An Overview

Jayan Jose Thomas

2.1 Introduction

This chapter examines the major trends in India's labour market, mainly during the 2000s.[1] A chapter of this nature is relevant for a number of reasons. First, India's GDP growth has experienced a marked acceleration, especially after the mid-2000s. India today has the distinction of being second only to China in terms of economic growth, among the large economies of the world. Second, market-oriented economic reforms, which began in India in 1991, have taken much deeper roots in the country by the 2000s. At the same time, there has also been an increasing recognition among India's policymakers and the political class that economic growth needs to be 'inclusive.' It is important to understand how India's labour market has behaved during such a period of far-reaching economic and policy changes. Third, this chapter is also relevant in the context of the general perception, particularly in the media, that India possesses the so-called demographic dividend. That is, India's large and relatively young population would prove to be a major advantage for the country's future economic growth. According to estimates by the World Bank, India's population in the age group of 15 to 59 years is expected to increase from 757 million in 2010 to 972 million in 2030, whereas population in the working age years is expected to decline in most developed regions of the world. Even in China, population in the age group of 15–59 years is projected to decline from 913 million to 847 million between 2010 and 2030. This implies that India could potentially contribute more than 200 million new workers over the next two decades, possibly accounting for a substantial chunk of the net increase in the global labour supply during this period.

The analysis in this chapter is based mainly on the NSSO reports on employment and unemployment in India.[2] All estimates in this chapter, unless otherwise specified, are based on the usual principal and usual subsidiary status (UPSS) of workers. The chapter points to some major structural changes occurring in India's labour market. The most important of these is the movement of the country's labour force away from agriculture, with the 2009–10 Survey registering for the first time an absolute decline in the size of the agricultural workforce. Secondly, there has been a noticeable rise in the population of students, including those unrolled for higher education, since the 2000s. This improvement has been marked in rural areas, among females, and among persons belonging to poor households.

On the other hand, however, there are severe obstacles to modernization of the labour force in India, given the slow rate of generation of non-agricultural jobs in the country. After 2004–05, construction has been the major source of non–agricultural employment in India, especially in rural areas, while employment growth decelerated in the manufacturing sector. The large-scale withdrawal of women from the labour force continues to be the most severe challenge for the progressive transformation of India's economy and society.

Section 2.2 of the chapter discusses the broad trends in labour absorption in the Indian economy. Section 2.3 deals with the important structural changes in India's labour market, and thereby tries to explain the seemingly sharp divergences in employment growth between the first and the second half of the 2000s. Section 2.4 is an analysis of the growth of non-agricultural employment in the country. Section 2.5 is on the low levels of female labour participation in India, and section 2.6 concludes the chapter.

2.2 Broad trends in labour absorption

A striking aspect of India's labour market is its relatively low labour participation rate (LPR). In 2012, LPR among persons aged 15 years and above was only 56 per cent in India compared to 71 per cent in China and 70 per cent in Brazil.[3] The labour participation rate indicates the proportion of the population that is economically active, which includes the employed as well as those unemployed but actively seeking jobs. The proportion of the population that is employed is denoted by workforce participation rate or worker population ratio. Persons who are not economically active comprise those who are too young or too old to work, students, renters, recipients of pensions or remittances, the disabled, as well as persons attending to 'domestic duties.'

Table 2.1 shows the usual principal and usual subsidiary status workers as a proportion of the total population of India over the years, as observed from the reports of the NSSO.[4] It is notable that despite far-reaching economic reforms, Workforce Participation Rates (WPR) in India have hardly improved since the 1990s, except in the case of urban males.

Another important feature is the extremely low rates of workforce participation among females – only 14.7 per cent among urban females in India in 2011–12. WPR declined in the case of rural females from 32.7 per cent in 2004–05 to 24.8 per cent in 2011–12 (see Table 2.1). In fact, India's low international ranking in terms of LPR is mainly on account of the low level of female participation in the labour force. In 2012, LPR among males was 81 per cent in India, marginally higher than China's 78 per cent. On the other hand, LPR among females in the same year was 64 per cent and 29 per cent respectively in China and India (for population aged 15 years and above).[5]

Table 2.1: Workforce participation rates in India – usual principal and usual subsidiary status workers as a proportion of population (all ages), in per cent

	1983	1993–94	1999–00	2004–05	2009–10	2011–12
Rural male	54.7	55.3	53.1	54.6	54.7	54.3
Rural female	34	32.8	29.9	32.7	26.1	24.8
Urban male	51.2	52.1	51.8	54.9	54.3	54.6
Urban female	15.1	15.5	13.9	16.6	13.8	14.7

Sources: NSSO (2006), NSSO (2011), and NSSO (2013)

The NSSO data provides reliable estimates of persons who are and who are not part of the labour force as proportions of the total population. The actual numbers of persons in each activity status (such as being in the labour force, unemployed, not in labour force due to old age, and so on) can be estimated by multiplying these proportions obtained from the National Sample Surveys with the total population figures available from the Census of India. Table 2.2 shows the distribution of India's population by activity status in 2011–12 and Table 2.3 shows the estimates of the country's workforce over the years. All estimates of workers in this chapter (unless otherwise specified) are based on the usual status of persons, considering both the usual principal and the usual subsidiary economic activities.

In 2011–12, out of India's total population of 1227.4 million, 472.5 million were workers and 10.8 million (or 0.9 per cent of the total population) were unemployed. Among the population that was not part of the labour force, there were 337.5 million students and another 232.4 million who, according to the official statistics, were described as attending to domestic duties (see Table 2.2). India's relatively low official unemployment figures actually conceal the large numbers of persons who are either underemployed and or who do not join the labour force due to lack of sufficient employment opportunities.

Table 2.2: Distribution of India's population by activity status, 2011–12, in million numbers

Activity status	Rural male	Rural female	Urban male	Urban female	Total
1. Employed	234.4	101.6	109.1	27.4	472.5 (38)
2. Unemployed	4.3	1.6	3.4	1.5	10.8 (0.9)
3. Labour force (1+2)	237.7	103.2	112.5	28.9	483.3 (39)
4. Students	129.1	102.0	58.1	48.2	337.5 (27)
5. Attending domestic duties only	0.4	68.9	0.4	65.9	135.6 (11)
6. Attending domestic duties and also engaged in other activities for household use	0.9	75.8	0.2	19.9	96.8 (8)
Population	431.7	409.8	199.8	186.1	1227.4 (100)

Notes: Estimates of population used in the calculations for this table correspond to 1 January 2012. Figures in brackets in the last column are proportions of the total population. Activity refers to the UPSS of workers.

Source: Estimates based on NSSO (2013).

Previous studies have pointed out that there was an upturn in the growth of non-agricultural employment opportunities in India's rural areas during the 1980s, which contributed to the rise in real agricultural wages and to the reduction of poverty during that decade (Sen, 1996). However, employment growth slowed down sharply in India during the 1990s, particularly in the rural areas. As Table 2.4 shows, the net increase in employment in India was 71 million between 1983 and 1993–94, but declined to 24 million only between 1993–94 and 1999–2000. Further, a substantial part of the incremental employment during the 1990s was of casual workers. These developments in India's labour market during the 1990s had given rise to much apprehension on the sustainability of the country's post-reform economic growth.

Employment growth in India revived impressively during the first half of the 2000s (between 1999–00 and 2004–05), with a net addition of 59.4 million new jobs (see Table 2.4). Some commentators argued that the survey in 2004–05 (61st round of the NSSO) provided proof that economic reforms had finally delivered on the employment front. However, the revival in employment growth during this period occurred along with a decline in the quality of employment (Chandrasekhar and Ghosh, 2006). Self-employed workers in agriculture, especially females, accounted for a significant part of the increase in employment (this aspect is discussed further in the next section). There was a decline in the average educational achievements of persons who were new entrants to the workforce between 1999–2000 and 2004–05 relative to the earlier periods (Thomas, 2011). Between 1993–94 and 2004–05, the growth of wages slowed down and wage inequalities increased (Karan and Selvaraj, 2008; Sarkar and Mehta, 2010). The size of the 'working poor' in the country was also found to be substantially large (Papola, 2008).

It was in the above context that the 66th round of the NSSO (in 2009–10) found that employment generation in the Indian economy decelerated sharply again, with only 4.7 million new jobs recorded between 2004–05 and 2009–10 (see Tables 2.3 and 2.4). Curiously, this employment-growth slowdown coincided with the acceleration in general economic growth in India (see Thomas, 2012). It is also notable that the employment generation in India during the second half of the 2000s fell far short of the target set by the Eleventh Five Year Plan of 50 million new jobs (EPW, 2011). The general discussions, particularly in the media, highlighted the 'jobless' nature of India's economic growth since the mid-2000s.

The NSSO's large (or 'thick') sample surveys on employment and unemployment are conducted normally at an interval of five years. However, breaking this tradition, NSSO conducted a large sample survey on employment and unemployment in 2011–12, just two years after the completion of its previous round in 2009–10. The 2011–12 survey showed some recovery in employment growth, with 10 million new jobs generated during the two years since 2009–10 (see Tables 2.3 and 2.4).

Table 2.3: Estimates of workers in India, by categories in various years, numbers in millions

Category	1983	1993–94	1999–2000	2004–05	2009–10	2011–12
Rural males	153.9	187.8	198.8	217.7	230.8	234.4
Rural females	90.7	104.8	105.8	123.5	104.5	101.6
Urban males	46.7	64.6	75.6	91.5	103.0	109.1
Urban females	12.1	17.2	18.2	25.2	24.2	27.4
Total	303.4	374.4	398.4	457.8	462.5	472.5

Notes: Refers to the UPSS of workers.

Population figures (based on Census of India) are from Sundaram (2007), Table 1 and NSSO (2013). The figures for 2004–05, 2009–10 and 2011–12 correspond to the estimates of population as on 1 January 2005, 1 January 2010 and 1 January 2012 respectively.

There are some differences between the estimates of workers reported in this article and those in Thomas (2012). This is because the population figures used in Thomas (2012) were projections based on the Census of India data until 2001. In this chapter, these population figures have been revised using data from the Census of India 2011.

Source: Estimates based on NSSO (1987), NSSO (1997), NSSO (2001), NSSO (2006), NSSO (2011), and NSSO (2013).

Table 2.4: Net increase in the number of workers in India, 1983 to 2011–12, in millions

Time periods	All workers	Agricultural workers	Non–agricultural workers
1983 to 1993–94	71.1	32.4	38.7
1993–94 to 2004–05	83.4	18.2	65.2
2004–05 to 2011–12	14.7	-33.3	48.0
Shorter time periods			
1993–94 to 1999–00	24.0	0.8	23.2

Time periods	All workers	Agricultural workers	Non–agricultural workers
1999–00 to 2004–05	59.4	17.4	41.9
2004–05 to 2009–10	4.7	-20.4	25.1
2009–10 to 2011–12	10.0	-12.9	22.9

Notes and Source: Same as Table 2.3.

2.3 'Jobless growth' or structural shifts in the labour market?

Much of the discussion in the previous section focused on the growth of overall employment in India. However, an analysis based solely on overall employment can be misleading, especially for a developing country like India. Overall employment refers to the sum of employment in agriculture and the non-agricultural sectors.

It is expected that employment in agriculture decline with economic development, both in relative terms as well as in absolute numbers. Arthur Lewis (Lewis, 1954) had famously modeled the movement of 'surplus labour' from the traditional (also agricultural or informal) to the modern (also industrial or formal) sectors. With the exhaustion of surplus labour reserves and with the absolute fall in the size of the agricultural work force, it was projected that real wages would rise in the economy (Fields, 2004). The East Asian tiger economies, Taiwan and South Korea, had reached such a turning point in development by the mid-1960s itself (Fei and Ranis, 1975). Some commentators argue that surplus labour in agriculture is depleting rather quickly in China too (Xiaobo, *et al.,* 2011).

In India, the share of agriculture and allied activities in GDP fell from 34.3 per cent in 1983 to 14.1 per cent in 2011–12. The share of these sectors in the country's total employment also declined during this period, from 68.2 per cent to 47.5 per cent (see Table 2.5). At the same time, while agriculture and related activities have suffered a slow and steady decline in their shares in total employment in India over a long period of time, an absolute fall in agricultural employment was not registered by statistical agencies in the country until the NSSO survey held in 2009–10.

In fact, it is remarkable that the size of the agricultural workforce in India showed an increase in absolute terms, by 17.4 million between 1999–2000 and 2004–05 (see Table 2.4). Notably, agricultural employment accounted for close to 30 per cent of the overall employment generation in India during the first half of the 2000s. On the other hand, agricultural employment declined in India during the second half of the 2000s. The overall increase in employment of only 4.7 million in India between 2004–05 and 2009–10 was the result of an absolute decline in agricultural employment, by 20.4 million, coupled with a modest increase in non-agricultural employment, by 25.1 million. A further decline in the size of India's agricultural workforce was observed in the NSSO survey held in 2011–12 (see Tables 2.4 and 2.6).

While, as noted above, an absolute fall in the size of India's agricultural workforce was observed for the first time in 2009–10 relative to 2004–05, this fall was observed only in the case of females. It was in the NSSO survey held in 2011–12 that the size of the male agricultural workforce registered an absolute decline for the first time in the country, falling by 5.9 million relative to the 2009–10 level.

The generation of non-agricultural employment in India was at the rate of 8.4 million a year between 1999–2000 and 2004–05, which slowed down to 5 million a year between 2004–05 and 2009–10, but accelerated again to 11.5 million a year between 2009–10 and 2011–12 (see Table 2.7). In fact, over the long term, the rate of generation of non-agricultural employment in the country improved from 5.9 million a year between 1993–94 and 2004–05 to 6.9 million a year between 2004–05 and 2011–12 (see Table 2.7). Clearly, therefore, there is very little justification for terming the employment growth in India since the mid-2000s as jobless.

2.3.1 The absolute decline in agricultural employment

What explains the rise in agricultural employment growth in India during the first half of the 2000s, and its subsequent decline after 2004–05? It is noteworthy here that the GDP growth in Indian agriculture had been statistically insignificant during the first half of the 2000s. On the other hand, the growth of agricultural incomes in the country improved somewhat after 2004–05 (see Thomas, 2012). How could agricultural employment have increased during a period when agricultural incomes stagnated, and later decreased when agricultural incomes revived?

2.3.1.1 Movement of women in and out of agricultural workforce

Out of India's 472.5 million workers in 2011–12, 52 per cent (or 245.3 million) were self-employed, 29 per cent were casual workers, and 19 per cent were regular employees (see Table 2.8). A major feature of employment growth in India during the first half of the 2000s was a massive increase (of 50 million) in the numbers of the self-employed. This trend was to some extent reversed since the middle of the 2000s. Between 2004–05 and 2011–12, there was a decline in the number of self-employed workers (by 13 million), which was compensated by the rise in the size of the regular and casual workforce (see Table 2.8; also see Thomas, 2012).

An overwhelming proportion of all persons who joined the agricultural labour force in India between 1999–00 and 2004–05 (15.5 million of 17.4 million) were self-employed, rural females (see Tables 2.4 and 2.9). Studies have argued that the entry of rural women into the agricultural labour force was to supplement the low household incomes, given the stagnancy in income growth in the countryside during this period (Abraham, 2009).

On the contrary, both 'push' and 'pull' factors appear to have caused the movement of the workforce away from agriculture after the mid-2000s. Between 2004–05 and 2009–10, the population of rural females engaged in agriculture and allied activities declined by 19.8 million in India, which accounted for almost the entire decline in the country's total agricultural workforce (by 20.4 million) during this period (see Tables 2.4 and 2.9).

The Mahatma Gandhi National Rural Employment Guarantee Act (MGNREGA) has produced a substantial impact on rural employment and rural wages. As per the current weekly status, casual workers engaged in public works numbered only 0.9 million in 2004–05, but rose to 6.6 million in 2009–10, which included 2.4 million jobs created through MGNREGA. Subsequently, however, the pace of creation of employment through public works programmes slowed down. In 2011–12, 6.7 million casual workers were engaged in public works, of which 2.9 million were employed through MGNREGA (see Table 2.10).

The daily real wages of rural female casual workers (aged 15–59 years) engaged in works other than public works grew at an average annual rate of only 1.4 per cent between 1999–2000 and 2004–05, but the wage growth accelerated to 4.4 per cent between 2004–05 and 2009–10, and to 7.2 per cent between 2004–05 and 2011–12 (see Table 2.11). A similar acceleration in wages occurred in the case of rural males as well. Usami (2012) found that the real wages of agricultural workers in India remained stagnant or even slightly declined between 1999–2000 and 2006–07 but began to rise after 2007–08. Thorat and Dubey (2012) noted acceleration in the growth of consumption expenditure and in the reduction of poverty in rural India between 2004–05 and 2009–10 across households belonging to the various socio-religious groups.

Between 1999–2000 and 2004–05, rural women who reported their economic status as 'attending to domestic duties only' declined in number, while rural females who were self-employed in agriculture grew in size. But this was reversed between 2004–05 and 2009–10. The numbers of rural females who were attending to domestic duties rose sharply, while those who were self-employed in agriculture declined (see Table 2.9). A possible reason for the movement of women back to work in their own households during the second half of the 2000s is the improvement in the availability of income–earning opportunities for male members of the family.[6]

There have been other factors too that led to the withdrawal of workers, including male workers, from agriculture. First is the marked acceleration in the growth of persons employed in construction in rural India after 2004–05, a significant part of which occurred in the less developed and chiefly agrarian states such as Uttar Pradesh, Rajasthan, Bihar and Madhya Pradesh. Secondly, the decline in number of people employed in agriculture occurred hand in hand with a marked rise in number of people attending educational institutions. It is noteworthy that the decline in agricultural employment in India between 2004–05 and 2011–12 was almost entirely among people who were younger than 35 years (see Table 2.8).

Of course, there have equally strong factors that appear to have pushed workers out of low productivity agriculture. Farmer suicides continue to be reported from several regions of the country. Surveys conducted by the Foundation for Agrarian Studies showed that a significant proportion of cultivator households in selected villages in Maharashtra and Andhra Pradesh had been earning negative incomes from crop production in 2005–06 (Ramachandran and Rawal, 2010). There have also been increasing instances across the country of farmlands being acquired for commercial and industrial purposes.

To sum up, the slow growth of overall employment in the Indian economy during the 2000s is partly on account of the structural changes occurring in the country's labour market. The most important of these changes is the absolute fall in the size of the agricultural labour force in the country. The decline in female agricultural employment during the second half of the 2000s is possibly due to an improvement, even if marginal – and not a worsening – in the economic conditions in rural India.

Table 2.5: Sector-wise distribution of India's GDP and employment, in per cent

Sectors	Shares in GDP (%)		Shares in employment (%)		Employment in millions
	1982–83	2011–12	1983	2011–12	2011–12
1. Agriculture and allied activities	34.3	14.1	68.2	47.5	224.4
2. Mining and quarrying	3.1	2.1	0.6	0.5	2.6
3. Manufacturing	14.3	15.7	10.6	13.0	61.3
4. Electricity, gas and water	1.6	1.9	0.3	0.5	2.5
5. Services and construction	45.9	66.3	19.9	38.5	181.7
5a. Construction	6.9	7.8	2.3	10.6	49.9
5b. Trade, hotels, transport and communication	17.3	27.5	8.8	16.5	77.9
5c. Financing, real estate and business services	8.9	18.1	0.7	2.9	13.5
5d. Community, social and personal service	12.9	12.8	8.1	8.6	40.4
GDP/total employment	100	100	100	100.0	472.5

Note: GDP at constant (2004–05) prices.

Source: Estimates based on NSSO (1987), NSSO (2013) and *National Accounts Statistics* (available with www.rbi.org.in).

Table 2.6: Net increase in employment (in million numbers) in India, sector-wise, 1983 to 2011–12

Sectors	1983 to 1993–94	1993–94 to 1999–2000	1999–2000 to 2004–05	2004–05 to 2009–10	2009–10 to 2011–12	2004–05 to 2011–12
1.Agriculture, hunting, forestry and fishing	32.4	0.8	17.4	−20.4	−12.9	−33.3
2. Mining and quarrying	0.9	−0.4	0.3	0.4	−0.2	0.2
3. Manufacturing	7.6	3.3	9.8	−3.0	8.1	5.1
4. Electricity, gas and water	−0.2	−0.4	0.2	0.1	0.3	0.3
5. Services and construction	31.1	22.1	31.3	27.0	15.6	42.7
5a. Construction	5.3	5.4	8.5	18.4	5.5	23.9
5b. Trade, hotels, transport and communication	12.6	13.4	12.9	4.8	4.7	9.5
5c.Financing, real estate and business services	1.6	1.4	3.0	2.5	3.3	5.8
5d.Community, social and personal services	11.6	2.0	7.0	1.3	2.1	3.4
Total employment	71.1	24.0	59.4	4.7	10.0	14.7

Notes and Source: Same as Table 2.3.

Table 2.7: Annual net increase in the number of workers (in millions) in India, 1983 to 2011–12

Time periods	All workers	Non–agricultural workers
1983 to 1993–94	6.8	3.7
1993–94 to 2004–05	7.6	5.9
2004–05 to 2011–12	2.1	6.9
Shorter time–periods		
1993–94 to 1999–00	4.0	3.9
1999–00 to 2004–05	11.9	8.4
2004–05 to 2009–10	0.9	5.0
2009–10 to 2011–12	5.0	11.5

Notes and Source: Same as Table 2.3.

Table 2.8: Net increase in employment between 2004–05 and 2011–12 and total in 2011–12, by activity status and age, in million numbers

| Category | Net increase, 2004–05 to 2011–12 | | | Total in: |
	5–34 years	35 years and above	All	2011–12
Self-employed, agriculture	−18.1	−1.0	−19.2	146.6
Self-employed, non-agriculture	−4.6	11.1	6.5	99.1
Self-employed, total	−22.5	10.1	−13.0	245.3
Regular, total	9.0	9.3	18.4	88.6
Casual, agriculture	−13.4	−0.2	−13.5	76.0
Casual, non-agriculture and public works	8.7	14.7	22.9	63.1

Category	Net increase, 2004–05 to 2011–12			Total in:
	5–34 years	35 years and above	All	2011–12
Casual, total	–4.6	14.6	9.3	139.1
Agriculture, total	–31.8	–1.3	–33.2	224.8
Non-agriculture, total	13.5	35.2	48.5	248.3
Total	–18.3	34.0	15.3	472.5

Source: Estimates based on NSSO (2006) and NSSO (2013).

Table 2.9: Net increases in the population of rural females by selected activity status, 1999–00 to 2011–12, in million numbers

Activity status	1999–00 to 2004–05	2004–05 to 2009–10	2009–10 to 2011–12
Self-employed in agriculture	15.5	–17.6	0.3
Casual work in agriculture	–2.7	–2.2	–7.0
Attending domestic duties	–6.3	25.4	–13.6
Attending domestic duties and also engaged other activities (such as tailoring) for household use (93)	5.7	10.8	19.4

Source: Estimates based on NSSO (2001), NSSO (2006), NSSO (2011) and NSSO (2013).

Table 2.10: Estimates of casual workers (by current weekly status) engaged in public works including MGNREGA in India, in million numbers

Activity status	Category	2004–05	2009–10	2011–12
Public works other than MGNREGA	Rural males	0.4	2	2.2
	Rural females	0.4	1.6	1.2
	All	0.9	4.2	3.8
MGNREGA	Rural males	0	1.2	1.3
	Rural females	0	1.2	1.6
	All	0	2.4	2.9

Activity status	Category	2004–05	2009–10	2011–12
Public works including MGNREGA	All	0.9	6.6	6.7

Source: Estimates based on NSSO (2006), NSSO (2011) and NSSO (2013).

Table 2.11: Annual average rates of growth (in per cent) of daily real wages of casual workers (aged 15–59 years) engaged in works other than public works in India

Period	Rural men	Rural women	Urban men	Urban women
1993–94 to 1999–2000	3.7	3.3	3.0	3.9
1999–2000 to 2004–05	1.7	1.4	−0.5	−1.2
2004–05 to 2009–10	3.0	4.4	3.0	2.9
2004–05 to 2011–12	5.9	7.2	4.8	5.4

Notes: Deflated using consumer price indices for agricultural labourers (1986–87 = 100) and for industrial workers (1982 = 100)
Source: Estimates based on NSSO (2011) and NSSO (2013)

2.3.2 Rise in the population of students

Another factor that has influenced India's labour market since the 2000s is a sharp rise in the population of students, notably in rural areas and among females. A major expansion of student enrolment at the primary and secondary level occurred in the country during the first half of the 2000s itself (see Thomas, 2012). Between 1999–00 and 2004–05, the ratio of students-to-population (SPR) among rural females in the age groups of 5–9 and 10–14 years rose by 14 and 13 percentage points, respectively. This improvement was particularly marked in rural areas and among females (Table 2.12).

After 2004–05, there has been a noticeable expansion of the population of students belonging to the 15–19 age group. During the seven years after 2004–05, SPR among rural males and females belonging to the 15–19 age group increased by 20 percentage points, reaching the levels of 64 per cent and 54 per cent respectively by 2011–12. SPR among urban males and females in the 15–19 age group increased too, by 13 percentage points during this period of time (see Table 2.12). A majority of the students who are 15–19 years old are likely to be pursuing education beyond the secondary levels. Therefore, the above numbers are indicative of some progress achieved in higher education in India after the mid-2000s. It is also notable that the population of students pursuing higher education is likely to be much higher in rural India than in urban India (Thomas, 2012).

There has been a remarkable reduction of disparity in access to education in India. Figure 2.1 shows the proportion of students among rural females in the age group of 5 to 24 years, and belonging to households with varying consumption-expenditure levels. The gap in this proportion between the richest and the poorest (in terms of consumption expenditure) deciles of households narrowed down considerably between 1999–00 and 2009–10 (see Figure 2.1).

The Public Report on Basic Education in India (PROBE) report on elementary education in India, which is based on surveys in eight North Indian states, also confirms that there was substantial improvement in student enrolment in the country between 1996 and 2006. The report adds that this positive change occurred due to public initiatives such as Sarva Shiksha Abhiyan, Supreme Court orders on mid-day meals, and also strong public campaigns (De, et al., 2011)

However, it may be noted here that the data on SPR provides little information on the quality of education that is offered, and indications from other studies give little to cheer about this aspect. Inadequacy of teachers and insufficient schooling infrastructure continue to remain as obstacles to improving the quality of education in India. It is striking that the PROBE report itself notes that there was little teaching activity in half of the government schools covered by the survey, at the time the (survey) investigators arrived (De, et al., 2011). Despite the achievements in enrolment ratios, the number of children in India in the age group of 6–14 years who were out of school was 22 million in 2009–10 (down from 65 million in 2001) (Rawal, 2012). Another reminder of the task ahead for the country in education comes from the Census of India 2011, which finds that the proportions of illiterates were 34.5 per cent and 17.9 per cent respectively among women and men in the country.

The increase in the population of students has had important implications for India's labour market. Between 2004–05 and 2011–12, while India's total population increased by 133 million, the population of students increased by 71 million – students thus accounting for 53 per cent of the country's incremental population. In fact, students accounted for 47 million (or 72 per cent) out of the incremental population of 65 million in India's rural areas during this period. A substantial part of the decline in India's agricultural workforce since the mid-2000s, which was marked among the younger age groups (as shown earlier), is associated with the increase in the population of students.

Table 2.12: SPR in India (in per cent), for various age groups: 1999–00 to 2011–12

Year	5–9 years				10–14 yrs.			
	RM	RF	UM	UF	RM	RF	UM	UF
1999–00	70.7	63.1	83.8	81	77.7	63.5	87.3	82.1
2004–05	80.2	76.8	88.7	87.4	85.8	76.1	89.8	87.8
2009–10	85.9	84.1	92.4	91.3	91	86.9	93.6	93.6
2011–12	86.9	87	93.4	92.4	93	89.4	94	94.2

Year	15–19 years				20–24 yrs.			
	RM	RF	UM	UF	RM	RF	UM	UF
1999–00	41.3	25.8	58.5	51.7	8.6	2.9	21.8	15.8
2004–05	43.6	31.5	58.7	56.7	9.1	3.9	21.5	14.9
2009–10	57.3	47.1	70.1	68.2	16.6	7.5	29.7	23.4
2011–12	63.5	53.6	71.9	70.1	19.4	9.4	32.1	24.3

Notes: RM = Rural males; RF = Rural females; UM = Urban males; UF = Urban females.
Source: Estimates based on NSSO (2001), NSSO (2006) and NSSO (2011) and NSSO (2013).

Figure 2.1: The ratio of students to population belonging to the 5–24 age group, among rural women in India, by household consumption-expenditure deciles, various years

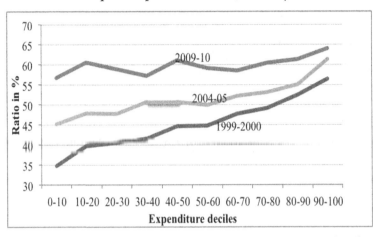

Source: Sourced from Thomas (2012), which was based on estimates from NSSO (2001), NSSO (2006) and NSSO (2011).

2.4 Slow growth of non-agricultural employment

There has been rapid growth in the supply of workers who could potentially join India's non-agricultural sector, especially after the mid-2000s. This is mainly on account of the country's demographic transition and also due to the growing shift of the country's workforce away from agriculture (as shown in the previous sections). The increase in the population of students who are 15 years and above reduces India's labour supply for now, but it increases the numbers of educated persons who would be demanding high quality jobs in the future. On the other hand, however, the expansion of employment opportunities in India's non-agricultural sector has been at a rather slow pace.

2.4.1 Deceleration in manufacturing employment

At the root of India's failure to diversify its employment structure is the relatively small size and slow growth of manufacturing sector in the country. In 2011–12, Indian manufacturing employed 61.3 million or 13 per cent of the country's total workforce (see Table 2.5). Between 2004–05 and 2011–12, manufacturing employment increased by 5.1 million, or just 10.6 per cent of the net increase in non-agricultural employment (of 48 million) in the country during this period (see Table 2.6). India's manufacturing sector consists of both the organized and unorganized sector workers. In 2009–10, organized manufacturing sector workers accounted for only 21 per cent of all manufacturing employment in India (see Thomas, 2012).

The Indian experience with respect to the role of manufacturing in economic growth stands in some contrast to those of East Asian countries and China. In China, industries in rural and semi-urban areas played a pivotal role in absorbing large numbers of that country's workforce. Between 1978 and 1996, employment in the Township and Village Enterprises (TVEs) increased from 28 million to 135 million, and output from the TVEs as a share of China's GDP increased from 6 per cent to 26 per cent (Naughton, 2007, 274–75). In 2005, the Chinese manufacturing sector employed 104 million 'regular' workers, which was almost double the size of India's total manufacturing workforce in that year (Ghose, 2008; Thomas, 2011).

Since the 1990s, the growth of manufacturing employment in India has exhibited high degree of unevenness over time. Manufacturing employment increased substantially, by 9.8 million, between 1999–00 and 2004–05 (see Table 2.6). This growth was led largely by export–oriented industries such as garments, textiles, leather and diamond cutting (Thomas, 2011). However, these very industries suffered sharp declines in employment by 2009–10, as they were hit by the downturn in export demand in the wake of the global financial crisis. India's manufacturing employment fell by 3 million between 2004–05 and 2009–10 (see Table 2.6). Manufacturing jobs were lost in most Indian states, notably Tamil Nadu (loss of 1 million jobs) and Gujarat (0.8 million jobs), two of the highly industrialized regions of the country (see Thomas, 2012).

Manufacturing employment in India recovered somewhat by 2011–12, as 8.1 million new manufacturing jobs were added in the country during the two years since 2009–10 (see Table 2.6). Nevertheless, there has been a clear deceleration in the growth of India's manufacturing employment after 2004–05 compared to the growth during its previous decade. The average annual growth of employment in Indian manufacturing was at the rate of 720,000 jobs a year during the 1980s, which accelerated to 1200,000 jobs a year between 1993–94 and 2004–05, but decelerated subsequently to 730,000 jobs a year between 2004–05 and 2011–12 (see Table 2.13).

Shortage of electricity, bottlenecks in infrastructure, volatility in exchange rate and prices (of raw material such as steel and cotton) have been some of the major factors that slowed down India's industrial growth during the late 2000s. Small scale industries have been affected in particular due to the inadequacy and high cost of credit. The worldwide economic slowdown during 2008–09 dealt a further blow to India's export oriented manufacturing units (Thomas, 2009; Thomas, 2013).

The sharp fluctuations in India's manufacturing employment during the 2000s is partly a result of the growing share of temporary and contract workers – who could be hired and fired easily – in India's manufacturing workforce. Women accounted for 40 per cent of the new manufacturing employment created in India during the first half of the 2000s. At the same time, 2.9 million out of the 3.0 million workers who lost jobs in Indian manufacturing during the second half of the 2000s were females too (see also Thomas, 2012).

2.4.2 Employment growth led by services and construction

Given the slow growth of manufacturing employment, the diversification of India's employment structure depended largely on the limited employment opportunities provided by services and construction.

During the 1980s, trade, hotels, transport and communication and community, social and personal services were the two major sources of services employment in India. Between them, they added 24.2 million new jobs or 62.5 per cent of the incremental non-agricultural employment created in the country during this period (see Table 2.6). Within the broad category of 'community, social and personal services', 'public administration and defense services' and 'education, scientific and research services' contributed 2.5 million and 1.8 million respectively to employment addition during the 1980s.[7]

During the 1990s trade, hotels, transport and communication, together, generated 13.4 million jobs, or 58 per cent of the net increase in non-agricultural employment during that decade. At the same time, employment growth under community, social and personal services decelerated sharply (see Table 2.6). More importantly, there has been a significant decline since the 1990s in the quality of jobs falling under this sector. An absolute decline in the number of jobs under public administration and defense services has occurred after 1993–94. Community, social and personal services recorded a jump in employment growth during the first half of the 2000s (7 million jobs during these five years), but a substantial part of the new jobs created were for female workers employed as domestic help (see Table 2.6 and also Thomas, 2011).

Since the 2000s, construction has become the major source of incremental employment in India. People employed in the construction industry increased by only 5.3 million during the 10 years between 1983 and 1993–94, and by 13.9 million during the 11 years between 1993–94 and 2004–05, but by 23.9 million during the seven years after 2004–05 (see Table 2.6). It needs to be highlighted that, between 2004–05 and 2011–12, the construction sector accounted for almost half (23.9 million out of 48 million) of the incremental non-agricultural employment generated in India, and almost all of the new employment opportunities that emerged in the country's rural areas (see Table 2.6).

There has been a growing dissociation in India between sectors that generate GDP and sectors that generate employment, possibly indicating a decline in the productivity and quality of new employment generated in the country. During the 1980s, construction contributed shares of a little over 7 per cent each to total GDP growth and to total employment growth in the Indian economy. The contribution made by construction to India's GDP growth did not increase much even during the post-1990 years. It was only 8.6 per cent even during the period from 2004–05 to 2009–10. On the other hand, construction accounted for 38 per cent of the incremental employment in India between 1993–94 and 2009–10, and 81 per cent of the incremental non–agricultural employment generated in the country between 2004–05 and 2009–10 (see Thomas, 2012).

Another noteworthy aspect of the increase in construction jobs in India after the mid-2000s is that an overwhelming proportion of this increase (20.5 million out of the net increase of 23.9 million between 2004–05 and 2011–12) occurred in rural areas. In fact, more than half of the incremental non-agricultural employment generated in India between 2004–05 and 2011–12 (27.3 million out of 48 million) was in the rural areas. This is a particularly interesting phenomenon given that India's GDP growth has been increasingly becoming more urban-centric over the same period.[8] This is also in sharp contrast to the growth trends in the country during the 1980s and 1990s when non-agricultural jobs were generated in larger numbers in urban areas than in rural areas (Thomas, 2012).

Particularly striking has been the regional distribution of this employment growth. The Indian states that registered the largest expansion of non-agricultural employment between 2004–05 and 2011–12 were Uttar Pradesh (UP), West Bengal and Rajasthan. Bihar and Madhya Pradesh were also in the top league in the list of Indian states with fast growth of non-agricultural employment. It is remarkable that the so-called 'BIMARU' states, which have long been considered development laggards, have figured prominently among states that recorded the fastest employment growth. In UP, Rajasthan and Madhya Pradesh at least 75 per cent of the incremental non-agricultural employment between 2004–05 and 2011–12 were generated in rural areas, and more than 70 per cent of this increase was due to construction (this was 63 per cent in Bihar).

How real are the reported increases in the numbers of persons employed in rural construction in states such as UP, Rajasthan and Bihar since the middle of the 2000s? The increase in development expenditures by governments in some of these states as also some of the initiatives by the central government such as the Pradhan Mantri Gram Sadak Yojana (PMGSY) for building rural roads may have aided rural employment generation.[9] It may also be noted here that the revival of real wages for agricultural and rural labour in India after 2007–08 was marked in the relatively poor states of Orissa, Bihar, Madhya Pradesh and UP (Usami, 2012).[10]

At the same time, it needs to be investigated whether at least a part of the increase in construction jobs for rural men is on account of the migration of rural workers to construction sites in urban areas. A number of reports indicate a marked increase in inter-state migration of workers, especially construction workers, in India in recent years.

2.4.3 Concentration of higher productivity jobs among urban males

It is a matter of concern for India's policymakers that the rate of employment generation has slowed down in the country in most sectors during the years from 2004–05 to 2011–12 compared to the years from 1993–94 to 2004–05 (see Table 2.13). The pace of employment generation has decelerated after 2004–05 in manufacturing, trade and repair, hotels and restaurants, transport and communication, and in community, social and personal services. The deceleration in employment growth in these sectors has been compensated, however, by a sharp increase the rate of generation of jobs in construction: from 1.3 million jobs a year between 1993–94 and 2004–05 to 3.7 million jobs a year between 2004–05 and 2011–12 (see Table 2.13).

Other than construction, the only sectors in which job creation accelerated in India after 2004–05 were financing, insurance, real estate and business services (see Table 2.13). This relatively high-productivity sector, which also comprises computer and related activities, added 5.8 million new jobs in India between 2004–05 and 2011–12 (see Table 2.6).

Men in urban areas obtained a relatively high share of jobs in non-agricultural sectors other than construction. Urban males comprised only 16 per cent of India's total population, but 77 per cent and 59 per cent respectively of all jobs in the country in computer and related activities and in public administration and defense in 2011–12 (see Table 2.14). Of the net employment increase in the country between 2004–05 and 2011–12, the share obtained by urban males was at least 55 per cent in manufacturing, trade and repair services, hotels, transport and communication, and in financing, real estate and business services (see Table 2.15).

The generation of high productivity urban jobs is also regionally concentrated. Maharashtra accounted for more than 20 per cent of all new urban jobs generated in India between 2004–05 and 2009–10. Maharashtra, Karnataka, Delhi, Gujarat, Kerala, and Andhra Pradesh, together, accounted for 91 per cent of the total of 2.3 million new jobs generated in the country under the category of finance and business services during the second half of the 2000s (see Thomas, 2012).

On the other hand, for India's rural residents, construction has virtually been the only source of non-agricultural employment after the mid-2000s. Between 2004–05 and 2011–12, 66 per cent of the net increase in non-agricultural employment among rural males (15.7 million out of 22.4 million) was in construction. Construction provided 4.8 million out of the 4.9 million non-agricultural jobs generated for rural females during this period (see Tables 2.14 and 2.15). Women, including urban women, received only a marginal share of the decent, high-productivity jobs generated in India during this period, an issue that has important implications for women's participation in the labour force (discussed in the next section).

Table 2.13: Annual averages of net increase in employment, in 100,000 numbers

Sectors	1983 to 1993–94	1993–94 to 1999–00	1993–94 to 2004–05	2004–05 to 2009–10	2004–05 to 2011–12
1. Agriculture and allied	30.8	1.3	16.5	−40.8	−47.6

Sectors	1983 to 1993–94	1993–94 to 1999–00	1993–94 to 2004–05	2004–05 to 2009–10	2004–05 to 2011–12
2. Manufacturing	7.2	5.6	12	−5.9	7.3
3. Construction	5.0	9.1	12.6	36.7	34.1
4. Trade, repair, hotels, transport and communications	12.0	22.3	23.9	9.6	13.6
5. Financing, insurance, real estate and business services	1.5	2.3	4	5.1	8.3
6. Community, social and personal services	11.0	3.3	8.1	2.6	4.9
6a. Public administration and defence	2.4	0.3	−1.2	2.3	−1
Total non-agricultural	36.9	38.7	59.2	50.2	68.6

Notes and Source: Same as Table 2.3.

Table 2.14: Employment in India in 2011–12, proportions (in per cent) across population categories

Sectors	RM	RF	UM	UF	Total
1. Agriculture and allied activities	62.0	34.0	2.8	1.3	100
2. Manufacturing	31.2	16.3	39.8	12.9	100
3. Construction	61.1	13.4	23.2	2.2	100
4. Trade, repair, hotels, transport, communication	38.4	4.0	52.6	5.0	100

Sectors	RM	RF	UM	UF	Total
5. Financing, insurance, real estate, business services	17.8	1.5	67.4	11.9	100
5a. Computer and related activities	3.8	0.0	76.9	15.4	100
6. Community, social and personal services	28.2	12.4	35.6	23.8	100
6a. Public administration and defence	28.9	3.6	59.0	8.4	100
6b. Education	29.7	18.6	26.9	24.8	100
Total non–agricultural	38.4	10.3	41.5	9.8	100

Notes and Source: Same as Table 2.3.

Table 2.15: Net increase in employment in India, 2004–05 to 2011–12: proportions (in per cent) across population categories

Sectors	RM	RF	UM	UF	Total
1. Manufacturing	37.3	–7.8	56.9	13.7	100
2. Construction	65.7	20.1	13.4	0.4	100
3. Trade, repair, hotels, transport and communication	39.6	–1.0	57.3	4.2	100
4. Financing, insurance, real estate and business services	15.5	5.2	63.8	15.5	100
4a. Computer and related activities	5.9	0.0	70.6	17.6	100
5. Community, social and personal services	2.9	11.8	41.2	44.1	100
5a. Education	28.6	21.4	25.0	25.0	100
Total non-agricultural	46.7	10.2	35.4	7.9	100

Notes and Source: Same as Table 2.3.

2.5 The missing women in the Indian economy

Arthur Lewis (1954, 404) pointed out that 'the transfer of women's work from the household to commercial employment is one of the most notable features of economic development.'[11] However, as shown earlier; India's record has been strikingly dismal with respect to the participation of females in the labour force.

A plot of female LPR against per capita incomes across 184 countries show that India's female LPR is considerably lower than what is predicted by the per capita income in the country (see Figure 2.2). Among the South Asian countries, Pakistan and Sri Lanka too have very low female LPR (24 per cent and 35 per cent respectively) while Bangladesh and Nepal have relatively high female LPR (57 per cent and 54 per cent respectively) (all in 2012).[12]

The other side of a low rate of female labour force participation is a substantially high proportion of females reporting their activity status as attending to domestic duties. In 2011–12, 35.3 per cent of all rural females and 46.1 per cent of all urban females in India were attending to domestic duties (see Table 2.16). The proportions of rural and urban women who attend to 'domestic duties only' (activity status 92) increased sharply between 2004–05 and 2009–10, but subsequently declined somewhat in 2011–12. The proportions of rural and urban females who attend to domestic duties and were also engaged in activities such as tailoring or weaving for household use (activity status 93) have increased considerably during the 2000s (see Table 2.16).[13]

In India, there are significant social restrictions on women's participation in the labour force. Often there are constraints on women's movements outside the household, and husbands and in-laws sometimes discourage women from working. But social factors alone do not explain the low female labour participation in the country. It needs to be noted that labour participation is strikingly low among females in urban areas and among the better educated – the very segments of the female population that are likely to face less social constraints on labour participation. In 2009–10, the proportion of females attending to domestic duties was nearly twice as high among urban females with graduate degrees as that among rural females with primary or middle school education (see Figure 2.3).

Women in India face various forms of discrimination at the workplace, particularly in terms of wages (Srivastava and Srivastava, 2010). Bardhan (1989) showed that there were significant differences between female and male wages in India during the late 1970s, even after accounting for variations in factors such as age, education, skill and caste. From a survey in 2004–05, Desai (2010) found that the ratio of female to male wage earnings in India was 73 per cent in the public sector and 53 per cent in the private sector. For all these, however, wage disparities cannot explain, to any great extent, the extremely low female labour participation in India. Women-men wage disparities exist in in the East Asian countries, such as South Korea and Japan, as well. In 1980, the ratio of female to male wage earnings was 44.5 per cent in South Korea and 48.2 per cent in Japan, according to Amsden (1989). Despite such disparities, female LPR is relatively high in these countries – unlike the case in India.

2.5.1 Absence of employment opportunities for women

It is likely that the most severe obstacle to female labour participation in India is the sheer absence of suitable employment opportunities. Females accounted for only a small share of the better paid and decent jobs generated in India in recent years. Between 2004–05 and 2011–12, the share of females in incremental employment was only 18 per cent in non–agricultural sectors as a whole, 21 per cent in financing, real estate and business services, 18 per cent in computer and related activities, and a meagre 3 per cent in trade, repair, hotels, transport, and communication combined (see Table 2.15). In 2011–12, female workers formed only 15 per cent or even less of the total employment in financing, real estate and business services, computer and related activities, and in public administration and defence (see Table 2.14).

In manufacturing, women find employment increasingly as temporary or contract workers. There is some evidence that female workers have been hit more acutely than male workers during periods of economic crisis. In 2009–10, Indian economy, and especially the manufacturing sector, was affected by the crisis and the slowdown in the global economy. In Table 2.17, actual employment in India in 2009–10 is compared with the employment estimated for that year assuming that employment growth between 2004–05 and 2009–10 was as fast as that between 2004–05 and 2011–12. It is found that that the actual employment in India's manufacturing and services in 2009–10 was less than the estimated employment by 10.9 per cent and 3.4 per cent respectively. But this employment deficit in 2009–10 was considerably higher in the case of females engaged in manufacturing and services: 17.4 per cent and 9.6

per cent respectively. Females lost disproportionately more jobs than males in export-oriented sectors such as textiles and garments as much as in the modern, highly skilled sectors such as computer and finance (see Table 2.17).

It appears that given the inadequacy in gainful employment opportunities, women tend to withdraw from the labour force, especially so in households where the male members do have some income earning opportunities. As shown in Figure 2.4, the proportion of females attending to domestic duties rises with household consumption expenditures, particularly in the urban areas.

Amartya Sen has written about the issue of the 'missing women' in India – pointing to the low women-men ratio in the country's population, which arises mainly on account of the disadvantages facing the female child (Sen, 1999). It can be seen that the phenomenon of the missing women in India's workforce is as crucial as the issue of the missing women in India's population. By missing women in workforce, the author is referring to the staggering numbers of women who have withdrawn from the labour force and attend to domestic duties (see also Thomas, 2011).

The population of women attending to domestic duties was 216 million in India in 2009–10, which was, in fact, bigger than the entire population of Brazil at that point in time. Women with secondary or higher-secondary school education and attending to domestic duties numbered 37 million – little more than the population of Canada. Women with graduate degrees or above and attending to domestic duties numbered 12.7 million in India , which was more than twice as big as the population of Singapore (all population figures in 2010) (see Table 2.18). Without doubt, such a massive withdrawal of women from the labour force involves a tremendous wastage of talent and huge opportunity cost for Indian economy. This is also the single biggest hurdle that India faces in achieving the demographic dividend.

Table 2.16: Females who attend to domestic duties as a per cent of all women in rural and urban India

	Rural women			Urban women		
Year	92	93	92 + 93	92	93	92 + 93
1993–94	15.8	13.3	29.1	33.1	8.6	41.7
1999–00	17.9	11.3	29.2	37.1	6.2	43.3
2004–05	15.1	12.1	27.2	33.4	9.4	42.8

	Rural women			Urban women		
Year	92	93	92 + 93	92	93	92 + 93
2009–10	20.6	14.1	34.7	38.9	7.6	46.5
2011–12	16.8	18.5	35.3	35.4	10.7	46.1

Notes: '92' refers to the activity status of persons who attended to domestic duties only (at the time of the survey). '93' refers to the activity status of persons who attended to domestic duties and were also engaged in free collection of goods (such as vegetables, firewood, and cattle feed) or in sewing, tailoring and weaving for household use. The table shows females in these two activity statuses as proportion of all females.

Source: Estimates based on NSSO (1997), NSSO (2001), NSSO (2006), NSSO (2011) and NSSO (2013).

Table 2.17: Difference between the actual and estimated values of employment as a proportion of the estimated value, in 2009–10, in per cent

Sectors	All categories	Women
A. Manufacturing	-10.9	-17.4
1. Textiles, garments, leather	-12.1	-20.6
2.Furniture, jewellery, toys, precision instruments	-12.6	-22.0
B. Services	-3.4	-9.6
1. Finance, real estate, business services	-10.4	-23.7
1a. Computer and related activities	1.3	-18.4
2. Community, social and personal services	-2.6	-8.5
2a. Private households with employed persons	-2.6	-13.6

Note: 'Estimated value': employment estimated for 2009–10 from the 2004–05 figures, based on the assumption that the rate of growth of employment between 2004–05 and 2009–10 was the same as that between 2004–05 and 2011–12.

Source: same as Table 2.2.

Figure 2.2: Log of per capita GDP and female labour participation rate, 2008, in 184 countries included in the ILO database

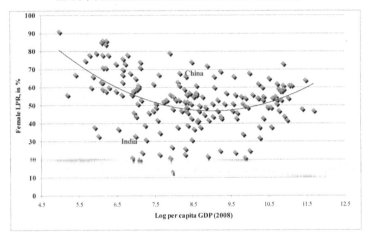

Note: LPR of population aged 15 years and above.

Source: Sourced from Thomas (2012), which was based on data obtained from International Labour Organization (ILO), available with World Development Indicators, World Bank (at http://data. worldbank. org/indicator.).

Figure 2.3: Females who are employed and who attend to domestic duties, as per cent of all females, rural and urban India, by education achievements, 2009–10

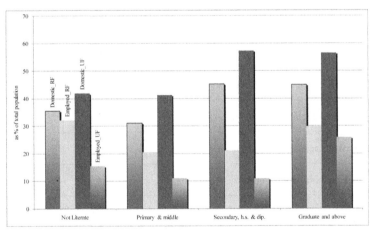

Notes: 'Domestic_UF' refers to the proportion of urban females attending to domestic duties. The various levels of education achievements are: not literate, primary- and middle-school, secondary, higher secondary and diploma, and graduate and above.

Source: Sourced from Thomas (2012), which was based on data from NSSO (2011).

Figure 2.4: Females who are employed and who attend to domestic duties, as per cent of all females in each household consumption-expenditure decile, rural and urban India, 2009–10

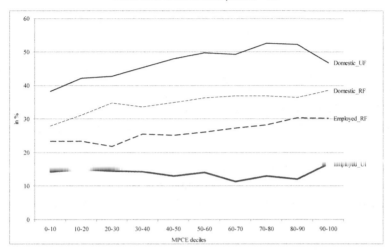

Notes: 'Domestic_UF' refers to the proportion of urban females attending to domestic duties.
Source: Sourced from Thomas (2012), which was based on estimates from NSSO (2011).

Table 2.18: The number of women who attend to domestic duties in India in 2009–10 and the increase in this number between 2004–05 and 2009–10, in millions

	Not literate	Primary and middle	Secondary, high school. and diploma	Graduate and above	Total in millions
In 2009–10	84.8	81.4	37.1	12.7	216.1
Increase between 2004–05 and 2009–10	13.0	16.8	14.4	4.6	49.4

Source: Sourced from Thomas (2012), which was based on data from NSSO (2011).

2.6 Conclusion

This chapter presents an overview of the major trends in India's labour market during the 2000s. The size of India's total workforce increased impressively, by

59.4 million, between 1999–2000 and 2004–05. But the next five years, 2004–05 to 2009–10, have widely been described as a period of 'jobless growth', as the net employment created by the economy fell sharply to 4.7 million only. The NSSO survey in 2011–12 has shown some recovery in employment growth, with 10 million new jobs generated during the two years since 2009–10. Nevertheless, this chapter argues that the above-discussed trends in the growth of overall employment conceal some major structural shifts in India's labour market, and that these structural changes are a source of both significant challenges as well as opportunities for India's future economic growth.

First is the absolute decline in the number of workers engaged in agriculture and related activities, which was observed for the first time in the country by the NSSO survey in 2009–10. The entry of rural females into self-employment in agriculture had contributed almost a third of the net increase in employment in India during the first half of the 2000s. But studies have shown that at least a part of this employment growth was driven by the absence of other income earning opportunities for the household, given the general agrarian distress that prevailed during this period.

On the other hand, the population of females engaged in agriculture declined equally sharply in India during the second half of the 2000s. At least to some extent, such a reversal in female agricultural employment could be linked to a marginal revival in India's rural economy after 2004–05, which appears to have benefited from some of the government initiatives. Between 2004–05 and 2011–12, casual employment in public works increased by an impressive 5.8 million, including 2.9 million jobs created due to MGNREGA. There was a clear improvement in rural wages during the second half of the 2000s as compared to the first half.

Secondly, there has been a marked rise in the population of students in India since the 2000s. In particular, the second half of the 2000s witnessed an expansion in the numbers of students aged 15 years and above, indicating considerable improvements in access to higher education in the country. Notably, these improvements in education have been marked among rural females and among people belonging to the poorer households.

It is clear that the supply of workers seeking decent jobs in the non-agricultural sectors is rising rapidly in India given the growing size of the working age population, its increasing shift away from agriculture, and with the improvements in education. On the other hand, however, the generation of employment in the country has been far from adequate to meet this challenge, as shown by the trends between 2004–05 and 2011–12.

First, of the net increase of 48 million new non-agricultural jobs in India between 2004–05 and 2011–12, 24 million or half of the total increase was on account of jobs in construction, which were, largely, in rural areas and casual in nature. At the same time, the manufacturing sector generated just 5 million new jobs during this period. A significant part of the incremental non-agricultural employment was generated in UP, Rajasthan and Bihar, states that are generally considered development laggards.

The absence of enough quality jobs has meant that women, especially the urban educated, are discouraged from entering the labour market, choosing instead to attend to domestic duties in their own households. The numbers of 'missing women' in India – women who withdraw from labour force and engage only in domestic duties – is a staggering 216 million in 2009–10, almost as large as the population of a country like Brazil. This is indeed the tallest hurdle for labour market modernization in India.

The gap between labour supply and labour demand will widen in India in the coming years, unless jobs are generated at a much faster pace to absorb the newer entrants to the labour force. The quality of jobs will have to increase too given the considerable expansion in the numbers of educated workers that will occur over the next few years.

Endnotes

1 This chapter has drawn extensively from the author's two previous studies on India's labour market. See Thomas (2012) and Thomas (2014).

2 This chapter has used concordance tables to compare the industry-wise distribution of workers in the various NSSO reports. The classification of industries is according to National Industrial Classification (NIC) 1970 in the 1983 NSSO report, according to NIC 1987 in the 1993–94 NSSO report, according to NIC 1998 in the NSSO reports for 1999–2000 and 2004–05, according to NIC 2004 in the 2009–10 NSSO report, and according to NIC 2008 in the 2011–12 NSSO report. See also Thomas (2011).

3 International Labour Organization (ILO) data available with World Development Indicators, World Bank.

4 NSSO defines usual principal status workers as people who worked for a relatively longer part of the 365 days preceding the date of survey. From the rest of the population, NSS identifies usual subsidiary status workers as persons who worked for at least 30 days during the reference period of 365 days preceding the date of survey.

5 ILO data available with World Development Indicators, World Bank.

6 At the same time, it needs to be investigated whether at least a part of the above-referred changes in women's employment is a result of some changes in the way NSSO measured women's activity statuses (especially self-employed in agriculture and attending to domestic duties).

7 Sen (1996) observed that increased government expenditure was an important stimulus to the growth of non-agricultural employment in India during the 1980s.

8 Sectors such as financing, real estate and business services, which are largely urban-based, have increased their weight in India's GDP during the recent decades.

9 There was an improvement in Bihar's development expenditures since the mid-2000s, although this improvement was not sustained, according to Das Gupta (2010).

10 The growth of non-agricultural employment in Uttar Pradesh until 2004–05 was distress-induced, notes Ranjan (2009). According to Rodgers and Rodgers (2011), migration has been the main trigger for labour market changes in rural Bihar.

11 Cited in Amsden (1989, p.203).

12 ILO data available with World Development Indicators, World Bank.

13 The reportedly low female labour force participation in India is partly on account of the methods employed to measure women's work. As is well known, women's domestic duties include childbirth, caring for the young and old, cooking, and a range of other activities that are crucial for the upkeep of the family. However, National Income Accounting or other statistical systems do not recognize such activities by women in their own households as economic activities (unlike the case of services by a paid domestic help, which is considered an economic activity and gets counted in the national income). It is probably true that the official statistical agencies undervalue women's contributions as does the society at large (Mazumdar and Neetha, 2011)

References

Abraham, Vinoj. 2009. 'Employment Growth in Rural India: Distress Driven?', *Economic and Political Weekly* 44(16): 97–104.

Amsden, Alice. H. 1989. *Asia's Next Giant – South Korea and Late Industrialisation*. New York: Oxford University Press.

Bardhan, Pranab. 1989. 'Poverty and Employment Characteristics of Urban Households in West Bengal, India: An Analysis of the Results of the National Sample Survey, 1977–78'. In *Urban Poverty and the Labour Market: Access to Jobs and Incomes in Asian and Latin American Cities*, edited by Gerry Rodgers. Geneva: International Labour Organization.

Chandrasekhar, C. P. and Jayati Ghosh. 2006. 'Working More for Less', *Macroscan: An Alternative Economics Webcentre*, 28 November 2006. Available at: www.macroscan.org. Accessed on 16 May 2010.

Das Gupta, Chirashree. 2010. 'Unravelling Bihar's "Growth Miracle"', *Economic and Political Weekly* 45(52): 50–62.

De, Anuradha, Reetika Khera, Meera Samson and A. K. Shiva Kumar. 2011. *PROBE Revisited: A Report on Elementary Education in India*. New Delhi: Oxford University Press.

Desai, Sonalde. 2010. 'The Other Half of the Demographic Dividend', *Economic and Political Weekly* 45(40): 12–14.

EPW. 2011. 'Don't Shoot the Messenger', *Economic and Political Weekly* July 9 46(28): 7–8.

Fei, C. H. John and Gustav. Ranis. 1975. 'A Model of Growth and Employment in the Open Dualistic Economy: The Cases of Korea and Taiwan', *Journal of Development Studies* 11(2): 32–63.

Fields, Gary S. 2004. 'Dualism in the Labour Market: A Perspective on the Lewis Model after Half a Century', *The Manchester School* 72(6): 724–35.

Ghose, Ajit K. 2008. 'The Growth Miracle, Institutional Reforms and Employment in China', *Economic and Political Weekly* 43(22): 47–56.

Karan, Anup K. and Sakthivel Selvaraj. 2008. 'Trends in Wages and Earnings in India: Increasing Wage Differentials in a Segmented Labour Market'. *Asia Pacific Working Paper Series*. New Delhi: International Labour Organization.

Lewis, Arthur. 1954. 'Economic Development with Unlimited Supplies of Labour'. In *The Economics of Underdevelopment*, edited by A. N. Agarwala and S. P. Singh. London: Oxford University Press.

Mazumdar, Indrani and N. Neetha. 2011. 'Gender Dimensions: Employment Trends in India, 1993–94 to 2009–10', *Economic and Political Weekly* 46(43): 118–126.

Naughton, Barry. 2007. *The Chinese Economy: Transitions and Growth.* Cambridge, Massachusetts: The MIT Press.

NSSO. 1987. *Report on the Third Quinquennial Survey on Employment and Unemployment.* Thirty Eighth Round, January-December 1983, Report No. 341. New Delhi: National Sample Survey Organization, Department of Statistics, Government of India.

_____. 1997. *Employment and Unemployment in India, 1993–94.* Fiftieth Round, July 1993-June 1994, Report No. 409. New Delhi: National Sample Survey Organization, Department of Statistics, Government of India.

_____. 2001. *Employment and Unemployment Situation in India 1999–2000.* Parts I and II. Fifty Fifth Round, July 1999–June 2000, Report No. 458. New Delhi: National Sample Survey Organization, Ministry of Statistics and Programme Implementation, Government of India.

_____. 2006. *Employment and Unemployment Situation in India 2004–05.* Parts I and II. Sixty First Round, July 2004–June 2005, Report No. 515. New Delhi: National Sample Survey Organization, Ministry of Statistics and Programme Implementation, Government of India.

_____. 2011. *Employment and Unemployment Situation in India 2009–10.* Sixty Sixth Round, July 2009–June 2010. New Delhi: National Sample Survey Organization, Ministry of Statistics and Programme Implementation, Government of India.

_____. 2013. *Key Indicators of Employment and Unemployment in India 2011–12.* Sixty Eighth Round, July 2011–June 2012. New Delhi: National Sample Survey Organization, Ministry of Statistics and Programme Implementation, Government of India.

Papola, T. S. 2008. 'Employment Challenge and Strategies in India', *Asia Pacific Working Paper Series*. New Delhi: International Labour Organization.

Ramachandran, V. K., and Vikas Rawal. 2010. 'The Impact of Liberalization and Globalization on India's Agrarian Economy', *Global Labour Journal* 1(1): 56–91.

Ranjan, Sharad. 2009. 'Growth of Rural Non–Farm Employment in Uttar Pradesh: Reflections from Recent Data', *Economic and Political Weekly* 44(4): 63–70.

Rawal, Vikas. 2011. 'Statistics on Elementary School Education in Rural India', *Review of Agrarian Studies* 1(2): 179–97.

Rodgers, Gerry and Janine Rodgers. 2011. 'Inclusive Development? Migration, Governance and Social Change in Rural Bihar', *Economic and Political Weekly* 46(23): 43–50.

Sarkar, Sandip and Balwant Singh Mehta. 2010. 'Income Inequality in India: Pre- and Post-Reform Periods', *Economic and Political Weekly* 45(37): 45–55.

Sen, Abhijit. 1996. 'Economic Reforms, Employment and Poverty: Trends and Options', *Economic and Political Weekly* 31(35/37): 2459–77.

Sen, Amartya. 1999. *Development as Freedom*. New Delhi: Oxford University Press.

Srivastava, Nisha and Ravi Srivastava. 2010. 'Women, Work and Employment Outcomes in Rural India', *Economic and Political Weekly* 45(28): 49–63.

Sundaram, K. 2007. 'Employment and Poverty in India, 2000–05', *Economic and Political Weekly* 42(30). 3121–31.

Thomas, Jayan Jose. 2009. 'Hurdles to Growth', *Frontline*, 10 October 26 (21).

_____. 2011. 'Locked in a Low–Skill Equilibrium? Trends in Labour Supply and Demand in India', *Indian Journal of Labour Economics* 54(2): 195–218.

_____. 2013. 'Explaining the "Jobless" Growth in Indian Manufacturing', *Journal of the Asia Pacific Economy* 18(4): 673–92.

_____. 2012. 'India's Labour Market during the 2000s: Surveying the Changes', *Economic and Political Weekly* 48(51): 39–51.

_____. 2014. 'The Demographic Challenge and Employment Growth in India', *Economic and Political Weekly* 49(6): 15–17.

Thorat, Sukhadeo and Amaresh Dubey. 2012. 'Has Growth Been Socially Inclusive During 1993–94–2009–10?', *Economic and Political Weekly* 47(10): 43–53.

Xiaobo, Zhang, Yang Jin and Wang Shenglin. 2011. 'China has Reached the Lewis Turning Point', *China Economic Review* 22(4): 542–54.

Usami, Yoshifumi 2012. 'Recent Trends in Wage Rates in Rural India: An Update', *Review of Agrarian Studies*. Available at: http://ras.org.in. Accessed on 16 August 2012.

3

Services-led Growth and Employment in India

Ajit K. Ghose

The Indian economy's transition to a high growth path in the 1990s is widely believed to have been triggered by accelerated growth of the service sector. And the acceleration in the growth of services has seemingly been fostered by globalization. These developments, when viewed in a perspective of international experience, appear quite extraordinary. In today's developed economies, manufacturing led the growth process in early stages of development and services took over the lead role only after a fairly high level of development had been reached.[1] The same pattern has also been observed in the East Asian 'tiger' economies and in China in more recent periods. In these Asian economies, moreover, openness to trade stimulated growth by stimulating growth of manufacturing and not growth of services.[2] India's recent experience appears to defy these patterns. Here services-led growth has come at an early stage of development and increased openness appears to have stimulated growth of services rather than growth of manufacturing.

Arguably, the 'stylized fact' about the role of services in economic growth is actually less than well established. Several studies claimed that, across countries, no significant relationship between the share of services in GDP and per capita GDP could be found.[3] Several others, however, did find a significant positive relationship between those variables.[4] A recent study seeks to reconcile these contradictory findings by proposing the idea of 'two waves of service-sector growth', a first wave coming at an early stage of development and a second wave at a relatively advanced stage of development.[5]

The steady growth of the share of manufacturing in output with per capita income, on the other hand, is a very well-established stylized fact. Against this backdrop, it has been argued that services have now acquired many of the characteristics of manufacturing ('learning by doing' effects at enterprise level, spill over effects at macroeconomic level and international tradability) so that it can serve as a lead sector in economic growth just as well as manufacturing.[6] Thus services-led growth in early stages of development may well be a new pattern that will be prominent in the new century and India's experience is perhaps a precursor of other experiences to come. The validity or otherwise of this conjecture will not be known for quite some time to come. What is known at this point of time is that India's experience of services-led growth stands out as quite exceptional.

The employment intensity of services in India also stands out as exceptional. It is known from general experience that services tend to be highly employment-intensive. So the services-led growth in India might have been expected to be rich in employment. It is widely believed, however, that growth of services in India has not been particularly employment-intensive.

It is hardly surprising, then, that India's services-led growth has generated much questioning and concern. What explains the premature appearance of services-led growth? Why has the growth of services been relatively jobless? Is services-led growth really sustainable? And if the low employment intensity of growth of services persists, how will India's mass of surplus labour ever be moved to productive employment?

This chapter takes a hard look at India's experience of services-led growth in an effort to answer these questions.

3.1 How exceptional is India's services-led growth?

India's transition to high growth and the role of services[7] in it can be read from Figure 3.1, which graphically presents five-year moving averages of annual growth rates of GDP and of services over the period 1951–2010.[8] The figure suggests two episodes of acceleration in GDP growth. The first acceleration occurs in the early 1980sand the second acceleration occurs toward the end of the 1990s.[9] Both of these accelerations in GDP growth appear to have been associated with accelerations in the growth of services. Thus it is not the case that India's services-led growth was triggered by the economic reforms of the early 1990s, which opened up India's hitherto quasi-closed economy to international trade and capital flows; the reforms at best strengthened a pre-existing tendency.[10]

Figure 3.1: Five-year moving averages of annual growth rates
of GDP and services

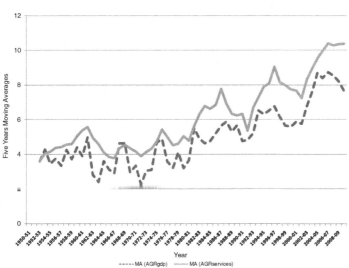

Source: Author's estimates based on data from Central Statistical Organisation, Government of India

Indeed, if growth is characterized as services-led when the contribution of services to GDP growth is higher than that of any of the other sectors, India's growth has always been services-led (Table 3.1). It was only during 1951–82 – the period of the so-called 'Hindu rate of growth' – that services grew at a slower rate than industry; throughout the post-1982 period, the growth of services was significantly faster than that of industry. But the share of services in GDP was already quite large (30 per cent) – much larger than that of industry (17 per cent) – in 1951 so that the contribution of services to even the 'Hindu rate of growth' was larger than that of any of the other sectors. What is distinctive about the post-1982 period is that the contribution of services to GDP growth was larger than the contributions of the other sectors put together.[11]

How unusual or exceptional is this pattern of growth of the post-1982 period in India? To answer this question, one needs to situate India's experience in the context of the experience of developing countries as a group.

Table 3.1: Pattern of growth

Sectors	Average annual rate of growth (%)			Contribution (%) sectors to GDP growth		
	1951–82	1983–99	2000–10	1951–82	1983–99	2000–10
Agriculture	2.1	3.1	2.6	26.4	17.1	6.9
Manufacturing	5.1	5.9	7.9	17.0	16.5	16.9
Construction	4.9	5.0	9.5	9.0	6.3	9.6
Other industries	5.7	6.7	5.0	5.3	6.4	3.3
Services	4.4	6.6	8.6	42.3	53.7	63.3
GDP	3.5	5.4	7.2			

Note: Other industries include 'mining and quarrying' and 'electricity, gas and water'.

Source: Author's estimates based on national accounts statistics from Central Statistical Office (CSO), Ministry of Statistics and Programme Implementation (MOSPI), Government of India (GOI).

In a first exercise, we look at the cross-sectional relationship between the share of services in GDP and the level of development (represented by per capita GDP in constant 2005 purchasing power parity or PPP dollars) in samples of developing countries (excluding India) in three periods: 2000, 2005 and 2010.[12] A simple linear regression equation, when fitted to the data for each of the three periods, yields results that are presented in Appendix Table A 3.1. These results are then used, together with the actual values of the independent variables for India in the three periods, to derive the predicted values for the share of services in GDP for India. Then there is a comparison of these predicted values with the actual values (Table 3.2). It turns out that the share of services in GDP in India is pretty much in line with what the international experience would lead one to expect.[13]

Table 3.2: Share of services in GDP, India, predicted and actual values (percentages)

	2000	2005	2010
Predicted value	52.6	53.9	56.4
Actual value	50.1	53.0	54.7

Note: Estimates of shares are based on data in current prices.

Source: Author's estimates based on data in Appendix Table A1 and national accounts statistics from CSO.

What is striking about India's growth experience is rather the exceptionally low share of industry in GDP. Cross-country comparisons show the share of industry in GDP in India to be significantly lower than what would be expected, given the share of services in GDP (Table 3.3). Thus while the share of services in GDP is not high in relation to per capita GDP, it is too high in relation to the share of industry in GDP. Essentially, given its level of development, agriculture in India is more important than it ought to be, industry is less important than it ought to be and services are about as important as they ought to be. India's services-led growth appears premature when viewed in this broader perspective.

Table 3.3: Share of industry in GDP, India, predicted and actual values (percentages)

	2000	2005	2010
Predicted value	32.6	32.4	32.8
Actual value	25.1	27.9	28.3

Note: Industry includes 'mining and quarrying', 'manufacturing', 'construction' and 'electricity, gas and water'. Estimates of shares are based on data in current prices.

Source: Author's estimates based on data in Appendix Table A3.2 and national accounts statistics from CSO.

The premature nature of services-led growth in India comes into particularly sharp focus when India's growth pattern is compared to that of three selected comparator countries: China, Indonesia and Thailand (Table 3.4). Both China and Thailand had industry-led growth throughout the 30-year period from 1980–2010. In the case of Indonesia, the economic crisis of 1997 appears to have changed the character of the growth process; its growth was industry-led in the pre-crisis period but services-led in the post-crisis period. Even in Indonesia, however, the contribution of industry to growth was important just as the contribution of services to growth was important in China and Thailand. In all three countries, the shares of both industry and services in GDP were high and growing together (Appendix Table A3.4). The peculiarity of India's experience, it emerges once again, lies in the 'marginalization' of industry, particularly of manufacturing, in the growth process by the rise of services (compare Tables 3.1 and 3.4).

Table 3.4: Pattern of growth: China, Indonesia and Thailand

	Contribution (%) of sectors to GDP growth		
	1980–95	1996–2010	2000–10
CHINA			
Agriculture	14.4	5.5	4.9
Industry	46.2	51.6	52.2
Manufacturing	32.3	34.1	33.6
Services	39.9	42.9	42.9
INDONESIA			
Agriculture	10.1	10.4	9.4
Industry	49.2	35	34
Manufacturing	32.2	25.8	23.1
Services	40.7	54.6	56.6
THAILAND			
Agriculture	5.1	6.2	4.7
Industry	48.2	57.5	55.7
Manufacturing	36.7	51.3	47.9
Services	46.7	36.3	39.6

Source: Author's estimates based on data from World Bank and World Development Indicators

Another aspect of India's growth experience is the exceptionally low employment intensity of services. Simple regression exercises show that, in general, the share of services in total employment in a developing economy tends to equal the share of services in GDP (Appendix Table A3.3). And the same pattern is observed in developed economies as well (Appendix Table A3.5). In India, however, the share of services in employment has been and remains far lower than the share in GDP (Table 3.5).

Table 3.5: Share of services in employment, India: predicted and actual values (percentages)

	2000	2005	2010
Predicted value	52.6	51.9	53.8
Actual value	25.7	27.4	28.9

Note: The predicted values are simple averages of predicted upper and lower values, which are estimated by alternately including and excluding the intercepts. The reason for doing this is that the intercepts are statistically insignificant.

Source: Author's estimates based on (1) data in Table 3.7, (2) data from World Bank, World Development Indicators, (3) National accounts data from CSO, and (4) data on employment from NSSO, MOSPI, and GOI.

To sum up, if one confines attention to a single variable, namely, the share of services in GDP, India's economy does not look like a significant outlier in the community of developing economies. But it does look like a very significant outlier when one considers two additional variables: the share of industry in GDP and the share of services in total employment in the economy.[14] Given the share of services in GDP, the values of these two variables should have been much higher than what they are. India's services sector is overdeveloped in relation to its industrial sector. And the share of services in employment is exceptionally low in relation to the share in GDP. The premature nature of India's services-led growth becomes apparent only when it is viewed from a broad perspective.

There is one other fact that also brings the exceptional nature of India's growth process into sharp focus. Since India's economy is dualistic in character, it is worth looking into the growth patterns in the two segments – organized and unorganized – separately.[15] The patterns, it turns out, have been remarkably similar; growth was services-led in both segments throughout the period 1981–2010 (Table 3.6). In the organized segment, the share of services in NDP steadily increased while that of industry steadily declined. In the unorganized segment, the share of services in NDP steadily increased while that of agriculture steadily declined. By 2010, services had become dominant in both organized and unorganized parts of the economy.

Table 3.6: Services-led growth in organized and unorganized sectors

	Contribution (%) to NDP growth		Share (%) of production sectors in NDP		
	1981–2000	2000–10	1981	2000	2010
Organized sector NDP					
Agriculture	2.7	1.0	11.1	5.6	3.0
Industry	38.3	35.8	44.4	36.2	34.8
Manufacturing	17.6	17.7	22.2	19.0	22.5
Services	59.0	63.2	44.5	58.2	62.2
Unorganized sector NDP					
Agriculture	30.7	12.0	50.2	39.0	26.5
Industry	15.1	20.8	16.1	15.1	17.7
Manufacturing	6.5	7.7	10.3	7.8	7.7
Services	54.2	67.3	33.7	45.9	55.8

Source: Author's estimates based on data on factor incomes from CSO.

3.2 Growth of services: Pace and pattern

What have been driving the rather exceptional growth of services in India? A first fact to note is the broad-based nature of growth of services (Table 3.7). Quite clearly, all types of services recorded speedy growth and most recorded growth acceleration.

For purposes of analysis, three basic groups of services can be defined: traditional services which include 'wholesale and retail trade, 'hotels and restaurants' and 'transport and storage'; modern services which include 'communication' (a category that includes telecom services), 'financial services' and 'real estate-renting-business services' (a category that includes software services); and social services which include 'public administration and defence' and 'community, social and personal services'. The traditional and the modern services are mostly in the private sector while the social services are mostly in the public sector. And as one shall see below, there are important differences in terms of employment structure between the traditional services on the one hand and the modern and the social services on the other.

Table 3.7: Pace and pattern of growth of services

	Average annual growth rate (%)		Contribution (%) to services growth	
	1981–2000	2000–10	1981–2000	2000–10
Services	*6.6*	*8.5*		
Trade (wholesale + retail)	6.6	9.1	28.7	30.8
Hotels and restaurants	7.7	9.8	2.6	2.9
Transport and storage	8.1	8.5	11.1	10.3
Traditional services	**7.0**	**9.0**	**42.4**	**44.0**
Communication	11.7	9.7	3.6	3.3
Financial services	8.5	7.7	13.8	10.7
Real estate, renting and business services	5.4	10.4	12.7	18.9
Modern services	**7.0**	**9.3**	**30.1**	**32.9**
Public administration and defence	5.7	7.2	11.5	11.0
Community, social and personal services	5.5	6.4	16.0	12.1
Social services	**5.6**	**6.8**	**27.5**	**23.1**

Source: Author's estimates based on data on factor incomes from CSO.

It is quite remarkable that the growth of modern services was really no faster than that of traditional services in either of the two periods. And while most services recorded significant growth acceleration between the periods, the exceptions were 'communication' and 'financial services', both modern services, which recorded slight deceleration. As a group, modern services nevertheless recorded growth acceleration because of large acceleration in the growth of 'real estate, renting and business services', which include software services.

The overall growth of services in both periods is actually attributable more to the speedy growth of traditional services than to the equally speedy growth of modern services.

This aggregate picture, however, does not say the full story and it is important to consider not just the growth of different types of services but also the growth of different types of services in each of the segments – organized and unorganized. The unorganized segment, though its importance has been declining over time, still accounts for more than 50 per cent of services output in the economy.[16] In both periods, the unorganized services grew only a little slower than the organized services (Table 3.8). The contribution of unorganized services to overall services growth, while it declined between the periods, was still above 50 per cent during 2000–10.

Table 3.8: Growth of organized and unorganized services

	Average annual rate of growth (%)		Contribution (%) to services growth	
	1981–2000	2000–10	1981–2000	2000–10
Services	6.6	8.5		
Organized services	7.0	9.1	40.6	46.9
Unorganized services	6.2	8.0	59.4	53.1

Source: Author's estimates based on data on factor incomes from CSO.

In both organized and unorganized sectors, all types of services recorded rapid growth in both periods and also recorded growth acceleration in the second period (Table 3.9). But there are important differences between the growth patterns in the two sectors as also between the two periods.

In the organized sector, during 1981–2000, social services (in large part, government services) were the most important contributor to the growth of services. This changed in the next period (2000–10) when modern services were the most important contributor. As already noted, however, the growth acceleration in modern services is wholly explained by the growth acceleration in 'business services', particularly in 'software services'.[17] One somewhat surprising fact is that traditional services in the organized segment not only recorded high growth during 1981–2000 but also recorded the largest acceleration in the next period. Organized 'wholesale and retail trade' and organized 'hotels and restaurants', in particular, recorded rapid growth in both periods.

Table 3.9: Pace and pattern of growth of organized and unorganized services

	Average annual growth rate (%)		Contribution (%) to services growth	
	1981–2000	2000–10	1981–2000	2000–10
Organized services	7.0	9.1		
Traditional	7.3	11.9	18.8	26.5
Modern	8.8	10.2	37.0	38.8
Social	5.9	6.8	44.2	34.7
Unorganized services	6.2	8.0		
Traditional	7.0	8.1	64.2	62.0
Modern	5.5	8.2	23.8	26.7
Social	4.8	6.9	12.1	11.3

Source: Author's estimates based on data on factor incomes from CSO.

In the unorganized segment, not too surprisingly, traditional services were by far the most important contributor to services growth. But modern services too grew rapidly in the second period. This essentially reflected quite spectacular growth of 'communication', which in turn reflected growth of mobile phone services. Social services in the context of the unorganized sector basically mean 'personal' services (services of security guards, gardeners, cooks, cleaners, and so on), and these also increased quite rapidly in the second period.

It is quite clear that the rapid growth of services was driven very largely by the growth of non-traded services, and thus by growth of domestic demand, in both periods. Even during 2000–10, when the growth of services exports was truly impressive, this made a relatively small contribution to the growth of services output. The estimates presented in Table 3.10 directly show these features. The contribution of growth of services exports to growth of services output was just 6 per cent for the period 1981–2000, which increased to 13 per cent for the period

2000–10. It also emerges that intermediate demand (including splintering) for services from industry and agriculture has been small and declined between the periods.[18] The rapid growth of services was clearly sustained very largely by the growth of domestic final demand.

Table 3.10: Contribution of different sources of demand to growth of services

	1981–2000	2000–10
Inputs into agriculture	1.2	0.7
Inputs into industry	8.9	7.8
Domestic final demand	84.0	78.0
Exports	5.9	13.4

Source: Appendix C.

The smallness of contribution of exports to growth of services should not really come as a surprise. The share of services exports (in value added terms) in services output was minuscule in the 1980s and the 1990s and, despite impressive growth in the 2000s, still remains small. This share hovered around 3.0 per cent between 1981 and 1997. It started growing only after that, reached a peak of 12 per cent in 2009 and declined thereafter.[19] Moreover, services exports have been and remain heavily concentrated; software exports accounted for about 34 per cent of services exports in 2000 and 52 per cent in 2010. For most of the years between 2000 and 2010, trade in services other than software services was actually in deficit. In short, only the exports of software services really recorded impressive growth.[20] But these exports constituted less than 1 per cent of services output in 2000 and less than 6 per cent in 2010. So while exports played a big role in stimulating growth of IT services, their role in stimulating growth of the services sector as a whole was rather small.

One intriguing question that arises is: How is it that India, a low income country with abundant supply of unskilled labour, has specialized in exports of skill-intensive software services rather than in exports of labour-intensive manufactures? The short answer is that it is the comparative advantage of the organized sector (and not of the economy as a whole) that counts and this sector's comparative advantage in skill-intensive activities has been created by policies, past and present. Already in the 1950s, India had adopted a growth strategy that accorded priority to heavy industries and thereby to increasing the availability of high skilled labour.[21] The education policy, therefore, had to be heavily biased toward tertiary education to the neglect of primary and secondary education. Thus, while universal primary education received little more than lip service, resources were concentrated in establishing centres of excellence in tertiary education. The government, moreover, provided large subsidy per student in tertiary education.[22] These biases have persisted to this day. The result has been availability of relatively cheap skilled labour. On the other hand, labour regulations had the effect of making unskilled/low-skilled labour relatively expensive in the organized sector. One can add that physical capital, like human capital, has also been subsidized in a variety of ways. Thus the factor endowments in the organized sector are (and have been) very different from the factor endowments of the economy; while the latter imply comparative advantage in labour-intensive activities, the former imply comparative advantage in capital-and-skill-intensive activities. It is the organized sector that exports services and it is really no surprise that skill-intensive services are being exported. Even India's manufactured exports are capital- and skill-intensive for similar reasons.[23]

One could ask: why has India specialized in skill-intensive services rather than in capital and skill-intensive manufacturing? The answer is that government policies have systematically privileged services vis-à-vis manufacturing. For one thing, services have been extremely lightly taxed while manufacturing has been heavily taxed.[24] For another, rules related to entry of FDI have been significantly less restrictive for services than for manufacturing and FDI inflows have been moving away from manufacturing towards services.[25] Moreover, policies have paid scant attention to development of physical infrastructure, which are far more important for production and export of manufactures than for production and export of services.[26] Thus, government policies, particularly in the post-reform period, seriously discriminated in favour of services and against manufacturing; they helped build the competitive strength of skill-intensive services on the one hand and eroded the competitive strength of manufacturing in general on the other.[27]

But, as noted above, growth of skill-intensive services exports ultimately provide only a small part of the explanation for the growth of services. To understand India's 'services revolution', therefore, one needs to answer one basic question: How is it that domestic final demand for services recorded such rapid growth in a low-income economy like India? The available evidence suggests three proximate explanatory factors: rapid growth of public consumption expenditure reflected in the rapid expansion of public services; high income elasticity of demand for services reflected in the rapidly rising share of services in private final consumption expenditure; and technological change involving both product innovations and price declines.

As observed earlier, expansion of government services was by far the most important contributor to the growth of organized services during 1981–2000 and remained an important contributor even during 2000–10. Behind such expansion was rapid growth of public final consumption expenditure. In real terms, public final consumption expenditure grew at 5.8 per cent per annum during 1981–2000 and at 5.2 per cent per annum during 2000–10.

Private final consumption expenditure (in real terms) also grew rapidly, particularly in the 2000s; the rate of growth was 4.3 per cent per annum during 1981–2000 and 6.4 per cent per annum during 2000–10. At the same time, the share of services in private final consumption expenditure was steadily growing.[28] Thus private final consumption expenditure on services was growing at a significantly faster rate than private final consumption expenditure in the aggregate. Indeed, private final consumption expenditure on services was growing at a faster rate than GDP, which suggests the income elasticity of demand for services to have been greater than unity. And the available estimates of the income/expenditure elasticity of demand for services confirm this.[29]

Given India's level of development, the observed greater than unity expenditure elasticity of demand for services comes as a surprise. Two basic developments seem to underlie the phenomenon. First, the 'electronics revolution' has produced new products whose availability has had the effect of altering the expenditure pattern of all income groups in favour of services. The availability of mobile telephones, for example, has obviously had the effect of creating/expanding demand for communication services even among the poor. Besides, rapid technological change resulted in declining prices; between 1997 and 2010, the deflator for communication services declined by more than 12 per cent per annum while the deflators for all other services were rising. Such price declines added further stimulus to demand growth. Something similar can be said of transport services, the demand for which is higher for every income group today than it was in the 1970s. On the one hand, spatial movements of people and goods have increased rapidly with economic growth. On the other hand, technological change has greatly expanded the availability and lowered the cost of transport (particularly air and land transport) services.

Second, income inequality has been growing and this too has had the effect of shifting the average expenditure pattern in favour of services. One cannot directly observe the trend in income inequality for lack of data; household surveys in India focus on consumption expenditure and not on income. Studies of distribution of household consumption expenditure do suggest significant growth of inequality.[30] It is known, moreover, that consumer expenditure surveys generally fail to adequately cover the top expenditure groups and hence underestimate both the extent and growth of expenditure inequality. And it is legitimate to assume that the growth of income inequality was larger than the growth of expenditure inequality. An important point to note here is that while the growth of inequality has aided growth of services, the growth of services has also contributed to growth of inequality.[31] The services-led growth has been feeding on itself to a certain extent.

3.3 Services-led growth and employment

Services in India, as already observed, are not employment-intensive (employment per unit of output is relatively low) and the employment intensity of growth of services also appears to have been low, particularly in the period of high growth (2000–10). However, the employment intensity of growth of services[32] was actually higher than that of manufacturing in both periods (Table 3.11). Since services output also grew significantly faster than manufacturing output, employment in services grew significantly faster than employment in manufacturing in both periods. Faster employment growth, combined with larger initial share of services in total employment in the economy, meant that the contribution of services to overall employment growth was much larger than that of manufacturing in both periods.

Table 3.11: Employment, 1983–2010

	Average annual rate of growth (%)		Employment intensity of growth		Contribution (%) to employment growth	
	1983–2000	2000–10	1983–2000	2000–10	1983–2000	2000–10
Economy	2.2	1.7	0.39	0.21		
Manufacturing	2.2	2.3	0.38	0.29	11.2	15.4
Services	3.7	2.9	0.51	0.33	38.3	45.7

Source: Author's estimates based on data from NSSO and CSO.

Employment, in Table 3.11, refers to the number of people in age–group (15–59) who are engaged in economically gainful activities for the major part of the reference year (employed in usual principal capacity (UPC) in the terminology used in Indian surveys). This measure of employment, which one uses in the rest of the chapter, focuses on the core workers in the economy. Even the core workers, however, do not all have full time employment; many of them remain unemployed for a minor part of the reference year.[33] It is for this reason that the ratio of employment growth to output growth has been called the employment intensity of growth rather than employment elasticity. And it is for this reason that one needs to do a more detailed analysis of the nature of employment growth so as to develop an adequate understanding of the employment effects of services-led growth. As it happens, for reasons of data availability, such analysis is possible only for the period 2000–10. Fortunately, this also is the period of rapid services-led growth.

The data in Table 3.12 shows the different types of employment that are found in India's economy. Regular employment is employment in which wages are paid on a regular, periodic basis (on a monthly basis, for example). The regular employees fall into two subcategories: regular-formal employees are those regular employees who have access to institutionalized social security and the rest of the regular employees are regular-informal employees.[34] Casual employees are those who are hired and paid on a daily basis. As it turns out, regular-formal employees, who exist only in the organized segment of the economy, also earn much higher wages than the regular-informal employees (Appendix Table A3.6). Casual employees, of course, not only face substantial underemployment but also earn substantially lower wage per workday than the regular-informal employees. In terms of quality of employment, therefore, there is a clear ranking of wage employment: regular-formal employment is the best and casual employment is the worst; regular-informal employment falls in between. In so far as the level of skill can be measured by the level of education, it can also be said that regular-formal employees are highly skilled, regular-informal employees are medium skilled and casual employees are low skilled (Appendix Table A3.6).

The average self-employed earns higher than even the average regular-informal employee (Appendix Table A3.6). The income of the self-employed, however, is not pure labour-income; it includes rent and profit. More importantly, the self-employed constitute a heterogeneous category that includes high income professionals (e.g., lawyers and doctors), prosperous small entrepreneurs as also a sizeable class of poor struggling to survive. This can be seen from the fact that the incidence of poverty among the self-employed is quite high; it is lower than that among the casual labourers but higher than that among the regular-formal and regular-informal employees (Appendix Table A3.6).The average level of education of the self-employed is also higher than that of the casual employees but lower than the other two categories of employees (Appendix Table A3.6).

Table 3.12: Structure of employment, 2010

	Organized segment share (%)	Percentage distribution of total employment by status			
		Regular formal	Regular informal	Casual	Selfem-ployed
Economy	15.0	8.0	10.9	34.2	46.9
Manufacturing	31.5	11.4	25.1	19.0	44.5
Services	30.0	20.9	23.9	8.1	47.1
Traditional services	9.6	4.2	20.2	10.0	65.6
Modern services	52.6	37.5	28.2	2.6	31.7
Social services	59.3	45.5	29.3	6.5	18.7

Source: Author's estimates based on unit-level data from NSSO surveys of employment and unemployment.

The data in Table 3.12, it can now be said, shows that employment in services, on average, is of better quality than employment in manufacturing. Of course, dualism is as prominent in services as in manufacturing, a large majority of the workers being outside the organized segment and in self-employment in both sectors. Also, in both organized manufacturing and organized services, there obviously is significant informal employment since the organized sector's share in total employment is much larger than the share of regular-formal employment in total employment. But the share of regular-formal employment in total employment is much higher (70 per cent in 2010) in organized services than in organized manufacturing (36 per cent in 2010).

As it has been seen, services divide rather neatly into traditional, modern and social services.[35] Traditional services are mostly produced in the unorganized sector and mainly by self-employed workers. Modern and social services are produced mostly in the organized sector and mainly by regular employees. These facts also tell one that traditional services employ mostly low-skilled (self-employed and casual) workers while modern and social services employ mostly high- and medium-skilled (regular-formal and regular-informal) workers. Naturally, labour productivity in traditional services is much lower than that in modern services; in 2010, modern services accounted for less than 11 per cent of total services employment and 38 per cent of services output, while traditional services accounted for 38 per cent of services employment and 40 per cent of services output.[36]

The evidence on wages and earnings from employment (Table 3.13) further confirms that services provide better quality employment than manufacturing and that modern services provide best quality employment. Labour income for each category of employed is higher in services than in manufacturing. And, except for casual employees (who constitute less than 3 per cent of all workers), labour-income is higher in modern services than in traditional and social services.

Table 3.13: Wage and income from employment, 2010

	Manufac-turing	Services	Traditional services	Modern services	Social services
Wage per day (current ₹)					
Regular-formal employees	461	538	509	656	511
Regular-informal employees	158	178	161	291	155
Casual employees	107	109	120	100	78
Mixed income per annum (current ₹)					
Self-employed	88015	223504	199093	409582	184223

Source: Wage per day: author's estimates based on unit-level data from NSSO surveys of employment and unemployment; mixed income of the self-employed: author's estimates based on data on factor incomes from CSO and data on employment from NSSO.

During 2000–10, there was substantial improvement in employment conditions in the economy (Table 3.14). Employment in the organized sector as also regular-formal employment grew at faster rates than overall employment. So there was transfer of workers from lower quality employment to higher quality employment. This improvement was due, to a large extent, to the growth of services, which produced rapid growth of organized sector employment as also of regular-formal employment. But growth of manufacturing also contributed substantially to improvement in employment conditions in the economy. Employment in organized manufacturing grew faster than total manufacturing employment and so did regular-formal employment in manufacturing.

Table 3.14: Pattern of employment growth, 2000–10

	Average annual rate of growth (%)		
	Economy	Manufacturing	Services
Organized segment	5.0	4.2	4.4
Unorganized segment	1.2	1.6	2.3
Regular-formal	3.3	2.7	3.3
Regular-informal	2.5	2.8	3.0
Casual	1.5	2.4	0.1
Self-employed	1.5	2.0	3.2
Total	1.7	2.3	2.9

Source: Author's estimates based on unit-level data from NSSO Surveys of Employment and Unemployment.

One remarkable fact is that services created many more jobs for highly skilled workers and far fewer jobs for low-skilled workers than manufacturing. Of the 28.5 million new jobs created in services between 2000 and 2010, 6.7 million (23.5 per cent) were for highly skilled workers (absorbed as regular-formal employees) while only 0.1 million (0.4 per cent) were for the low-skilled (absorbed as casual employees). In contrast, of the 8.9 million new jobs created in manufacturing, 1.2 million (12.8 per cent) were for the highly skilled (absorbed as regular-formal employees) while 1.9 million (19.6 per cent) were for the low-skilled (absorbed as casual employees).

To complete the analysis, one considers the evidence on growth of labour-incomes (Table 3.15). A remarkable fact that emerges from this evidence is that, despite the differences in the pattern of employment growth between manufacturing and services, the pattern of growth of labour incomes has actually been very similar. That said, two interesting aspects of the pattern of growth of labour incomes are worth noting. First, while wage growth for the highly skilled (regular-formal employees) was significantly faster than that for the low-skilled (casual employees), wage growth for the low-skilled was faster than that for the medium-skilled (regular-informal employees) in both manufacturing and services (except in modern services). There is something of a puzzle here; growth in this period created many more jobs for the medium skilled than for the low-skilled, and yet the low-skilled appear to have gained much more in terms of wage growth.[37] Second, income growth for the self-employed was significantly faster than wage growth for the regular-formal employees in both manufacturing and services. The explanation for faster wage growth for casual employees than for regular-informal employees very probably lies here. For, it is the growth of labour incomes in self-employment that drives the growth of casual wage.[38]

Table 3.15: Growth of real wage and real income from employment, 2000–10

	Average annual rate of growth (%)				
	Manu-facturing	Services	Traditional services	Modern services	Social services
Wage per day (₹ 2000)					
Regular-formal employees	3.0	3.0	3.3	2.9	2.7
Regular-informal employees	0.3	0.1	0.0	1.6	–2.6
Casual employees	1.6	2.2	2.3	1.1	1.0
Mixed income per annum (₹ 2000)					
Self-employed	4.1	5.3	4.2	9.3	4.5

Source: Wage per day: author's estimates based on unit-level data from NSSO surveys of employment and unemployment; mixed income of the self-employed: author's estimates based on data on factor incomes from CSO and data on employment from NSSO.

3.4 Conclusion

India has had services-led growth in the entire post-1980 period. Economic reforms of the early 1990s did not usher in services-led growth; they merely strengthened it. At independence, India had inherited a services heavy economy created by the British colonial administration (see Appendix Table A3.7). The growth strategy that India adopted in the 1950s then laid the foundation for premature services-led growth. For it accorded strategic priority to tertiary education, cheap capital and the public sector. Labour regulations designed to create decent conditions of work in the organized part of the economy (then dominated by the public sector) also contributed by making the relative price of low skilled labour vis à vis high skilled labour (which was relatively cheap because its production was heavily subsidized) high. The organized sector of the economy steadily acquired comparative advantage in the production of capital and skill-intensive products. To add to this, certain later policies favoured services and disadvantaged manufacturing. Compared to manufacturing, services have been lightly taxed. Inadequate attention to development of physical infrastructure constrained manufacturing far more than services. And trade and foreign investment regimes for services have been more liberal than those for manufacturing. In short, India's premature services-led growth has very much been a product of policies.

But this is a supply-side story and one needs to add a demand-side story. Contrary to a widely held perception, growth of services was driven primarily by growth of domestic final demand and not by growth of exports. During 1981–2000, services exports were of marginal significance. Even during 2000–10, when services exports boomed, their contribution to overall growth of services was far less important than the contribution of the growth of domestic demand. The only surprise here is India's specialization in skill-intensive services (essentially software services). The explanation is that the organized part of India's economy actually has comparative advantage in capital and skill-intensive products. Even India's manufactured exports are capital and skill-intensive. The rapid growth of domestic demand for services is explained partly by the rapid growth of final consumption expenditure, both public and private, and partly by a greater-than-unity income elasticity of private demand for services. The surprise here is the observed greater-than-unity income elasticity of private demand for services. Two particular developments explain this. The 'electronics revolution', by producing new and relatively cheap products, has caused a shift in the expenditure pattern of all income groups in favour of services. And income inequality has also been growing.

Contrary to another widely-held perception, India's services-led growth has not been 'jobless'. It has in fact been associated with substantial improvement in employment conditions in the economy. The share of the organized sector in total employment has increased substantially as has the share of regular-formal employment. Real wages of both regular-formal and casual employees have also increased though the former have gained much more than the latter. And while self-employment has remained the dominant form of employment in the economy, real incomes of the self-employed have shown significant growth.

What nevertheless remains true is that the share of services in total employment has remained much too low in relation to their share in GDP. Here is a colonial legacy that more than 60 years of development has not undone. In British India, the share of services in employment was far below the share in GDP. In independent India, the change in GDP share of services has been higher, in terms of percentage points, than the change in employment share. Between 1946 and 2010, the share of services in GDP increased by 20 percentage points, while the share of services in total employment in the economy increased by 14 percentage points. (Appendix Table A3.7). The already large gap between the two shares, inherited from the past, has grown larger.

Compared to manufacturing, services have not just generated employment at a faster pace but have also generated better quality employment. So it cannot be argued that manufacturing-led growth would have done more to improve overall employment conditions than services-led growth. However, while services generated few employment opportunities for the low-skilled, manufacturing generated substantial employment opportunities for them. What can be said, therefore, is that manufacturing-led growth would have done more to shift labour out of agriculture and to thus reduce underemployment and poverty. Quite possibly, moreover, it would have prevented (or at least moderated) the rise in income inequality.

Will services-led growth be sustained even if the existing policy biases are maintained? The answer is 'yes but'; services-led growth can be sustained but only at a much lower level. The slowdown of growth in the developed world and the emergence of other players (such as China and the Philippines) in software services will make it difficult to sustain high growth of service exports. It is true that many services other than software services – medical, education, financial, travel, transportation, etc. – are being increasingly traded. But India's success has thus far been confined to exports of software services and it is not clear that ability to export other services can be easily and quickly developed. On the whole, there are good reasons to think that growth of services exports will slow down. The growth of domestic demand can also be expected to slow down. Except in the unlikely event of another technological revolution, there will be no new shift in the pattern of private expenditure and the income elasticity of private demand for services will decline.

Most importantly, rapid services-led growth will be made impossible by endemic balance of payments difficulties.[39] A large mismatch between the structure of domestic absorption and that of domestic production has already emerged in India's economy. On very rough calculations, the share of goods in domestic absorption was 67 per cent in 2010 while the share of goods in domestic production was only 43 per cent.[40] This means that around 26 per cent of the domestic demand for goods (amounting to around 27 per cent of GDP) had to be met through import in that year. On the other hand, net exports of services in that year constituted just 3 per cent of GDP, i.e., could conceivably have financed imports worth 3 per cent of GDP. Since, with continued services-led growth, the gap between domestic absorption and domestic production of goods must be expected to widen, it is hard to see how the resources required to fill the gap in domestic absorption of goods through imports would be found.

Our conclusion is that sustaining rapid economic growth would require a transition from services-led growth to manufacturing-led growth. This would not mean stagnation of services just as services-led growth thus far has not meant stagnation of manufacturing. It would mean significant acceleration in manufacturing growth and perhaps some deceleration in services growth. Policy reforms will be required to facilitate this transition. Particular emphasis would have to be placed on building of physical infrastructure. Subsidies on physical and human capital would need to be reduced and labour regulations would need to be reformed so that the relative price of low skilled labour vis à vis capital and high skilled labour is not maintained at an artificially high level. And the existing biases in tax, trade and foreign investment regimes that disadvantage manufacturing vis à vis services would have to be removed.

On the basis of past evidence, it can be said that a transition to manufacturing-led growth would alter the pattern of employment growth. Growth of employment opportunities for the low-skilled would accelerate while growth of employment opportunities for the highly skilled would perhaps slow down a little. To put it differently, growth of regular-formal employment would slow down a little while growth of regular-informal and casual employment would accelerate. There would be faster shift of labour out of agriculture as a result. The consequent faster growth of labour productivity in agriculture would mean faster growth of wages of low skilled labour in both agriculture and non-agriculture. And regular-formal employment should continue to grow faster than the labour force. Rapid manufacturing-led growth, therefore, should continue to rapidly improve overall employment conditions and in a healthier manner.

Appendix A

Table A3.1: Share of services in GDP and level of development, regression results (Dependent variable: Percentage of share of services in GDP)

Independent variables	Regression coefficients		
	2000	2005	2010
GDP per capita	0.204	0.171	0.199
Significance level	*0.004*	*0.022*	*0.009*
Share (%) of services in exports	0.249	0.254	0.244
Significance level	*0.046*	*0.035*	*0.030*
Constant	43.85	43.97	45.47
Significance level	*0.000*	*0.000*	*0.000*
R^2	0.303	0.219	0.290
n	32	32	32

Note: GDP per capita, measured in constant 2005 PPP dollars, is indexed with the value for the Republic of Korea as 100. Estimates of shares are based on data in current prices.

Source: Author's estimates based on data from World Bank, World Development Indicators.

Table A3.2: Services-industry relation, regression results
(Dependent variable: Percentage of share of industry in GDP)

Independent variable	Regression coefficients		
	2000	2005	2010
% share of services in GDP	-0.40	-0.51	-0.56
Significance level	*0.005*	*0.00*	*0.000*
Constant	52.91	60.15	63.74
Significance level	*0.000*	*0.000*	*0.000*
R^2	0.215	0.306	0.470
n	32	32	32

Source: Author's estimates based on data from World Bank, World Development Indicators.

Table A3.3: Employment-output relation in services, regression results
(Dependent variable: Percentage of share of services in employment)

Independent variable	Regression coefficients		
	2000	2005	2010
% share of services in GDP	1.18	0.993	0.995
Significance level	*0.00*	*0.00*	*0.00*
Constant	−14.62	−3.62	−2.06
Significance level	*0.207*	*0.785*	*0.886*
R^2	0.550	0.339	0.397
n	29	32	27

Source: Author's estimates based on data from World Bank, World Development Indicators.

Table A3.4: Shares percentage of sectors in GDP

	1980	2000	2010
China			
Agriculture	37.3	15.1	8.4
Industry	34.1	45.9	50.1
Manufacturing	25.8	32.1	32.9
Services	28.6	39.0	41.5
Indonesia			
Agriculture	25.1	15.6	13.2
Industry	37.4	10.9	11.1
Manufacturing	13.0	27.7	25.8
Services	37.5	38.5	45.7
Thailand			
Agriculture	19.9	10.3	8.3
Industry	30.1	44.4	48.7
Manufacturing	23.1	36.4	40.7
Services	50.0	45.3	43.0

Source: World Bank, World Development Indicators.

Table A3.5: Share percentage of services in GDP and in employment, 2010

Countries	Share (%) of services in GDP	Share (%) of services in employment
Austria	69.4	69.9
Belgium	77.6	75.3
Denmark	77.0	77.9
Finland	67.9	71.9
Germany	71.2	70.0
Japan	71.5	69.7
Netherlands	74.2	71.6
Sweden	71.8	77.7
United Kingdom	77.6	78.9
United States	78.8	81.2

Source: World Bank, World Development Indicators.

Table A3.6: Wage-income per annum (₹), wage per day (₹), average years of education and incidence of poverty, 2010

	Average wage income per annum	Average wage per day	Average mixed income per annum	Average years of education	Incidence of poverty (%)
Employees					
Organized segment	201894	362		10.2	12.5
Unorganized segment	44359	107		5.3	35.4
Regular-formal		522		11.9	4.7
Regular-informal		174		8.5	17.2
Casual		96		3.7	47.5
Self-employed			133479	6.1	28.3

Source: Average wage-income per annum and average mixed income per annum are estimated by combining data on employment from NSSO with data on factor incomes from CSO. The estimates of average wage per day, average years of education and incidence of poverty are based on unit level data from NSSO Surveys of Employment and Unemployment.

Table A3.7: Structure of output and employment (percentage distribution)

	1901	1926	1946	2010
GDP				
Agriculture	47.3	39.4	34.4	14.6
Industry	24.6	26.3	28.3	28.1
Services	28.1	34.3	37.3	57.3
Employment				
Agriculture	74.8	76.3	74.3	47.9
Industry	10.8	9.4	10.5	23.2
Services	14.4	14.3	15.2	28.9

Source: For the years 1900, 1925 and 1946, Sivasubramonian (2000). For the year 2010, author's estimates based on data from NSSO and CSO.

Appendix B: List of countries in the samples used for cross-country regressions

Core sample

Argentina, Bangladesh, Botswana, Brazil, Chile, China, Costa Rica, Dominican Republic, Egypt. El Salvador, Honduras, Indonesia, Jordan, Korea (Republic),

Malaysia, Mauritius, Mexico, Mongolia, Morocco, Nicaragua, Pakistan, Panama, Paraguay, Peru, Philippines, South Africa, Sri Lanka, Thailand

Additional countries in

The sample for 2000: Colombia, Madagascar, Mali, Turkey

The sample for 2005: Colombia, Jamaica, Madagascar, Mali

The sample for 2010: Syria, Turkey, Uganda, Uruguay

Data on share of services in total employment were missing for

Madagascar, Mali and Sri Lanka in the sample for 2000

Bangladesh, Botswana, Honduras, Nicaragua and Uruguay in the sample for 2010

A note

In each of the samples, there are a few countries for which data for the precise year were not available. In such cases, data for either the preceding or the following year were used.

Appendix C: Estimation of the contribution of domestic final demand to services growth

The following identity is used at the start:

$S = a. A + i. I + XS + CS$, where S, A and I are value added in Services, industry and agriculture, XS denotes value added in services exports, CS represents domestic consumption of services, a is services input per unit of value added in agriculture, and i is services input per unit of value added in industry.

Then:

$\Delta S = \Delta (a. A) + \Delta (i. I) + \Delta XS + \Delta CS$, where Δ denotes change over a period,

$\Delta S/S = \Delta (a. A)/S + \Delta (i. I)/S + \Delta XS/S + \Delta CS/S$

$= a. (\Delta A/A). (A/S) + i. (\Delta I/I). (I/S) + (\Delta XS/XS). (XS/S) + (\Delta CS/CS). (CS/S)$

A/S, I/S, XS/S and CS/S are interpreted as initial values for the period under study.

For the period 1981–2000, one considers the input-output tables for 1979–80,

1989–90, 1993–94 and 1998–99 and use the average values for a and i: a = 0.041, i = 0.181, and use the input-output table for 1989–90 to derive the share of value added in a unit of services exports, which is 0.760. One also has: $\Delta S/S$ = 2.673, $\Delta I/I$ = 1.914, I/S = 0.687, $\Delta A/A$ = 0.838, A/S = 0.953, $\Delta XS/XS$ = 5.049 and XS*(0.760)/S = 0.031. So,

$(\Delta CS/CS)$. (CS/S) = 2.673 – (0.041). (0.838). (0.953) – (0.181). (1.914). (0.687) – (5.049). (0.031)

= 2.673 – 0.033 – 0.238 – 0.157

= 2.245

Thus

2.673 = 0.033 + 0.238 + 0.157 + 2.245

100 = (1.234 + 8.904) + 5.874 + 83.988

= 10.138 + 5.874 + 83.988

For the period 2000–10, the input-output table for 2006–07 is used to derive the values - a = 0.075 and i = 0.165 – and use the input-output table for 1998–99 to derive the share of value added in a unit of services exports as 0.692. We also have: $\Delta S/S$ = 1.251, $\Delta I/I$ = 1.095, I/S = 0.545, $\Delta A/A$ = 0.250, A/S = 0.477, $\Delta XS/XS$ = 3.287 and XS*(0.692)/S = 0.051. So,

$(\Delta CS/CS)$. (CS/S) = 1.251 – (0.075). (0.250). (0.477) – (0.165). (1.095). (0.545) – (3.287). (0.051)

= 1.251 – 0.009 – 0.098 – 0.168

= 0.976

Thus

1.251 = 0.009 + 0.098 + 0.168 + 0.976

100 = (0.719 + 7.834) + 13.429 + 78.817

=8.553 + 13.429 + 78.018

Endnotes

1 The general patterns of structural change were first derived by Kuznets (1957) and subsequently confirmed by the more comprehensive analysis of Chenery (1960), Kuznets (1971) and Chenery and Syrquin (1975). Kaldor (1966) used insights from Young (1928) and Arrow

(1962) to develop a general explanation for the observed tendency of the manufacturing sector to play the lead role at early stages.

2   There is a large literature on growth and structural change in East Asian economies. See, for example, World Bank (1993); Amsden (1989); Chen (1979); Kwon (1990); Galenson (1979) and Brandt and Rawski (2008).

3   Among these are the well-known studies of Kuznets (1957) and Chenery (1960).

4   See, for example, Chenery and Syrquin (1975) and Kongsamut, et al. (2001).

5   See Eichengreen and Gupta (2013).

6   See Dasgupta and Singh (2005, 2006).

7   Here and throughout this chapter, services exclude 'electricity, gas and water' and 'construction' (UN's ISIC treats these as services).

8   The base data are from Central Statistical Office, Ministry of Statistics and Programme Implementation (Government of India). Statistical data generally refers to the financial year in India (which runs from April of year zero to March of year 1). The years, therefore, are recorded as 1950–51, 1951–52 and so on. Here I have adopted the convention of referring to 1950–51 as 1951, 1951–52 as 1952 and so on.

9   Econometric exercises confirm the timing of the first growth acceleration in India. See, for example, De Long (2003), Wallack (2003), Rodrik and Subramanian (2005) and Balakrishnan and Parameswaran (2007). The timing of the second acceleration remains a matter of controversy. Balakrishnan (2010) finds the second growth acceleration to have occurred around 1992 but this is not widely accepted. Some have argued that growth in the 1990s was really no higher than that in the 1980s. See Kotwal, Ramswami and Wadhwa (2011), for example. On the other hand, that growth in the 2000s was higher than in the 1990s is not in dispute.

10 Papola (2006) is one of the very few to have noticed this.

11 There is evidence to suggest that, in India, growth of services has a positive effect on growth of industry but growth of industry has no effect on growth of services. This seems to hold for the entire period since 1951. See Balakrishnan and Parameswaran (2007). This also says that economic growth in India has always been services-led.

12 Detailed lists of countries included in the samples are presented in Appendix B.

13 A similar finding is reported in Gordon and Gupta (2004) and Eichengreen and Gupta (2011).

14 Some other studies have also reported similar findings. See, for example, Kochar, et al., (2006).

15 In India, the organized sector is defined to include all government, public sector and private corporate sector establishments, and all private non-corporate sector establishments with 10 or more employees. While the share of the organized sector in total NDP has been growing, it remained well below 50 per cent even in 2010. This share was 35 per cent in 1981, 42 per cent in 2000 and 45 per cent in 2010.

16 The share of the unorganized segment in services output in the economy was 65.2 per cent in 1981, 59.3 per cent in 2000 and 53.3 per cent in 2010.

17 'Real estate and renting' services are mainly in the unorganized segment while 'business services' (which includes 'software services') are mainly in the organized segment.

18 Several other studies – Gordon and Gupta (2004), Singh (2006), Eichengreen and Gupta

(2010) and Nayyar (2012) – have noted that the growth of intermediate demand for services from agriculture and industry was quite small.

19 In contrast, exports of manufactures (in value added terms) constituted 13.7 per cent of output of manufactures in 1981, and this percentage increased to 23.1 by 2010.

20 India's software exports increased from US$ 4 million in 1980 to US$ 105 million in 1990, then to US$ 5287 million in 2000 and then to US$ 37300 million in 2010. See Dossani (2012) and Murthy (2012). The implied growth rate per annum was 38.6 per cent during 1980–90, 48.0 per cent during 1990–2000 and 21.6 per cent during 2000–10.

21 Kochar *et al.* (2006) provide empirical evidence to show that India, in contrast to other developing countries, had actually specialized in capital and skill-intensive manufacturing industries. They also show that this feature has not been altered by the economic reforms implemented since the early 1990s.

22 For example, data from the World Bank (World Development Indicators) shows that the ratio of public expenditure per student in tertiary education to that in primary education was 6.2 in India in 2006, 2.1 in Indonesia in 2007 and 1.6 in Thailand in 2004.

23 Veeramani (2011) provides evidence to show that India's manufactured exports have become increasingly capital and skill-intensive in the period since the mid-1990s. This also reflects the peculiar nature of factor endowments in India's organized sector.

24 Hansda (2002) shows that while the share of services in GDP crossed 50 per cent in the 1990s, services accounted for only about 10 per cent of the government's tax revenue.

25 See Rakshit (2007), Banga (2005) and Chanda (2012).

26 See Rakshit (2007).

27 Estimates of RCA, derived from World Bank data, suggest that India has always (i.e., throughout the period 1980–2010) had comparative advantage in services and no comparative advantage in manufactures. However, till 1993, the RCA of manufactures was increasing while that for services was declining; the two were in fact equal (0.99) in 1993. There was a reversal of trends after 1993; the RCA of manufactures steadily declined and that for services steadily increased. However, the growth of RCA of services seems to have been due entirely to growth of RCA in 'software services'. In fact, as Chanda (2012) shows, India's comparative advantage is exclusively in 'software services'. Balakrishnan (2006) discusses how state policies helped build this comparative advantage.

28 Nayyar (2012) estimates this share to have been 16.8 per cent in 1981, 20.9 per cent in 1991, 27.2 per cent in 2000 and 44.3 per cent in 2009.

29 Rakshit (2007) uses national accounts statistics to estimate the household income elasticity of demand for services to have been 1.5 for the period 1998–2005. Nayyar (2012) uses data on consumer expenditure generated by the National Sample Surveys to estimate household expenditure elasticity of demand for services, which turns out to be significantly greater than unity.

30 See, for example, ADB (2012).

31 In general, if the growth of incomes is higher for the high income, highly skilled persons, then the domestic demand will also be skewed in favour of goods and services produced by highly skilled labour. For concrete evidence, see Azam (2009) and Mehta, *et al.*, (2013).

32 This ratio is defined as the rate of growth of employment to the rate of growth of output but do not call it employment elasticity for reasons that will shortly be made clear. For estimating

growth rates of both output and employment here, I have used the compound interest method with initial and terminal values.

33 Our definition minimizes but does not eliminate the possibility. If children, older people and those who are employed in usual subsidiary capacity were included (i.e., who are in employment for only a minor part of the reference year), underemployment would have been much higher so that the number of persons in employment would have been a far less meaningful measure of employment.

34 Regular-formal employees refer to those regular employees in the organized sector who are eligible for one, some or all of the following benefits: provident fund, pension, gratuity, health care and maternity. Those regular employees, who are not eligible for any of those benefits, are categorized as regular-informal employees. Such employees are found in both organized and unorganized sectors.

35 Ideally, real estate and renting services should have been included in traditional services, while business services should have been included in modern services. But one faces practical difficulties in separating these.

36 Social services are left out of account here. The reason is that, in the case of organized social services, wages and salaries account for a very large part (around 90 per cent) of the output so that comparisons of output or labour productivity are not particularly meaningful.

37 It has been argued that while services expanded jobs for the highly skilled faster than jobs for the medium-skilled, the supply of highly skilled workers increased at a slower rate than the supply of medium-skilled workers (Azam, 2009; Mehta, et al., 2013). This seems a plausible explanation for the stagnation of wages for the regular-informal employees who are medium-skilled. However, it is not quite consistent with the fact that the wage of regular-informal employees did increase in modern services. Also, one needs a separate explanation for the observed growth of wages for low-skilled workers.

38 Ghose (2012) discusses the link between the income of the self-employed and the wage of casual labour.

39 This point has been made by other observers, notably, by Rakshit (2007) and Papola (2006).

40 Domestic absorption is defined as the sum of private consumption, government consumption and fixed capital formation, all measured in constant prices. In 2010, the share of goods in private consumption was 55 per cent and the share of goods in government consumption was 38 per cent (the share of 'compensation to employees' in government consumption was 62 per cent so that the share of goods could be takes as 38 per cent). And the share of goods in fixed capital formation is taken to be 100 per cent.

References

ADB. 2012. *Asian Development Outlook 2012*, Chapter 2. Manila: Asian Development Bank

Amsden, A. H. 1989. *Asia's Next Giant: South Korea and Late Industrialization*. New York: Oxford University Press

Arrow, K. J. 1962. 'The Economic Implications of Learning by Doing', *Review of Economic Studies* 29(3): 155–73

Azam, M. 2009. 'India's Increasing Skill Premium: Role of Demand and Supply'. *Discussion Paper no. 3968*. Bonn: IZA – Institute for the Study of Labour.

Balakrishnan, P. 2006. 'Benign Neglect or Strategic Intent? Contested Lineage of Indian Software Industry', *Economic and Political Weekly* 41(36): 3865–72

_____. 2010. *Economic Growth in India: History and Prospect.* New Delhi: Oxford University Press

Balakrishnan, P. and M. Parameswaran. 2007. 'Understanding Economic Growth in India: A Prerequisite', *Economic and Political Weekly* 47(27/28): 2915–22.

Banga, R. 2005. 'Critical Issues in India's Service-led Growth'. *ICRIER Working Paper no. 171.*

Basu, K. and A. Maertens, (eds.). 2012. *The New Oxford Companion to Economics in India.* New Delhi: Oxford University Press.

Brandt, L. and T. Rawski. 2008. *China's Great Economic Transformation.* New York: Cambridge University Press.

Chanda, R. 2012. 'Services-led growth'. In *The New Oxford Companion to Economics in India*, edited by K. Basu and A. Maertens, 624–32.

Chen, E. K. Y. 1979. *Hypergrowth in Asian Economies: A Comparative Survey of Hong Kong, Japan, Korea, Singapore and Taiwan.* London: Macmillan

Chenery, H. B. 1960. 'Patterns of Industrial Growth', *American Economic Review* 50(4): 624–54

Chenery, H. B. and M. Syrquin. 1975. *Patterns of Development, 1950–1970.* London: Oxford University Press.

Dasgupta, S. and A. Singh. 2005. 'Will Services be the New Engine of Indian Economic Growth?', *Development and Change* 36(6): 1035–58.

_____. 2006. 'Manufacturing, Services and Premature Deindustrialization in Developing Countries'. *A Kaldorian Analysis. Research Paper no. 2006/49.* Helsinki: UNU-WIDER.

De Long, J. B. 2003. 'India Since Independence: An Analytic Growth Narrative'. In *In Search of Prosperity: Analytic Narratives on Economic Growth*, edited by D. Rodrik. Princeton and Oxford: Princeton University Press.

Dossani, R. 2012. 'IT-enabled Services'. In *The New Oxford Companion to Economics in India*, edited by Basu and Maertens, 424–27.

Eichengreen, B. and P. Gupta. 2011. 'The Service Sector as India's Road to Economic Growth'. *Working Paper no. 16757.* Cambridge, Massachusetts: National Bureau of Economic Research.

_____. 2013. 'The Two Waves of Services Sector Growth', *Oxford Economic Papers* 65(1): 124–46

Galenson, W., (eds.). 1979. *Economic Growth and Structural Change in Taiwan.* Ithaca, NY: Cornell University Press.

Ghose, A. K. 2012. 'Employment: The Fault Line in India's Emerging Economy', *Comparative Economic Studies* 54: 765–86.

Gordon, J. and P. Gupta. 2004. 'Understanding India's Services Revolution'. *Working Paper no. 04/171.* Washington DC: International Monetary Fund.

Hansda, S. K. 2002. 'Services Sector in the Indian Growth Process: Myths and Realities', *The Journal of Income and Wealth* 24(1/2): 80–94

Kaldor, N. 1966. *Causes of the Slow Rate of Economic Growth of the United Kingdom.* Cambridge: Cambridge University Press.

Kochar, K., U. Kumar, R. Rajan, A. Subramanian and I. Tokatlidis. 2006. 'India's Pattern of Development: What Happened, What Follows?', *Journal of Monetary Economics* 53(5): 981–1019.

Kongsamut, P., S. Rebelo and D. Xie. 2001. 'Beyond Balanced Growth', *Review of Economic Studies* 68(4): 869–82.

Kotwal, A., B. Ramaswami and W. Wadhwa. 2011. 'Economic Liberalization and Indian Economic Growth: What's the Evidence?', *Journal of Economic Literature* 49(4): 1152–99.

Kuznets, S. 1957. 'Quantitative Aspects of the Economic Growth of Nations', *Economic Development and Cultural Change* 5(4): 2–80.

Kuznets, S. 1971. *Economic Growth of Nations: Total Output and Production Structure*. Cambridge, Massachusetts: Harvard University Press.

Kuznets, J. K., (edu.), 1990. *Modern Economic Development*, New York: Greenwood.

Mehta, A., J. Phelipe, P. Quising and S. Camingue. 2013. 'Where Have All the Educated Workers Gone? Services and Wage Inequality in Three Asian Economies', *Metroeconomica* 64(3): 466–97.

Murthy, N. R. N. 2012. 'Software and Services Exports'. In *The New Oxford Companion to Economics in India*, edited by Basu and Maertens, 645–48.

Nayyar, G. 2012. *The Services Sector in India's Development*. New Delhi: Cambridge University Press.

Papola, T. S. 2006. 'Emerging Structure of Indian Economy: Implications for Growing Intersectoral Imbalances', *Indian Economic Journal* 54(1): 5–25

Rakshit, M. 2007. 'Services-led Growth: The Indian Experience', *Money and Finance* (ICRA Bulletin): 91–126..

Rodrik, D. and A. Subramanian. 2005. 'From "Hindu Growth" to Productivity Surge: The Mystery of the Indian Growth Transition', *IMF Staff Papers* 52(2): 193–228.

Sivasubramonian, S. 2000. *The National Income of India in the Twentieth Century*. New Delhi: Oxford University Press.

Wallack, J. S. 2003. 'Structural Breaks in Indian Macroeconomic Data', *Economic and Political Weekly* 38(41): 4312–15.

World Bank. 1993. *The East Asian Miracle*. New York: Oxford University Press.

Young, A. 1928. 'Increasing Returns and Economic Progress', *Economic Journal* 38(152): 527–42.

Veeramani, C. 2011. 'Anatomy of India's Merchandize Export Growth, 1993/94 to 2010/11', *Economic and Political Weekly* 47(1): 94–104.

4

Growth, Structural Change and Poverty Reduction
Evidence from India

Rana Hasan, Sneha Lamba and Abhijit Sen Gupta

4.1 Introduction

After three decades of generally low growth, the Indian economy experienced a growth acceleration that started in the 1980s. Growth in gross domestic product per capita, only 1.4 per cent annually from the 1950s through 1970s, accelerated steadily from average annual growth rates of 3.5 per cent in the 1980s, to 3.7 per cent in the 1990s, and 5.5 per cent in the new millennium. While a slowdown in growth since early 2011 has led to a vigorous debate about the Indian economy's 'growth potential' and its ability to sustain growth rates of around 6 per cent and higher (in per capita terms) for long stretches of time, a more enduring debate has been about the inclusiveness of India's growth.

What has been the impact of India's growth on poverty? What factors explain the strength of the growth–poverty relationship in India? What, if anything, can be done to make the growth process more effective in reducing poverty? This chapter examines these questions through the lens of structural transformation – i.e., changes in an economy's structure of output and employment.[1] Such an approach is important since, although there are many causes of poverty, ultimately the poor are poor because the work they do earns them so little. Consequently, understanding the relationships between growth, changes in the structure of output and employment, and poverty reduction is crucial for policymaking.

The chapter provides a snapshot of the empirical relationship between economic growth and poverty reduction in India since the 1980s. (A detailed discussion of data and variable construction is provided in the Appendix.) The snapshot indicates that while growth in India has been associated with an unambiguous decline in poverty, the extent of poverty reduction in India has been considerably less than in other high-growth economies in Asia. The next section then considers the proximate factors that can explain the relatively weak link between growth and poverty reduction in India. Drawing upon previous literature and some simple analysis of the evolving sectoral composition of output and employment in India, it is noted that the impact of growth on poverty is influenced by the production sectors that drive growth. This is because in India, as is the case in developing countries more generally, sectors differ vastly in terms of their (labour) productivity.[2] Of course, sectors also differ in terms of how many people they employ. Since productivity influences earnings, differential performance of sectors in terms of growth in output and productivity will have important implications for workers' earnings and thus poverty.[3] In general, growth will have a larger impact on poverty when the former is driven by increases in productivity in sectors that employ a large proportion of an economy's workers. However, growth can also be driven by a reallocation of workers from low productivity (and low earning) sectors to higher productivity (higher earning) sectors.[4] Growth that is driven by such a reallocation can also be expected to reduce poverty.

The following section uses state-level data on poverty and productivity across 11 broad sectors of production from 1987 to 2009 to explore the impact of aggregate labour productivity growth and its components – within-sector productivity growth and productivity growth due to reallocation of labour – on poverty reduction.[5] A key finding is that the movement of workers from lower productivity to higher productivity sectors is an important channel through which increases in productivity translate into poverty reduction. Significantly, the relative importance of this phenomenon, which is known as structural change[6] and which should be distinguished from the broader concept of structural transformation – varies across states.

Some exploratory regression analysis indicates that the extent of structural change responds to policies and the institutional environment. In particular, states with better functioning credit markets and pro-competitive regulations are more likely to see greater reallocation of labour from lower productivity to higher productivity sectors. The chapter concludes with a discussion of the policy implications of the findings, including what types of policy changes may be needed for growth to have a bigger impact on poverty reduction.

4.2 Growth and poverty reduction in India

After three decades of low and volatile growth, India experienced an acceleration in economic growth in the 1980s.[7] As Figure 4.1 shows, prior to the 1980s, growth in GDP per capita (in terms of five year moving averages) tended to fluctuate between 1 per cent and 2 per cent.[8] However, growth rates started increasing in the early 1980s and continued to do so well into the 2000s. Thus, while GDP per capita grew by an average of around 1.2 per cent annually in the 1960s and 1970s, each subsequent decade has seen a steady climb in growth rates – from average annual growth rates of 3.5 per cent in the 1980s, to 3.7 per cent in the 1990s, to 5.5 per cent in the new millennium. Table 4.1 shows that India's growth acceleration has put it among the fastest-growing economies in the world.[9]

Viewed from the lens of poverty and household expenditure data (on which computations of poverty in India are based), growth in India has been inclusive. As Figure 4.2 indicates, poverty rates in India have declined for a variety of poverty lines, national and international. The insensitivity of trends in poverty to different poverty lines is not surprising when one considers that per capita expenditures adjusted for both temporal and spatial price differentials have increased for every statistical percentile group of individuals in India (Figure 4.3). Thus, regardless of the poverty line used, it is clear that the proportion of people living in poverty has been declining. Indeed, the data indicate that even the number of extremely poor in India has begun to decline since the mid-2000s (or even mid-1990s, depending on the particular poverty line used). Thus, while the number of poor (based on the Expert Group 2009 poverty lines) increased marginally from 403.7 million in 1993–94 to 407.2 million in 2004–05, the number of poor had fallen to 354.7 million in 2009–10.[9] This is in sharp contrast to the situation in the 1950s and 1960s when the number of poor was expanding rapidly in India (in terms of a variant of the national poverty line used by Datt and Ravallion).[10] Based on this alternative poverty line, the number of poor only began declining after some point in the mid-1990s.

Figure 4.1: India's growth performance: Five year moving averages of GDP per capita, 1951–52 to 2011–12

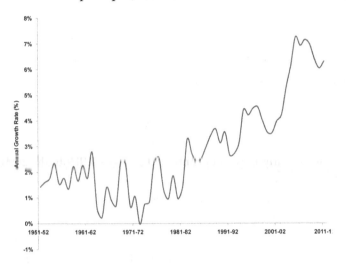

Source: Database on Indian Economy, Reserve Bank of India

Table 4.1: International comparison of economic growth

Region	Period	GDP	GDP per worker
India	1960–80	3.4	1.3
	1980–2004	5.8	3.7
People's Republic of China (PRC)	1960–80	4.0	1.8
	1980–2003	9.5	7.8
South Asia	1960–80	3.6	1.4
	1980–2003	5.5	3.4
East Asia without PRC	1960–80	7.0	4.0
	1980–2003	6.1	3.7
Latin America	1960–80	5.7	2.7
	1980–2003	2.0	−0.6

Region	Period	GDP	GDP per worker
Africa	1960–80	4.4	1.9
	1980–2003	2.2	–0.6
Middle East	1960–80	5.4	3.2
	1980–2003	3.8	0.8
Industrial Countries	1960–80	4.2	2.9
	1980–2003	2.6	1.6

Source: Bosworth, Collins and Virmani (2007).

Figure 4.2: Poverty decline in India using different poverty lines

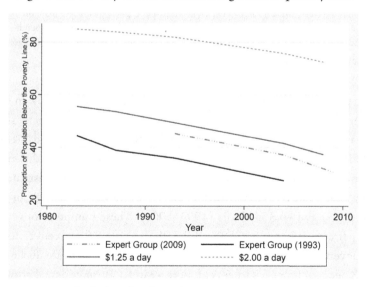

Source: Government of India (2012) and PovcalNet.

Figure 4.3: Growth in per capita expenditures by percentiles of the population, 1993–94 to 2009–10

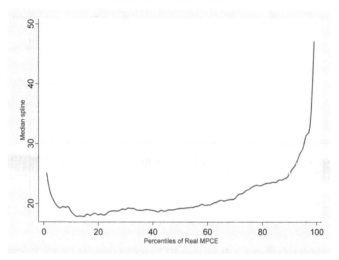

Note: Computed using Uniform Recall Period monthly per capita expenditure from the National Sample Survey Organization's Consumer Expenditure Survey data and adjusting expenditures for spatial and inter-temporal differences in prices using the implicit consumer price index generated from the Expert Group (2009) poverty lines.

Source: Authors' estimates.

The pace of poverty reduction has, however, been relatively slow in India. As Figure 4.4 shows, India's pace of poverty reduction has been clearly slower than that of the People's Republic of China (PRC), Indonesia, and Vietnam. Interestingly, differentials in GDP growth rates do not explain the differential performance in poverty reduction. Consider the following elasticities of poverty reduction to GDP growth reported by Ravallion,[11] –0.8 for PRC (1981–2005) and –0.3 for India (1993–2005). These numbers convey that for a 1 per cent increase in GDP in PRC, there was a 0.8 per cent reduction in the poverty rate. In India, on the other hand, the poverty rate declined by only 0.3 per cent for every 1 per cent increase in GDP. Since actual growth in PRC was also much higher than in India, the net effect of growth on poverty was that much greater.

Figure 4.4: Poverty reduction in India as compared to selected economies

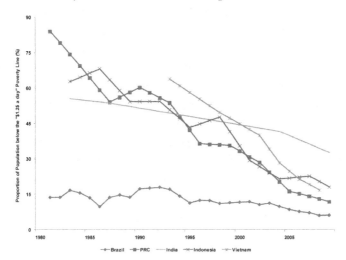

Note: Poverty Head Count Ratios are based on the '$ 1.25 a day' at 2005 Purchasing Power Parity poverty lines.

Significantly, Datt and Ravallion's analysis of the growth-poverty relationship in India from 1951 to 2006 indicates that the pace of poverty reduction failed to picked up after the reforms of 1991 (although it must be noted that more recently released data reveals that the pace of poverty reduction has distinctly picked up between 2004 and 2009).[12] Since economic growth has been faster in the post-1991 period, the elasticity of poverty reduction to growth in GDP, in fact, declined a little if data until 2006 is considered.

Why has growth in India not led to faster poverty reduction? There are several proximate factors that can explain the relatively weak link between growth and poverty reduction in India. First, India's 'initial conditions' in terms of human development – encompassing nutritional, health, and educational status – have been weaker. Given the findings of Datt and Ravallion that Indian states with better initial levels of human development had higher growth elasticities of poverty reduction, the growth-poverty linkage in India might be weaker on account of its more limited progress on the nutrition, health, and education front as compared to many East and Southeast Asian countries.[13] Second, growth has tended to be lower in states that account for a large proportion of India's poor. As Figure 4.5 shows, among Indian states that accounted for more than 3.5 per cent each of India's total poor in 1993, there has been a clear tendency for states with greater numbers of poor to grow more slowly from 1993 to 2009. Similarly, growth in rural India, which has accounted for between 81.5 per cent and 78 per cent of India's poor over 1993 and 2009, has been considerably slower than growth in urban India. Estimates from the High Powered Expert Committee (HPEC) indicate that the faster growth of urban areas has resulted in their contribution to GDP increasing from 51.7 per cent in 1999–2000 to around 62 per cent in 2009–10.[14] Interestingly, however, this differential growth between rural and urban areas may not have as strong a role in explaining the relatively weak growth-poverty relationship post-1991 as it had prior to 1991. Datt and Ravallion find that, whereas rural economic growth was more important than urban economic growth for overall poverty reduction, urban economic growth has begun having a significant impact on poverty reduction in the post-1991 period.[15]

Figure 4.5: Initial incidence of poverty and economic growth across states

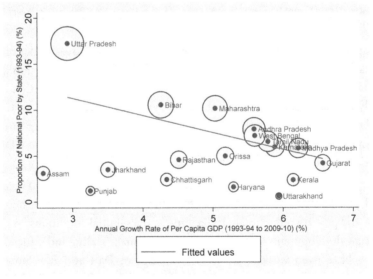

Notes: The fitted line is based on states with more than 3.5 per cent of India's total poor in 1993–94.

Source: Authors' estimates.

Finally, and perhaps more importantly, the sectoral composition of India's growth seems to have been such that it has generated relatively fewer productive employment opportunities for the poor Consider Figure 4.6, which describes the sectoral contribution to GDP growth in India from 1980 to 2011. Three features are apparent. First, the contribution of agriculture to aggregate growth has been declining over time. Second, the main driver of growth in India has been service industries such as finance, insurance, and real estate; transport services and communications; and wholesale and retail trade. Third, while growth in manufacturing (and construction) has also played an important role, this has been on account of the registered or formal manufacturing sector; the contribution of unregistered or informal manufacturing sector to growth has been low and unchanged over time.

In and of itself, the first of these features is not problematic. Indeed, it is natural for agriculture's contribution to growth to decline as an economy develops. The problem comes in when we recognize that the structure of employment in India has changed far less than the structure of output. In particular, the share of agriculture in total employment declined from 68 per cent in 1983 to 51 per cent in 2009. Given that the share of agriculture in total output declined from 37.1 per cent to 14.7 per cent over the same period, the implication is that far too many of India's workers have remained in a sector that has displayed insufficient productivity growth.[16] Similarly, while the rapid growth of services relative to industry or manufacturing is also not problematic per se (though it does go against the pattern experienced by high-performing East Asian economies that have also been very successful in poverty reduction), the lacklustre growth of India's unregistered manufacturing sector – which employs around 80 per cent of manufacturing workers and tends to be very labour-intensive in contrast to the skill and/or capital-intensive registered manufacturing sector – is. In particular, it suggests that employment opportunities in a non-agricultural sector (widely believed to have considerable potential for absorbing less skilled workers at higher productivity than agriculture) expanded at a slow pace.[17]

Figure 4.6: Sectoral contribution to GDP growth, selected periods

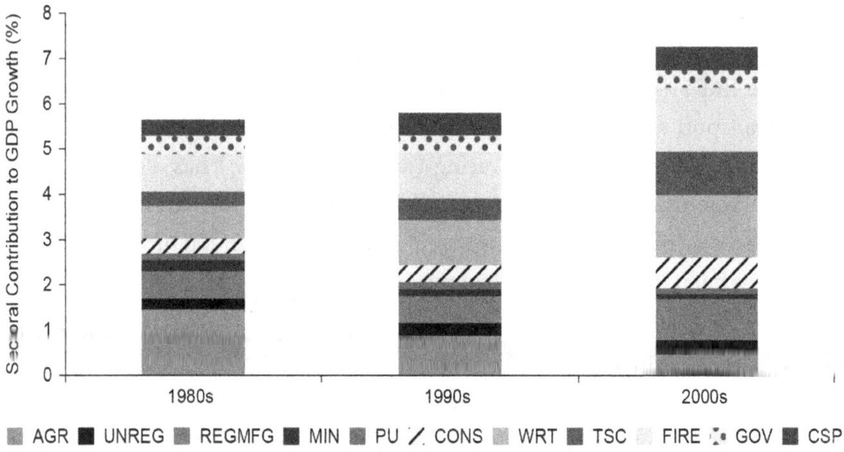

AGR = Agriculture and Allied Activities, CONS = Construction, CSP = Community, Social and Personal Services, FIRE = Finance, Insurance and Real Estate, GOV = Public Administration; Government Services, MIN = Mining and Quarrying, PU = Public Utilities, REG = Registered Manufacturing, TSC = Transport, Storage and Communications, UNREG = Unregistered Manufacturing, and WRT = Wholesale and Retail Trade, Restaurants and Hotels.

Notes: Computed using national accounts data from the Central Statistical Organization. GDP and sectoral growth rates are averages over the 10–year period reported.

Source: Authors' estimates.

Put differently, India's changing structure of production, characterized by the declining importance of agriculture, would have been more poverty reducing had it been accompanied by larger increases in agricultural productivity and larger changes in the structure of employment with labour moving out of agriculture to higher productivity sectors.[18] Figure 4.7, which uses India-wide data from 2009 to describe how India's workers are distributed across sectors along with the levels of sectoral labour productivity (relative to the national average), shows this quite clearly.[19] As may be seen, around half of India's workers are engaged in the agriculture sector. Given the extremely low productivity of the sector – only 29 per cent of average productivity nationally – the implication is that a near majority of India's workers are trapped in a vicious cycle of low productivity and low earnings. For growth to be associated with rapid poverty reduction, India would have to raise productivity in the agriculture sector on one hand, and ensure that job opportunities come up in higher productivity sectors elsewhere.

Figure 4.7: Employment shares and labour productivity differentials across sectors, 2009–10

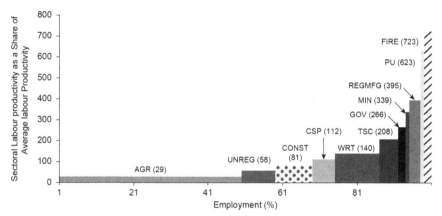

AGR = Agriculture and Allied Activities, CONST = Construction, CSP = Community, Social and Personal Services, FIRE = Finance, Insurance and Real Estate, GOV = Public Administration; Government Services, MIN = Mining and Quarrying, PU = Public Utilities, REGMFG = Registered Manufacturing, TSC = Transport, Storage and Communications, UNREG = Unregistered Manufacturing, and WRT = Wholesale and Retail Trade, Restaurants and Hotels.

Source: Authors' estimates based on CSO and NSSO reports.

Which sectors will these be? As Figure 4.7 reveals, there are certainly sectors in which productivity levels are very high. The difficulty is that many of these sectors – such as finance, insurance, and real estate; mining; and public utilities – have low potential for generating jobs on a large scale for semiskilled workers. One sector with considerable untapped potential for generating reasonably high productivity jobs is manufacturing. Unfortunately, employment in this sector has been fairly stable at around 12–15 per cent. The policy reasons behind India's pattern of growth in output and employment, and thus the relationship betw een growth and poverty, are something we will come back to later in this chapter.

4.3 Productivity growth, structural change and poverty reduction

The foregoing discussion suggests that the impact of aggregate growth on poverty depends on the sectoral composition of growth for two reasons. First, production sectors differ vastly in terms of their productivity. Since earnings are influenced by productivity, this differential has implications for cross-sector earnings. Indeed, as Figure 4.8 shows, average wages tend to be higher (lower) in sectors with higher (lower) productivity.[20] Second, employment shares vary considerably across sectors. The implication is that differential performance of sectors should have implications for the extent of new employment opportunities generated, earnings, and thus poverty.

Figure 4.8: Average wages and productivity across sectors, 2004–05

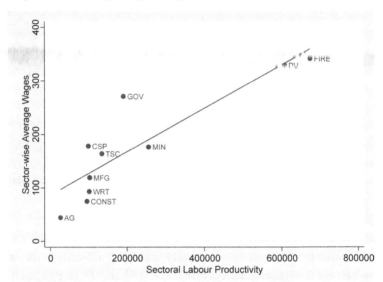

Notes: Average daily wages and annual labour productivity are expressed in nominal 2004–05 ₹.

AGR = Agriculture and Allied Activities; CONST = Construction; CSP = Community, Social and Personal Services; FIRE = Finance, Insurance and Real Estate; GOV = Public Administration, Government Services; MFG = Manufacturing; MIN = Mining and Quarrying; PU = Public Utilities; REGMFG = Registered Manufacturing; TSC = Transport, Storage and Communications; and WRT = Wholesale and Retail Trade, Restaurants and Hotels.

Source: Authors' estimates based on National Sample Survey Organization reports.

An implication of Figure 4.7 is that increases in aggregate growth need not stem only from improvements in productivity within a given production sector; they can also arise from a reallocation of resources, especially employment, from lower productivity to higher productivity sectors.[21] In fact, in their analysis of productivity growth and its drivers in developing countries from around the world, McMillan and Rodrik note an important feature that distinguishes the experience of Asia, the region with the highest increases in aggregate productivity, from Africa and Latin America. While all three regions have experienced increases in within-sector productivity, it is mainly in Asia that these have additionally been accompanied by a reallocation of employment from lower productivity to higher productivity sectors. The result has been fairly high increases in aggregate productivity. In contrast, in Africa and Latin America, employment changes toward higher productivity sectors have been minor (or even actually moved to lower productivity sectors). One reason for this is that the expansion of aggregate output and productivity in Latin America and Africa has been often driven by increases in productivity within highly capital-intensive sectors (for example, mining).

The implications for poverty reduction follow quite clearly. Growth will have a larger impact on poverty when it is driven by sectors that employ a large proportion of an economy's rank and file workers (such as agriculture). However, growth can also be driven by a reallocation of workers from low productivity (and low earnings) sectors to higher productivity (higher earnings) sectors. Growth that is driven by such a reallocation should also be poverty reducing.

In what follows, we use data on poverty, employment, and productivity for 15 states (based on pre-2000 state definitions, as noted earlier, and spanning 1987–2009) to explore how aggregate (labour) productivity, the proximate driver of economic growth, affects poverty. Following the work of McMillan and Rodrik, we break down states' aggregate productivity growth into two components: within-sector productivity growth and that due to structural change or reallocation of labour. The relationships are captured by the following equation:

$$\Delta Y_t = \sum_{i=n} \varnothing_{i,t-k} \Delta y_{i,t} + \sum_{i=n} y_{i,t} \Delta \varnothing_{i,t} \qquad \text{(Equation 4.1)}$$

where ΔY_t is the change in productivity at the economy wide level. The first term on the right hand side of the equation reflects the weighted sum of productivity growth within the individual production sectors, with the weights, $\varnothing_{i,t-k}$, being the share of employment at the beginning of the period. The second term indicates the change in labour productivity due to reallocation of employment across sectors. McMillan and Rodrik refer to this term as 'structural change'.[22]

4.3.1 Productivity growth across states

We first examine how productivity and its two components have evolved across India's major states from 1987 to 2009. The bars of Figure 4.9 present the productivity growth numbers expressed in annualized growth rates.[23] The numbers above the bar denote the ranking of states in terms of how important structural change has been as a driver of growth. As may be seen from the figure, both within-sector productivity growth and structural change have contributed positively to aggregate labour productivity growth in all states, although the extent of the contribution of the two components have varied significantly across the states. The contribution of structural change to aggregate labour productivity is highest in Karnataka, Maharashtra, and Haryana (as may be seen from the number above) and lowest in Punjab, Bihar, and West Bengal.

Figure 4.9: Within-sector productivity growth and structural change in Indian states, 1987–2009

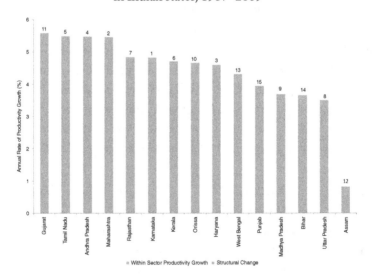

Notes: All values are in annualized percentage terms. States are sorted in order of the highest magnitude of total productivity growth. The numbers above the bars indicates how each state ranks with respect to the proportion of structural change in total productivity growth, i.e., the length of the black bar.

Source: Author estimates based on Central Statistical Organization reports.

4.3.2 Impact of productivity growth on poverty reduction

We next consider the experience of states with regard to poverty reduction. Figure 4.10 ranks states according to their annual rates of poverty reduction. The southern states of Kerala, Tamil Nadu, Karnataka, and Andhra Pradesh have the highest rates of poverty reduction (4 per cent per annum or higher), while the states with the lowest rates of poverty reduction are Madhya Pradesh, Bihar, Punjab and Assam (less than 2 per cent per annum). Figure 4.11 shows that both a higher pace of structural change (upper panel), as well as a higher pace of within-sector productivity growth (lower panel) are positively associated with a higher pace of poverty reduction. Of course, the relationships are not watertight. As may be seen, given the rates of structural change and within-sector productivity growth that Kerala has experienced, the extent of poverty reduction in the state has been far higher than what the simple linear relationship between poverty reduction and the two components of productivity growth would suggest.[24] To a lesser extent, Madhya Pradesh also emerges as an outlier, though in a direction opposite to that of Kerala. In this state, the extent of poverty reduction has been considerably less than what the pace of structural change and within-sector productivity growth would suggest.

Figure 4.10: Annual rate of poverty reduction in Indian states, 1987–2009

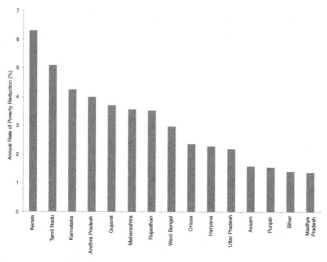

Notes: All values are in annualized percentage terms. States are sorted in order of highest magnitude of annual rate of poverty reduction.

Source: Authors' estimates based on National Sample Survey Organization reports.

Figure 4.11: Productivity and poverty reduction in Indian states, 1987–2009

Figure 4.11.a: Structural change and poverty reduction (1987–2009)

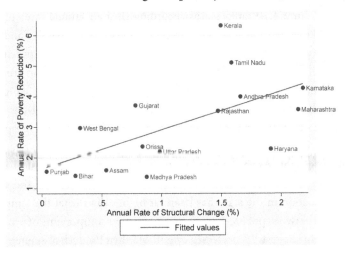

Source: Authors' estimates

Figure 4.11.b: Within-sector productivity growth and poverty reduction (1987–2009)

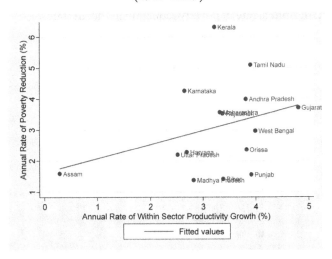

Source: Authors' estimates

To probe a bit further into the relationship between productivity growth, its two components, and poverty we carry out some simple regression analysis involving the following regression specification:

$$\Delta Pov_{j,t,t=k} = \alpha + \beta \Delta X_{j,t,t-k} + \varepsilon \qquad \text{(Equation 4.2)}$$

where $\Delta Pov_{j,t,t-k}$ and $\Delta Xov_{j,t,t-k}$ are the annual rates of change in poverty headcount ratios and productivity growth for state j over $(t-k)^{th}$ and t^{th} years.

Table 4.2 describes the results of the regression analysis. These indicate that the higher is overall productivity growth, as well as its two components – productivity growth occurring due to the reallocation of labour (i.e., the 'structural change' term) and 'within-sector productivity growth' – the faster is the pace of poverty reduction. This holds for the full time period examined (i.e., 1987–2009; columns 1–3) as well as for only the post-liberalization years, 1993–2009 (columns 4–6). To understand the magnitude of the estimated relationship between productivity growth and poverty reduction, consider column (1). The estimated coefficient on the productivity growth term implies that a 1 percentage point increase in the annual rate of productivity growth leads to a 0.64 percentage point increase in the annual rate of poverty *reduction*. Taking the case of Andhra Pradesh, which experienced an increase of productivity growth from 4.6 per cent per annum over 1993–2004 to 9 per cent per annum over 2004–09, the estimated coefficient suggests that Andhra Pradesh's poverty rate should have declined from 29.7 per cent in 2004 to 22.01 per cent by 2009. Had there been no increase in productivity growth, so that the latter remained at 4.6 per cent per annum, the poverty rate by 2009 would be around 25.6 per cent. As it happens, an increase in productivity of 4.4 percentage points per annum took place from 2004–09 and Andhra Pradesh's headcount ratio ended up at 21.1 per cent by 2009, a little lower than if productivity growth were the only factor determining the extent of poverty reduction.

Interestingly, all productivity growth coefficients are larger in the post–liberalization period. Also, the coefficient for the 'structural change' term is larger in absolute terms than the 'within-sector productivity growth' term for both time periods, strongly suggesting that the reallocation of labour from lower productivity to higher productivity sectors is an important means through which growth reduces poverty.

Table 4.2: Effect of total productivity growth and its components on poverty

	Dependent variable: Annual rate of change in poverty rates					
	All years (1987–2009)			Post-liberalization years (1993–2009)		
	(1)	(2)	(3)	(4)	(5)	(6)
Constant	−0.0027	−0.0058	−0.0279***	0.0030	−0.0009	−0.0265***
	[−0.399]	[−0.803]	[−5.893]	[0.358]	[−0.098]	[−4.011]
Average labour Produc- tivity growth	0.6409***			−0.7183***		
	[−5.439]			[−5.381]		
Within- sector Produc- tivity growth		−0.6989***			−0.8109***	
		[−4.526]			[−4.455]	
Structural change			−0.7784**			−0.9546**
			[−2.597]			[−2.541]
Observa- tions	45	45	45	30	30	30
R-squared	0.4076	0.3227	0.1356	0.5084	0.4148	0.1874

Notes: The independent variables are in annualized rate of change terms. Specifications (1)–(3) estimate the coefficient for all the time periods under consideration, i.e. the periods 1987–1993, 1993–2004 and 2004–09, while specifications (4)–(6) estimates coefficients for only post-liberalization years, i.e., the time periods 1993–2004 and 2004–09. All values are in annualized percentage terms. t-statistics in parentheses; *** p<0.01, ** p<0.05, * p<0.1.

Source: Authors' estimates.

Indeed, a closer look at the drivers of aggregate productivity growth among states with strong and weak performance on poverty reduction is instructive. Of the states where the poverty rate declined by at least 4 per cent per annum over 1987–2009 (Kerala, Tamil Nadu, Karnataka, and Andhra Pradesh), all four performed well on the structural change component of aggregate productivity growth relative to most other states. Their relative performance on the within-sector component is more mixed. The starkest case is that of Karnataka, which had the second largest structural change component among the 15 states but experienced within-sector productivity growth that was one of the weakest (third lowest).[25] Among the weak performers on poverty reduction – i.e., states where the poverty rate declined by less than 2 per cent per annum over 1987–2009 (Madhya Pradesh, Bihar, Punjab, and Assam) – the situation is somewhat converse. For example, while Punjab ranked favourably in terms of within-sector productivity growth (among the top three states), it experienced the second lowest amount of structural change. Similarly, while Bihar's within-sector productivity growth was middling (rank 7 out of 15), it had the third lowest structural change term.[26]

Figure 4.12 allows us to delve deeper into how individual sector experiences vis-à-vis the two components of productivity growth may be shaping the broader productivity growth–poverty reduction relationship. The figure displays by state, the extent of structural change and within-sector productivity growth in each of the 11 production sectors considered in this chapter. As per equation (4.1), negative values for structural change in any given sector imply a reduction in its share in total state employment; negative values for within-sector productivity growth imply a reduction in sectoral labour productivity between 1987 and 2009. Production sectors appear across states in the figure based on (ascending) order of state and sector-specific labour productivity in 2009.

Figure 4.12: Productivity growth decomposition by
state and sector: 1987–2009

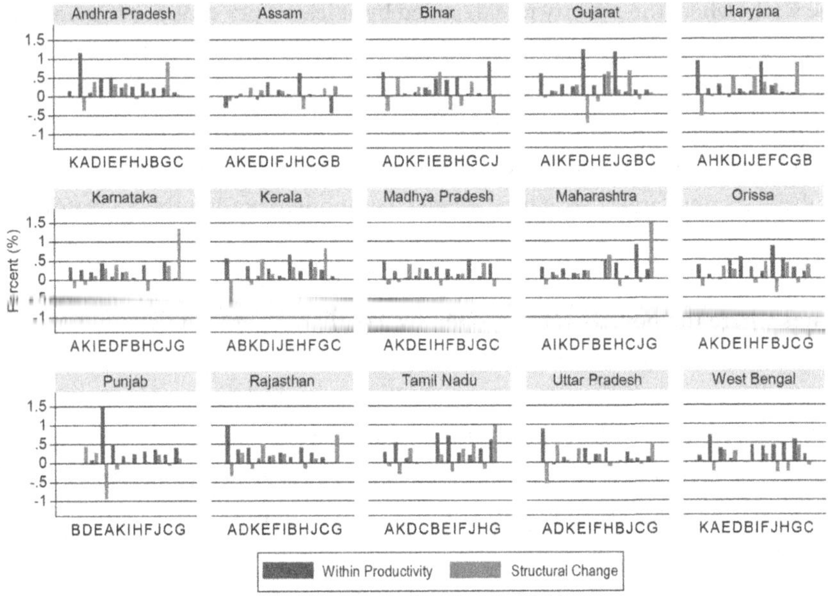

A = Agriculture and Allied Activities; B = Mining and Quarrying; C = Public Utilities;
D = Construction; E = Wholesale and Retail Trade, Restaurants and Hotels; F = Transport,
Storage, and Communications; G = Finance, Insurance and Real Estate; H = Government
Services; I = Community, Social and Personal Services; J = Registered Manufacturing, and
K = Unregistered Manufacturing.

Source: Authors' estimates.

Focusing on the cases of Bihar, Karnataka, and Punjab, the following salient
features may be noted. First, while labour reallocated out of agriculture in Bihar
– the state's lowest productivity sector (as in 11 other states, the exceptions being
in Andhra Pradesh, Punjab, and West Bengal) – it seems to have been primarily
to relatively low productivity construction sector activities.[27] At the same time,
several high productivity sectors saw decline in employment shares (which may
be inferred from the negative values of the bars representing structural change).
Interestingly, registered manufacturing was one of these latter sectors. Not only
was it Bihar's highest productivity sector in 2009, it also showed the largest
within-sector productivity increases over 1987–2009. In conjunction with the
fact that unregistered manufacturing in Bihar displayed negligible increases in
both of the two components of aggregate productivity (the third set of bars
from the left), and that within-sector productivity in agriculture *increased,*

a fairly plausible narrative for the weak response of poverty to aggregate productivity growth in Bihar would include the state's inability to generate dynamism in modern, labour-intensive manufacturing.

Second, as in the case of Bihar, Karnataka experienced reallocation of employment out of agriculture. To the extent that some of this employment moved into the second lowest productivity sector (unregistered manufacturing), it did so to a sector that was experiencing some improvements in within-sector productivity (certainly much more so than the construction sector in Bihar). Moreover, the employment share of unregistered manufacturing itself declined so that overall employment shares should have moved unambiguously to significantly higher productivity sectors that would have pulled people out of poverty. Two other striking differences from the case of Bihar are the fact that the high productivity registered manufacturing sector not only experienced a relatively high degree of within-sector productivity growth but also an increase in its share of the state's employment, and that the highest productivity sector (encompassing finance, insurance, and real estate services) contributed significantly to the total structural change in the state. While one usually thinks of these sectors as mainly generating employment opportunities for high skilled (and therefore non-poor) workers, recent work has begun to identify linkages between the growth of modern services sectors and employment opportunities for less skilled workers.[28]

Finally, in the case of Punjab – which experienced weak poverty reduction like Bihar (albeit starting with initially low poverty rates) – it is interesting to note that although the share of agriculture in state employment declined as elsewhere, agriculture has not been the lowest productivity sector. In fact, three other sectors had lower productivity than agriculture. Moreover, employment shares in two of these sectors increased (i.e., construction and wholesale as well as retail trade, hotels, and restaurants). Given these patterns, it is not surprising to note that an exit from agriculture has coexisted with weak structural change in the aggregate. Finally, the fact that agriculture in Punjab also experienced the highest amount of within-sector productivity change across all sectors and states (the result of healthy productivity growth and the large employment share of agriculture) serves to emphasize that poverty reduction requires not just an improvement in agricultural productivity. It also requires the emergence of modern, labour-intensive sectors that will make up for the exit of the workforce from agriculture.

4.3.3 Determinants of structural change

We conclude with an attempt to shed exploratory light on the policy or policy-amenable factors that may influence the extent of structural change – the component of productivity growth that Table 4.2 shows is more strongly associated poverty reduction. We consider the initial employment shares in agriculture, initial education levels (in terms of average number of years of schooling), and indicators of labour market regulations, product market regulations, and financial development at the state level.[29] Initial employment shares in agriculture can be looked upon as capturing the potential for structural change in a state, since a larger initial share of workers engaged in low productivity agriculture implies a larger share of workers who can reallocate out of agriculture. Similarly, since education is widely believed to provide workers greater occupational mobility, states with a higher initial share of educated workers can be expected to experience greater structural change. Finally, states with better developed financial systems, more competitive product markets, and greater labour market flexibility are likely to be those with a more dynamic economic environment, allowing for a greater reallocation of resources from one economic activity to another. They may therefore be more likely to experience growth-enhancing structural change. As with the measures of poverty and productivity, details on these variables are provided in the Appendix.

Table 4.3 provides the results of our exploratory regression analysis. Each of the columns of the table includes as explanatory variables the initial share of workers in agriculture and workers years' of education. While the coefficient on average years of schooling fails to be statistically significant, that on the initial share of agriculture is significant across some of the specifications. It is positive in both instances, consistent with the idea that the variable captures the potential for structural change. Turning to the variables capturing elements of the investment climate, each is positive and statistically significant when introduced one at a time. The results suggest that states with better developed financial systems, more competitive product markets, and greater labour market flexibility experience faster structural change. When introduced simultaneously, however, it is only the financial development variable that retains its statistical significance. This should not be too surprising, however, since the labour market and product market regulation indicators pertain mainly to the manufacturing sector. On the other hand, the financial development variable used here captures the state of financial development for the state as a whole.

Table 4.3: The determinants of structural change

	Dependent variable: annual growth rate of structural change				
	(1)	(2)	(3)	(4)	(5)
Constant	0.0234	−0.0535**	−0.0208	0.0171	−0.0555*
	[0.816]	[−2.538]	[−0.763]	[0.715]	−2.193]
Initial employment Share in agriculture	−0.0138	0.0506**	0.0283	0.0018	0.0541**
	[−0.418]	[2.341]	[0.944]	[0.065]	[2.264]
Initial average years of schooling	−0.0010	0.0018	0.0032	−0.0020	0.0027
	[−0.349]	[1.092]	[1.168]	[−0.804]	[1.196]
Index of financial development		0.0051***			0.0043**
		[5.427]			[2.967]
Index of Labour Market flexibility			0.0106**		0.0034
			[2.883]		[0.973]
Index of product Market competition				0.0054**	0.0001
				[2.542]	[0.041]
Observations	15	15	15	15	15
R-squared	0.0145	0.7320	0.4387	0.3793	0.7594

Note: t-statistics in parentheses; *** $p<0.01$, ** $p<0.05$, * $p<0.1$.
Source: Authors' estimates.

4.4 Conclusion

Our review of recent empirical studies and our analysis of the links between growth, structural transformation, and poverty reduction lead one to note the following. First, viewed from the perspective of poverty reduction, growth in India has been inclusive However, as comparisons with the experiences of East and Southeast Asian economies reveal, there appears to be considerable scope to increase the impact of growth on poverty reduction in India.

Second, while India's relatively weak performance in improving the health and educational status of its population may well be an important factor in explaining the muted link between growth and poverty reduction, as highlighted by previous literature, India's specific pattern of structural transformation is likely to have played an important role. In particular, significant reductions in the share of aggregate output contributed by agriculture – a sector that employed more than two thirds of India's labour force as recently as the 1980s and continues to employ around a half today – have taken place without significant increases in the productivity of agriculture and expansion of output in sectors with high potential to employ semiskilled workers productively, such as modern, labour-intensive manufacturing.

Indeed, the results of this chapter indicate that the latter process, especially the reallocation of workers from lower to higher productivity sectors – and referred to as growth enhancing structural change by recent literature – is intimately connected to poverty reduction. States with the best performance in poverty reduction over 1987–2009 (such as Tamil Nadu, Karnataka, and Andhra Pradesh) have tended to be precisely the ones registering a high degree of structural change. Conversely, states with the weakest track record in poverty reduction (such as Bihar, Madhya Pradesh, and Assam) have tended to be the ones registering a low degree of structural change.

Particularly instructive is the comparison between Bihar and Karnataka. Judged by the metric of within-sector productivity growth, Bihar's performance was the better of the two. However, of the reallocation of workers that took place across sectors, very little was from lower to significantly higher productivity sectors in Bihar. In fact, Bihar ranked 14th out of 15 states in terms of the extent of structural change, leading its overall productivity growth to be among the lowest of the 15 states. In contrast, structural change in Karnataka was the strongest in the country, leading the state to register a decent growth rate in aggregate productivity (sixth out of 15 states) and third best performance in poverty reduction (4.3 per cent reduction annually in its poverty rate).

Third, our exploratory analysis of the drivers of structural change suggests that better functioning credit markets, competitive business regulations, and relatively flexible labour regulations are associated with a larger reallocation of labour from lower to higher productivity sectors. These findings are consistent with the view that a better investment climate is not only good for business, it is also an important means for making growth more pro-poor in a labour abundant country. By highlighting the importance of reallocation of resources to both growth and poverty reduction, the findings of this chapter strongly suggest the need for more micro-oriented research, for example, using firm level data, on the links between different types of economic policies and the decisions of economic agents on entry and exit across and within sectors of production and how these decisions influence employment opportunities.

Appendix

We describe here the data used in their analysis of state–level productivity growth, structural change, and poverty reduction over the time period 1987–88 to 2009–10. As noted earlier, we work with 15 major states of India defined in terms of their pre-2000 state boundaries.[30]

Poverty

Our measure of (absolute consumption) poverty is the poverty rate, i.e., the proportion of the population living below a given poverty line. We use the state-specific poverty lines developed by the Expert Group 2009 (Government of India, 2009) for the years 1993–94, 2004–05, and 2009–10 (as updated by the Indian Planning Commission following the recommendations of the Expert Group). These poverty lines are then applied to the large scale or quinquennial round consumer expenditure surveys carried out by the NSSO to obtain combined poverty rates for both rural and urban areas in the 15 major states that we consider in their analysis.[31] Owing to the controversy surrounding the NSSO's consumer expenditure survey for 1999–2000 (on account of side by side placement of 7 and 30-day recall periods for consumption items in the survey questionnaire), we drop this year from their analysis entirely.[32]

However, given that the starting year for our analysis is 1987–88 we are still left with the task of estimating the poverty rates for this year. To do so, we follow Cain, Hasan, and Mitra in extending the Expert Group's poverty lines back to 1987–88. Cain, Hasan, and Mitra use Deaton's Fischer price indexes for 1993–94 relative to 1987–88[33] to translate the Expert Group's state and sector-specific poverty lines for 1993–94 to come up with their corresponding 1987–88 values. They then use these poverty lines against the expenditure data reported in the 1987–88 consumer expenditure survey to estimate poverty rates in that year. Cain, Hasan, and Mitra follow the procedures of the Expert Group so that, rather than use household expenditures reported on a uniform 30-day basis for their computations, they use 'mixed reference period' expenditures whereby the 30-day expenditures for high frequency consumption items (food, fuels, etc.) are combined with 365-

day expenditures for low frequency consumption items (clothing, footwear and durables) duly prorated to 30 days.[34] Tables A4.1 and A4.2 describe the state-specific poverty lines and poverty rates used in this chapter.

Table A4.1: Poverty lines

	Round 43		Round 50		Round 61		Round 66	
	1987–88		1993–94		2004–05		2009–10	
State	Rural	Urban	Rural	Urban	Rural	Urban	Rural	Urban
Andhra Pradesh	138.9	159.2	244.1	282.0	433.4	563.2	693.8	926.4
Assam	153.4	172.7	266.3	306.8	478.0	600.0	691.7	871.0
Bihar	147.8	161.7	236.1	266.9	433.4	526.2	655.8	773.3
Chhattisgarh			229.1	283.5	398.9	513.7	617.3	806.7
Gujarat	163.8	193.9	279.4	320.7	501.6	659.2	725.9	951.4
Jharkhand			227.7	304.1	404.79	531.3	616.3	831.2
Haryana	168.7	175.7	294.1	312.1	529.4	626.4	791.6	975.4
Karnataka	152.4	166.6	266.9	294.8	417.8	588.1	629.4	908.0
Kerala	166.5	166.9	286.5	289.2	537.3	584.7	775.3	830.7
Madhya Pradesh	135.3	160.7	232.5	274.5	408.4	532.3	631.9	771.7
Maharashtra	155.5	181.9	268.6	329.0	484.9	632.9	743.7	961.1
Orissa	136.1	166.4	224.2	279.3	407.8	497.3	567.1	736.0
Punjab	150.5	183.0	286.9	342.3	543.5	642.5	830.0	960.8
Rajasthan	163.0	174.9	271.9	300.5	478.0	568.2	755.0	846.0
Tamil Nadu	150.7	169.2	252.6	288.2	441.7	559.8	639.0	800.8
Uttar Pradesh	145.5	170.1	244.3	281.3	435.1	532.1	663.7	799.9
Uttaranchal			249.5	306.7	486.2	602.4	719.5	898.6
West Bengal	141.4	173.0	235.5	295.2	445.4	572.5	643.2	830.6

Notes: Poverty lines are drawn from Amoranto and Hasan (2010) and Cain, Hasan, and Mitra (2010) for the 43rd round and Government of India (2009 and 2012) for the 50th, 61st and 66th rounds. State and sector-specific poverty lines are used in conjunction with NSS consumer expenditure survey data to obtain poverty rates for each state as a whole (i.e., rural + urban).

Source: Amoranto and Hasan, 2010; Cain, Hasan and Mitra, 2010 and Government of India, 2009 and 2012

Table A4.2: Poverty rates

	1987–88	1993–94	2004–05	2009–10
Andhra Pradesh	51.8	44.6	29.7	21.1
Assam	54.0	51.8	34.5	37.9
Bihar	68.8	60.5	52.2	50.3
Gujarat	52.9	37.8	31.7	23.0
Haryana	33.4 ˙	36.0	24.1	20.1
Karnataka	61.5	49.5	33.4	23.6
Kerala	50.4	31.3	19.6	12.0
Madhya Pradesh	55.3	46.4	48.9	40.7
Maharashtra	54.5	47.9	38.3	24.5
Orissa	62.6	59.1	57.2	37.0
Punjab	22.5	22.4	20.9	15.9
Rajasthan	54.7	38.3	34.4	24.8
Tamil Nadu	54.2	44.8	29.4	17.1
Uttar Pradesh	59.9	47.7	40.5	36.7
West Bengal	51.9	39.4	34.2	26.7

Notes: Bihar, Madhya Pradesh, and Uttar Pradesh are defined in terms of their pre–2000 boundaries (and thus include Jharkhand, Chhattisgarh, and Uttaranchal, respectively).
Source: Cain, Hasan, and Mitra (2010) for 1987 and Government of India (2009 and 2012) for the years 1993, 2004, and 2009.

Output

Our data on state domestic product and its sectoral composition is from the CSO and the Government of India. We organize the real sectoral output data into eleven broad sectors, namely: (1) agriculture and allied activities; (2) mining and quarrying; (3) registered manufacturing; (4) unregistered manufacturing; (5) construction; (6) public utilities that include electricity, water supply and gas; (7) transport, storage and communications; (8) wholesale and retail trade; hotels and restaurants; (9) finance, insurance and real estate; (10) government services; and (11) community, personal and social services. The data on output from 1983–84 to 2009–10 is available for four different base years: 1980–81, 1993–94, 1999–2000 and 2004–05 with several overlapping years across different bases. To arrive at a uniform base, 2004–05 in the chapter, we create linking factors at the sector level. These linking factors are based on the average ratios of sector output available over the common years.

Employment

We use the employment–unemployment surveys of the NSSO for the years 1987–88, 1993–94, 2004–05, and 2009–10 to get estimates of employment across industries and states. We follow the principal usual activity status to determine employment status and the national industrial classification code corresponding to the usual status to determine the broad sector of employment for the worker. Principal usual status defines the employed as those who (1) work in household enterprises, i.e., self-employed or own account workers; (2) work as helpers in household enterprises (unpaid family workers); (3) work for regular salaries or wages; and (4) work as casual wage earners. We consider workers of all ages.

We supplement the information from the employment–unemployment surveys with data on employment in registered manufacturing from the Annual Survey of Industries (ASI).[35] This addition is crucial for constructing real value added and employment data separately for the registered manufacturing and unregistered manufacturing. Since the NSSO employment-unemployment survey data provides employment figures for the manufacturing sector as a whole, we compute employment numbers for unregistered manufacturing by subtracting registered manufacturing employment (ASI) from total manufacturing employment (NSSO). In doing this exercise, we are careful to match and harmonize the data across years and data sources, using the National Industry Classification (NIC) codes so that a consistency in definitions of the broad sectors is maintained throughout. Table A4.3 describes the NIC codes used in various NSSO survey rounds. Table A4.4 explains how we have harmonized NIC codes for the 10 broad industry groups (at the two digit level of classification).

Table A4.3: NICs across National Sample Survey Rounds

Round	Year	NIC classification
38	1983	1970
43	1987–88	1970
50	1993–94	1987
55	1999–2000	1998
61	2004–05	1998
66	2009–10	2004

Source: Various NSSO reports

Table A4.4: Harmonizing NIC codes over time at the two-digit level

Name of broad industry group	Industry	Round 43 NIC 1970	Round 50 NIC 1987	Round 61 NIC 1998	Round 66 NIC 2004	Harmonized Industry Code
Agriculture and allied industries (hunting, forestry and fishing)	AG	0	0	01,02 and 05	01,02 and 05	1
Mining and quarrying	MIN	1	1	10 to 14	10 to 14	2
Manufacturing	MFG	2 and 3	2 and 3	15 to 37	15 to 37	3
Electricity, gas and water	PU	4	4	40and41	40and41	4
Construction	CONST	5	5	45	45	5
Wholesale and retail trade: restaurants and hotels	WRT	6	6	50 to 52 and 55	50 to 52 and 55	6
Transport, storage and communications	TSC	7	7	60 to 64	60 to 64	7
Finance, insurance, real estate	FIRE	8	8	65 to 67 and 70 to 74	65 to 67 and 70 to 74	8
Public administration; government services	GOV	90	90	75	75	9
Community, social and personal services	CSP	91 to 99	91 to 99	80,85,90 to 93 and 95	80,85,90 to 93 and 95	10

Source: Various National Sample Survey Organization Reports

Table A4.5: Concordance of education categories across National Sample Survey rounds and number of years of education

Round 43		Round 50		Round 61		Round 66		Harmonized codes	Number of years of education
Code	Description	Code	Description	Code	Description	Code	Description		
0	not literate	1	not literate	1	not literate	1	not literate	1 = Below Primary	0
1	literate w/o formal schooling	2	literate through attending NFEC/AEC	2	literate through attending EGS/NFEC/AEC	2	literate through attending EGS/NFEC/AEC		1
		3	TLC	3	TLC	3	TLC		1
		4	Others	4	Others	4	Others		1
2	literate but below primary	5	literate but below primary	5	literate but below primary	5	literate but below primary		2.5
3	primary	6	primary	6	primary	6	primary	2 = Primary	5
4	middle	7	middle	7	middle	7	middle		8
5	secondary	8	secondary	8	secondary	8	secondary	3 = Secondary	12
		9	higher secondary	10	Higher secondary	10	Higher secondary		12
				11	Diploma/certificate course	11	Diploma/certificate course		12
7	Graduate and above in engineering/technology	11	Graduate and above in engineering/technology	12 or 13	Graduate/ postgraduate and above	12 or 13	Graduate/ postgraduate and above	4 = Tertiary and above	15
8	Graduate and above in medicine	12	Graduate and above in medicine						15
9	Graduate and above in other subjects	13	Graduate and above in other subjects						15

Note: AEC = Adult Education Centres; EGS = Education Guarantee Scheme; NFEC = Non-formal Education Courses; TLC = Total Literacy Campaign.

Source: Cain, Hasan, Magsombol, and Tandon (2010) and authors' estimates

Other variables

We capture initial conditions in states through the 1987 share of employment in agriculture and average number of years of schooling among the employed. For constructing the initial average number of years of schooling, we closely follow Cain, Hasan, Magsombol, and Tandon (2010). Table A4.5 generates a variable denoting the number of years of schooling corresponding to each general education code in the 43rd NSSO survey round. Information on other rounds is provided for reference. We restrict our attention to those defined as employed on a principal activity status basis and construct the average years of education over this group.

To capture the state–level policy environment, we consider measures of labour market flexibility, product market competition (PMC), and financial development (FINDEV). These measures are taken from Hasan, Mitra, and Ramaswamy (2007); Gupta, Hasan, and Kumar (2009); and Cain, Hasan, and Mitra (2010) respectively.[36] Table A4.6 reports the values taken for these and the initial conditions variables.

Table A4.6: State characteristics

State	Initial employment shares in agriculture (1987)	Initial average years of schooling (1987)	Labour market regulations (FLEX)	Product market regulations (PMR)	Initial level of financial development (1987) (FINDEV)
Andhra Pradesh	0.67	2.02	1	0	6.39
Assam	0.70	3.83	0	-1	2.69
Bihar	0.74	2.47	0	-1	3.37
Gujarat	0.56	3.48	1	0	5.67
Haryana	0.57	4.02	0	1	6.09
Karnataka	0.66	3.03	1	1	7.04
Kerala	0.47	5.72	0	0	6.66
Madhya Pradesh	0.77	2.13	0	-1	5.09
Maharashtra	0.63	3.70	1	1	6.42

State	Initial employment shares in agriculture (1987)	Initial average years of schooling (1987)	Labour market regulations (FLEX)	Product market regulations (PMR)	Initial level of financial development (1987) (FINDEV)
Orissa	0.68	2.27	0	−1	4.49
Punjab	0.52	4.51	0	1	4.65
Rajasthan	0.64	1.94	1	−1	4.97
Tamil Nadu	0.51	3.52	1	1	7.78
Uttar Pradesh	0.70	2.86	0	0	4.10
West Bengal	0.52	3.73	0	−1	4.91

Notes: 1. Labour market flexibility measure (FLEX) is based on Hasan, Mitra and Ramaswamy (2007); 1 refers to flexible and 0 refers to inflexible labour regulations. 2. Product Market Regulations (PMR) measure is based on Gupta, Hasan and Kumar (2009); 1 refers to competitive, 0 refers to neutral and −1 refers to cumbersome product market regulations. 3. Financial Development (FINDEV) is interpolated for 1987 and is based on the Financial Infrastructure Development Index (for years between 1971–72 and 1997–98) quoted in Ghosh and De (2004). Larger values of FINDEV represent states with a relatively well-developed financial system.

Endnotes

1 Structural transformation in an economy is usually thought to encompass three processes: (1) changes in sectoral composition of output; (2) changes in sectoral composition of employment; and (3) changes in the rural-urban composition of output and employment. Our focus in this chapter is on the first two processes only.

2 McMillan and Rodrik (2011).

3 Increases in productivity may also lead to a reduction in the price of output. In this case, the relationship between productivity and poverty would run through the gains the poor experience as consumers of a product whose (relative) price is falling. Of course, the significance of this effect will depend on the importance of the product in the consumption basket of the poor.

4 McMillan and Rodrik (2011).

5 Our state level analysis is based on data from 15 major Indian states using pre-2000 boundaries of three large states: Andhra Pradesh, Assam, Bihar (including what is now Jharkhand), Gujarat, Haryana, Karnataka, Kerala, Madhya Pradesh (including what is now Chhattisgarh), Maharashtra, Orissa, Punjab, Rajasthan, Tamil Nadu, Uttar Pradesh (including what is now Uttarakhand) and West Bengal.

6 Following the terminology of McMillan and Rodrik (2011).

7 The exact timing of India's growth acceleration and its causes are the subject of debate. For

example, while Rodrik and Subramaniam (2005) have emphasized the role of 'pro-business' reforms of the early 1980s, and thus downplayed the importance of the dramatic trade liberalization and industrial policy delicensing that took place in 1991, Panagariya (2008) has argued that unsustainable increases in public expenditures and foreign borrowings were important drivers of growth in the 1980s, and thus that without the reforms of 1991, India's growth acceleration of the 1980s would have proved to be short-lived.

8 The figure considers a five year moving average of annual growth rates of GDP per capita since there is a lot of year-to-year fluctuation in growth rates, particularly in the earlier years when India's economy was especially influenced by the often fickle monsoons.

9 Press Note on Poverty Estimates, 2009–10, Planning Commission, Government of India, March 2012.

10 Datt and Ravallion (2011).

11 Ravallion (2009).

12 Datt and Ravallion (2011).

13 Datt and Ravallion (1999).

14 HPEC (2011).

15 Datt and Ravallion (2011).

16 Papola and Sahu (2012).

17 Using data on Indian poverty and production from 1951 to 1991, Ravallion and Datt (1996) find output growth in the primary and tertiary sectors to be poverty reducing. Growth in the secondary sector is found to have no impact on poverty reduction. These patterns show up both in the aggregate as well as for rural and urban India, separately. A consistent set of results is obtained by Hasan, Quibria, and Kim (2003) who use cross-country data and find that poverty reduction in South Asia has been more closely associated with growth in the primary and tertiary sectors – unlike the case of East Asia where the growth in the secondary sector has been an important driver of poverty reduction. Both findings are consistent with the point being made here. That is, while India's manufacturing sector grew, its expansion was driven by the skill and/or capital intensive registered manufacturing sector. The labour-intensive unregistered manufacturing sector experienced limited growth. Since the fortunes of the poor are likely to be more intimately linked with the performance of unregistered manufacturing given the dualism in Indian manufacturing, it would not be surprising to find that growth in manufacturing, driven by an expansion of registered manufacturing, to not be particularly poverty reducing.

18 In their analysis of the effects of agricultural productivity on poverty in India, Datt and Ravallion (1998) find increases in agricultural productivity to be associated with lower poverty through several channels including higher yields, an expansion of employment opportunities, increases in wages, and/or declines in relative food prices.

19 Output data is from the CSO while employment data is drawn from the employment–unemployment surveys of the NSSO. Information on usual principal status of individuals is used for determining employment across states and industries.

20 Our measure of average wages is derived from the NSSO's employment–unemployment survey of 2004–05 for the 15 major states. In particular, we took data on weekly earnings and number of half days worked (over a 7 day period) by regular and casual wage employees to calculate daily wages for workers. These were averaged over each of the production sectors we

work with in this chapter. However, as the survey data does not allow us to distinguish between unregistered and registered manufacturing, we consider a single, consolidated manufacturing sector for computing both average wages as well as average labour productivity by sector.

21 This implication is highlighted by McMillan and Rodrik.

22 McMillan and Rodrik (2011).

23 These are computed as follows: First, we calculate the annual growth rate of overall productivity. Next, we compute what proportion of the total productivity change in absolute terms is accounted for by structural transformation and within–sector productivity respectively. These proportions are then multiplied by the annual growth rate of overall productivity to obtain the annualized growth rate of structural transformation and within-sector productivity growth, respectively. This closely follows the methodology used by McMillian and Rodrik as explained by Ahsan and Mitra (2013).

24 Whether Kerala's superior poverty reduction is on account of its superior human capital endowments à la Ravallion and Datt (1999) or mechanisms related to transfers (either public or private, such as through remittances from Kerala's diaspora spread across India and abroad) cannot be addressed by the data here.

25 The relative rankings of the structural change and within-sector productivity growth components for each of the four states are, respectively: 5 out of 15 and 10 out of 15 for Kerala; 3 out of 15 and 4 out of 15 for Tamil Nadu; 2 out of 15 and 13 out of 15 for Karnataka; and 4 out of 15 and 6 out of 15 for Andhra Pradesh.

26 The relative rankings of the structural change and within-sector productivity growth components for each of the four states are, respectively: 9 out of 15 and 11 out of 15 for Madhya Pradesh; 13 out of 15 and 7 out of 15 for Bihar; 14 out of 15 and 3 out of 15 for Punjab; and 15 out of 15 and 15 out of 15 for Assam.

27 As in almost every other state (the exception of Punjab), labour productivity in Bihar's construction sector is higher than that in agriculture. However, the agriculture-construction sector differential in productivity is among the lowest in the case of Bihar. Coupled with the fact that the level of agricultural productivity in Bihar is among the lowest in the 15 states, we consider here (only Madhya Pradesh's was lower in 2009), the relatively low differential in productivity between the two sectors is probably an important reason for the shift of employment from agriculture to construction in Bihar to not be particularly poverty reducing.

28 Dehejia and Panagariya (2012).

29 Along the lines of McMillan and Rodrik.

30 The states covered in this chapter includes Andhra Pradesh, Assam, Bihar, Chhattisgarh, Gujarat, Haryana, Jharkhand, Karnataka, Kerala, Madhya Pradesh, Maharashtra, Orissa, Punjab, Rajasthan, Tamil Nadu, Uttar Pradesh, Uttarakhand, and West Bengal. To maintain consistency in state boundaries over time, the newer states of Chhatisgarh, Jharkhand, and Uttarakhand have been merged with the states from which they were carved out, i.e., Madhya Pradesh, Bihar, and Uttar Pradesh, respectively.

31 Combined rural and urban poverty estimates for any given state are simple averages of the corresponding rural and urban poverty estimates, each weighted by the sector's share in the combined population (as derived from the consumer expenditure survey data).

32 See Cain, Hasan, and Mitra (2010) for a detailed summary of the debates surrounding poverty lines in India. Also see Deaton (2003).

33 Deaton (2003).

34 The Expert Group's procedures for estimating poverty in 1993–1994, 2004–2005 and 2009–2010 rely on monthly per capita expenditures based on a 'mixed reference period' of 365 days for 'low frequency' items of consumption (pro-rated to 30 days and covering clothing, footwear, durables, and expenditures on education and health (institutional)) and 30 days for the remaining items, including food. The consumer expenditure survey for 1987–88 collected expenditures on a 365-day basis for three of the low frequency groups, i.e., clothing, footwear and durables; education and health expenditures were only collected on a 30 day basis. However, this is unlikely to raise serious comparability issues vis-à-vis the other two rounds since the weight of these items in total consumption expenditures is not very high.

35 ASI time series data (1998–99 to 2007–08) is available at: http://mospi.nic.in/Mospi_New/upload/asi/ASI_main.htm?status=1&menu_id=88. ASI unit level data is used for computing employment figures in registered manufacturing for 1987 and 1993.

36 These papers use information and indexes created by a number of other researchers and studies including Besley and Burgess (2004) on labour regulations; OECD (2007) and World Bank (2004) on product market regulations and the investment climate, respectively; and Ghosh and De (2004) on financial development across India's states. Ghosh and De construct an index of states' financial development using information from 1981 to 1997 on credit-to-deposit ratios in nationalized banks, share of state tax revenue in net state domestic product, and the number of post offices per 10,000 of the population.

References

Ahsan, R. N. and D. Mitra. 2013. 'Can the Whole Actually Be Greater Than the Sum of Its Parts? Lessons from India's Growing Economy and its Evolving Structure'. Unpublished Mimeograph.

Amoranto, G. V. and R. Hasan. 2010. *A Note on Updating Poverty Lines over Time: An Application to India*. Mimeo. Manila: Economics and Research Department, Asian Development Bank.

Besley, T. and R. Burgess. 2004. 'Can Regulation Hinder Economics Performance? Evidence from India', *The Quarterly Journal of Economics* 119(1): 91–134.

Bosworth, B., S. M. Collins and A. Virmani. 2007. 'Sources of Growth in the Indian Economy'. *NBER Working Papers 12901*. Cambridge, Massachusetts, USA: National Bureau of Economic Research, Inc.

Cain, J. S., R. Hasan, R. Magsombol and A. Tandon. 2010. 'Accounting for Inequality in India: Evidence from Household Expenditures', *World Development* 38(3): 282–97.

Cain, J. S., R. Hasan and D. Mitra. 2010. 'Trade Liberalization and Poverty Reduction: New Evidence from Indian States'. *Columbia Program on Indian Economic Policies Working Paper No. 2010-3*. New York: School of International and Public Affairs, Columbia University.

Datt, G. and M. Ravallion. 2011. 'Has India's Economic Growth Become More Pro-Poor in the Wake of Economic Reforms?', *World Bank Economic Review* 25(2): 157–89.

_____. 1998. 'Farm Productivity and Rural Poverty in India', *Journal of Development Studies* 34(4): 62–85.

Deaton, A. 2003. 'Prices and Poverty in India, 1987–2000', *Economic and Political Weekly* 38(4): 362–68.

Dehejia, R. and A. Panagariya. 2012. 'Services Growth in India: A Look Inside the Black Box'. In *Reforms and Economic Transformation in India*, edited by Jagdish Bhagwati and Arvind Panagariya, 86–118. New York: Oxford University Press.

Ghosh, B. and P. De. 2004. 'How Do Different Categories of Infrastructure Affect Development?', *Economic and Political Weekly* 39(42): 4645–57.

Government of India. 2009. *Report of the Expert Group to Review the Methodology for Estimation of Poverty*. New Delhi: Planning Commission.

———. 2012. *Press Note on Poverty Estimates, 2009–10*. New Delhi: Planning Commission.

Gupta, P., R. Hasan and U. Kumar. 2009. 'Big Reforms but Small Payoffs: Explaining the Weak Record of Growth in Indian Manufacturing', *India Policy Forum* 5(1): 59–123.

Hasan, R., D. Mitra and K. V. Ramaswamy. 2007. 'Trade Reforms, Labor Regulations, and Labor-Demand Elasticities: Empirical Evidence from India', *The Review of Economics and Statistics* 89(3): 466–81.

Hasan, R., M. G. Quibria and Y. Kim. 2003. 'Poverty and Economic Freedom: Evidence from Cross-Country Data'. *Economics Study Area Working Papers 60*. Honolulu, Hawaii, USA: East-West Centre.

High Powered Expert Committee (HPEC). 2011. *Report on Indian Urban Infrastructure and Services*. The HPEC for estimating the investment requirements for urban infrastructure services.

McMillan, M. S. and D. Rodrik. 2011. 'Globalization, Structural Change and Productivity Growth'. *NBER Working Papers 17143*. Cambridge, Massachusetts, USA: National Bureau of Economic Research.

Organization for Economic Co-operation and Development. 2007. *OECD Economic Surveys: India 2007* (14).

Panagariya, A. 2008. *India: The Emerging Giant*. USA: Oxford University Press.

Papola, T. S. and P. P. Sahu. 2012. *Growth and Structure of Employment in India: Long Term and Post Reform Performance and the Emerging Challenge*. ISID Report.

Ravallion, M. 2009. 'A Comparative Perspective on Poverty Reduction in Brazil, [People's Republic of] China, and India'. *Policy Research Working Paper 5080*. Washington, DC: World Bank.

Ravallion, M. and G. Datt. 1996. 'How Important to India's Poor is the Sectoral Composition of Economic Growth?', *World Bank Economic Review* 10(1): 1–25.

———. 1999. 'When is Growth Pro-Poor? Evidence from the Diverse Experiences of India's States'. *Policy Research Working Paper Series 2263*. Washington, DC: World Bank.

Rodrik, D. and A. Subramanian. 2005. 'From "Hindu Growth", to Productivity Surge: The Mystery of the Indian Growth Transition', *IMF Staff Papers* 52(2): 193–228.

World Bank. 2004. *India Investment Climate Assessment 2004: Improving Manufacturing Competitiveness*. Washington, DC: World Bank.

5

Age Structure Transition, Population Ageing and Economic Growth
New Evidence and Implications for India

M. R. Narayana

5.1 Introduction

Age structure of a population refers to distribution of population by age, either by single year or age groups. Broadly speaking, the total population by age may be divided into young (age 0–14 years), youth (age 15–24 years), working (age 25–59 years) and elderly (age 60 years and above). Over a period of time, proportion of total population in these age groups may undergo a transition from a higher (lower) share to a lower (higher) or declining (increasing) share due to the interactive effects of fertility and mortality. This transition is called the age structure transition. For instance, a long-term decline in fertility and mortality (or longer life expectancy of life) may lead to a decline in the young and youth population and a rise in working age or elderly population. Consequently, a country with more younger and youth population today may eventually become an ageing country. Though age structure transition is a demographic phenomenon, its effects are ultimately economic in nature because population is a source of supply of labour in production and demand for goods and services in consumption and both may vary across individual years or age groups. Knowledge of age-specific aggregate production and consumption is useful to determine whether a country may be well-off or worse-off in terms of production effects and/or consumption effects of age structure transition. To quantify these macroeconomic effects of age structure transition, framework that introduces age into National Income and Product Accounts (NIPA) is needed as a basis for calculation of age profile of aggregate production and consumption and to explain and predict the long-term relationships between the age structure transition, population ageing, and economic growth. Such a framework should be useful for answering three important research questions.

(1) Does age structure transition impact national economic growth?

(2) Does population ageing retard economic growth by increasing old-age dependency ratio?

(3) Does population ageing impose a total burden on tax paying working population to financing of public support systems (e.g. universal old age pension scheme).

This chapter argues that the NTA, developed by Professor Ronald Lee at University of California (Berkeley) and Professor Andrew Mason at University of Hawaii (Manao), is a plausible framework to answer the above research questions. It is a new macro-economic methodology for introduction of age into NIPA. As individuals pass through their life-cycle from young to youth, youth to working and from working to old age, both production and consumption changes create deficits (consumption exceeding production) and surplus (consumption less than production). As an accounting framework, NTA aims at (a) quantifying the nature and magnitude of these economic lifecycle changes and (b) developing the public and private institutional mechanisms by which deficits are financed by surplus generated during the working ages through age reallocations in terms of transfers and asset-based reallocations. These aims are accomplished by developing a conceptual framework for measurement and calculation of age profiles of consumption, production and age reallocations. This framework establishes the Flow Account of NTA, which gives new accounting relationships through inter-age flows (i.e. inflows and outflows) of the variables for an accounting year in monetary terms and at national level of aggregation.

The main purpose of this chapter is to explain and predict the economic relationship between age structure transition, population ageing and economic growth (measured by growth rate of national income per effective consumer) in India by using the NTA methodology. For this purpose, (1) a framework for calculation of growth effects of age structure transition through the FDD with special reference to population ageing effects has been presented; and (2) the public cost of financing a universal old age pension scheme and its effects on financing lifecycle deficit for elderly population in India is estimated. The period of the chapter is from 2004–05 through to 2049–50. The FDD approach is useful in distinguishing population ageing effect from the viewpoint of economic growth. Financing lifecycle deficit is relevant to derive implications on inter-generational equity with reference to elderly population. Thus, the approach of this chapter offers new evidence and implications to the empirical knowledge in the existing non-NTA and NTA-based studies on impact of age structure transition, population ageing and economic growth for India (e.g. Park and Shin, 2012; Aiyar and Mody, 2011; Bloom, et al., 2010; Choudhry and Elhorst, 2010; and Ogawa, et al., 2009).

Rest of the chapter is organized as follows. Section 5.2 provides an overview of India's age structure transition and population ageing over the period 1961 to 2100. Framework for analyses by using NTA methodology is outlined in section 5.3. Data and variable descriptions are given in section 5.4. Main results and their economic interpretations are given in section 5.5. Major conclusions and implications are included in section 5.6.

5.2 India's age structure transition and population ageing

Using the single year age distribution of population in the Census of India from 1961 to 2011 and projected population from the United Nations (2013a) from 2021 to 2100, trends in India's age structure transition and population ageing (i.e., increase in proportion of population at age 60 and above) is shown in Figure 5.1. Before 1991, share of young population (0–14) was higher than the working age population (25–59). In 1991, the two curves intersected with share of total population at about 37 per cent. Since 1991, young population shows a continuous and rapid decline in contrast with a rising working age population. Thus, the two curves show a scissor's shape. Age structure transition is also characterized by changes in youth population and elderly population. Share of the youth population shows a gradual increase from about 17 per cent in 1961 to about 19 per cent in 2011 and a decline from about 17 per cent in 2021 to about 13 per cent in 2051 and to 10 per cent in 2100. On the other hand, share of elderly population shows a gradual increase from about 6 per cent in 1961 to about 7 per cent in 2001 and a rapid increase from about 8 per cent in 2011 to about 22 per cent in 2050 and to 37 per cent in 2100. Consequently, total projected population by these age groups in 2050 (or 2100) is as follows. young: 319 (or 235) million, youth: 229 (or 166) million, working: 818 (or 655) million and elderly: 376 (or 622) million. An obvious impact of India's projected age structure transition would be on the changing dependency ratios. Figure 5.2 shows India's young, youth and old-age dependency transition over the period 1961–2100. The decline in young and youth dependency ratio and a rise in old-age dependency ratio are the remarkable features of India's dependency transition over the period up to 2100.

Figure 5.1: Age structure transition, India, 1961–2000

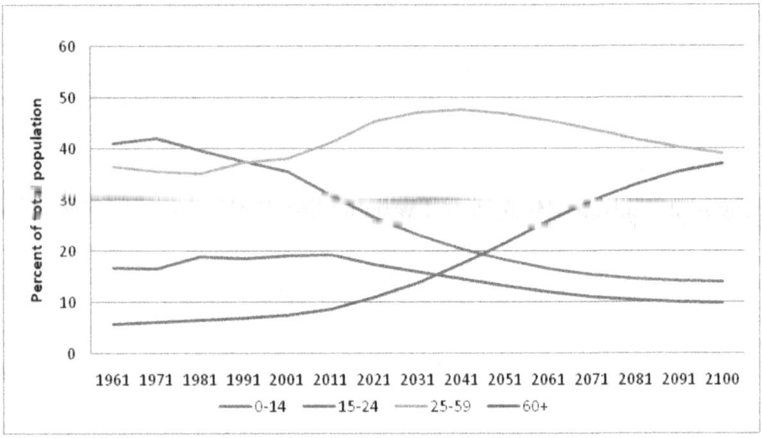

Source: Author by using the basic data from Census of India reports and United Nations (2013a).

Figure 5.2: Dependency transition, India, 1961–2000

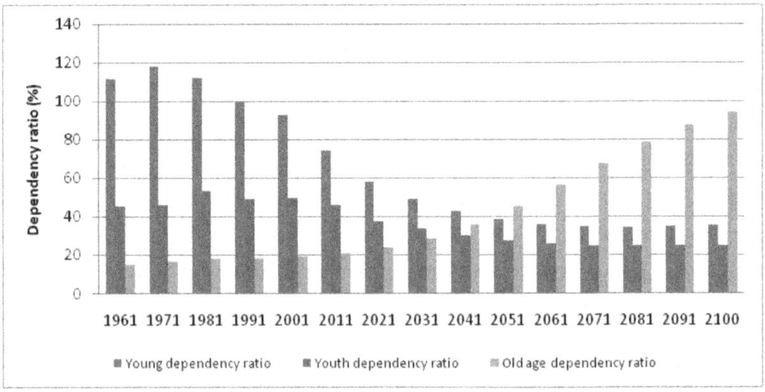

Source: Author by using the basic data from Census of India reports – various issues and United Nations (2013a).

How do the above changes in age structure and population ageing impact the long-term economic growth of India? A framework to answer this question is presented below.

5.3 Framework for analysis

The NTA methodology is applied for quantitative impact analysis of age structure transition and population ageing on India's economic growth, and to calculate the lifecycle deficit of elderly population and cost and financing of the deficit by a universal old age pension scheme. This methodology draws heavily from Mason and Lee (2007) and Lee and Mason (2011).

5.3.1 Age structure and economic growth

To introduce age structure into economic growth, we first formulate a measure of per capita income adjusted for age structure transition in terms of income per effective consumers.

Let $Y(t)$ be the national income in year t, $L(t)$ be the total number of effective producers or workers and $N(t)$ be the total number of effective consumers. Effective number of producers and consumers are measured respectively by

$$L(t) = \Sigma \gamma(a)P(a,t) \qquad \text{(Equation 5.1)}$$

$$N(t) = \Sigma \varphi(a)P(a,t) \qquad \text{(Equation 5.2)}$$

where $\gamma(a)$ is productivity at age–a or productivity age profile; $\varphi(a)$ is consumption needs at age–a or consumption age profile; $P(a,t)$ is population at age–a and time–t; and the summation is over all ages (i.e. from 0 to 90).

Using (5.1) and (5.2), income per effective consumer $[Y(t)/N(t)]$ can be expressed as a product of (a) income per effective producer $[Y(t)/L(t)]$ or labour productivity and (b) proportion of effective number of producers or workers to effective consumers $[L(t)/N(t)]$. That is,

$$Y(t)/N(t) = \{Y(t)/L(t)\}\{L(t)/N(t)\} \qquad \text{(Equation 5.3)}$$

In technical terms, $[L(t)/N(t)]$ is called the economic support ratio (ESR) or ratio of effective number of producers to effective number of consumers of goods and services.[1] Age structure transition leads to large shifts in support ratios and interacts with labour productivity to determine the economic growth. The period during which growth of support ratio leads to an increase in economic growth (or growth of national income per effective consumer) is called FDD. In other words, FDD is rate of growth of economic support ratio, which rises or falls, subject to age compositional transformation in the process of demographic transition. However, equation (5.3) is the standard growth accounting equation except for adjusting the variables for age structure changes.[2]

Taking natural log of both sides of equation (5.3) and differentiating with respect to time, economic growth is equal to the sum of growth rates of labour productivity and economic support ratio.

$$g[Y(t)/N(t)] = g[Y(t)/L(t)] + g[L(t)/N(t)] \qquad \text{(Equation 5.4)}$$

NTA is a useful framework for calculation and projection of growth rate in (5.4) because it provides a macroeconomic foundation for calculating the productivity and consumption age profiles by introducing age into NIPA. This foundation, consistent with the National Income Identity, is established by the following NTA-Flow Account Identity (suffix 'f' stands for private sector, 'g' for public sector and 'i' refers to individual or age group).

$$Y_{L,i} + Y_{A,i} + (T_{f,i}^{+} + T_{g,i}^{+}) = (C_{f,i} + C_{g,i}) + S_i + (T_{f,i}^{-} + T_{g,i}^{-}) \qquad \text{(Equation 5.5)}$$

where $Y_{L,i}$ is labour income, $Y_{A,i}$ is non-labour or asset income, $T_{f,i}^{+}$ and $T_{f,i}^{-}$ are private transfer inflows and outflows respectively; $C_{f,i}$ is private consumption expenditure, $C_{g,i}$ is public (government) consumption expenditure, S_i is savings, $T_{g,i}^{+}$ and $T_{g,i}^{-}$ are public transfer inflows and outflows respectively. The left hand side of equation (5.5) shows total inflows and the right hand side shows total outflows. Net exports are indirectly introduced in (5.5) to take care of Rest-of-World (ROW) by including net compensation of employees from ROW in $Y_{L,i}$ and net entrepreneurial income from ROW in $Y_{A,i}$. This implies that (5.5) is consistent with an open macroeconomy. However, individual is the fundamental entity in the NTA and all flows are disaggregated at individual level by age.

Construction of NTA Flow Account is useful to derive many insightful results and implications. First, LCD, defined by the difference between total value of goods and services consumed and produced by an age group can be calculated by: $LCD_i = (C_{f,i} + C_{g,i}) - Y_{L,i}$. This shows which age group/s has/have surplus ($LCD_i < 0$) or deficit ($LCD_i > 0$) in an accounting year. Second, financing of LCD can be calculated by age reallocations in terms of public and private transfers and asset-based reallocations. If (5.5) is constructable over a period of time, age reallocations show the evolution of instruments and nature and magnitude of their impact on financing deficit consumption, or intergenerational equity, including for elderly population.

In the context of this chapter, equation (5.5) is a macroeconomic basis to calculate the age profiles of labour productivity or labour income and total consumption of goods and services. Given these profiles and projected population by age, and assuming that labour productivity to remain constant throughout, equation (5.4) can be calculated to explain the impact of age structure transition and population ageing on economic growth.

5.3.2 Calculation of age profiles

The NTA methodology for calculation of age profiles of variables in (5.5) is detailed in NTA (2013) and United Nations (2013b). In particular, NTA methodology calculates aggregate labour income profile by combining individual income from wages and salaries and household income from self-employment. Aggregate consumption profile is obtained by combining public and private consumption. Both public and private consumptions are disaggregated by education, health and others. Aggregate consumption profile is obtained by three steps: first, age profile of education, health and other consumption are obtained by public and private sectors; second, aggregate public and private consumption profiles are calculated by combining the individual profiles of education, health and others; and third, aggregate consumption profile is obtained by combining the public and private consumption profiles. Further, age profile of taxes is included in the calculation of public sector transfer outflows in (5.5). Tax profiles are separated by direct and indirect taxes; and direct taxes by personal income tax and corporation tax.

For lack of time series data for calculation of age profile of labour income, consumption and taxes, this chapter focuses on calculation of these profiles for 2004–05 and assume their constancy from 2005 through 2050. Data and variable descriptions for calculation of cross-sectional age profiles are elaborated below.

5.4 Data and variable descriptions

Data, variable descriptions and measurements, and NTA age allocation rules are given in Table 5.1. Throughout, United Nations (2013a) projected population (*The 2012 Revision and Medium Variant*) for India by sex by single year age (i.e. from age 0 through 90) from 2005 to 2050 is used.

Table 5.1: Data, variable descriptions and measurements, and NTA age allocation rules, India: 2004–05

Aggregate controls	Measurement of aggregate controls	Age allocation methods and data sources
1. Labour income	Compensation of employees + (2/3) of mixed income + net compensation of employees from ROW	Age profile is based on the income from salaries and wages and self-employment, using the individual income from wage and salary and household income from self-employment (i.e., farm income and non-farm business income) in India Human Development Survey 2005 (Desai, *et al.*, 2008). Age profile of self-employment income at household level is derived through the following allocation rule. That is, self employment income of household is allocated to individual in a household who reported as self-employed, using the age profile of mean earnings of employees. Accordingly, self-employment income accruing to ith individual in household j [YLSij(x)] is equal to YLSj.γ(x) and γ(x)= w(x).SEj(x)]/ Σ w(a).SEj(a), where x is the age of ith household; SEj(a) is number of people in household j who are self-employed or unpaid workers of age a; w(a) is average earnings of employees. This means that γ(x) is the share of total household self-employment labour income allocated to each self-employed who is at age x. Summing across all households, total self-employment labour income is computed at age x.
2. Public consumption	Government Final Consumption Expenditure (GFCE)	
2.1. Public education consumption	Expenditure on education services under GFCE	Age profile is derived by public formal and informal education. Public formal education age profile is based on computed per student public education consumption by levels of education. This computation is based on the following enrolment rates and public expenditure by level of education. First, using estimated attendance data from the 61st Round of National Sample Survey Organization (July 2004–June 2005) on Status of Education and Vocational Training in India 2004–05, share of attendance in public

Aggregate controls	Measurement of aggregate controls	Age allocation methods and data sources
		institutions by levels of education is computed. This share is applied for total enrolment data in the Government of India's Education Statistics 2004–05 to obtain attendance in public institutions (i.e., government and local body institutions). Second, using Indian Public Finance Statistics 2006–07 (Government of India, 2007), revenue expenditure on education by all levels of governments (including non-education departments) is obtained. Public education consumption is presumed to be proportional to revenue expenditure by levels of education. Per student public education consumption is obtained by using the computed enrolment data in public institutions. Public informal education consumption is equal to expenditure on adult education and training and allocated on per capita basis for age group 30–59.
2.2. Public health consumption	Expenditure on health and other services under GFCE	Age profile is drawn by using the individual level data on utilization of public health facilities in the 60th Round of National Sample Survey on Healthcare, Morbidity and Conditions of aged in India in 2004, Public health facilities refers to health services provided by public hospitals and dispensaries (including Primary Health Centres, Sub-centres and Community Health Centres). Utilization is proxied by expenditure incurred on treatment for hospitalized or in-patient (during 365 days prior to the survey), non-hospitalized or out-patient (during 15 days prior to the survey) and other expenditure (e.g. transport expenses to and from the hospital visits).
2.3. Public consumption other	Expenditure on non-education and non-health services under GFCE	Public consumption other includes general public services; defense; housing and other community amenities; cultural, recreational, and religious services; economic services (e.g., agriculture, mining, transport, and communication). This variable is allocated on per capita basis.
3. Private consumption	Private Final Consumption Expenditure (PFCE) net of indirect taxes	

Aggregate controls	Measurement of aggregate controls	Age allocation methods and data sources
3.1. Private education consumption	PFCE on education net of indirect taxes. Indirect taxes on private education consumption are assumed equal to share of PFCE on education in PFCE.	Age profile is drawn by using the individual level data on private education expenditure in the India Human Development Survey 2004–05 (Desai, *et al.*, 2008). Private education expenditure refers to expenditure incurred by currently enrolled students in elementary, secondary and tertiary level education on school/college fees, books uniform and other materials, transportation and private tuition.
3.2. Private health consumption	PFCE on medical care and health services net of indirect taxes. Indirect taxes on private health consumption are assumed to be equal to share of PFCE on medical care and health services in PFCE.	Age profile is drawn by using the individual level data on private health expenditure in the India Human Development Survey 2004 05 (Desai, et al., 2008). Private health expenditure refers to sum of expenditure incurred for in-patient as well as out-patient treatment services for short term morbidity during last one month and major morbidity during 12 months. Treatment expenses included hospital surgery, medicine and tests and others (e.g. tips, bus/train/taxi fares or lodging while getting treatment).
3.3. Private consumption other	PFCE on non-education, and non-medical care and health services. This expenditure is net of indirect taxes where indirect taxes are assumed to equal to share of PFCE other in PFCE.	Private consumption other includes food and beverages, clothing and footwear; fuel and power; furniture, furnishing, appliances; transport and communication; and recreation and cultural services. Age profile is derived by using Equivalence Scale. The scale is equal to 1 for adults aged twenty or older, declines linearly from age 20 to 0.4 at age 4, and is constant at 0.4 for those age 4 or younger. That is, $\lambda(a)$ = $(1-0.6)$, $(a \leq 4)$; $\lambda(a) = 1 - [0.6.(20-a)/16]$, $(4 < a < 20)$; and $\lambda(a) = 1$, $(a \geq 20)$. Using the above formula, intra-household allocation of private other consumption is equal to: CFX_{ij} = $[CFX_j.\lambda(x)/\Sigma\lambda(a).M_j(a)]$, where x is the age of the ith household member.
4. Taxes		
4.1. Personal income tax	Non-corporation taxes in Statement 43	Age profile is calculated by assuming that the tax paid is proportional to total labour income of individuals. Labour income by age is calculated as detailed in item (1) above. However, it is important to mention that personal income tax is levied above an exemption limit with differential rates by income slabs. To incorporate these features into the tax profile, we need

Aggregate controls	Measurement of aggregate controls	Age allocation methods and data sources
		a household survey that includes income tax payments to tabulate the taxes directly from the survey and then scale them with the appropriate macro-control. That is to (a) calculate age profile for income below and above the exemption limit; and (b) tax age profiles separately for each income range that conforms to the tax schedule and to obtain age-specific tax rate. At present, no national sample survey of households on consumption expenditure and employment in India includes information on the tax payment details.
4.2. Corporation tax	Corporation tax in Statement 43	Age profile is calculated by assuming that the tax paid is proportional to total asset income (e.g., rent and dividends or capital gains) of individuals. Source: India Human Development Survey 2005 (Desai, et al., 2008).
4.3. Indirect or consumption tax	Total indirect taxes in Statement 43	Age profile is derived by applying the age profile of private other (i.e. non-education and non-health) consumption as given in item (3.3) above.

Note: (a) All aggregate controls are derived and measured by using the data in Government of India (2007). (b) Except for public education and public health, age allocation rule for all other aggregate controls variables follows the NTA general methodology [NTA (2013) and United Nations (2013)].

Source: Author

Growth rate of productivity cannot be calculated from the cross–section productivity age profile in 2004–05. To overcome this measurement problem, growth of per capita labour productivity is computed (exogenously, however) by using the basic data on gross value added (at 1999–00 prices) and total workers over the period 1999–2000 to 2004–05 in Government of India (2008). The computed annual growth rate of labour productivity is 3.01 per cent.

5.5 Results and economic interpretations

5.5.1 Pattern of age profiles

Figure 5.3 presents the age profile of per capita labour productivity or income and consumption for India in 2004–05. Shape of this profile increases rapidly and then slowly, peaking in the early or mid-40s. Per capita consumption rises very fast up to the age 23 and then stabilizes beyond 30 years. The crossing age from net consumers to net producers is 27 years and from net producers to

net consumers is 61 years. This does not imply that the duration of stay in the
workforce is 33 years because a person can be in the workforce even if his/her
consumption is greater than labour income.[3] Elderly individuals account for a
portion of aggregate labour income. This equals to 4.26 per cent of aggregate
labour income of all ages (₹15845.35 billion). Labour income for elderly is
mainly due to prevalence of informal employment (e.g. self-employment),
especially in agriculture and service sectors.[4] In the same way, the elderly share
8.46 per cent of aggregate consumption (₹18448 billion).

Figure 5.3: Age profile of per capita labour income and consumption,
India, 2004–05

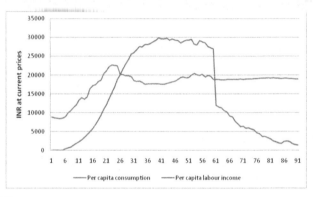

Source: Author

A recent UNFPA (2012) report on the status of elderly in India offers
supportive information, among others, for work and income status.[5] Of the
elderly individuals, 24.2 (or 63.8) per cent were currently working (or ever
worked). Of the currently working elderly individuals, about 81 (or 94) per
cent worked for more than 6 months per year (or 4 hours per day). Economic
compulsion was the main reason for 71 per cent of currently working elderly.
The percentage of elderly households who received no retirement and pension
benefits was about 84 per cent because more than 86 per cent of them worked
in informal sector (including self-employment). Further, about 43.3 per cent of
elderly individuals reported no personal income. This group of elderly individuals
did constitute the complete dependents on family, government and other
sources for their expenditure needs. For instance, 74 per cent received economic
support from the family members (i.e. son, spouse, daughter and others). The
rest of the elderly individuals sourced their income from salary/wages (12 per
cent), employers' pension (11.40 per cent), social/civilian pension, such as, old

age pension, (18.3 per cent), agriculture/farm income (12.90 per cent) and other sources including asset income from land, housing and savings (9.30 per cent). These incomes were the bases for elderly individuals' support to different household expenditures, children education, medical expenses, loan repayment and special events (e.g. marriage and social ceremonies).

The above results indicate that elderly population as such cannot be considered as totally dependent for their consumption needs on non-elderly population. Implications of this result are further evident below in the calculated economic support ratios.

5.5.2 Growth effects of age structure transition

Table 5.2 gives the growth effects of age structure transition over the period 2005–50. Economic support ratios increase up to 2045. The period or duration of FDD ends by 2045 because the annual growth rate of support ratios is negative from 2045. Further, given the productivity growth rate of 3.01, the FDD or growth rate of national income per effective workers is higher than the productivity growth rate and ranges from 3.49 per cent in 2005–10 to 3.17 per cent in 2025–30 and 3.04 per cent in 2035–40. Subsequently, growth rate of national income per effective workers is less than productivity growth rate due to declining support ratios. Growth rate of support ratio is remarkably different between total population and elderly population (Figure 5.4). For instance, unlike for total population, growth rate of support ratio for elderly population is negative throughout.

Figure 5.4: Growth rate of support ratio, India, 2000–50

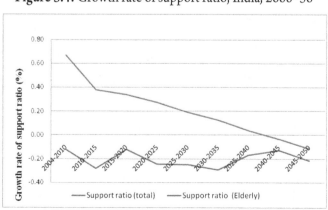

Source: Author

Table 5.2: Growth effects of age structure transition, India, 2005–50

Year	Support ratio	Year	Annual growth rate of support ratio	FDD
2005	0.867			
2010	0.892	2005–10	0.480	3.49
2015	0.909	2010–15	0.316	3.33
2020	0.924	2015–20	0.281	3.29
2025	0.937	2002–25	0.228	3.24
2030	0.946	2025–30	0.158	3.17
2035	0.952	2030–35	0.104	3.11
2040	0.954	2025–40	0.031	3.04
2045	0.952	2040–45	−0.030	2.98
2050	0.946	2045–50	−0.097	2.91

Source: Author's calculations based on equation (5.4).

Our results are different from the previous studies due, among others, to using country-specific age profiles, actual productivity growth rates, and recent UN Population Projections 2012. For instance, Ogawa *et al.* (2009) estimated, among others, the FDD for 14 Economic and Social Council for Asia and the Pacific (ESCAP) member-countries including India. The age profile of per capita income and consumption refers to 'per capita age–specific profiles for developing Asia'. This is the combined age profile of four Asian countries: India, Indonesia, Thailand and Philippines. The estimates show that India's FDD over the period from 1974 to 2044 with a total duration of 70 years at an annual growth rate of 0.55 per cent (over the period 2000–10); 0.57 per cent (2010–20); 0.48 per cent (2020–30); 0.28 per cent (2030–40); and −0.03 per cent (2040–50).

Table 5.3: Financial implications of proposed UOAPS in India, 2004–05 to 2009–10

Year	Labour income of elderly individuals as a percentage of GDP (at market prices)	Expenditure on proposed UOAPS as a percentage of					
		GDP (at market prices)	Labour income of elderly individuals	Indirect tax payments by elderly individuals	Direct tax payment by elderly individual	Combined revenue expenditure of the central and state governments	Combined revenue expenditure of the central and state governments net of direct and indirect tax payments by elderly individuals
2004–05	2.00	5.75 (4.01)	287.03 (200.13)	575.42 (401.20)	561.21 (391.29)	26.63 (18.57)	29.39 (20.49)
2005–06	1.80	5.18 (3.50)	287.33 (194.13)	507.25 (342.70)	460.20 (310.92)	24.24 (16.38)	26.94 (18.20)
2006–07	1.59	4.58 (2.91)	288.65 (183.56)	434.38 (276.23)	341.71 (217.30)	21.34 (13.57)	24.02 (15.27)
2007–08	1.40	4.05 (2.43)	289.67 (174.06)	391.07 (234.99)	261.00 (156.83)	19.95 (11.99)	22.87 (13.74)
2008–09	1.27	3.68 (1.92)	289.97 (151.25)	387.57 (202.16)	248.65 (129.70)	16.06 (8.38)	17.97 (9.37)
2009–10	1.14	3.30 (1.06)	289.23 (93.34)	386.73 (124.81)	228.81 (73.84)	13.86 (4.47)	15.34 (4.95)
2010–11	0.99	2.84 (0.68)	287.64 (69.37)	206.61 (49.83)	527.74 (127.28)	11.90 (2.87)	12.94 (3.12)

Notes: (a) Figures in parentheses exclude the combined revenue expenditure on the pension and other retirement benefits to employees of the central and state governments and on Indira Gandhi National Old Age Pension Scheme. (b) Figures for 2010–11 refer to revised estimates.

Source: Author's calculations based on the labour income profile in Figure 5.3, and basic data on GDP and taxes in Central Statistical Office, Government of India (2013) and Government of India (2012).

Further, given the annual growth of labour productivity at 3.01 per cent, the growth effects of age structure transition in Table 5.3 are remarkably lower than the growth effects of productivity. This result is consistent with the available findings on India's growth effects of age structure transition before 2000. For instance, Bloom *et al.* (2010) provide an interesting decomposition of sources of growth (or annual average growth rate of GDP per capita) for India over the periods 1970–80 and 1980–2000. In both the periods, the largest source of growth is evident for growth of labour productivity (or growth rate of real GDP per worker) as compared to age structure transition (or growth rate of ratio of population aged 15–64 to total population). In particular, growth rate of labour productivity accounted for about 86 (or 108) per cent; the age structure transition about 21 (or 8) per cent to India's economic growth over the period 1970–80 (or 1980–2000); and the rest was explained by negative growth of labour participation rate (i.e. share of workers to working-age population). Most recently, Government of India's (2013) reported estimates of the decomposition of India's source of growth over the period 1991–2011 showed that increase in working age population contributed so little (on an average, 0.5 percentage points) and rest of the remarkable contribution came from greater labour productivity for India's economic growth. This experience of India is also shown to be comparable with China since 1979, South Korea since 1973 and Indonesia since 1967.

The above FDD may be called the potential FDD because it shows the maximum economic growth if all people are productively employed as per the age productivity profile in Figure 5.3. However, realization of this potential FDD into actual FDD needs many complementary measures. For instance, Choudhry and Elhorst (2010) note that the realization depends on the creation of more productive and better skilled workforce, and stimulation of investment especially in infrastructure that can absorb unskilled labour and expand the market for goods and services. These factors complement to what Bloom *et al.* (2010) noted as the policy environment in terms of governmental institutions, labour legislation, macroeconomic management, openness to trade and education policy.

In the absence of any other changes, however, age structure transition beyond 2045 may reduce the economic growth rate further due to population ageing. Mason and Lee (2012) argue that societies can respond to this situation in many ways, such as, (1) change policies or behaviour that link change in population age structure and economic support ratio (e.g. delaying retirement); (2) increase investment in human capital to enhance labour productivity; and (3) increase savings to fund a longer period of retirement. These changes are contributory for societies to reap the Second Demographic Dividend (SDD), which operates through productivity growth by inducing the accumulation of wealth and capital deepening. Wealth affects lifecycle consumption in two ways. First, older persons rely on transfer wealth (i.e. present value of expected net public and/or private transfers received in current and future time periods) to finance their deficit consumption. Second, adult persons may rely on capital accumulation during working ages to finance consumption at older ages. At the same time, however, capital accumulation (including deepening human capital as well through increased investment in education and health care of children) impacts on economic growth through changes in productivity. This dynamic effect of capital accumulation on economic growth is a source of SDD and a topic of future research.

5.5.3 Universal Old Age Pension Scheme (UOAPS)

Public debates on the needs and amount of old age pension for unorganized workers are not new in India. Way back in 2005, the National Commission for Enterprises in the Unorganized Sector (NCEUS) had recommended for the monthly old age pension of ₹ 200 per month to all poor (BPL or Below Poverty Level families) old aged (60+) workers. In contrast, the *Pension Parishad*, a non-governmental initiative to ensure universal, publicly funded, non-means related and non-contributory pension in India, has recently demanded for a uniform amount of ₹ 2000 per person per month to all persons in the pensionable ages: 55 years for men; 50 years for women; and 45 years for specially deprived communities. About 100 million people are expected beneficiaries of this proposed scheme. However, the number of beneficiaries is reduced to 80 million, if the income–tax payers are excluded and the benefit is extended to all at 60+.[6]

5.5.3.1 Financing UOAPS

Financial implications of the above *Pension Parishad's* UOAPS can be calculated by applying NTA age profiles of labour income, consumption and taxes, and the actual GDP at market prices. In particular, we obtain the financial estimates if the proposed UOAPS by the *Pension Parishad* (i.e., ₹ 2000 per worker per month) were to be implemented from 2004–05 through 2009–10 for all elderly individuals in India. The results are new and interesting (Table 5.3). Ratio of elderly labour income to GDP is lower than the ratio of UOAPS payments to GDP in all years. This indicates that cost of supporting the UOAPS is substantially higher than the elderly contribution to national labour income. Ratio of UOAPS payments to labour income marginally increases from about 287 per cent in 2004–05 to 288 per cent in 2010–11. The share of old age pension payment to total indirect (or direct) taxes paid by the elderly population ranges from 575 (or 561) per cent in 2004–05 to 207 (or 528) per cent in 2010–11.[7] These figures indicate the implicit and partial direct and indirect tax financing of the UOAPS by the elderly population themselves. UOAPS payments cost the public exchequer about 29 per cent of combined total revenue expenditure of the centre and state governments in 2004–05 and declines to 13 per cent by 2010–11. A comparison of pension payments as a percentage of the combined revenue expenditure and that expenditure net of direct and indirect taxes paid by elderly individuals shows a tendency towards greater self-financing of old age pension payments by elderly individuals themselves.

Figures in parentheses of Table 5.3 shows the UOAPS payments to elderly individuals net of the combined revenue expenditure net of (1) pension and other retirement benefits to employees of central and state governments; and (2) Indira Gandhi National Old Age Pension Scheme (IGNOAPS).[8] This is relevant because the population of elderly includes pensioners of these government employees and beneficiaries of the IGNOAPS. The calculated figures show that the cost of the UOAPS is considerably reduced as a percentage of GDP, labour income of elderly individuals, indirect and direct tax payments by elderly individuals and combined revenue expenditure of the central and state governments. For instance, pension payments decline from 20 per cent in 2004–05 to 3 per cent in 2010–11 when the combined total revenue expenditure is net of indirect taxes paid by the elderly individuals.

All the ratios in Table 5.3 show a decline over the period 2004–05 to 2009–10 except the ratio of pension payments to direct tax payments by elderly individuals.[9] The decline is due to larger and faster growth of GDP; and its resultant increase in private consumption other and, hence, the increase in indirect tax revenues. Thus, for the elderly, the ratio of labour income to total indirect tax payments declines over the period. The ratio of pension payments to elderly labour income shows the total public resource requirements (e.g. tax revenues) for the UOAPS in terms of their labour income.

Expenditure on UOAPS in Table 5.3 is unadjusted for its growth. In what follows, growth of this expenditure is adjusted for annual inflation rate and income elasticity of UOAPS. This analysis is useful to examine the implications of current and future financing of UOAPS.

Table 5.4 shows the changes in public expenditure on UOAPS at different rates (from 1 per cent to 10 per cent) of annual inflation as a percentage of GDP (at current market prices). These percentages are remarkably different from the unadjusted figures in column 3 of Table 5.3. For instance, at 5 per cent annual rate of inflation, expenditure on UOAPS as a percentage of GDP increases to 6.67 in 2004–05 4.69 in 2007–08 and 3.29 in 2010–11.

Table 5.4: Sensitivity of public expenditure on proposed
UOAPS to inflation rate

Year	Public expenditure on UOAPS as per cent of GDP: sensitivity to inflation rates									
	1%	2%	3%	4%	5%	6%	7%	8%	9%	10%
2004–05	5.81	5.93	6.10	6.35	6.67	7.07	7.56	8.16	8.90	9.79
2005–06	5.23	5.34	5.50	5.72	6.00	6.36	6.81	7.35	8.01	8.82
2006–07	4.62	4.71	4.86	5.05	5.30	5.62	6.01	6.50	7.08	7.79
2007–08	4.09	4.17	4.29	4.46	4.69	4.97	5.32	5.74	6.26	6.88
2008–09	3.72	3.79	3.91	4.06	4.27	4.52	4.84	5.23	5.70	6.27
2009–10	3.33	3.40	3.50	3.64	3.82	4.05	4.33	4.68	5.10	5.61
2010–11	2.87	2.92	3.01	3.13	3.29	3.48	3.73	4.03	4.39	4.83

Source: Author's calculations.

Income elasticity of UOAPS is calculated as annual per cent change in GDP divided by per cent change in public expenditure on UOAPS. The elasticity is distinguished at 0.5, 1.0 and 1.5 and assumed to represent a policy of less generous, generous and more generous public expenditure on UOAPS respectively. Given the annual growth rate of GDP at market prices from 2005–06 to 2010–11, required size and annual growth of expenditure on UOAPS at these elasticities are calculated for each year. In addition, the required amount is expressed as a percentage of the GDP. Results are given in Table 5.5. Apparently, if a more generous policy (or income elasticity =1.5) were to be implemented from 2004–05, it would have cost more in terms of required increase in the public expenditure on UOAPS. Thus, the results in Table 5.5 offer a range of generosity policy scenarios if policymakers were to consider implementation of UOAPS from 2004–05 through 2010–11.

Table 5.5: Sensitivity of public expenditure on proposed UOAPS to income elasticity

| | Actual expenditure on UOAPS | | Public expenditure on UOAPS: Sensitivity to income elasticity of UOAP | | | | | | | | |
| | | | Income elasticity=0.5 | | | Income elasticity=1.0 | | | Income elasticity=1.5 | | |
Year	Total expenditure (₹ crore)	Annual increase (%)	Required annual increase in expenditure on UOAPS (%)	Required amount of expenditure on UOAPS (₹ crore)	Required expenditure on UOAPS as percentage of GDP at current market prices	Required annual increase in expenditure on UOAPS (%)	Required amount of expenditure on UOAPS (₹ crore)	Required expenditure on UOAPS as a percentage of GDP at current market prices	Required annual increase in expenditure on UOAPS (%)	Required amount of expenditure on UOAPS (₹ crore)	Required expenditure on UOAPS as a percentage of GDP at current market prices
2005–06	191316	2.58	4.38	194677	6.00	11.34	207653	5.40	18.30	220630	6.80
2006–07	196547	2.73	5.41	201658	5.46	13.55	217233	5.38	21.69	232807	6.30
2007–08	201758	2.65	5.41	207181	4.82	13.47	223024	5.19	21.53	238868	5.56
2008–09	207297	2.75	3.70	209225	4.20	10.15	222231	4.16	16.59	235237	4.72
2009–10	213656	3.07	4.46	216544	3.85	11.99	232151	4.12	19.52	247758	4.40
2010–11	221150	3.51	6.66	227890	3.52	16.83	249617	3.55	27.00	271344	4.19

Note: One crore = 10 million

Source: Author's calculations.

5.5.3.2 Lifecycle deficit of elderly and UOAPS

Using the age profiles of labour income and consumption profiles in Figure 5.3 and the projected population over the period 2005 to 2050, aggregate lifecycle deficit for elderly [LCD(e)] is calculated by the following equation.

$$LCD(e) = \Sigma\varphi(e)P(e,t) - \Sigma\gamma(e)P(e,t) \qquad \text{(Eqaution 5.6)}$$

Where $\gamma(e)$ is per capita labour productivity at age 60 and above; $\varphi(e)$ is per capita consumption at age 60 and above; $P(e,t)$ is population at age 60 and above in year–t. The summation is from age 60 to 90.

Equation (5.6) assumes that per capita age profiles remains constant throughout. Further, assuming that the amount of UOAPS remains the same at ₹ 2000 per month throughout, total amount of LCD and UOAPS are calculated from 2005 through 2050. The results, as given in column two to four in Table 5.6, indicate that the computed ratio of UOAPS to elderly LCD is about 200 per cent for all years. This implies that the UOAPS is empirically supportable to financing the deficit consumption of elderly population.

Table 5.6: Financing lifecycle deficit of elderly by proposed UOAPS, India, 2005–50

Year	LCD unadjusted for inflation and UOAPS unadjusted for both inflation and income elasticity			Lifecycle deficit (LCD) of elderly adjusted for annual rate of inflation at 5% (₹ billion)	UOAPS adjusted for annual rate of inflation (5%) and income elasticity (1.0)		UOAPS adjusted for annual rate of inflation (5%) and income elasticity (0.5)	
	LCD of elderly (₹ crore)	Total expenditure on UOAPS (₹ crore)	UOAPS as a percentage of LCD of elderly		Total expenditure on UOAPS (₹ crore)	UOAPS as a percentage of inflation adjusted-LCD of elderly	Total expenditure on UOAPS (₹ crore)	UOAPS as a percentage of inflation adjusted-LCD of elderly
2015	124435	269984	216.97	130656	347688	266.10	278713	213.32
2020	150129	324005	215.82	157636	542523	344.16	349883	221.96
2025	179098	3822.94	213.46	188053	839923	446.64	437429	232.61
2030	211662	4469.06	211.14	222245	1291479	581.11	544930	245.19
2035	247183	5162.67	208.86	259542	1975252	761.05	676968	260.83
2040	286586	5948.73	207.57	300916	3000275	997.05	837981	278.48

Year	LCD unadjusted for inflation and UOAPS unadjusted for both inflation and income elasticity			Lifecycle deficit (LCD) of elderly adjusted for annual rate of inflation at 5% (₹ billion)	UOAPS adjusted for annual rate of inflation (5%) and income elasticity (1.0)		UOAPS adjusted for annual rate of inflation (5%) and income elasticity (0.5)	
	LCD of elderly (₹ crore)	Total expenditure on UOAPS (₹ crore)	UOAPS as a percentage of LCD of elderly		Total expenditure on UOAPS (₹ crore)	UOAPS as a percentage of inflation adjusted-LCD of elderly	Total expenditure on UOAPS (₹ crore)	UOAPS as a percentage of inflation adjusted-LCD of elderly
2045	330531	6770.28	206.33	344947	4527112	1312.41	1033715	299.67
2050	373488	7647.22	204.75	393162	6790734	1727.21	1271257	323.34

Note: Crore=10 million

Source: Author's calculations based on equation (6).

Further, Table 5.6 gives the sensitivity results for computed value of LCD and UOAPS when the growth of LCD is adjusted for annual inflation rate of 5 per cent and growth of UOAPS is simultaneously adjusted for both annual inflation rate at 5 per cent and income elasticity of UOAPS at 0.5 and 1.0. Apparently, a generous public policy of UOAPS (income elasticity is 1.0) leads to higher expenditure on UOAPS that what is needed to financing the LCD of elderly individuals. This implies that from the viewpoint of inter-generational equity for elderly or total financing of elderly deficit consumption, public expenditure requirements on UOAPS would be far less than the adjusted expenditure for inflation and income elasticity.

5.6 Conclusion

This chapter has examined the linkages between age structure transition, population ageing and economic growth of India by using the new methodology of NTA. This approach provides with a macroeconomic foundation for calculation of age profiles of labour income, consumption and taxes. Usefulness of these profiles is shown by calculating the growth effects of age structure transition and population ageing over the period up to 2050. These effects are called the FDD. In addition, the profiles are useful to assess the cost and financing a proposed UOAPS scheme and draw the scheme's implications for financing deficit consumption of elderly in India. Major conclusions and implications of this analysis are as follows.

Over the period from 2005 to 2050, the growth effect of India's age structure transition is positive due to the FDD and largely contributed by productivity growth. Policy efforts are required to enhance and strengthen the productivity of workers including elderly age groups in order to delay or halt the ending of FDD. These efforts are also essential to translate the potential FDD into actual FDD for India.

Population ageing as such may not have negative implications on India's economic growth because all elderly individuals are not out of labour force, do not have zero economic support ratio and do not impose total burden on tax paying working population to public financing of old age consumption of goods and services and other public support systems. This conclusion is mainly driven by the presence of informal sector jobs for elderly individuals with no formal age of retirement, and their labour and non-labour incomes are contributory for direct and indirect (or consumption-based) taxes of the general government and a partial source of financing the old age support systems, such as, a publicly-funded universal old age pension scheme.

The cost of a universal old age pension scheme for the elderly individuals is misunderstood to be entirely financed by taxing the working adults. This misunderstanding must be cleared in the minds of policy makers and adult tax payers by informing the valuable economic contribution of India's elderly population towards labour income and direct and indirect taxes. In fact, these taxes do implicitly and partially pay for their proposed publicly-funded, non-contributory, non-means related UOAPS. Most surprisingly, such public expenditure on UOAPS is more than what is required to finance the LCD of elderly individuals in India even if growth of the expenditure is unadjusted for inflation and income elasticity of UOAPS. These results imply that policy makers may have to work on calculating the net tax fiscal burden of financing a UOAPS before the scheme is considered for implementation in future. In addition, this analysis needs to be extended by examining the impact of total financing of UOAPS in terms of sustainability of fiscal policy and intergenerational tax burden.

This chapter has recognized the importance of the role of informal employment as a source of income in general and for the elderly labour income in particular. However, policy efforts are essential to enhance and strengthen productivity of existing and future labourers in informal sector for attainment of higher economic growth through demographic dividends. Further, due to continued elderly work participation, special policy efforts (e.g. training programmes for skill formation) may also be necessary for enhancement and strengthening of labour productivity for elderly labour force to maximize the growth effects and to neutralize the negative growth effects of population ageing. This implies a need for overall policy efforts to enhance and strengthen the productivity of all workers and expand employment opportunities including in elderly age groups in order to delay or halt the ending of FDD and to translate the potential FDD into actual FDD for India.

The conclusions and implications of this chapter must be qualified by data limitations to calculate the age profiles and the underlying assumptions, such as, constancy of cross-sectional age profiles of labour income and consumption, and growth rate of labour productivity. Subject to the availability of newer or finer data in future, this data limitation may be overcome. Further, many realities of Indian economy, such as, gender differences, rural-urban distinctions and inter-state variations in demographic transition deserve to be newly explored in the framework of the NTA.

Endnotes

1   It is important to note that Economic Support Ratio (ESR) for young, youth and elderly population can be different from their dependency ratios in Figure 5.2 if $\gamma(a) \geq 0$ and $\varphi(a) > 0$ for all a. This implies that ESR cannot be interpreted as a dependency ratio unless $\gamma(a)=0$ for $60 \leq a \leq 24$.

2   Non-NTA studies have accounted for growth by decomposing the other sources. For instance, Park and Shin (2012) accounted for sources of per capita GDP by per capita labour force (or work participation rate) and ratio of income to labour force (or labour productivity). Bloom et al. (2010) identified three sources of per capita income growth by income per worker (or labour productivity), ratio of labour force to working age population (or labour participation) and share of working age population to total population.

3   For a recent international comparison of age profiles of labour income and consumption among developing Asian countries, see, for instance, ADB (2011).

4   For instance, labour force participation rate (LFPR) is 39.4 per cent at 60 and above in the 61st Round of NSS on Employment and Unemployment 2004–05. The United Nations (2007) projected the LFPR at age 65+ in 2020 is 27.3 per cent for India. An excellent analysis of work participation rates by broad age groups from 1983 through 2007–08 is available in Mahendra Dev and Venkatanarayana (2011).

5   The report is based on a sample survey of 8329 elderly households (i.e. having at least one elderly member aged 60+) or 9852 elderly individuals in seven states (Himachal Pradesh, Kerala, Maharashtra, Odisha, Punjab, Tamil Nadu and West Bengal) in May-September 2011. The sample states were selected as they had a higher percentage of elderly population above the national average.

6   For details, see Pension Parishad's website: http://pensionparishad.org/pension/about-pension-parishad/

7   Direct taxes are calculated based on the combined age profile of personal income tax and corporate income tax. Indirect taxes exclude service tax on education and health consumption because education consumption is not yet taxed and health consumption is taxed from 2010–11 (i.e. service tax on health services provided by hospitals and medical enterprises).

8   Of these pension schemes, expenditure on IGNOAPS constituted less than 5 per cent from 2004–05 through 2010–11.

9   The increase in elderly share in direct tax in 2010–11 is due to a remarkable annual increase in direct tax revenue by about 19 per cent.

References

ADB. 2011. *Asian Development Outlook 2011 Update, Preparing for Demographic Transition*. Manila: Asian Development Bank.

Aiyar, S. and A. Mody. 2011. 'The Demographic Dividend: Evidence from Indian States'. IMF *Working Paper No.WP/11/38*. Washington: International Monetary Fund.

Bloom, D. E., D. Canning, L. Hu, Y. Liu, A. Mahal and W. Yip. 2010. 'The Contribution of Population Health and Demographic Change to Economic Growth in China and India', *Journal of Comparative Economics* 38(1): 17–33.

Central Statistical Office. 2013. *National Accounts Statistics 2013*. New Delhi: Ministry of Statistics and Programme Implementation, Government of India.

Choudhry, M. T. and J. Paul Elhorst. 2010. 'Demographic Transition and Economic Growth in China, India and Pakistan', *Economic Systems* 34(3): 218–36.

Desai, Sonalde, Amaresh Dubey, B. L. Joshi, Mitali Sen, Abusaleh Shariff and Reeve Vanneman. 2009. *India Human Development Survey (IHDS) [Computer file]*. ICPSR22626-v2. University of Maryland and National Council of Applied Economic Research, New Delhi [producers], 2007; Ann Arbor, MI: Inter-university Consortium for Political and Social Research [distributor], 30 June 2009.

Government of India. 2013. 'Seizing the Demographic Dividend', Chapter 2. *Economic Survey 2013-13*. New Delhi: Oxford University Press.

_____. 2012. *Indian Public Finance Statistics 2011-12*. New Delhi: Department of Economic Affairs, Ministry of Finance.

_____. 2008, *Report on Definition and Statistical Issues Relating to Informal Economy*. New Delhi: National Commission for Enterprises in the Unorganized Sector.

_____. 2007. *National Accounts Statistics 20073*. New Delhi: Central Statistical Organization, Government of India.

Lee, R. and A. Mason. 2011. 'Introducing Age into National Accounts'. In *Population Aging and the Generational Economy*, edited by Ronald Lee and Andrew Mason, 55–78. Cheltenham: Edward Elgar.

Mahendra Dev, S. and M. Venkatanarayana. 2011. 'Youth Employment and Unemployment in India'. *Working Paper#2011-09*. Mumbai: Indira Gandhi Institute of Development Research.

Mason, A. and R. Lee. 2007. 'Transfers, Capital and Consumption over the Demographic Transition'. In: *Population Aging, Intergenerational Transfers and the Macroeconomy*, edited by Robert Clark, Naohiro Ogawa and Andrew Mason, 128–62. Northampton: Edward Elgar.

Mason, A. and L. Sang-Hyop. 2012. 'Population, Wealth and Economic Growth in Asian and the Pacific'. In *Ageing, Economic Growth, And Old-Age Security in Asia*, edited by Donghyun Park, Sang-Hyop Lee and Andrew Mason, 32–82. Cheltenham: Edward Elgar.

NTA. 2013. Available at: http://www.ntaccounts.org/web/nta/show/Documents/Methods. Accessed on 1 January 2013.

Ogawa, N., A. Chawla and R. Matsukura. 2009. 'Some New Insights into the Demographic Transition and Changing Age Structure in the ESCAP Region', *Asia-Pacific Population Journal* 24(1): 87–116.

Park, D. and K. Shin. 2012. 'Impact of Population Aging on Asia's Future Growth'. In *Aging, Economic Growth, and Old-Age Security in Asia*, edited by Donghyun Park, Sang-Hyop Lee and Andrew Mason, 83–110. Cheltenham: Edward Elgar.

UNFPA. 2012. *Report on the Status of Elderly in Select States of India, 2011*. New Delhi: United Nations Population Fund.

United Nations. 2013a. *World Population Prospects: The 2012 Revision*. New York: Population Division, Department of Economic and Social Affairs, United Nations.

_____. 2013b. 'National Transfer Accounts Manual: Measuring and Analysing the Generational Economy'. *ESA/P.WP/226*. New York: Population Division, Department of Economic and Social Affairs.

_____. 2007. *World Population Ageing 2007*. New York: United Nations.

6

Labour Intensity in Indian Manufacturing
Measurement, Patterns and Determinants

Deb Kusum Das, Kunal Sen and Pilu Chandra Das

6.1 Introduction

India's disappointing performance in labour-intensive manufacturing is one of the compelling and least understood aspects of India's post-reform economic development (Kochhar, *et al.*, 2006; Joshi, 2010). Given the large numbers of surplus labour in low productivity agriculture in India, the expectation was with the economic reforms of 1991, and the removal (at least in part) of existing distortions in factor and capital markets, India's structure of production would shift more towards labour-intensive sectors, and there would be an increase in labour-intensity across the board in Indian manufacturing. Yet as Hasan *et al.* (2013) show, India uses more capital-intensive techniques of production than countries at similar levels of development.[1] More surprisingly, controlling for factor prices, India specializes in more capital-intensive varieties within broad industry groups than the United States, which is a much more capital-abundant country.

In this chapter, we analyse the patterns and determinants of labour-intensity in Indian manufacturing. To do this, we need to know which industries can be classified as labour-intensive and which cannot be. We propose and implement a simple method of classifying industries by labour-intensity. Using this classification, we examine broad trends and patterns in labour-intensity (that is, the ratio of workers to fixed capital stock) in the sectors we identify from 1980–81 to 2009–10. We then examine possible determinants of the growth of labour-intensive sectors in Indian manufacturing using states as units of analysis. But first, we begin with a discussion of the overall phenomenon of jobless growth in India, and locate the issue of the weak performance of the labour-intensive manufacturing industries within this wider phenomenon.

6.2 Phenomenon of Jobless growth in India

India has witnessed the fastest rates of economic growth since the 1991 economic reforms in its post-independence period. However, this process of economic growth has not been job creating. The employment elasticity of output – the per cent increase in employment for a 1 per cent increase in GDP – has fallen from 0.40 in 1983–1993 to 0.29 in 1993–2004. Employment growth was 1.79 per cent per annum in 1993–2004 as compared to 1.99 per cent per annum, in spite of a higher rate of economic growth in the 1990s as compared to the 1980s. The overall low rate of employment creation in the 1990s and early 2000s masks changes in patterns of employment creation within skill categories. Perhaps the most relevant indicator of job creation from a poverty reduction perspective is the rate of employment growth for unskilled workers. Kotwal *et al.* (2011) find that in the 1980s, the fastest growing sectors hardly provided any unskilled labour employment. In fact, many of the fastest growing sectors shed unskilled labour. This changed in the 1990s, when many of the fastest growing sectors used unskilled labour abundantly. The most important of the fast growing sectors from the point of view of providing unskilled labour employment were the trade (retail and wholesale trade) and construction sectors, which increased their share in GDP rapidly since the early 1990s. There was also less evidence of labour shedding in the 1990s. Non-farm employment increased strongly in 1993–2004 by 60.2 million workers as compared to an increase of 35.9 million workers in 1983–93.

This suggests that the phenomenon of jobless growth may not hold true for all skill categories (and in particular, for unskilled workers, who form the bulk of India's poor) and for all fast growing sectors (and in particular, those components of the tertiary sectors which use unskilled labour intensively). In fact, much of the phenomenon of jobless growth in the post–reform period is confined to the organized segment of the manufacturing sector. The annual rate of growth of employment in organized manufacturing was -0.38 per cent in 1993–2004 as compared to 1.1 per cent in 1983–93. In contrast, employment growth in unorganized manufacturing increased from 2.3 per cent per annum in 1983–93 to 4.3 per cent per annum in 1993–2004.

As is commonly known, all the major Asian economies, starting with Japan, then Korea, Singapore, and Taiwan, and now more recently, China and Vietnam, have moved from the import substituting phases of their economic development to an export-oriented development strategy that involved a strong growth in the labour intensive segment of the manufacturing sector in the initial years (Riedel, 1988; Haggard, 1996; Krueger, 1997). In all these countries, as their economies integrated more closely with world markets, economic growth and structural transformation from an agriculture-based to a manufacturing-based economy went hand in hand, and surplus labour was pulled from less productive agriculture to the more productive manufacturing sector. This has not happened in India. In fact, the share of the labour-intensive textile, clothing and footwear industries actually contracted from the mid 1970s to the late 1990s in organized manufacturing production and employment, in spite of India's apparent comparative advantage in labour intensive industries (Wood and Calandrino 2000; Sen, 2008). This was not accompanied by an increase in the share of the informal/unorganized sector in output and employment in the same industries (Raj and Sen, 2012). The lack of strong growth in the labour–intensive manufacturing sector can explain in great part the phenomenon of jobless growth in Indian manufacturing.

Intuitively, overall labour-intensity in Indian manufacturing is dependent on how labour-intensive is each industry in the manufacturing sector along with the weight of the labour-intensive industries in overall manufacturing. Clearly, the best scenario for increasing overall labour-intensity is an increase in labour–intensity in each industry and an increase in the share of the labour-intensive industries in aggregate manufacturing. In our analysis of labour-intensity of Indian manufacturing, we keep sight of both these variables. Before we move on to the analysis, we propose a method of identifying the labour-intensive industries.

6.3 Identifying the labour-intensive manufacturing industries of India

For identifying labour-intensive industries, we computed the labour–intensity[2] for the entire three-digit (NIC, 1998) organized manufacturing industries for every year, and for each industry an average labour-intensity ratio was calculated for the period 1980–81 to 2009–10. The average labour-intensity (L/K) ratio for all industries taken together was found to be 0.84. All the industries or sectors with average labour-intensity ratio greater than 0.84 were considered as labour-intensive industries and all those industries with a ratio less than 0.84 were labelled capital intensive. According to this definition, we found 13 industries that were labour intensive industries out of 52 three-digit industry groups. Box 6.1 below provides the description of the labour-intensive industries.

Box 6.1: Identified labour-intensive manufacturing industries

NIC-1998	Industry description
153	Grain mills products, starches and starch products and prepared animal feeds
154	Other food products
160	Tobacco products
173	Knitted and crocheted fabrics and articles
181	Wearing apparel, except for fur
182	Dressing and dyeing of fur, manufacture of articles of fur
191	Tanning and dressing of leather, manufacture of luggage hand bags, saddler and harness
192	Manufacture of footwear
201	Saw milling and planing of wood
202	Products of wood, cork, straw and plaiting materials
352	Railway and tramway locomotives and rolling stock
361	Manufacture of furniture
369	Manufacturing n.e.c

Source: Authors' calculations

Figure 6.1: Level and distribution of overall labour-intensive industries: 1980–81 to 2009–10

Panel A

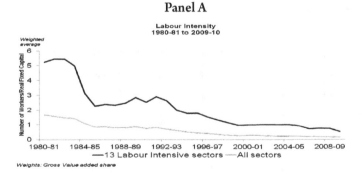

Panel B

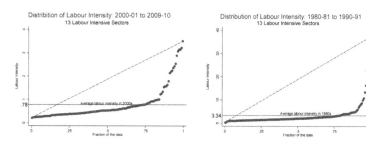

Source: Authors' calculations

Our estimates indicate that over the last 30 years there has been a decline in levels of labour intensity across organized manufacturing. Labour intensity across 52 NIC three digits sectors have fallen from average 1.45 in 1980s to 0.33 in 2000s. The pace of decline has been much steeper for the labour intensive sectors (for 13 labour-intensive sectors, it has fallen from average 3.34 in 1980s to 0.78 in 2000s) in comparison to all organized manufacturing as evident from panel B of Figure 6.1. Further, the pace of fall in labour intensity was highest during the period of 1980 (fell by 27 per cent), moderate during 1990s (fell by 19 per cent) and slowed by 2000s (4.8 per cent).

The overall decline in levels of labour intensity is spread across all the industry groups– ranging from food products, wearing apparel, to railway transport equipment's as is evident from Figure 6.2 below. The pace of decline in the 1990s and 2000s at the aggregate level holds true even at the broad product groups.

Figure 6.2: Levels of labour-intensity across manufacturing industries: 1980–81 to 2009–10

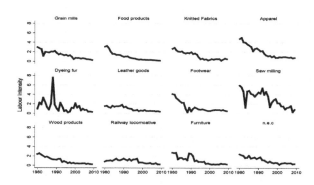

Source: Authors' calculations

It is worthwhile to examine the contribution of Labour-Intensive (LI) industries to the overall manufacturing value added to understand their importance in a labour surplus country like India. Panel A of Figure 6.3 shows the GVA share of 13 labour intensive sectors as against the overall growth in GVA for organized manufacturing. We found that the share of the labour-intensive industries in the overall manufacturing value added remained constant (12 per cent of organized manufacturing) for almost two decades beginning 1980 with sharp fall at the beginning of the decade of 2000s.

Figure 6.3: Overall and individual labour-intensive manufacturing industries: value added shares

Panel A

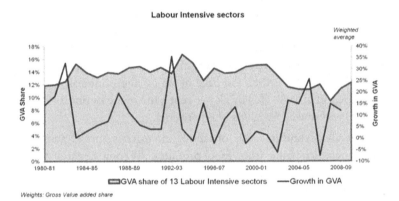

Panel B

Source: Authors' calculations

From panel B of the Figure 6.3, we found that in 1980–81 food products (154), railway locomotives (352) and tobacco manufacturing (160) contributed more than 60 per cent of the value added share of the labour-intensive groups. The 1990s saw apparel (181) and leather footwear (192) increase its share substantially. The beginning of the 2000s (2000–01) saw the share of labour-intensive sectors improve to around 15 per cent, mainly through doubling the share of apparel industries. In recent times, the aggregate share of labour intensive sectors in GVA has come down to around 12 per cent mainly through the falling share of food and apparel industries.

6.4 Patterns in labour intensity in Indian manufacturing: Growth, employment and productivity

In this section, we discuss the observable patterns in the identified labour intensive sectors for the period 1980–2010. As discussed in section 6.3, the share of labour-intensive industries has remained more or less unchanged for a large part of the time period. Yet to understand the dynamics of the sector, we need to look at the individual industries. We look at some yardsticks of performances – growth in value added, employment growth, labour productivity, wages and workers per factory.

6.4.1 Growth in value added

As regards the growth of VA across different industries of the labour-intensive sector, we found evidence of sharp inter-industry variations. In addition, we found that the apparel sectors (173, 181, 182 and 369) drive the growth in the labour intensive by recording more than 10 per cent growth in value added for the 30 year period.

Table 6.1: Growth in real value added – labour-intensive manufacturing industries

NIC–98	1980–81 to 1990–91	1991–92 to 1999–2000	2000–01 to 2009–10	1980–81 to 2009–10
153	7.64	8.7	7.84	8.04
154	11.69	5.04	3.68	6.87
160	7.87	7.96	0.59	5.39

NIC–98	1980–81 to 1990–91	1991–92 to 1999–2000	2000–01 to 2009–10	1980–81 to 2009–10
173	15.83	15.46	9.34	13.48
181	18.39	15.83	7.76	13.93
182	14.86	2.34	23.57	13.98
191	9.31	2.05	10.39	7.43
192	16.01	2.36	9.12	9.4
201	1.12	–15.51	3.13	–3.35
202	7.44	–7.2	10.11	3.82
352	3.45	–13.74	14.15	1.8
361	–9.25	14.38	8.76	4.29
369	5.71	24.94	6.97	12.11

Source: Authors' calculations

6.4.2 Employment generation

Second, turning our attention to employment generation by the labour-intensive sectors we found that the employment share of LI industries increased from 26 per cent in 1980s to 29 per cent in 1990s and further increase to 31 per cent in 2000s. Further, the 1990s show a substantial jump in employment growth of LI industries from -0.1 per cent on an average during 1980s to 3.0 per cent in 1990s and again 3.3 per cent in 2000s. In terms of employment growth at the level of individual industries, we observed that the industry group food products has the largest employment share (25 per cent) followed by apparel (21 per cent) and tobacco (14 per cent) in 2009–10. Further, we found that the apparel, leather, gems and jewellery has contributed the highest to employment generation during the 30 year period from 1980–2010. Rest of the labour-intensive industries exhibits evidence of poor employment generation during the same 30 year period. In addition, the employment growths of different LI industries across different periods are provided in the panel b of Figure 6.4 below.

Figure 6.4: Overall and individual labour-intensive
industries – employment share and growth

Panel A

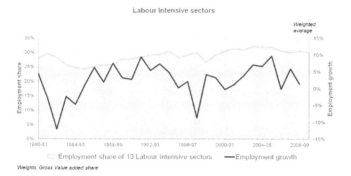

Panel B

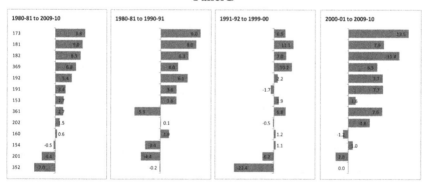

Source: Authors' calculations

The employment elasticity of the labour-intensive (LI) industries witnessed a decline in 2000s after showing signs of improvements in the 1990s, keeping in line with the decline in real value added growth for the same period. It may be important to underline here that LI manufacturing industries like textiles and garments, leather and footwear, gems and jewellery, and food processing must be allowed to adjust labour force in relation to fluctuating in demand and in the process simplify the regulatory frameworks, which act as barriers to employment expansions.

6.4.3 Labour productivity performance

Finally, we look at the productivity performance of these identified sectors. Productivity is defined as value added per worker. We observed that the labour productivity growth was relatively very low to the aggregate organized manufacturing. In addition, we found continuous divergence in labour productivity between labour intensive sectors and organized manufacturing as a whole. It is worth noting that after 2000–01 organized manufacturing experienced a substantial jump in labour productivity but there is not much contribution from the labour intensive industries.

Figure 6.5: Growth in labour productivity: all manufacturing versus overall labour-intensive manufacturing industries

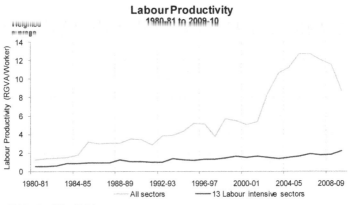

Weights: Gross Value added share

Source: Authors' calculations

Majority of the industry record growth in labour productivity of around 4 per cent and above with the highest growth recorded by the transport equipment sector (8 per cent per annum) for the 30 year period. An important aspect of these numbers is to ascertain if the worker in question is a skilled worker or unskilled worker and this may be particularly relevant for sectors like railway transport equipment, gems and jewellery, food and beverages etc. The decline in capital productivity (in terms of falling labour intensity) could be a possible determinant of low growth in labour productivity in the labour-intensive industries. The answer may lie in increase in accumulation of capital in LI sectors but if capital productivity does not improve within these sectors it leads to constraints in achieving growth in labour productivity.

It remains to be seen how does this overall performance in growth in labour productivity reflects across different industries. Table 6.2 below documents the evidence on labour productivity growth by industry and sub-periods.

Table 6.2: Growth in labour productivity – labour-intensive manufacturing industries

NIC–98	1980–81 to 2009–10	1980–81 to 1990–91	1991–92 to 1999–00	2000–01 to 2009–10
153	5.34	4.03	5.81	6.21
154	7.4	15.13	3.99	2.73
160	4.78	5.97	6.79	1.78
173	3.68	6.83	8.94	–4.19
181	4.98	10.35	4.76	–0.19
182	5.7	8.58	–4.65	12.15
191	4.05	5.71	3.75	2.65
192	3.96	9.94	0.13	1.41
201	1.09	5.56	–9.27	5.96
202	2.28	7.34	–6.7	5.31
352	8.81	3.62	8.61	14.17
361	1.62	–3.32	7.63	1.16
369	5.36	1.76	14.76	0.5

Source: Authors' calculations

6.4.4 Wage share and workers per factory

Our final assertion is to explore the poor performance of the LI industries by examining the wage share to GVA and workers per factory. The decline in labour intensity across industry groups for successive time periods reflects in the share of labour income in value added declining from around 53 per cent in 1980–81 to about 31 per cent in 2009–10. Our findings indicate that this declining pattern also holds across all industry groups and for all time periods (refer appendix Table A6.1).

Figure 6.6: Growth rate of wage and wage share in GVA

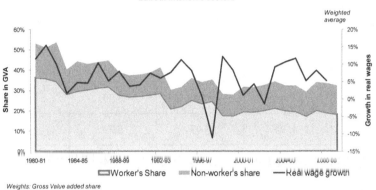

Weights: Gross Value added share

Source: Authors' calculations

Further, examining the workers per factory over time, we do not find any evidence of an increase in the number of workers resulting in LI firms not being able to reap the economies of scale. This is surprising, given the removal of licenses and de-reservation, and may be linked to labour laws and infrastructural and skill constraints.

Table 6.3: Number of workers per factory – labour-intensive manufacturing industries

NIC–98	1980–81 to 1990–91	1991–92 to 1999–00	2000–01 to 2009–10	1980–81 to 2009–10
153	19	20	19	19
154	100	98	93	97
160	46	89	147	93
173	20	27	65	37
181	43	64	116	74
182	19	34	65	39
191	43	35	41	40
192	61	60	80	67
201	9	7	6	8

NIC–98	1980–81 to 1990–91	1991–92 to 1999–00	2000–01 to 2009–10	1980–81 to 2009–10
202	31	25	19	25
352	638	459	69	394
361	27	23	30	26
369	26	44	68	46

Source: Authors' calculations

6.5 Possible constraints to the growth of labour-intensive manufacturing in India

There is a small but growing literature on why labour-intensive sectors in Indian manufacturing have not exhibited strong growth in the post-reform period.[3] This literature identifies four sets of factors that inhibit the growth of labour-intensive sectors in India. Firstly, it is argued that the nature of the trade regime in India is still biased towards capital-intensive manufacturing, in spite of reforms which have reduced the protection towards the capital goods and intermediate goods sectors. Tariffs in India still remain high as compared to the regional average (Athukorala, 2009). In addition, as recent as 1996–2000, the shares of intermediate inputs and consumer goods subject to non-tariff barriers were as high as 28 and 33 per cent respectively (Das, 2003). Secondly, several papers have shown that stringent employment protection legislation – among the most protective of formal workers in the world – has reduced the incentive of firms, especially those in the purview of employment protection legislation, to hire workers on permanent contracts and pushed them towards more capital intensive modes of production, than warranted by existing costs of labour relative to capital. Dougherty (2009) finds that for large firms (that is, firms with 100 or more workers), almost all the increase in employment has been in the form of contract workers – workers employed through intermediaries who do not benefit from employment protection legislation – while the employment of permanent workers has decreased for these firms. Employment protection legislation is applicable to firms with 100 workers or more, so this shows that labour laws have led to firms shedding regular labour in favour of temporary labour. On the other hand, the employment of permanent workers increased for firms with less than 100 workers. Perhaps the seminal paper here is Gupta, Hasan and Kumar (2009), who use a three-dimensional state-industry-year panel to examine the determinants of industrial growth at the three digit ASI level such as labour regulations, infrastructure, skills and financial development and find that Indian states with relatively inflexible labour legislation have experienced slower growth in labour–intensive industries and slower employment growth overall. Saha, Sen and Maiti (2013) find that states with labour legislation that favour permanent workers have shown a higher growth of contract workers relative to regular workers.

A third explanation offered for poor performance of labour–intensive sectors are infrastructural bottlenecks (especially in access to electricity) as well as the lack of access to bank credit for the small and medium-sized firms that comprise the majority of firms in the labour–intensive sectors (Panagariya, 2008).[4] Finally, poor skills and low literacy rates among unskilled workers in India are seen as key impediments to the growth of the labour-intensive sectors that employ these workers more intensely than the capital-intensive sectors (Sen, 2008).

6.6 Explaining success in labour-intensive manufacturing in Indian states

In section 6.4, we observed wide variation in labour intensity in Indian manufacturing, both across industries and over time. We now examine possible determinants of labour intensity, using Indian states as units of analysis. We first see which states have been more successful in the labour-intensive industries that we had identified in section 6.3. We then present some descriptive statistics on correlates of labour intensity. Finally, we undertake econometric analysis of the determinants of success in labour intensity manufacturing across states and over time.

6.6.1 How is success in labour-intensive manufacturing measured for Indian states?

All major states have some presence of labour intensive industries. How do we establish which state has been more successful in the competitiveness of their labour-intensive sectors relative to other states? We determine their relative competitiveness in labour intensive sectors by using a modified version of the Revealed Comparative Advantage (RCA) measure. This measure is usually used to compute the relative advantage or disadvantage of a certain country in a certain class of goods or services as evidenced by trade flows, and is based on the Ricardian comparative advantage concept (see Kumar *et al.*, 2003 for an application to Indian trade data). For their purposes, we calculate the relative advantage or disadvantage of the state in question in labour–intensive sectors relative to the aggregate manufacturing sector. We only look at this measure for the 15 major states in which about 95 per cent of India's population resides.

We define RCA, i denotes state and t time.

RCA_{it} = [(*Sum of Gross Value Added of Labour Intensive Sectors in the state in time t/Sum of Gross Value Added of Labour Intensive Sectors in All 15 States in time t*)]/[(*Sum of Gross Value Added of All Manufacturing Sectors in the state at time t*)/(*Sum of Gross Value Added of Sectors of All Manufacturing Sectors in All 15 States at time t*)].

Table 6.4: RCA of labour-intensive manufacturing in each state

State	1980–81	1991–92	2000–01	2009–10
Andhra Pradesh	1.51	1.44	1.37	0.82
Assam	6.22	4.24	2.74	3.12
Bihar	0.40	0.71	3.01	3.38
Gujarat	0.43	0.39	0.33	0.60
Haryana	0.43	0.75	1.28	1.37
Karnataka	0.93	0.95	1.87	1.29
Kerala	1.08	1.81	1.12	0.12
Madhya Pradesh	0.33	0.14	0.50	0.67
Maharashtra	0.59	0.81	0.87	0.81
Odisha	0.36	0.27	0.30	0.22
Punjab	1.03	1.28	1.22	1.36
Rajasthan	0.49	0.47	0.44	0.74
Tamil Nadu	1.09	1.32	1.25	1.33
Uttar Pradesh	2.02	1.08	1.71	2.70
West Bengal	1.16	0.90	1.05	1.51

Source: Authors' calculations

We present the results of their calculations for the years 1980–81, 1991–92, 2000–01 and 2009–2010 in Table 6.4, with the calculations of the numerator and denominator in the RCA formula presented in Tables 6.5 and 6.6.

We find from Table 6.4 that Andhra Pradesh has seen a decline in the relative advantage of their labour-intensive industries. On the other hand, Bihar and Haryana have seen an increase in the relative advantage of their labour-intensive industries. The other states show no clear trend in their RCAs over the 20 year period.

The RCA for the state can increase either if the share of the state in total value added of the labour-intensive manufacturing sectors at the all India level has increased, and/or if the total manufacturing value added of the state has fallen (while the labour-intensive segment has not), relative to the total manufacturing value added at the all India level. We see from Tables 6.5 and 6.6 that the increase in RCA we observed in Bihar is mostly due to a falling share of the state's manufacturing value added in all India value added, while the increase in RCA in Haryana is mostly due to an increase in the value added of the state's labour-intensive industries in total value added of labour intensive manufacturing at the all India level.

Table 6.5: Share of value added of labour-intensive sectors in each state in total manufacturing value added of labour-intensive sectors for all states

State	1980–81	1991–92	2000–01	2009–10
Andhra Pradesh	7.5	9.4	8.5	5.9
Assam	6.3	5.8	2.5	2.6
Bihar	2.5	4.2	1.5	1.3
Gujarat	4.2	3.1	4.2	9.4
Haryana	1.5	2.3	5.1	6.4
Karnataka	4.7	5.7	10.7	8.0
Kerala	3.4	5.2	2.6	0.1
Madhya Pradesh	1.7	0.7	2.1	1.7
Maharashtra	14.0	15.8	18.4	15.6
Odisha	0.7	0.7	0.5	0.6
Punjab	3.4	4.8	3.6	3.4

State	1980–81	1991–92	2000–01	2009–10
Rajasthan	1.4	1.5	1.6	2.5
Tamil Nadu	10.9	14.5	14.2	13.7
Uttar Pradesh	12.1	11.8	11.9	14.4
West Bengal	12.4	5.8	4.2	4.9

Source: Authors' calculations

Table 6.6: Share of value added of all manufacturing sectors in each state in total manufacturing value added for all states

State	1980–81	1991–92	2000–01	2009–10
Andhra Pradesh	5	6.5	6.2	7.1
Assam	1	1.4	0.9	0.8
Bihar	6.1	5.9	0.5	0.4
Gujarat	9.6	7.9	12.9	15.5
Haryana	3.5	3.1	4	4.6
Karnataka	5.1	6	5.7	6.2
Kerala	3.2	2.9	2.3	1.2
Madhya Pradesh	5	5.2	4.2	2.5
Maharashtra	23.6	19.5	21.1	19.4
Odisha	1.9	2.5	1.7	2.6
Punjab	3.3	3.8	2.9	2.5
Rajasthan	2.8	3.2	3.6	3.4
Tamil Nadu	10	11	11.4	10.3
Uttar Pradesh	6	10.9	7	5.3
West Bengal	10.7	6.4	4	3.3

Source: Authors' calculations

6.6.2 What explains the success in labour-intensive manufacturing in Indian states?

We have already noted in section 6.5 that most studies of India's labour-intensive manufacturing sectors point to labour regulations, infrastructure, electricity, trade openness, bank credit to labour-intensive sectors, and skills (as proxied by literacy rates) as being important constraints to the growth of labour-intensive manufacturing in India. We now examine to what extent these factors can explain the differences we observed in the RCAs both across states and over time.

To capture the variation in labour regulation across states, we use the commonly used Besley-Burgess (2004) measure of labour regulation. Industrial relations in India fall under the joint jurisdiction of the central and state governments. The rationale for the Besley-Burgess measure is as follows. The key piece of central legislation in industrial relations is the Industrial Disputes Act (IDA) of 1947, which sets out the conciliation, arbitration and adjudication procedures to be followed in the case of an industrial dispute. The IDA specifies a multi-tier conciliation cum adjudication system, where the tiers are created and maintained by state governments. In general, across all states IDA imposes significant restrictions on employers regarding layoff, retrenchment and closure. As a consequence, India's labour laws earned notoriety for being among the most restrictive in the world, especially on the question of retrenchment. According to the rigidity of employment index proposed by the World Bank, which is a summary indicator of different aspects of labour legislation across countries, Indian labour laws are more protective than the international average or an average of a group of comparator countries composed of large developing countries and countries in East and South Asia (Ahsan and Pages, 2009). The IDA has been extensively amended by state governments during the post-independence period. Besley and Burgess code each state amendment to labour laws as neutral, pro-worker or pro-employer. For neutral amendments, they assign a score of zero, for a pro-worker amendment a score of +1 and for a pro-employer amendment a score of -1. They then cumulate the scores over time for the period 1947–97. In their sample, the state of West Bengal has the most pro-worker labour institutions with a score of +4 in 1997, and Andhra Pradesh and Tamil Nadu the most pro-employer labour institutions, each with a score of -2 in 1997.

As we have noted previously, infrastructure and skills are important determinants of the competitiveness of the labour-intensive sectors. Indian states have differed widely in their ability to provide electricity to manufacturing firms, in part due to the very different performance of state electricity boards, the main agency responsible for transmission and distribution, across Indian states (Krueger and Chinoy, 2002; Panagariya, 2008). Therefore, electricity provision has differed widely across Indian states. We measure the quality of electricity provision by the percentage of transmission and distribution losses across states. In addition, transportation links differ widely across Indian states. For labour-intensive sectors, which have inherently low profit margins, low density of transportation links (as measured by the presence of railway networks) can lead to higher transactions costs and make them un-competitive. Finally, we measure skills by the literacy rate in the state.

In India, government regulations made it mandatory for commercial banks to lend a large proportion of their funds to small and medium enterprises in the formal manufacturing sector (which are mostly the units that are making the transition from the informal sector) along with farmer-households in the agricultural sector – these regulations were called priority sector lending requirements (Sen and Vaidya, 1997). We captured differential access to formal sector credit for small and medium enterprises across Indian states and over time by the share of bank lending going to priority sectors for 1989–90, 1994–95, 2000–01 and 2005–06.

We had noted in section 6.5 that trade openness is also seen as an important determinant of labour intensity. However, measures of trade openness such as tariffs and quotas tend to vary across industries and over time and not by region. In the Indian context, Marjit, Kar and Maiti (2007) have constructed a regional openness for Indian states from 1980–81 to 2002–03. This index captures to what extent the state's production is in the exporting and importing industries. We use this as our preferred measure to assess the impact of trade openness on RCA in their empirical analysis.

In Appendix figures A6.1 to A6.6, we present scatter plots of the Length of Railway Network, Besley-Burgess labour regulation measure, the Marjit-Kar-Maiti regional openness measure, literacy rates, transmission and distribution losses and priority sector lending, all against RCA for the 15 major Indian states. We observe a weak positive relationship between RCA and regional openness, and between RCA and priority sector lending. We also notice a negative relationship between length of rail network and RCA. There is no clear relationship between RCA on one hand and labour regulation and literacy rates on the other hand.

We now proceed to multivariate analysis. Our regression specification is as follows:

$RCA_{it} = \alpha_0 + \alpha_1$ Besley Burges$_{it} + \alpha_2$ Length of Rail Network$_{it} + \alpha_3$ Literacy Rate$_{it} + \alpha_4$ Reginal Open–ness$_{it} + \alpha_5$ Transmission and Distribution losses$_{it} + \alpha_6$ Priority Sector Lending$_{it} + \alpha_7 t + e_{it}$ (Equation 6.1)

where, i=state, t=1980–81, 1991–92, 2000–01 and 2009–10. We capture common trends in the RCA by a time trend variable t. We use both state fixed effects and random effects to estimate the regression. Labour regulation data till 1997 comes from Besley and Burgess (2004), and we have updated it using similar coding procedures till 2009. Data on priority sector lending comes from an annual publication titled Statistical Tables Relating to Banks in India published by the Reserve Bank of India (RBI). The state-level data on the transmission and distribution losses comes from the report on Energy published by the Centre for Monitoring Indian Economy. The data on length of rail network and literacy rates comes from the Statistical Abstracts of India, and the regional openness measure comes from Marjit *et al.* (2007).

Table 6.7: Descriptive statistics

Variable	Observations	Mean	Std.dev.	Min	Max
RCA	60	1.2	1.1	0.1	6.2
Besley-Burgess labour measure	60	0.1	1.3	–2	4
Length of railway network	60	3939.7	1937	1050	8726
Regional openness	60	8	2.7	2.5	14.5
Literacy rate	60	59.9	16.2	28.4	93.9
Transmission and distribution losses	60	26.5	8.4	15	46
Priority sector lending to small scale sector	60	32.9	10	10.4	58.2

Source: Authors' calculations

Table 6.8: Regression results

Explanatory variables	Coefficients	P>|t|
Besley-Burgess labour regulation measure	−0.16	0.473
Length of railway network	0.00	0.434
Regional openness	−0.13	0.024
Literacy rate	0.07	0.027
Transmission and distribution losses	−0.02	0.360
Priority sector lending	0.00	0.915
Time	−0.68	0.061
Number of obs	60	
R-sq	0.0171	

Source: Authors' calculations

We provide the summary statistics in Table 6.7 and the regression results in Table 6.8. We found that while the Besley-Burgess measure has the right sign – that is, negative – it is not statistically significant. In fact, the only variable that is statistically significant is the literacy rate. Higher rates of literacy lead to greater competitiveness in labour–intensive manufacturing sectors, as we would expect. None of the other variables are statistically significant. Our regression results, though suggestive, do indicate that the key explanatory variable at the state level for the competitiveness of labour intensive manufacturing is the availability of skills, and not so much labour regulations, infrastructure, financial development and trade openness.

6.7 Conclusion

Our study concludes that there has been a continuous decline in the levels of labour intensity for all the identified labour-intensive manufacturing industries. In particular, labour intensity has fallen from average 3.34 in 1980s to 0.78 in 2000s. The pace of fall in labour intensity was highest during 1980s (fell by 27.5 per cent), moderated during 1990s (19.8 per cent) and slowed in 2000s (4.8 per cent). Further, their estimates indicate that over the last 30 years there has been a decline in levels of labour intensity across organized manufacturing. The pace of decline has been much steeper for the labour-intensive sectors.

The observable patterns in the identified labour-intensive sectors for the period 1980–2010 show sharp variations over time as well as across manufacturing industries. We do observe that the selected labour-intensive industries registered positive output growth, however the growth was not commensurate with employment growth, resulting in low employment elasticity of labour intensive industries. Labour productivity gain was very low relative to the aggregate organized manufacturing. The decline in capital productivity across all the industries could have had a negative effect on the growth in labour productivity. It may be pertinent to point out that in the post-reform period there is no evidence of an increase in contribution of labour-intensive industries to organized manufacturing value added.

The poor performance of India's labour-intensive manufacturing sectors point to labour regulations, infrastructure, electricity, trade openness, bank credit to labour-intensive sectors, and skills as being important constraints to the growth of labour intensive manufacturing in India. However the initial econometric analysis of determinants of RCA of labour-intensive sectors at the state-level was not successful in picking up any statistically significant indicators except the literacy rate. To the extent that literacy rate is a good proxy for basic skill capability (human capital) skill differences can be said to play an important role. More systematic analysis is needed on industry-level barriers to understand the puzzling phenomenon of falling labour intensity and employment elasticity, along with a stagnant share of the labour-intensive sectors in manufacturing. This forms the core of follow up research.

Appendix

Table A6.1: Growth in wage share by labour-intensive industries

NIC–98	1980–81 to 2009–10	1980–81 to 1990–91	1991–92 to 1999–00	2000–01 to 2009–10
173	0.68	−0.4	−4.86	6.76
181	−0.28	−6.71	0.73	5.24
201	−0.56	−0.77	0.24	−1.06
191	−1.00	−2.97	−1.85	1.74
182	−1.05	−8.92	10.47	−3.53
202	−1.48	−2.52	0.74	−2.42
192	−1.97	−10.12	1.41	3.13
369	−2.03	1.51	−11.47	2.93
154	−2.26	−2.36	−2.87	−1.62
361	−2.30	1.98	−8.89	−0.65
153	−3.03	−1.72	−3.39	−4.01
160	−4.05	−4.03	−6.45	−1.92
352	−6.06	0.51	−6.74	−12.01

Source: Authors' calculations

Figure A6.1: Length of rail network and RCA, 2009–10

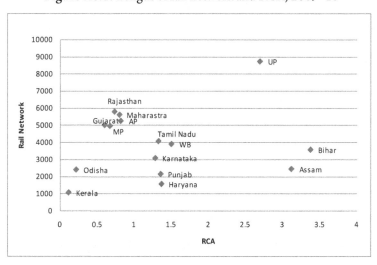

Source: Authors' calculations

Figure A6.2: Besley-Burgess labour regulation measure and RCA, 2009–10

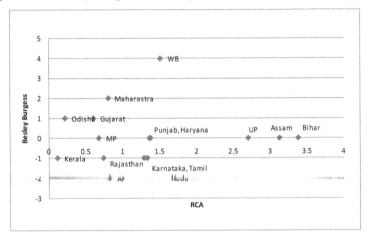

Source: Authors' calculations

Figure A6.3: Regional openness and RCA, 2009–10

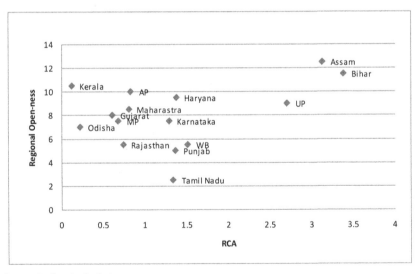

Source: Authors' calculations

Figure A6.4: Literacy and RCA, 2009–10

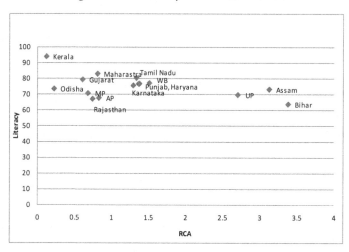

Source: Authors' calculations

Figure A6.5: Transmission and distribution losses and RCA, 2009–10

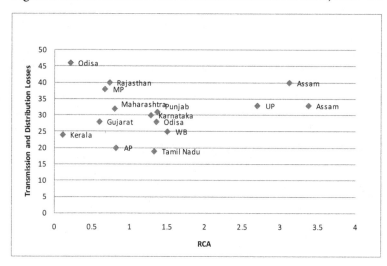

Source: Authors' calculations

Figure A6.6: Priority sector lending and RCA, 2009–10

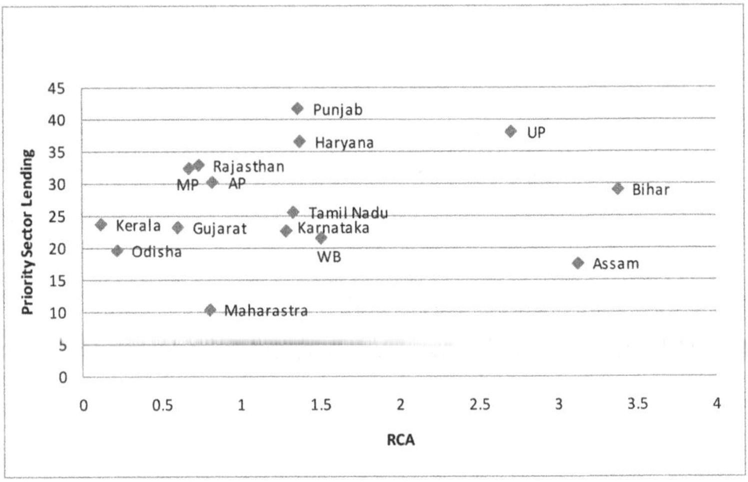

Source: Authors' calculations

Endnotes

1   A chapter commissioned by National Manufacturing Competitive Council of India to study the employment potential of labour-intensive manufacturing in India showed decline in levels of labour intensity across organized manufacturing in India for the period 1980–2004. Refer, ' A chapter on Labor Intensity and Employment potential of Indian Manufacturing' ICRIER (2008).

2   Labour intensity is defined as a ratio of number of workers to real fixed capital. The data source is ASI Summary Results for various years.

3   Das and Kalita (2009) using survey-based evidence across five labour-intensive sectors,– apparel, leather products, sports goods, bicycles and gems and jewellery attribute a host of factors that inhibit employment generation. In particular, the chapter points to lack of skilled workforce, low quality of machinery used and non-competitive export orientation as primary findings from a survey of 250 labour-intensive manufacturing enterprises.

4   Panagariya (2011) argues that there still remain binding restrictions on the expansion of labour–intensive sectors and these needs to be addressed. He highlights amongst many such constraints, laws related to 'Transparent Bankruptcy' and 'Land Acquisition.'

References

Ahsan, A. and C. Pagés. 2009. 'Are All Labor Regulations Equal? Evidence from Indian Manufacturing', *Journal of Comparative Economics* 37(1): 62–75.

Athukorala, P. 2009. 'Export Performance in the Post Reform Era: Has India Regained the Lost Ground?' In *The Indian Economy Sixty Years After Independence*, edited by R. Jha. London: Palgrave Macmillan.

Besley, T. and R. Burgess. 2004. 'Can Labor Regulation Hinder Economic Performance? Evidence from India', *The Quarterly Journal of Economics* 119(1): 91–134.

Das, D. K. 2003. 'Quantifying Trade Barriers: Has Protection Declined Substantially in Indian Manufacturing'. *Working Paper No. 105*. New Delhi: ICRIER.

Das, D. K. and G. Kalita. 2009. 'Are Labour-intensive Industries Generating Employment in India? Evidence from Firm Level Survey', *The Indian Journal of Labour Economics* 52(3): 411–32.

Dougherty, S. M. 2009. 'Labour Regulation and Employment Dynamics at the State Level in India', *Review of Market Integration* 1(3): 295–337.

Gupta, P., R. Hasan and U. Kumar. April 2009. 'Big Reforms but Small Payoffs: Explaining the Weak Record of Growth in Indian Manufacturing', *India Policy Forum* 5(1): 59–123. New Delhi: Sage Publications.

ICRIER. 2008. *Report on Labour Intensity and Employment Potential of Indian Manufacturing*. New Delhi, India: National Manufacturing Competitiveness Council (NMCC).

Joshi, V. 2010. 'Economic Resurgence, Lopsided Reform and Jobless Growth'. In *Continuity and Change in Contemporary India: Politics, Economics and Society*, edited by A. Heath and R. Jeffrey, Oxford: Oxford University Press.

Haggard, S. 1996. 'Lessons from Successful Reformers: Korea and Taiwan', *Economic Reform Today, Constructing a Market Economy* 2: 15–22.

Hasan, R., D. Mitra and A. Sundaram. 2013. 'What Explains the High Capital Intensity of Indian Manufacturing?', *Indian Growth and Development Review* 62(2): 212–41.

Kochhar, K., U. Kumar, R. Rajan, A. Subramanian and I. Tokatlidis. 2006. 'India's Pattern of Development: What Happened, What Follows?', *Journal of Monetary Economics* 53(5): 981–1019.

Kotwal, Ashok, Bharat Ramaswami and Wilima Wadhwa. 2011. 'Economic Liberalization and Indian Economic Growth: What's the Evidence?', *Journal of Economic Literature* 49(4): 1152–99.

Krueger, A. 1997. 'Trade Policy and Economic Development: What Have we Learned?', *American Economic Review* 87(1): 1–22.

Krueger, A. O. and S. Chinoy. 2002. 'The Indian Economy in a Global Context'. In *Economic Policy Reforms and the Indian Economy*, edited by A. O. Krueger. Chicago: University of Chicago Press.

Kumar, A. G., K. Sen and R. R. Vaidya. 2003. *International Competitiveness, Investment and Finance: A Case-study of India*. London: Routledge, UK.

Mazumdar, D. and S. Sarkar. 2008. *Globalisation, Labor Markets and Inequality in India*. London: Routledge.

Marjit, S., S. Kar and D. S. Maiti. 2007. 'Regional Trade Openness Index and Income Disparity: A New Methodology and the Indian Experiment', *Economic and Political Weekly* 24(9): 757–69.

Panagariya, A. 2008. *India: The Emerging Giant*. New York: Oxford University Press.

_____. 2011. 'Avoiding Lopsided Spatial Transformation'. In *Reshaping Tomorrow: Is South Asia Ready for the Big Leap?*, edited by Ejaz Ghani. New Delhi: Oxford University Press.

Raj, R. S .N. and K. Sen. 2012. 'Did International Trade Destroy or Create Jobs in Indian Manufacturing?', *European Journal of Development Research* 24(3): 359–81.

Riedel, J. 1988. 'Economic Development in East Asia: Doing What Comes Naturally?' In *Achieving Industrialisation in East Asia*, edited by H. Hughes. Cambridge: Cambridge University Press.

Saha, B., K. Sen and D. Maiti. 2013. 'Trade Open-ness, Labour Institutions and Flexibilisation: Theory and Evidence from India', *Labor Economics* 24(October): 180–95.

Sen, K. and R. R. Vaidya. 1997. *The Process of Financial Liberalization in India*. New Delhi: Oxford University Press.

Sen, K. 2008. *Trade Policy, Inequality, and Performance in Indian Manufacturing*. London: Routledge Advances in South Asian Studies.

_____. 2009. 'What a Long, Strange Trip It's Been: Reflections on the Causes of India's Growth Miracle', *Contemporary South Asia*. 17(4): 363–77.

Kathuria, V., R. S. N. Raj and K. Sen. 2010. 'Organised versus Unorganised Manufacturing Performance Growth in the Post-Reform Period', *Economic and Political Weekly* 45(24): 55–64.

Wood, A. and M. Calandrino. 2000. 'When the Other Giant Awakens: Trade and Human Resources in India', *Economic and Political Weekly* 35(52–53): 4677–94.

7

Gender Discrimination in Manufacturing Employment in India, 1999–2009

Bishwanath Goldar and Suresh Chand Aggarwal

7.1 Introduction

There have been a number of studies on gender discrimination in India. A common finding of these studies is that after controlling for endowments and certain other factors, the wages received by women are relatively lower than those received by men (see, for instance, Reilly and Vasudeva-Dutta, 2005; Menon and Rodgers, 2007; Khanna, 2012; Krishna and Bino Paul, 2012; and Paul and Paul, 2013). In this chapter, a different dimension of discrimination is studied, namely discrimination in job tenure (regular wage jobs versus casual jobs).[1] The analysis is confined to Indian manufacturing, as in the paper of Menon and Rodgers (2007). The main hypothesis tested econometrically is that after controlling for endowments and industry affiliation, the women tend to get discriminated in the matter of getting regular jobs. A related hypothesis is about the effect of economic reforms, particularly trade liberalization, on gender discrimination. There are reasons to believe that liberalization of trade and industrial policies, inasmuch as it leads to increased competition, will reduce gender discrimination in wages. This view is based on a theory of discrimination (see Becker, 1971). The argument is that gender discrimination is costly and the employers do discrimination despite it being costly because of the nature of their preferences. Hence, the employers will have to curb their preference for discrimination if competitive forces bring down their profit margin.

A question of particular interest to this chapter is the inter-state differences in the extent of gender-based discrimination in manufacturing employment. The focus, as mentioned above, is on the tenure of employment i.e., how far women tend to be discriminated against in the matter of getting regular jobs. It would be interesting to find out which are the Indian states where the extent of gender discrimination in manufacturing employment is relatively high, and the states in which it is relatively low. What is more important is to look for an explanation of the observed inter-state differences. For this purpose, two factors are considered: (1) women's social status and women empowerment in different states as reflected in the proportion of women among entrepreneurs in small and medium scale manufacturing enterprises of the state and a number of other indicators including female school enrolment ratios; and (2) inter-state differences in the degree of rigidity in the industrial labour market. Arguably, if women enjoy a more equal social status as compared to men in a state than in other states, the gender based discrimination in employment is expected to be relatively lower in that state. Hence, one would expect a negative relationship to arise between women's social status and the extent of gender-based discrimination in manufacturing employment. As regards labour market rigidity, it should bear a positive relationship with the extent of casualization in manufacturing firms (see Goldar and Aggarwal, 2012a and 2012b). Whether labour market rigidity should lead to greater gender discrimination is not clear a priori. However, that is certainly a possibility. It would be interesting to examine empirically if the extent of gender discrimination shows a positive relationship with the degree of labour market rigidity.

The rest of the chapter is organized as follows. Section 7.2 describes the data used for the analysis and presents a preliminary analysis of the data. Section 7.3 discusses the econometric model used for the analysis and presents the results. Section 7.4 is devoted to an analysis of inter-state differences in the extent of gender discrimination in manufacturing employment. Finally, section 7.5 summarizes and concludes.

7.2 Data and preliminary analysis

7.2.1 Data used for the analysis

The main data source used for the present chapter is the EUS conducted by the NSSO, Government of India. We use the data collected in the quinquennial rounds of 1999–2000 (55th round), 2004–05(61st round) and 2009–10 (66th round). Thus, the chapter covers the period, 1999–00 to 2009–10. From the unit-level data of these surveys, it is possible to identify the workers by their work status as well as the principal and subsidiary status of employed persons. Broadly, workers are categorized on the basis of status codes into self-employed (codes 11 to 21), regular workers (code 31) and casual workers (codes 41 and 51). NSSO (2013, page A-5) defines casual wage worker as 'A person who was casually engaged in other's farm and non-farm enterprises (both household and non-household) and, in return, received wages according to the terms of the daily or periodic work contract.' A regular salaried/wage worker, on the other hand, is defined as a person 'who worked in other's farm or non-farm enterprises (both household and non-household) and, in turn received salary or wages on a regular basis.' This category includes those persons who are getting time wage as well as those people who receive piece wage. It covers people getting a salary and paid apprentices, both full time and part time.

The analysis in the chapter is confined to those workers who according to their UPSS are engaged in manufacturing.[2] The preliminary analysis presented in this part of the chapter covers all UPSS workers in manufacturing. The econometric analysis presented in section 7.3, however, is confined only to paid workers, i.e., it leaves out the self-employed and considers the dichotomy between regular wage workers and casual wage workers.

7.2.2 Preliminary analysis of the data: Aggregate level and manufacturing industries

Table 7.1 shows the proportion of female workers in the total workforce in India and rural and urban sectors of the economy. It reveals that between 1999 and 2009 the share of females in total workforce has declined from 29.05 per cent to 27.55 per cent at the aggregate level. In rural India, the share of female workers in the total workforce is only about one third, and this share has reduced by over three percentage points over the period from 1999 to 2009. The implication is that the growth rate of employment in rural sector has been faster for male workers than for the female workers.

The share of female workers is smaller in urban India at 22.7 per cent in 2009. However, contrary to the trends observed for the rural sector, women's share has increased marginally in the urban sector over the period from 1999 to 2009. As a result of these employment growth trends, the composition of female workforce between rural and urban sectors has shifted in favour of urban female workforce. While in 1999, about two-thirds of the female workers were employed in rural areas, the share in 2009 was only 58 per cent – a decline of 9 percentage points.

Table 7.1: Proportion of female workers in rural and urban India

Sector/area	NSS rounds		
	66th (2009–10)	61st (2004–05)	55th (1999–00)
Rural	32.59	37.32	35.98
	57.99	64.35	67.14
Urban	22.71	23.57	20.85
	42.01	35.65	32.86
Total	27.55	30.89	29.05
	100	100	100

Note: The first row gives the proportion of female workers within the sector and second row gives the proportion out of total female workers.

Source: Authors' computations from NSS data on employment.

The distribution of women workers by work status is given in Table 7.2. A look at Table 7.2 makes it clear that not only are women losing in terms of their share in total workforce, which shows a downward trend, but there is also a tendency of casualization of female workforce. While the share of female workers has reduced both as self-employed and regular wage workers, their

Table 7.2: Proportion of female workers by work status

Work status	NSS rounds		
	66th (2009–10)	61st (2004–05)	55th (1999–00)
Self-employed	39.64	43.83	41.74
	69.43	71.67	74.47
Regular-wage	10.05	13.00	11.87
	11.81	13.12	12.39
Casual labour	26.67	25.67	21.42
	18.76	15.21	13.14
Total	27.55	30.89	29.05
	100	100	100

Note: The first row gives the proportion within the category and second row gives the proportion out of total females workers.

Source: Authors' computations from NSS data on employment.

Table 7.3: Proportion of female workers by education

Level of education (general education)	NSS Rounds		
	66th (2009–10)	61st (2004–05)	55th (1999–00)
Up to primary	37.25	40.76	39.87
	66.19	76.41	81.55
Middle to Hr. secondary	20.44	19.37	14.51
	30.58	21.22	17.22
Above Hr. secondary	9.06	8.89	5.88
	3.23	2.38	1.23
Total	27.55	30.89	29.05
	100	100	100

Note: The first row gives the proportion within the category and second row gives the proportion out of total female workers.

Source: Authors' computations from NSS data on employment.

share as casual labour has increased. The casualization of female workforce has taken place despite female workers acquiring higher education (see Table 7.3). The share of female workers with no or up to primary education has substantially reduced from four–fifths (81 per cent) of total female workforce in 1999 to two-thirds (66 per cent) in 2009. There are reasons to believe that improvement in the level of education among female workers should reduce the proportion of casual workers among them (Goldar and Aggarwal, 2012a, 2012b, and econometric findings of this study presented later in the chapter). It is thus remarkable to note that the extent of casualization has increased significantly among women workers despite their acquiring higher education.

Having discussed the overall situation, we now turn to manufacturing. The industry-wise distribution of female workers employed as regular workers or casual workers is shown in Tables A7.3 and A7.4. This is shown for various two-digit industries according to the NIC. Some key data are reproduced in Figures 7.1 and 7.2.

Figure 7.1: Proportion of female workers among regular workers, manufacturing, by industry and year

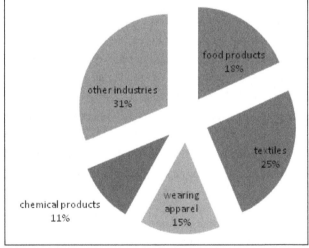

Source and *note:* Authors' computations from NSS data on employment. For description of industries, see Table A7.2. The industries in which the proportion in question was below 10 per cent in 2009–10 are not shown in the figure.

Figure 7.2: Industry-wise distribution of female workers in manufacturing having regular work status, 2009–10

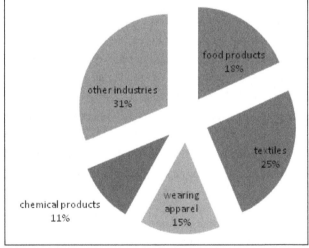

Source: Authors' computations from NSS data on employment.

The female workers intensity as regular employees is high only in industry 16 (manufacture of tobacco products). However, it is interesting to observe that the proportion of women employed among regular workers in this industry has declined from 85 per cent to just 54 per cent during the period from 1999 to 2009. In some of the industries, the share of women among regular workers is between 10 and 15 per cent, and it is lower in the rest of the industries. Considering the distribution of regularly employed women workers among various manufacturing industries, it is found that the industries which are the biggest source of regular employment to female workers are 15 (food products), 17 (textiles), 18 (wearing apparel), and 24 (chemical products). These four industries, together, account for almost two-thirds of the total regular female employment in manufacturing (Figure 7.2).

Because of increased casualization of female workers, we found that the proportion of women among casual workers was quite high in 2009 in several manufacturing industries (see Table A7.3). The proportion in question is relatively high in the following industries: 15 (food products), 16 (tobacco products), 17 (textiles), 18 (wearing apparel), 21 (paper and paper products), 22 (printing), 24 (chemical products), 26 (non-metallic mineral products), and 27 (basic metals) (see Figure 7.3). The share of females among casual workers has increased rapidly between 1999 and 2009 in some of these industries. These industries are 16 (tobacco products), 22 (printing), and 24 (chemical products), where it now is more than half.

Figure 7.3: Proportion of females among casual workers, manufacturing, by industry, 2009–10

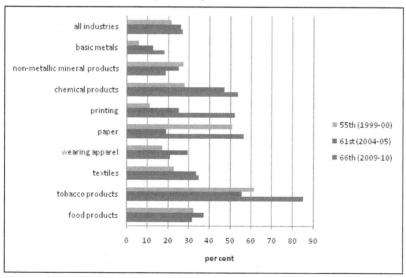

Source: Authors' computations from NSS data on employment.

The major industries which, account for bulk of the female casual workers within manufacturing are 15 (food products), 16 (tobacco products), 17 (textiles), and 26 (non-metallic mineral products). Taken together, these industries accounted for about 80 per cent of total female workforce engaged as casual workers in manufacturing in 2009–10.

Table 7.4 shows the distribution of male and female workers of manufacturing according to work status. The proportion of regular wage workers is relatively higher among males than females at the aggregate level and also for most industries. Also, it is interesting to note that while in certain industries almost all female workers have regular wage employment, in certain other industries (for example, tobacco products and non-metallic mineral products) only a small percentage of female workers have regular wage job.

Table 7.4: Distribution of male and female workers by work status, manufacturing, 2009–10

Industry (NIC code)	Male				Female			
	Self-employed	Regular wage	Casual labour	Total	Self-employed	Regular wage	Casual labour	Total
15	44.5	37.0	18.5	100	55.3	20.9	23.8	100
16	76.0	8.3	15.8	100	76.4	2.3	21.3	100
17	35.6	43.1	21.3	100	65.2	14.0	20.8	100
18	64.2	26.4	9.4	100	87.2	8.7	4.2	100
19	36.2	50.1	13.7	100	61.8	34.7	3.5	100
20	68.5	9.3	22.3	100	95.5	0.7	3.8	100
21	28.8	62.8	8.4	100	41.2	23.6	35.3	100
22	39.3	57.3	3.4	100	20.1	41.0	38.9	100
23	8.0	72.5	19.5	100	0.0	100.0	0.0	100
24	7.1	85.5	7.3	100	44.8	35.7	19.5	100
25	17.0	69.1	13.9	100	20.3	64.3	15.5	100
26	27.8	17.3	54.9	100	41.5	6.2	52.4	100
27	16.3	68.4	15.3	100	9.4	23.3	67.4	100
28	33.0	45.9	21.1	100	51.9	19.3	28.8	100

	Male				Female			
Industry (NIC code)	Self-employed	Regular wage	Casual labour	Total	Self-employed	Regular wage	Casual labour	Total
29	24.0	64.4	11.6	100	38.1	49.8	12.1	100
30	30.6	69.4	0.0	100	0.0	100.0	0.0	100
31	25.2	66.6	8.2	100	10.7	71.2	18.1	100
32	38.2	59.9	2.0	100	0.0	66.0	34.0	100
33	7.0	80.5	12.6	100	32.0	58.4	9.6	100
34	2.3	91.4	6.4	100	0.0	89.1	10.9	100
35	19.6	73.0	7.4	100	0.0	100.0	0.0	100
36	51.3	28.3	20.4	100	82.9	9.2	8.0	100
All	40.49	40.03	19.48	100	69.72	11.73	18.55	100

Source: Authors' computations from NSS data on employment.

The discrimination again female workers becomes visible more clearly when a comparison is made of the proportion of casual workers out of paid workers between males and females. This is shown in Figure 7.4. At the aggregate level, there is a gap of about 30 percentage points. The proportion of casual workers out of paid workers is about 33 per cent among male workers while the corresponding figure is about 61 per cent for female workers. For several two-digit industries, a large gap in the proportion of casual workers out of paid workers between males and females is visible in Figure 7.4. These include 27 (basic metals), 21 (paper and paper products), 32 (radio, television and communication equipment and apparatus), 28 (fabricated metal products), 16(tobacco products) and 17 (textiles). The gap is about 25 percentage points or more.

Figure 7.4: Casual worker percentage paid workers in manufacturing, males and females, by two-digit industries

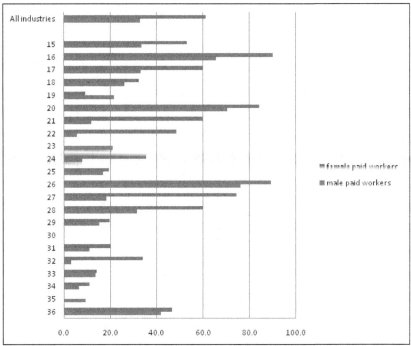

Source: Based on Table 7.4.

7.2.3 Preliminary analysis of the data: State-wise analysis for manufacturing industries

We now try to get a picture of gender discrimination in major States of India. The analysis is confined to major states. We first identify those states where the employment of female workers in manufacturing is noticeable (i.e., their share in total female workers in manufacturing is noticeable). The subsequent analysis is then done only for those states.

Table 7.5 provides the distribution of male and female workers by work-status in manufacturing in 2009–10 for major states. It is evident that overall the proportion of self-employed is higher among female workers (70 per cent approximately) as compared to male workers (40 per cent), while the opposite is true for regular and casual workers. The implication is that female workers are relatively more vulnerable in the job market and are less likely to get paid employment either as a regular or as a casual worker. The major states where self-employment among female workers (within manufacturing) is very high are Andhra Pradesh, Bihar, Chhattisgarh, Himachal Pradesh, Jammu and Kashmir, Jharkhand, Madhya Pradesh, Orissa, Rajasthan, Uttar Pradesh and West Bengal. Each of these states has more than 70 per cent self-employment among female workers. Casualization among female workers is high (more than 20 per cent) in the states of Assam, Chhattisgarh, Gujarat, Jharkhand, Kerala, Pondicherry, Tamil Nadu and West Bengal.

Figure 7.5 shows the extent of casualization among paid workers of manufacturing in different states, separately for males and females. It is evident that the extent of casualization among paid workers is greater among females than males. At the All-India level, the gap is about 30 percentage points, as noted earlier. The gap is relatively large in Bihar, Chhattisgarh, MP, UP and West Bengal. It is also interesting to observe that the extent of casualization among paid female workers of manufacturing differs widely across states. It ranges from 3 per cent in Uttaranchal to about 90 per cent or more in Bihar, Chhattisgarh, Jharkhand, UP and West Bengal. Let one consider the case of Jharkhand. About 80 per cent of the women workers in manufacturing are self-employed (presumably, these are mostly unpaid family workers employed in the family enterprises). Of the remaining 20 per cent of women workers covered in the survey, almost all are employed as casual workers and virtually none is employed as regular worker. Contrast this to the situation in Maharashtra. Out of the paid women workers in manufacturing, about two-thirds are working as regular workers and one third are working as casual workers. Why do we have so much inter-state differences in casualization of female paid workers in manufacturing, is an interesting question. This is obviously connected with gender discrimination in manufacturing employment. This issue is explored in section 7.4 of the chapter.

Table 7.5: Distribution of male and female worker by work status, manufacturing, 2009–10

State	Male				Female			
	Self-employed	Regular wage	Casual labour	Total	Self-employed	Regular wage	Casual labour	Total
Andhra Pradesh	40.58	37.98	21.44	100	71.18	13.04	15.77	100
Assam	53.7	19.84	26.45	100	42.85	7.93	49.23	100
Bihar	71.17	13.26	15.57	100	96.99	0	3.01	100
Chhattisgarh	44.44	28.38	27.19	100	77.30	0.16	22.20	100
Delhi	34.57	63.87	1.57	100	29.88	70.12	0	100
Gujarat	28.26	52.03	19.71	100	64.19	15.14	20.66	100
Haryana	21	72.98	6.02	100	55.7	27.75	16.54	100
Himachal Pradesh	45.84	32.18	21.98	100	78.18	9.94	11.88	100
Jharkhand	36.98	17.39	45.64	100	77.95	0	22.05	100
Karnataka	40.59	40.14	19.27	100	63.65	18.58	17.76	100
Kerala	34.41	28.42	37.17	100	39.95	15.92	44.13	100
Madhya Pradesh	60.22	31.24	8.54	100	87.03	5.45	7.52	100
Maharashtra	23.53	63.53	12.94	100	60.59	26.29	13.12	100
Orissa	57.93	24.53	17.53	100	88.42	3.89	7.7	100
Punjab	31.35	51.2	17.45	100	69.54	15.41	15.06	100
Rajasthan	57.55	27.53	14.92	100	80.09	7.66	12.24	100
Tamil Nadu	28.77	48.25	22.98	100	54.1	20.56	25.35	100
Uttar Pradesh	52.77	23.96	23.27	100	88.12	1.28	10.6	100
Uttaranchal	37.16	47.87	14.97	100	75.37	23.95	0.68	100
West Bengal	45.17	28.77	26.06	100	74.08	2.52	23.39	100
Total	**40.49**	**40.03**	**19.48**	**100**	**69.72**	**11.73**	**18.55**	**100**

Source: Authors' computations from NSS data on employment.

Figure 7.5: Casual worker percentage paid workers in manufacturing, males and females, by state

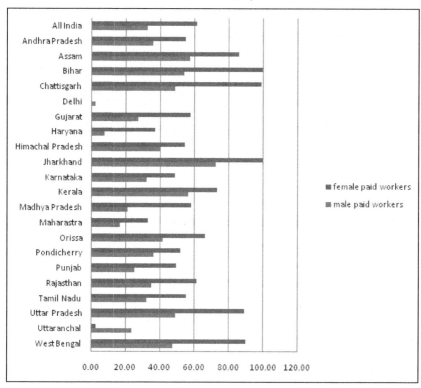

Source: Based on Table 7.5.

Details of employment of female among regular and casual workers in different industries in different major states in 2009 are provided in Tables A7.5 and A7.6.[3] An examination of female employment intensities given in these appendices reveals that there are only four major states, namely Andhra Pradesh, Karnataka, Kerala and Tamil Nadu where the share of female workers out of regular workers in manufacturing is around 20 per cent or more. The intensity of female workers employment among regular workers is relatively high mainly in industries 15 (food products), 16 (tobacco products), 17 (textiles), 22 (printing) and 25 (rubber and plastic products). However, in different states, it is a different set of industries which employ more of female regular workers. Andhra Pradesh has a high proportion of female workers among regular workers in industries 15, 16, 17, 18, 25, 26, 29 and 32; the ratio is highest in industry 18 (manufacture of wearing apparel; dressing and dyeing of fur), where 74 per cent of the regular workers are females. On the other hand, in Tamil Nadu, the intensity of female workers among regular workers is high in industry 16 (manufacture of tobacco products).

For casual female workers, the distribution is more scattered (see Table A7.6). In almost all major states there exists female employment in casual labour in significant proportion. It is high – more than 30 per cent – in the states of Andhra Pradesh, Assam, Haryana, Karnataka, Kerala, Madhya Pradesh, Tamil Nadu and West Bengal. However, the concentration of female casual workers is again different in different industries in these States. While in the State of Andhra Pradesh, the proportion of female worker out of casual workers is relatively high in industries 16, 18 and 22, in the State of Kerala the intensity is relatively high in the industries 15, 16, 17, 18 and 24.

7.3 Econometric model and results

As mentioned above, the econometric analysis is confined to the paid workers in manufacturing. The self-employed workers are excluded from the analysis. The question asked is what factors determine the work status of a worker, the dichotomy between regular wage employment and casual wage employment. A Logit model has been estimated for the analysis using data on both male and female paid workers in manufacturing.

7.3.1 Specification of the model

The econometric model for explaining work status of a person engaged in manufacturing is specified as follows:

SW = f (education, age, sex, ORG, urban area dummy, SC/ST dummy, industry dummies) (Equation 7.1)

The dependent variable (SW) is the status of the worker. It takes value one for a casual worker and zero for regular wage worker. The explanatory variables include the age and education level of the individual. To represent education, a set of dummy variables corresponding to different levels of education have been used. Whether the individual belongs to Scheduled Castes/Scheduled Tribes (SC/ST) community is taken as a dummy variable. It takes value one if the individual belongs to SC/ST community This allows for the possibility that an individual belonging to SC/ST community may be at a disadvantage in getting a regular job in manufacturing even if he/she is of the same age, experience and education level as that of an individual not belonging to SC/ST community.

To take into account inter-industry differences, industry dummies are included in the model. Industries may differ in regard to the scale of demand fluctuations they face. They may differ also in terms of the nature of work done by the workers. These factors would give rise to inter-industry differences in the extent of casual employment. Indeed, the discussion in the previous section brought out that there are significant differences in the extent of casualization among different manufacturing industries. It is important to incorporate this aspect into the econometric analysis, which is done by including industry dummies in the model.

Two other variables used in the model are based on the nature of the enterprise where the individual works. One dummy variable reflects whether the enterprise is situated in an urban area. The other dummy variable (ORG) reflects whether the enterprise is in the organized sector (i.e., employing 10 or more workers with power or 20 or more workers without power).

Gender discrimination is captured by introducing a dummy variable (sex of the worker) in the model. It takes value one for female workers and zero for male workers. A positive coefficient of this dummy variable signifies gender discrimination. The higher the coefficient, the greater is the gender discrimination.

Estimation of parameters has been done by applying the Logit model. Unit level data of the employment-unemployment survey of the three rounds, 55th, 61st and 66th are utilized. In some cases, the data of the three rounds are pooled. In other cases, the data of the three rounds are used separately. When the model in equation (7.1) above is estimated from data pooled across three rounds, 55th, 61st and 66th rounds, dummy variables for the rounds are included in the model.

7.3.2 Aggregate level analysis

Table 7.6 shows the estimates of the model obtained when data for all states and manufacturing industries are combined. The results in the first three columns are respectively for the three rounds being considered for this study. In the last two columns, the data for the three rounds have been pooled. In one of these models, dummy variables for rounds have been included, and in the other one this has not been done.

The results indicate that with age (reflecting experience) and education, a person enhances his/her prospects of getting a regular job rather than a casual job. The coefficients of the education related dummy variables are significantly negative and increase in numerical value with the level of education considered. The interpretation of this finding is that the probability of being in a regular job increases with education. The higher the level of education of an individual, the greater is the likelihood of his/her being in a regular job. This is consistent with the findings of Goldar and Aggarwal (2012a, 2012b).

The coefficients of the organized sector dummy and urban area dummy are negative and statistically significant. These findings imply that a person working in an organized sector manufacturing enterprise is more likely to be in a regular job as compared to a similar person working in an unorganized sector manufacturing enterprise. Similarly, a person working in a manufacturing enterprise in urban areas is more likely to be in regular job than a similar person working in a manufacturing enterprise in rural areas.

The finding of a positive and statistically significant coefficient of the dummy variable for persons belonging to SC/ST community points to some disadvantage such persons have in getting a regular job. The coefficient is, however, low in numerical value and therefore it seems that the disadvantage is probably not large.

Table 7.6: Estimates of the logit model explaining casual employment in Indian manufacturing

Explanatory variables	66th round (2009–10)	61st round (2004–05)	55th round (1999–00)	Pooled	Pooled (with round dummies)
Organized sector enterprise (dummy)	-0.937 (-10.64)	-0.820 (-11.07)	-0.799 (-13.70)	-0.880 (20.14)	-0.878 (-20.07)
Urban area enterprise (dummy)	-0.975 (-11.22)	-0.885 (-12.49)	-0.936 (-16.07)	-0.931 (21.99)	-0.935 (-21.93)
Age	-0.003 (-0.83)	-0.014 (-4.72)	-0.013 (-5.27)	-0.009 (-5.48)	-0.010 (-5.76)
Education:					
Primary	-0.484 (-3.83)	-0.391 (-4.23)	-0.399 (-5.03)	-0.402(-6.83)	-0.412 (-7.00)

Explanatory variables	66th round (2009–10)	61st round (2004–05)	55th round (1999–00)	Pooled	Pooled (with round dummies)
Middle	-0.525 (-4.67)	-0.647 (-6.72)	-0.496 (-6.89)	-0.525 (-9.58)	-0.538 (-9.79)
Secondary	-1.069 (-8.77)	-1.114 (-9.29)	-1.103 (-12.24)	-1.065 (-16.48)	-1.08 (-16.67)
Hr. secondary	-1.480 (-7.86)	-1.801 (-8.71)	-1.883 (-2.25)	-1.561 (-11.93)	-1.60 (-12.10)
Diploma	-2.229 (-4.74)	-1.921(-7.73)	-4.825 (-6.31)	-.2.067 (-9.09)	-2.087 (-9.23)
Graduate and above	-2.221 (-9.47)	-3.470 (-8.54)	-2.448 (-10.98)	-2.516 (-15.97)	-2.546 (-16.23)
Belongs to SC/ST (dummy)	0.283 (6.27)	0.064 (0.82)	0.162 (2.67)	0.162 (3.49)	0.119 (2.53)
Female worker (dummy)	0.801 (6.27)	0.716 (7.26)	0.409 (5.44)	0.669 (10.99)	0.667 (10.92)
Industry dummies	Yes	Yes	Yes	Yes	Yes
Round 2 (dummy)					-0.034 (−0.78)
Round 3 (dummy)					0.151 (2.95)
No. of observations	9090	11561	15497	36219	36219
Wald chi-square (df)	1063.6(32)	1263.9(33)	1793.4 (32)	3537.6(33)	3539.0 (35)
Pseudo-R-squared	0.299	0.279	0.237	0.265	0.266

Note: The dependent variable is a dichotomous one representing the status of the worker. It takes value one for casual workers and zero for regular workers ('t' statistics).

Source: Authors' computations from NSS data on employment.

The coefficient of the gender dummy variable is positive and statistically significant. It seems therefore that there is significant gender discrimination in manufacturing employment.[4] Other things being equal, a women worker is more likely to be in a casual job than a male worker. It is interesting to observe that the coefficient estimated from data for the 61st round (2004–05) is higher than that estimated from data for the 56th round (1999–2000). There is a further increase in the numerical value of the coefficient when data for the 66th round (2009–10) are used. Evidently, the results do not show a downward trend in gender based discrimination in manufacturing employment in the period 1999 to 2009. Rather, there are signs of an upward trend. Thus, the hypothesis that economic reform would lower gender based discrimination in manufacturing employment is not supported by the data. These results are in harmony with the findings of Menon and Rodgers (2007) who have investigated the impact of industrial concentration and international trade competition on the residual male-female wage gap in Indian manufacturing industries. They use data for the period 1983 to 2004–05 and find that openness to trade is associated with a widening of the male-female wage gap. Clearly, this is consistent with the findings of the present chapter.

7.3.3 State-level analysis

The analysis presented in earlier revealed marked differences across states in the extent of casualization of women workers in manufacturing. A part of the observed differences in casualization is attributable to difference in the industry composition across states (industry composition will make an impact because the proportion of casual workers varies significantly from one industry to another). Also, the women workers of different states may differ in terms of their educational attainments. Thus, for a proper assessment of gender discrimination in manufacturing employment in different states, the Logit model described in Section 3.1 above needs to be estimated separately for different states. This has been done and the results are reported in Table A7.7.

Estimation of the Logit model has been done for only for those states for which at least 300 observations could be obtained after pooling data for the three rounds, 55th, 61st and 66th. Accordingly, model estimation has been done for 17 states. An exception has been allowed in the cases of Chhattisgarh and Uttaranchal. The model has been estimated for these two states even though the number of observations after pooling of data from the three rounds falls short of 300. Thus, altogether, the estimation of the model has been done for 19 states.

From the model estimates given in Table A7.7, it is seen that there is a good deal of similarity in the results of the Logit model obtained for different states. In most cases, the coefficients of the organized sector dummy variable and the urban area dummy variable are negative and statistically significant.

The coefficient of age is negative in most cases and statistically significant in many of them. The state level results uniformly indicate that with higher level of education, the probability of being in a regular job goes up and the probability of being in a casual job goes down.

Table 7.7: Inter-state variation in the estimated coefficient of the female worker dummy and the proportion casual workers among female paid workers in manufacturing

State	Coefficient of female worker dummy (t-ratio in parentheses)	Casual worker % paid female workers in manufacturing
Jharkhand	5.329 (3.81)	100.00
Chhattisgarh	3.026 (2.59)	99.30
Assam	2.413 (3.31)	86.13
Gujarat	1.835 (5.63)	57.71
Haryana	1.513(3.58)	37.34
West Bengal	1.255(5.26)	90.27
Rajasthan	1.251(3.87)	61.51
Uttar Pradesh	1.109(3.82)	89.23
Bihar	0.914(1.84)	100.00
Kerala	0.731 (4.05)	73.49
Maharashtra	0.535 (2.68)	33.29
Karnataka	0.527 (1.77)	48.87
Madhya Pradesh	0.523 (2.30)	57.98
Orissa	0.376 (0.84)	66.44
Punjab	0.285(0.71)	49.43
Tamil Nadu	0.274 (2.28)	55.22
Andhra Pradesh	–0.155 (–0.55)	54.74
Pondicherry	–0.437 (0.87)	52.03
Uttaranchal	–2.466 (–2.13)	2.76

Source: Based on Table A7.7 and Table 7.5.

As regards the coefficient of the female worker dummy variable which is the main variable of interest, the coefficient varies widely across states, both in terms of numerical value and the level of statistical significant. In some cases (Andhra Pradesh, Pondicherry and Uttaranchal), the coefficient is found to be negative. The results indicate that there is very little or no gender discrimination in manufacturing employment in these states. By contrast, the coefficient is positive, relatively high in numerical value and statistically significant in the estimates obtained for Assam, Chhattisgarh, Gujarat, Haryana and Jharkhand. It seems that gender discrimination in manufacturing employment is relatively greater in these states.

Table 7.7 compares the estimated coefficient of the female worker dummy for the 19 states for which the econometric model has been estimated and the proportion casual female workers out of female paid workers in manufacturing in 2009–10. In the table, the states have been ordered according to the numerical value of the estimated coefficient of the female worker dummy. The estimated coefficient obtained from the Logit model which may be interpreted as an indicator of gender discrimination bears a positive correlation with the extent of casualization shown in the last column of the table. The correlation coefficient is 0.72. It is statistically significant. It seems the observed inter-state variation in the extent of casualization of female labour engaged in manufacturing has a lot to do with discrimination against women in manufacturing employment.

7.4 Explaining inter-state differences in gender discrimination

From the results of the econometric analysis presented in the previous section, it appears that there are substantial inter-state differences in the degree of gender based discrimination in manufacturing employment. What explains these differences? Two factors are considered in this chapter: (1) labour market rigidity; and (2) women's social status and empowerment.

To assess the effect of labour market rigidity, the econometric model specified in equation (7.1) above has been estimated separately for two groups of states, one marked by flexible labour market, the other by inflexible labour market. The results for 55th round and 66th round are reported in Table 7.8. The classification of states of India into these two groups follows that used by Ramaswamy (2013, Table A4, 40; a modified classification based on Besley and Burgess, 2004). According to Ramaswamy, the states with flexible labour market are Andhra Pradesh, Gujarat, Karnataka, Rajasthan, Uttar Pradesh and

Tamil Nadu. The states with inflexible labour market include Assam, Bihar, Jharkhand, Haryana, Kerala, Madhya Pradesh, Chhattisgarh, Maharashtra, Orissa, Punjab and West Bengal.

Table 7.8: Estimates of the Logit model explaining casual employment, 55th Round (1999–2000) and 66th Round (2009–10), states grouped according to the degree of labour market flexibility

Explanatory variables	55th Round, 1999–00		66th Round, 2009–00	
	States with flexible labour market	States with inflexible labour market	States with flexible labour market	States with inflexible labour market
Organized sector enterprise (dummy)	-0.809 (-10.18)	-0.850 (-9.26)	-1.004 (-8.05)	-0.979 (-7.60)
Urban area enterprise (dummy)	-0.606 (-7.62)	-1.403 (-15.99)	-0.957 (-7.48)	-1.037(-8.43)
Age	-0.0115 (-3.39)	-0.0170 (-4.78)	0.0031(0.65)	-0.0104 (-2.21)
Education:				
Primary	-0.485 (-4.39)	-0.379(-3.21)	-0.659 (-3.48)	-0.263 (-1.62)
Middle	-0.529(-5.37)	-0.515(-4.80)	-0.519 (-3.16)	-0.587 (-3.60)
Secondary	-1.101 (-8.37)	-1.104 (-8.37)	-1.118 (-6.45)	-0.958 (-5.21)
Hr. secondary	-0.908 (-1.00)	@	-1.64 (-6.29)	-1.095 (-4.27)
Diploma	-5.381 (-5.22)	-4.56(-4.25)	-2.165 (-3.47)	-2.347 (-4.89)
Graduate and above	-2.588 (-8.40)	-2.263 (-7.04)	-2.433 (-6.46)	-2.011 (-6.42)
Belongs to SC/ST (dummy)	0.228 (2.47)	0.221 (2.25)	0.391 (1.75)	0.138 (0.83)
Female worker (dummy)	0.180 (1.73)	0.887 (7.63)	0.596 (3.38)	1.130(7.23)
Industry dummies	Yes	Yes	Yes	Yes
No. of observations	7177	7211	3742	4671

Explanatory variables	55th Round, 1999–00		66th Round, 2009–00	
	States with flexible labour market	States with inflexible labour market	States with flexible labour market	States with inflexible labour market
Wald chi-square (df)	893.2 (32)	1149.2 (30)	515.7 (30)	653.2(32)
Pseudo-R-squared	0.21	0.33	0.27	0.35

Notes: The dependent variable is a dichotomous one representing the status of the worker. It takes value one for casual workers and zero for regular workers. States have been divided into three groups: (a) those with flexible labour market, (b) those with inflexible labour market, and (c) other states. The results for groups (a) and (b) are shown. The results for group (c) are not shown.

@ In the model estimates for Round 55, states with inflexible labour market, the individuals with higher secondary education (39 observations) get dropped from the Logit model, as the model predicts the worker status perfectly for those cases ('t' statistics).

Source: Authors' computations from NSS data on employment

It is seen from Table 7.8 that the estimated coefficient of the model estimated for states with flexible labour market are quite similar to the estimated coefficients of the model estimated for the states with inflexible labour market. The coefficient of the female worker dummy, however, differs considerably. The coefficient is lower for the states with greater labour market flexibility. This pattern is seen in the results for the 55th round as well as the results for the 66th round (the same pattern is seen in the results for 61st round which have not been reported in the table). The results suggest that gender discrimination in manufacturing thrives when the labour market is rigid, and the extent of discrimination comes down as the labour market becomes more flexible.

To examine the relationship between gender based discrimination and women's social status and empowerment, correlation coefficients have been computed between the estimated coefficients of the women workers dummy obtained for different states (see Table 7.7) and a set of variables representing women's social status and empowerment. A negative correlation coefficient is expected, and it is seen from Table 7.9 that the computed correlation coefficient is indeed negative in five of the seven variables considered. In some cases, the coefficient is found to be statistically significant at five per cent level.

Table 7.9: Correlation coefficients between the estimated degree of gender discrimination and variables representing women's social status and empowerment across states

Variable representing women's social status and empowerment		Correlation coefficient with the estimated degree of gender discrimination in manufacturing employment (rank correlation coefficient in parentheses)
Variable no.	Description	
V1	Proportion of women among entrepreneurs of micro, small and medium industrial enterprises in different states	-0.27 (-0.46)
V2	Gross enrolment ratio in classes I–V among female children of age 6 to 10 years	0 .42(0.13)
V3	Gross enrolment ratio in classes VI–VIII among female children of age 11 to 13 years	-0.48 (-0.53)
V4	Percentage of women of age 20–49 who have at least 10 years of education	-0.42 (-0.43)
V5	Among women of age 15–49 employed in the past 12 months (at the time of NFHS-3 {National Family Health Survey} survey) the percentage in professional/ technical/ managerial occupations	-0.18 (-0.24)
V6	Percentage of women of age 15 to 49 with a bank or savings account they themselves use	-0.30 (-0.38)
V7	Currently married women of age 15–49 who are employed for cash and who have the main say alone or jointly, in how their earnings are used (percentage)	0.21(0.17)

Source: V1: Computed from Final Report of the Fourth All India Census of Micro, Small and Medium Enterprises, 2006–07, Registered Sector, Development Commissioner, MSME, Ministry of Micro, Small and Medium Enterprises, Government of India. V2 and V3: Statistics of School Education, 2010–11 (provisional). V4–V7: Kishor and Gupta (2009), based on NFHS-3.

7.5 Conclusion

In this chapter, gender discrimination in job tenure (regular jobs versus casual jobs) in manufacturing employment was examined using unit level data of NSS employment-unemployment surveys for 1999–2000, 2004–05 and 2009–10. The results of the analysis revealed that there is significant gender discrimination in manufacturing employment in India. Though there is grounds to expect that trade liberalization would lower the extent of gender discrimination in India, the results of the analysis presented in the chapter did not reveal any downward trend in gender based discrimination, confirming the findings of some earlier studies.

State-level analysis revealed significant variation in the extent of gender discrimination across states. It is found that the extent of gender discrimination bears an inverse relationship with labour market flexibility. Thus, gender discrimination is relatively less for those states which have a more flexible industrial labour market. There are indications from the empirical analysis that the extent of gender discrimination in manufacturing employment is relatively less in the states that have better social status of women and greater women empowerment.

The results of the econometric analysis raise several questions. Why increased competition in Indian manufacturing in the post-reform period has not been associated with a reduction in gender-based discrimination remains a puzzle. Why labour market flexibility should result in lower gender-based discrimination is another puzzle. There are indications from our results that increased labour market flexibility tends to reduce use of casual labour. But, why the reduction should be relatively more for female workers than male workers needs explanation. These are some of the questions that will be addressed in future research.

The results of our analysis relating to the impact of women's social status and empowerment on gender based discrimination revealed a negative correlation between the two. Separate analysis of gender-based discrimination for women belonging to different social classes can provide further insight. This is an issue we hope to take up in our future research.

Appendix

Table A7.1: Distribution of female workers in manufacturing by work status, according to UPSS and UPS

Work status	66th round (2009–10)		61st round (2004–05)		55th round (1999–2000)	
	UPSS	UPS	UPSS	UPS	UPSS	UPS
Self-employed	69.72	67.42	71.84	68.10	74.51	70.45
Regular-wage	11.73	14.16	13.04	15.95	12.40	15.45
Casual labour	18.55	18.43	15.12	15.95	13.10	14.10
Total	100	100	100	100	100	100

Source: Authors' computations from NSS data on employment.

Table A7.2: List of manufacturing industries, according to NIC, 1998

NIC 1998 code	Industry description
15	manufacture of food products and beverages
16	manufacture of tobacco products
17	manufacture of textiles
18	manufacture of wearing apparel; dressing and dyeing of fur
19	tanning and dressing of leather; manufacture of luggage, handbags, saddlery, harness and footwear
20	manufacture of wood and of products of wood and cork, except furniture; manufacture of articles of straw and plaiting
21	manufacture of paper and paper products
22	publishing, printing and reproduction of recorded media
23	manufacture of coke, refined petroleum products and nuclear fuel
24	manufacture of chemicals and chemical products
25	manufacture of rubber and plastics products
26	manufacture of other non-metallic mineral products

NIC 1998 code	Industry description
27	manufacture of basic metals
28	manufacture of fabricated metal products, except machinery and equipment
29	manufacture of machinery and equipment N.E.C.
30	manufacture of office, accounting and computing machinery
31	manufacture of electrical machinery and apparatus N.E.C.
32	manufacture of radio, television and communication equipment and apparatus
33	manufacture of medical, precision and optical instruments, watches and clocks
34	manufacture of motor vehicles, trailers and semi-trailers
35	manufacture of other transport equipment
36	manufacture of furniture; manufacturing N.E.C.
37	recycling

Table A7.3: Proportion of regular employed female workers in different manufacturing industries

Industry / rounds→	66th (2009–10)	61st (2004–05)	55th (1999–2000)
15	16.78	12.47	8.62
	18.44	9.16	8.90
16	54.12	73.23	85.68
	4.72	25.18	24.96
17	14.99	10.30	13.24
	25.15	13.34	18.36
18	16.73	18.88	26.57
	14.77	10.90	11.09
19	7.50	18.17	10.39
	2.06	5.58	2.24
20	1.92	3.94	5.86
	0.31	0.63	1.03

Industry / rounds→	66th (2009–10)	61st (2004–05)	55th (1999–2000)
21	10.54	4.36	8.30
	1.72	0.69	1.44
22	6.32	12.89	10.09
	2.25	3.86	3.05
24	14.72	22.32	13.75
	10.56	12.84	9.19
25	13.16	5.87	5.55
	3.79	1.53	2.08
26	7.99	9.13	6.25
	3.13	2.76	2.06
27	1.61	1.30	4.27
	0.90	0.42	1.92
28	2.21	2.94	1.48
	1.33	1.68	1.03
29	2.71	5.13	2.27
	1.67	2.12	1.10
31	5.39	8.25	10.62
	2.12	1.55	4.84
34	4.15	0.87	1.83
	1.68	0.23	0.26
35	0.73	4.41	4.51
	0.27	0.72	0.73
36	4.49	6.85	5.78
	3.02	3.83	2.43
All	10.05	13.00	11.87
	100	100	100

Note: The first row gives the proportion within the sector/ industry (females among regular workers) and second row gives the proportion of total female regular workers in manufacturing. The description of industries is given in Table A7.2.

Source: Authors' computations from NSS data on employment.

Table A7.4: Proportion of casually employed female workers in different manufacturing industries

Rounds→	66th (2009–10)	61st (2004–05)	55th (1999–2000)
Industry			
15	31.41	37.00	32.08
	13.18	17.65	21.91
16	85.11	55.45	61.32
	27.53	10.19	12.61
17	34.65	33.30	22.70
	23.79	24.61	19.60
18	20.87	29.24	17.07
	4.33	3.78	3.05
19	2.23	4.23	10.38
	0.10	0.33	1.60
20	4.63	8.44	3.18
	1.18	2.37	1.26
21	56.27	18.91	50.82
	1.55	0.54	0.67
22	52.08	24.77	11.08
	1.37	0.50	0.58
24	53.57	46.79	27.83
	3.69	7.54	4.07
25	16.42	29.19	14.62
	0.58	0.96	1.09
26	18.56	24.74	27.17
	16.67	24.87	25.76
27	17.87	12.46	5.55
	1.68	0.88	0.56
28	6.65	1.33	3.17
	1.23	0.25	0.75
29	3.68	6.82	3.01
	0.26	0.36	0.25

Rounds→	66th (2009–10)	61st (2004–05)	55th (1999–2000)
Industry			
31	10.53	39.21	18.98
	0.34	0.74	0.51
34	7.12	19.43	13.98
	0.13	0.62	0.46
35	0.00	0.00	0.62
	0.00	0.00	0.01
36	5.58	10.02	9.73
	1.72	3.56	3.92
All	26.67	25.67	21.42
	100	100	100

Note: The first row gives the proportion within the sector/industry (females among casual workers) and second row gives the proportion of total female casual workers in manufacturing. The description of industries is given in Table A7.2.

Source: Authors' computations from NSS data on employment.

210 | Bishwanath Goldar and Suresh Chand Aggarwal

Table A7.5: Proportion of female workers among regular workers in each manufacturing industry for each of the major states (66th round, 2009–10)

State↓/industry→	15	16	17	18	19	22	24	25	26	27	28	29	31	32	33	35	36	Total
Andhra Pradesh	38.4	49.1	27.9	73.8	0.0	0.9	7.8	24.9	26.1	1.4	0.0	25.0	7.3	26.5	0.0	3.5	18.4	20.0
Assam	5.0	–	65.2	0.0	–	–	0.0	0.0	0.0	–	–	0.0	–	–	–	–	0.0	8.7
Chhattisgarh	0	–	0	–	–	0	0	0	–	–	–	●	0	17.2	0	0	0	0.1
Delhi	0.0	–	69.7	12.7	0.0	0.0	0.0	0.0	0.0	0.0	0.0	0.0	12.4	0.0	0.0	0.0	0.0	4.8
Goa	0.0	–	0.0	–	–	–	8.2	0.0	0.0	6.4	12.9	0.0	0.0	–	0.0	0.0	0.0	9.7
Gujarat	0.0	0.0	8.6	0.0	0.0	0.0	7.5	0.0	0.0	0.0	38.7	0.0	0.0	0.0	26.3	0.0	1.1	4.7
Haryana	0.0	0.0	22.7	13.6	0.0	0.0	1.0	0.0	24.0	0.0	5.3	0.0	0.0	0.0	0.0	0.0	0.0	6.9
Himachal Pradesh	0.0	0.0	–	0.0	0.0	42.1	16.2	0.0	0.0	–	0.0	–	0.0	–	–	–	0.0	7.1
Karnataka	34.6	100.0	11.7	33.8	100.0	40.1	9.3	34.8	4.8	25.2	0.0	0.0	23.0	37.7	0.0	0.0	0.0	19.6
Kerala	72.4	–	47.9	82.4	0.0	5.3	0.0	20.3	19.1	0.0	0.0	0.0	10.6	18.8	0.0	3.7	1.0	30.5
Maharashtra	3.6	6.0	4.3	18.5	0.0	5.3	21.5	0.0	15.0	1.0	0.0	4.1	5.8	0.0	0.0	1.1	9.6	7.8
Madhya Pradesh	2.5	0.0	2.3	0.0	25.8	26.3	0.0	40.3	0.0	5.4	0.0	5.3	14.6	–	83.7	0.0	0.0	9.6
Orissa	26.3	95.1	0.0	0.0	–	15.9	0.0	0.0	0.0	2.0	0.0	0.0	0.0	0.0	–	0.0	0.0	8.9
Punjab	11.7	–	10.2	7.4	17.8	0.0	13.9	0.0	0.0	12.5	0.0	0.2	0.0	0.0	0.0	0.0	0.0	5.2
Rajasthan	17.0	100.0	11.6	8.3	–	48.0	0.0	0.0	0.0	0.0	0.0	0.0	0.0	0.0	–	0.0	0.0	7.9
Tamil Nadu	15.8	97.0	26.8	21.1	25.1	3.6	37.6	24.9	26.0	0.0	4.7	3.6	0.0	0.0	33.1	0.0	16.6	19.8
Uttaranchal	17.6	–	0.0	0.0	0.0	0.0	22.9	0.0	0.0	0.0	0.0	0.0	0.0	0.0	–	0.0	0.0	6.7
West Bengal	13.2	84.0	2.3	0.0	0.0	0.0	7.5	0.0	2.1	0.0	0.0	0.0	0.0	0.0	0.0	0.0	0.0	4.6

Note: The proportions are out of total regular workers in a particular industry in a particular state.

Source: Authors' computations from NSS data on employment.

Table A7.6: Proportion of female workers among casual workers in each manufacturing industry for each of the major states (66th round, 2009–10)

State ↓ / industry →	15	16	17	18	19	22	24	25	26	27	28	29	31	32	33	35	36	Total
Andhra Pradesh	25.9	80.5	37.3	47.6	0.0	76.4	0.0	10.7	30.4	3.3	0.0	0.0	–	–	–	0.0	3.2	34.8
Assam	73.3	100.0	62.1	–	–	–	0.0	–	13.9	–	0.0	–	–	–	–	–	0.0	30.7
Chhattisgarh	29.2	6.2	–	0.0	–	–	–	–	8.8	19.6	0.0	–	–	–	–	–	0.0	16.7
Gujarat	7.9	–	54.5	0.0	0.0	0.0	1.5	9.5	0.0	8.2	0.0	0.0	0.0	–	54.3	0.0	3.7	15.1
Haryana	0.0	–	67.7	45.6	–	–	–	0.0	17.6	0.0	–	0.0	0.0	–	–	–	100.0	34.7
Himachal Pradesh	0.0	–	–	–	–	–	–	–	26.8	–	–	–	–	–	–	–	–	11.7
Jharkhand	100.0	2.2	0.0	0.0	–	–	0.0	–	20.4	0.0	0.0	28.5	–	–	–	0.0	–	15.8
Karnataka	37.5	100.0	38.6	33.3	–	0.0	73.0	0.0	36.7	0.0	0.0	0.0	0.0	–	–	0.0	6.2	32.7
Kerala	80.0	99.1	68.2	63.2	0.0	16.5	88.0	0.0	19.3	–	2.2	0.0	0.0	–	–	0.0	3.1	48.2
Maharashtra	24.8	86.2	7.5	41.0	0.0	0.0	0.0	0.0	26.7	4.5	0.0	0.0	0.0	83.2	0.0	0.0	0.0	17.2
Madhya Pradesh	44.0	100.0	13.8	0.0	–	0.0	100.0	0.0	40.8	–	0.0	–	0.0	–	–	–	100.0	34.8
Orissa	26.2	100.0	36.0	20.2	–	–	0.0	–	21.1	18.3	0.0	0.0	–	–	–	–	0.0	21.2
Punjab	0.0	–	61.6	–	–	–	0.0	100.0	12.8	0.0	0.0	0.0	0.0	–	–	–	0.0	13.6
Rajasthan	0.0	81.1	22.7	0.0	–	–	100.0	–	30.0	0.0	0.0	0.0	0.0	–	–	–	0.0	20.2
Tamil Nadu	37.8	100.0	50.2	25.2	0.0	62.0	50.9	43.0	25.3	70.2	23.4	0.0	0.0	–	–	–	14.6	38.9
Uttar Pradesh	0.0	47.5	10.4	0.0	0.0	–	0.0	0.0	12.4	0.0	0.0	0.0	22.3	0.0	0.0	–	8.5	10.7
West Bengal	5.9	97.0	16.0	3.0	4.1	51.0	0.0	4.9	8.3	2.9	2.8	18.7	54.8	–	–	0.0	0.0	33.3

Note: The proportions are out of total casual workers in a particular industry in a particular state.
Source: Authors' computations from NSS data on employment.

Table A7.7: State-wise estimates of the model explaining casual employment (data for three rounds are pooled)

Explanatory variables	Punjab	Haryana	Rajasthan	Uttar Pradesh
Organized sector enterprise (dummy)	0.261 (1.06)	-0.362 (-1.07)	0.790 (-3.09)	-0.799 (-5.77)
Urban area enterprise (dummy)	-0.962 (-2.79)	-0.713 (-2.22)	-0.991 (-4.11)	-1.076 (-7.79)
Age	-0.0009 (-0.11)	-0.0108 (-0.83)	-0.0046 (-0.41)	0.0071 (-1.39)
Education:				
Primary	-0.402 (-1.44)	-0.214 (-0.59)	0.243 (0.81)	-0.855 (-4.68)
Middle	-0.839 (-2.54)	-0.407 (-0.93)	-0.414 (-1.42)	-0.581 (-3.43)
Secondary	-0.921 (-3.09)	-1.103 (-2.05)	-1.067 (-2.27)	-1.556 (-7.54)
Hr. secondary	-2.234 (-3.18)	-0.449 (-0.59)	-1.040 (-1.44)	-2.221 (-5.67)
Diploma		0.971 (0.55)		-3.844 (-3.92)
Graduate and above	-6.091 (-5.74)	-2.915 (-2.51)	-4.403 (-4.13)	-2.426 (-5.86)
Belongs to SC/ST (dummy)	0.732 (2.13)	0.729 (2.03)	-0.153 (0.50)	0.686 (4.26)
Female worker (dummy)	0.285 (0.71)	1.513 (3.58)	1.251 (3.87)	1.109 (3.82)
Industry dummies	Yes	Yes	Yes	Yes
Round dummies	Yes	Yes	Yes	Yes
No. of observations	1507	867	910	3305
Wald chi-square (df)	271.2 (27)	172.7 (26)	163.1 (27)	556.9 (32)
Pseudo-R-squared	0.355	0.459	0.239	0.339

Note: The dependent variable is a dichotomous one representing the status of the worker. It takes value one for casual workers and zero for regular workers ('t' statistics).

Source: Authors' computations from NSS data on employment.

Table A7.7: State-wise estimates of the model explaining casual employment (data for three rounds are pooled) (*continued*)

Explanatory variables	Andhra Pradesh	Karnataka	Bihar	West Bengal
Organized sector enterprise (dummy)	-0.746 (-3.88)	-1.128 (-4.75)	-1.042 (-3.00)	-1.062 (-6.52)
Urban area enterprise (dummy)	-0.962 (-5.40)	-0.844 (-3.87)	-0.574 (-1.72)	-0.422 (-2.85)
Age	0.0052 (0.77)	-0.0175 (2.10)	-0.0434 (-3.22)	-0.0329 (-6.08)
Education:				
Primary	-0.459 (-1.49)	-0.685 (-2.31)	-0.832 (-1.42)	-0.347 (-2.02)
Middle	-1.005 (-4.38)	-0.817 (-2.58)	-2.119 (-4.17)	-1.161 (-5.85)
Secondary	-1.506 (-5.99)	-0.957 (-3.48)	-2.021 (-3.03)	-0.896 (-3.68)
Hr. secondary	-3.425 (-4.47)	-1.332 (-2.72)	-1.122 (-1.16)	-1.744 (-4.61)
Diploma	-2.721 (-5.02)	-2.522 (-2.97)		-1.371 (-2.43)
Graduate and above	-3.634 (-5.51)	-4.123 (-7.39)	-4.597 (-4.40)	-2.455 (-6.39)
Belongs to SC/ST (dummy)	-0.093 (-0.49)	0.307 (1.62)	0.834 (1.89)	-0.099 (-0.65)
Female worker (dummy)	-0.155 (-0.55)	0.527 (1.77)	0.914 (1.84)	1.255 (5.26)
Industry dummies	Yes	Yes	Yes	Yes
Round dummies	Yes	Yes	Yes	Yes
No. of observations	2418	1748	833	3170
Wald chi-square (df)	341.2 (32)	312.2 (33)	214.5 (28)	507.3 (33)
Pseudo-R-squared	0.292	0.365	0.487	0.310

Note: The dependent variable is a dichotomous one representing the status of the worker. It takes value one for casual workers and zero for regular workers ('t' statistics).

Source: Authors' computations from NSS data on employment.

Table A7.7: State-wise estimates of the model explaining casual employment (data for three rounds are pooled) (*continued*)

Explanatory variables	Orissa	Madhya Pradesh	Gujarat	Maharashtra
Organized sector enterprise (dummy)	-0.813 (-2.47)	-1.673 (-7.64)	-0.646 (-4.04)	-0.958 (-7.06)
Urban area enterprise (dummy)	-1.355 (-4.44)	-0.118 (-0.51)	-1.302 (-7.70)	-1.177 (-8.09)
Age	0.0414 (3.32)	-0.0343 (-4.61)	-0.0233 (-3.20)	-0.0127 (-2.28)
Education:				
Primary	-0.794 (-1.64)	-1.314 (-5.31)	-0.460 (-1.94)	-0.357 (-2.01)
Middle	-2.062 (-5.07)	-0.400 (-1.43)	-0.236 (-1.09)	-0.469 (-2.71)
Secondary	-1.150 (-3.35)	-1.260 (-2.92)	-1.045 (-4.57)	-0.952 (-4.70)
Hr. secondary	-3.682 (-3.77)	-1.353 (-2.31)	-1.302 (-3.28)	-1.199 (-3.28)
Diploma	-4.676 (-4.13)		-1.465 (-2.52)	-2.396 (-5.16)
Graduate and above	-3.803 (-3.81)	-4.037 (-5.93)	-2.079 (-4.24)	-2.247 (-5.08)
Belongs to SC/ST (dummy)	-0.098 (-0.30)	0.442 (1.89)	0.185 (1.03)	0.269 (1.99)
Female workers (dummy)	0.376 (0.84)	0.523 (2.30)	1.835 (5.63)	0.535 (2.68)
Industry dummies	Yes	Yes	Yes	Yes
Round dummies	Yes	Yes	Yes	Yes
No. of observations	721	1391	2853	4475
Wald chi-square (df)	200.0(28)	301.0 (28)	402.6 (32)	411.4(32)
Pseudo-R-squared	0.467	0.367	0.288	0.271

Note: The dependent variable is a dichotomous one representing the status of the worker. It takes value one for casual workers and zero for regular workers ('t' statistics).

Source: Authors' computations from NSS data on employment.

Table A7.7: State-wise estimates of the model explaining casual employment (data for three rounds are pooled) (*continued*)

Explanatory variables	Chhattisgarh	Jharkhand	Assam	Uttaranchal
Organized sector enterprise (dummy)	-1.492 (-2.72)	-1.100 (-1.48)	-1.129 (-2.15)	-2.003 (-2.24)
Urban area enterprise (dummy)	0.747 (1.33)	-1.694 (-3.08)	-1.163 (-3.09)	-0.516 (-0.57)
Age	0.0266 (1.06)	-0.1055 (-4.46)	-0.0040 (-0.26)	0.0380 (1.18)
Education:				
Primary	-0.398 (-0.67)	-1.169 (-1.44)	-0.290 (-0.57)	-0.356 (-0.37)
Middle	-0.073 (-0.09)	-1.500 (-1.85)	-0.659 (-1.01)	-0.193(-0.20)
Secondary	-0.436 (-0.56)	-2.360 (-2.74)	-1.315 (-1.84)	-3.606 (-3.47)
Hr. secondary	1.573 (1.72)	-2.463 (-2.45)	-2.240 (-2.41)	
Diploma		-2.920 (-2.22)		
Graduate and above	-0.767 (-1.04)	-5.937 (-5.52)	-2.522 (-2.30)	-4.603(-3.28)
Belongs to SC/ST (dummy)	0.358 (0.74)	-1.031 (1.47)	-0.448 (-0.92)	0.276(0.28)
Female worker (dummy)	3.026 (2.59)	5.329 (3.81)	2.413 (3.31)	-2.466 (-2.13)
Industry dummies	Yes	Yes	Yes	Yes
Round dummies	Yes	Yes	Yes	Yes
No. of observations	274	385	363	153
Wald chi-square (df)	76.6 (20)	149.0 (24)	104.8 (21)	59.3(21)
Pseudo-R-squared	0.422	0.639	0.355	0.532

Note: The dependent variable is a dichotomous one representing the status of the worker. It takes value one for casual workers and zero for regular workers ('t' statistics).

Source: Authors' computations from NSS data on employment.

Table A7.7: State-wise estimates of the model explaining casual employment (data for three rounds are pooled) (*continued*)

Explanatory variables	Kerala	Tamil Nadu	Pondicherry
Organized sector enterprise (dummy)	-1.168 (-7.16)	-0.899 (-7.95)	-0.324 (-0.73)
Urban area enterprise (dummy)	-0.423 (-2.77)	-0.430 (-3.95)	-0.850 (-2.26)
Age	-0.0261 (-3.54)	-0.0099 (-2.15)	-0.0206 (-1.19)
Education:			
Primary	0.120 (0.049)	0.317 (2.18)	0.222 (0.39)
Middle	-0.359 (-1.56)	-0.477 (-3.16)	-1.275 (-2.27)
Secondary	-1.085(-3.96)	-0.903 (-5.03)	-2.090 (-3.83)
Hr. secondary	-1.160 (-1.96)	-1.250 (-3.71)	-2.645 (-2.61)
Diploma	-1.709 (-3.79)	-2.918 (-4.59)	-5.275 (-5.52)
Graduate and above	-2.746 (-5.19)	-2.507 (-4.67)	
Belongs to SC/ST (dummy)	0.052 (0.27)	1.299 (4.26)	-0.672 (1.09)
Female workers (dummy)	0.731 (4.05)	0.274 (2.28)	-0.437 (0.87)
Industry dummies	Yes	Yes	Yes
Round dummies	Yes	Yes	Yes
No. of observations	2043	4501	408
Wald chi-square (df)	314.0 (34)	421.0 (32)	115.2 (28)
Pseudo-R-squared	0.247	0.198	0.311

Note: The dependent variable is a dichotomous one representing the status of the worker. It takes value one for casual workers and zero for regular workers ('t' statistics).

Source: Authors' computations from NSS data on employment.

Endnotes

1   A crucial issue that requires discussion here is whether greater casualization among women amounts to discrimination among them. One may argue that given that women are usually the 'second bread earner', in inflexible labour markets women may agree more easily to work as casual labour, and therefore, a higher proportion of women may turn out to be casual workers without the entrepreneurs effectively discriminating against them. We do not find this line of

argument convincing. For, by the same logic, if women pick up less paid jobs (being a second bread earner) and therefore women's wage rate after controlling for endowments is relatively less then there is no discrimination because the women have willing chosen to take up the less paid jobs. This will go against the framework underlying a large number of studies on women wage discrimination that have been done for India and other countries. The key question is whether women actually want a less regular job than men. In this regard, we feel that there is no reason to believe that women want a less regular job. Rather, one may argue that men may opt for high risk, high return jobs, while women may go for more stable jobs. If this is right and yet a higher proportion of women are found to be in casual job (which is less paid than regular jobs) as compared to the corresponding proportion among men, then there is ground to believe that there is some sort of discrimination.

2   The use of employment data according to UPSS criterion tends to understate the proportion of women workers in manufacturing who have regular jobs. UPSS workers include a small section of subsidiary workers (those who works a minor part of the year) who are mostly women and are unlikely to be regular even in terms of most broad definition of regular workers used by NSSO. Indeed, our computations show that the proportion of women workers in manufacturing having a regular job is relatively higher when employment data according to Usual Principal Status (UPS) are used rather than UPSS. This may be seen from Table A7.1. The implication is that the use data on employment according to UPSS may exaggerate somewhat the discrimination (in regard to work tenure) again women. This is a limitation of the analysis presented in the chapter. We, however, did not attempt to address this issue by shifting to UPS employment data. Since many studies in employment in India have been based on the UPSS criterion (including our own studies on casualization in manufacturing), we felt that for maintaining comparability, the UPSS concept should be used in this study too.

3   There is need for a great deal of caution in interpreting the estimates shown in different cells of the tables in these two appendices. These estimates which are cross-classified by industry and state are based on a small number of observations and thus subject to sampling error. Yet, it is useful to study how the intensity of regular women workers in manufacturing for a state varies across different two-digit industries.

4   In one version of the model (results not reported in the chapter), an interaction term between the urban area dummy and the gender dummy variable has been used as an additional explanatory variable. The coefficient of the interaction term is found to be statistically significant. The results suggest that the disadvantage of women in getting a regular job in manufacturing is more in urban areas than that in rural areas.

References

Becker, G. 1971. *The Economics of Discrimination*, Second Edition. Chicago: University of Chicago Press.

Goldar, B. and S. C. Aggrawal. June 2012a. 'Informalization of Industrial Labor in India: Effects of Labor Market Rigidities and Import Competition', *Developing Economies* 50(2): 141–69.

_____. 2012b. 'Employment of Casual Workers in Organized Manufacturing in India: Analysis of Trends and the Impact of Labour Reforms'. Paper presented at the National Seminar on 'Globalisation, Labour Markets and Employment Relations in India' organized at Mumbai by the Institute for Human Development and the Indian Society of Labour Economics, 9–10 July 2012.

Khanna, S. 2012. 'Gender Wage Discrimination in India: Glass Ceiling or Sticky Floor?', *Working Paper No. 214.* New Delhi: Centre for Development Economics, Department of Economics, Delhi School of Economics.

Kishor, S. and K. Gupta. 2009. *Gender Equality and Women's Empowerment in India. National Family Health Survey (NFHS-3), 2005–06.* Mumbai: International Institute of Population Sciences.

Krishna, M. and G. D. Bino Paul. 2012. 'What Explains Wage in India?'. *Discussion Paper #15.* Deonar, Mumbai: Labour Market Research Facility, School of Management and Labour Studies, Tata Institute of Social Sciences.

Menon, N. and Y. van der Meulen Rodgers. 2007. *International Trade Competition, Market Power, and Gender Wage Differentials in India's Manufacturing Sector.* New Brunswick, NJ: Women's and Gender Studies Department, Rutgers University.

NSSO. 2013. *Key Indicators of Employment and Unemployment in India-NSS 68th Round.* New Delhi.

Paul, S. and S. B. Paul. 2013. 'Trade Reforms and Gender Wage Gap in India'. Paper presented at Population Association of America, Annual Meeting, 2013. Available at: http://paa2013. princeton.edu/papers/131268. Accessed on 19 August 2013.

Ramaswamy, K. V. 2013. 'Understanding the "Missing Middle" in Indian Manufacturing: The Role of Size-dependent Labour Regulations and Fiscal Incentive'. *VRF series no. 480.* Tokyo, Japan: Institute of Developing Economies.

Reilly, B. and P. Vasudeva-Dutta. 2005. 'The Gender Pay Gap and Trade Liberalization: Evidence for India'. *PRUS Working Paper no. 32.* Sussex: Policy Research Unit, Sussex University.

Part 2

Employment
and
Labour Law

8

From Rigidity to Flexibility

Changes in the Indian Labour Market

Bibhas Saha

8.1 Introduction

For decades the Indian labour market has been regarded as highly rigid. Seeing it from the employers' perspective, it is clear that the employers have been *legally* restricted to restructure their labour force or layoff even a single worker, thanks to some job security provisions of the Industrial Disputes Act. When militant unions and bureaucratic red tapes are added to the job security laws, one gets the picture of an economy where large industries will be reluctant to make new hiring, because it will be difficult to shed them later.

It is also the case that the last 15 years' growth in the Indian economy, at least the manufacturing component of it, has led to a disproportionate expansion of the informal sector, accompanied by outsourcing and substitution of permanent labour for contract labour. Overall, the informal sector employment and the hiring of contract workers in the formal sector have gone up significantly. Critics might call these developments a swing to the other end of the rigidity scale – rampant flexibilization, or informalization of the Indian workforce. For a number of reasons one need not see this as a healthy trend. If the informal sector workers do not experience significant income gains, then the prospect of urban poverty reduction is grim. It is also the case that the informal firms are unlikely to graduate to the formal sector and offer a somewhat secure work environment to their workers. They are still regulation free like a 'wild west of the cowboy capitalists'.

The question is whether there is an evolution of the middle ground, or is the labour market acting like a seesaw, or are these simply subversive acts?

The rigidity has not disappeared, not in *law* and *labour regulations*, but the *practice* has allowed flexibility. Since practice is hard to regulate, the nature of flexibility will be determined by the incentives created by external and domestic opportunities, as well as the physical capabilities to respond to opportunities. For instance, to meet a large export order, whether a formal sector firm will hire permanent workers, or contract workers, or outsource to an informal firm, depends on the union it faces, the links it has with the local informal sector, and crucially the infrastructural bottlenecks all firms face. In this chapter this issue is discussed by drawing from some of the theoretical and empirical researches.

8.2 Understanding and detecting rigidity

There are several ways to understand rigidity. To begin with let one thing be absolutely clear. Nowhere is labour market completely free from any regulations. Labour market is very different from markets for physical goods. For a number of reasons completely unrestricted functioning of the labour market is neither possible nor desirable. Even in the informal sector both employers and workers try to engage in long-term contracts making transactions across time. Clearly, this will not be possible unless social norm allows them to trust each other and make promises and honour them in return.

At a conceptual level, labour market interventions are just like any other interventions needed for correcting market failures. Labour market failure occurs due to distributional conflicts as well as asymmetric information and uncertainty. Of course all interventions come at some cost, the magnitude of which depends on the design of interventions and the legal and political institutions. There are three approaches to explain labour market institutions: institutional theory, political power theory and legal theory. A brief discussion of each is provided here.

The institutional theory: North (1990) argued that institutions help achieve efficiency by reducing transaction costs, which would otherwise cause market failures and restrict social welfare. In the context of the labour market, for example, the workers and their employer cannot costlessly negotiate on how to share the organizational surplus. This is because the employer has superior information on the true size of the organizational surplus and therefore has incentive to understate it. The workers in turn cannot trust the employer, and therefore they have to engage in a costly and lengthy process of negotiations, which might lead to strikes or lock-out. These actions are socially inefficient and cause market failures. Therefore, regulations should aim to restrict opportunistic behaviours or impose obligations to disclose private information, in order to make negotiations as smooth as possible.

The political power theory: According to political power theory, those who capture political power will transfer resources from those who are not in power, and this task is accomplished by designing the appropriate regulations and institutions. The origin of this argument is found in Marx; but it has been refined and adapted to modern settings in the works of Olson (1965), Stigler (1971), and Becker (1983). It comes in various flavours. Marx was concerned about capitalist exploitation and appropriation of surplus labour, and he saw a political system was designed to facilitate this exploitation. The only way this could be rectified, in his view, was abolition of private property (at least the large industrial units) through a new political system brought about possibly by revolution. But in modern democracies with universal suffrage, where political power can be acquired only by winning elections, resources are transferred to pressure groups. The ideology of the ruling party can also be important. A pro-labour party will legislate in favour of the workers regarding the regulation of working conditions and/or industrial disputes. One may recall that when the former Prime Minister Indira Gandhi introduced the Chapter VB restriction in Industrial Disputes Act in 1976 prohibiting layoffs and retrenchment in factories of 300 or more workers, she had already declared emergency throughout the country, which virtually ruled out strikes, protests and any form of workers' unrest. This made her appear like pro-employer. So perhaps to avoid that unfavourable tag, she moved to the other extreme and introduced this extremely pro-labour legislation, which later on proved to be controversial.

The legal theory: One may view legal theory as a part of institutional theory, because all laws are formal institutions. However, a separate discussion of it is warranted on the ground that historically today's legal systems around the world come from two major (and distinct) legal traditions in Western Europe, namely common law and civil law. These two traditions are very old going back to twelfth century and they were transported to different countries via colonization. The common law tradition emerged in England and it is characterized by the importance of decision-making by juries, independent judges, and more importantly by the emphasis on judicial discretion as opposed to codes. India, like all other British colonies, inherited this tradition. Civil law, on the other hand, evolved from Roman law through the middle ages, and was incorporated into civil codes in France and Germany in the nineteenth century.

Civil law is characterized by a greater role of both substantive and procedural codes as opposed to judicial discretion and independent judiciaries. Much of modern Europe, North and West Africa, all of Latin America, and some parts of Asia have inherited this system.

It is generally argued that common law countries tend to regulate less and rely more on markets and contracts, whereas civil law countries legislate and regulate more and try to directly control businesses (Djankov, *et al.*, 2003). The legal tradition matters not only for the extent of legislation, but also for the enforcement practice, and its effect on the behaviours of the economic agents.

In a seminal paper Botero *et al.*, (2004) investigate the institutions of labour markets in 85 countries by categorising the laws and regulations under three broad heads: employment regulations, collective bargaining regulations, and social security laws. They find that the leftist ideology of political parties is associated with more stringent regulations as a whole and common law countries have less labour regulations. Stringent regulation of labour also causes lower labour force participation and higher youth unemployment.

There is now a substantial research on the economic effect of labour market rigidity. Earlier economists used a so-called labour demand approach due to Nickell (1986) in which the effect of any restrictive regulation will be detected from a depression of the labour demand curve.[1] This approach was taken by Fallon and Lucas (1991, 1993) and Dutta Roy (2003). Fallon and Lucas (1991, 1993) modelled the effect of the introduction of the job security provision via Chapter VB of the ID Act in 1976. They showed that the job security regulation of 1976 did not affect the adjustment cost (i.e., no change in the rigidity), but it reduced the long run industrial employment by 17.5 per cent on the aggregate. 11 of the 35 (two-digit) industries suffered loss in employment. In particular, cotton textile industry had a loss of 36.1 per cent employment, soaps and cosmetics 33.3 per cent, and silk and synthetics as high as 44.8 per cent.[2] Dutta Roy (2003) developed a simultaneous equation system of dynamic labour and capital demands with labour further disaggregated between workers and supervisors and covering longer time period (1960–94). No doubt hers is by far the best modelling of dynamic labour demand available for the Indian industry. She tested for long run adjustment costs through the identification of rigidity, and then examined whether the job security provisions of 1976 and 1982 have worsened it. Her findings are mixed and industry-specific. More importantly, in some industries, there was no effect of the legislation on the rigidity, and in other industries the rigidities were seen to exist well before 1976. Her findings suggest that there are deeper structural characteristics that have contributed more to the rigidities than the legislative provisions of job security.

This brings one to the question of to what extent additional legislations add or alter the labour market rigidity. Perhaps a better approach would be to take all the labour laws and regulations together and try to quantify its effect on output or employment. Besley and Burgess (2004) have precisely taken such an approach. They exploited a key historical fact that all states in India started from the same set of labour laws in 1947, but subsequently diverged from each other through various amendments of the ID Act. The amendments were at times pro-workers and at other times pro-employer or neutral. So the aggregate effect of these amendments over time can be seen as an outcome of which changes were dominant. If a state has made most of the changes in favour of the employers, then after many years it should turn out as a pro-employer state. Following this logic, they classified four states, namely Gujarat, Maharashtra, Orissa and West Bengal as pro-workers, while Andhra Pradesh, Madhya Pradesh, Rajasthan, Tamil Nadu, Karnataka and Kerala as pro-employers, and the remaining states as neutral.

Next, by using the quantitative measure of the bias in labour regulations as an explanatory variable, they show that the state registered manufacturing outputs fell with pro-labour legislation, and while the state unregistered manufacturing showed a stronger positive relationship with labour rigidity. Their point is that pro–worker states have lost out on the registered manufacturing.

Several other studies utilized the Besley-Burgess classification of labour rigidity and explored a number of related issues. These are notably, Aghion *et al.*, (2008), Hasan *et al.*, (2007), Ahsan and Pagés (2009), Adhvaryu *et al.*, (2013),and Saha *et al.*, (2013), all confirming the negative effects of rigidity.[3] However, there is a criticism of the Besley-Burgess approach raised by Bhattacharjea (2006) who found several errors in coding of the labour laws, with some of the changes significantly affecting the aggregate score for some states. Ahsan and Pagés (2009) took this modification into account and showed that those alleged errors do not affect the general conclusion. Moreover, they segregated the labour laws in two broad categories – employment protection legislation and the dispute resolution legislations, and show that their effects on employment and outputs are different. So there is now ample evidence that labour rigidity is causing significant loss of employment and other ill effects, and no longer can people afford to ignore it.

8.3 Imperfect flexibility

In the early 1990s, the Indian Government was so concerned about the job security provision and its possible links with liquidation difficulty with bankrupt firms (commonly called as sick industrial units) that it asked an expert committee to come up with an exit policy document. This gave rise to an expectation that the rigid labour laws would be reformed, which was not only advised by academics and policy experts, but also demanded by the Indian corporates and foreign investors. But politicians did not dare touch the labour laws, even though the old architecture of industrial regulation, licensing and trade protections was dismantled one by one within a relatively short span of time. The reason for leaving the labour laws unchanged was political. Despite representing only 10 per cent of the workers, large unions remained a grand symbol of labour interests, and anti-union measures were, and are still, eared to be judged anti-people.

So in replacement of legal reforms, flexibility was offered in practice. The 1972 Contract Labour Regulation Act provided a compromise, allowing firms to hire workers on contract, who can be fired at will and kept out of unions. The unions did not see that as a major challenge to their role as rent-sharer. Moreover, contract employment is better than outsourcing, which poses a much bigger threat to their rents and eventually to their jobs. The share of contract workers increased from 12 per cent in 1985 to 26 per cent in 2004. The trend is much stronger in states like Andhra Pradesh, Madhya Pradesh, Maharashtra and Rajasthan. Between 1998 and 2004 the share of contract workers in organized manufacturing employment has gone up from 15 per cent to 51 in Andhra Pradesh, from 16 per cent to 28 per cent in Madhya Pradesh, from 15 per cent to 27 per cent in Punjab and from 21 per cent to 33 per cent in Rajasthan. Some of the states like Bihar, Uttar Pradesh and Orissa already had much proportion of contract labour. On the other hands, states like Kerala, Tamil Nadu, Karnataka, Assam and West Bengal have much lower incidence of contract labour, though in all of these states there has been an increasing trend (Saha et al., 2013).

Outsourcing also thrived, though, largely at the expense of in-house employment, rather than current employment; firms tend to outsource often to meet a sudden spike in demand. So this may not necessarily be seen as a union-busting strategy. Besides there is a limit to outsourcing as the economics of 'make or buy' strategy calls for striking a balance between cost of coordination and quality control and the benefit of lower costs. Ramaswamy (1999) noted that the incidence of outsourcing is significant in large labour-intensive factories (which employ more than 50 workers). For instance, in 1992–93 the share of outsourcing in the value-added was in the order of 56 per cent in textile industries. His disaggregated analysis provides a further insight that the consumer non-durables industries have the highest subcontracting intensity and their average labour intensity is also the highest. In contrast the intermediate goods industries have the lowest sub-contracting intensity and value-added share.[4]

But flexible practice does not fully make up for the lack of flexible labour laws. For one thing, practice is rarely going to be transparent and easily transferable knowledge. One needs to invest in relationships and network to carry out profitable and reliable outsourcing or contract hiring; further, this may not be uniform across India, as each state has modified the Contract Labour Act and the Industrial Disputes Act in their own ways to make the local labour markets sufficiently opaque to deter new entrants or foreign investors, who largely respond to the central government's call. So for the foreign firm, entering India and choosing a particular state as an entry point will require substantial research resulting in higher entry costs. Existing Indian firms do have some advantage in this regard. Nothing is more important than a transparent legal and regulatory system that can attract large volumes of foreign investment.

Take the case of China. During the planning era, local and regional bureaucrats in China used to allocate workers to factories very much like physical inputs. This was also linked to a household registration system, which could allow a worker to move to another city or town only after he could secure a residence there; this was known as the *Hukou* system. Enterprises were also required to make room for new workers regardless of their needs. Three important labour reforms were carried out between 1984 and 1994: (1) wage reform; (2) elimination of bureaucratic labour allocation system; and (3) introduction of new labour laws permitting hire and fire.

Most of the labour laws that regulate China's industrial relations are new – legislated after 1985. Among these notable are Trade Unions Act, 1992 (amended in 2001), Labour Act, 1994 and Regulations on Collective Contracts, 2004 (Decree 22 of the Ministry of Labour and Social Security). (See Chan, 2000; Solinger, 2002 for more).

The Trade Unions Act, 1992, which drastically replaced the 1950 version of the same Act, has granted all workers everywhere the right to form union.

But the union must be affiliated to the All China Federation of Trade Unions (ACFTU), the only trade union nationally recognized. Thus, China has ruled out multiple trade unions. Critics point out that the Trade unions Act does not mention 'strike' anywhere and workers are advised to behave in a disciplined manner during a dispute. The Labour Act, 1994 acknowledges labour as a contractible object, and paved the way for several new phenomena such as 'collective contracts', 'floating wage rules' and 'layoffs and retrenchments'. The contracts can be firm- and/or job-specific, and fixed term, with no promise of renewal. Further, the employing enterprise can breach the contract on grounds of financial distress. However, dismissal requires a notice of 30 days and payment of compensations. The Regulations on Collective Contracts, 2004 specifies that a collective contract should be determined by 'collective bargaining'. For more on this see Saha (2006).

It is clear from the above discussion that China completely revamped its labour legislations; this was needed to exercise greater control on its labour force, but to inform the outside world that China is ready to do business. Not only can the abundantly cheap and relatively skilled workers be hired and fired at will, but the industrial disputes will be efficiently resolved by the intervention of the State. In fact, the disputes were to be pre-empted by the state's labour arm ACFTU. The result of a clear cut labour regime is there for all to see.

In contrast, India chose to disengage from the management of the industrial disputes regulations, leaving things to the unions and firms to fight it out. Therefore, labour practice became more important than labour law. One may criticize the Besley-Burgess classification of the Indian states on the ground that legal changes do not matter much; practices are far more important. Though Kerala was classified by them as pro-employer, Gujarat and Maharashtra as pro-worker, going by the experience on the ground one would claim that Kerala is pro-worker and Gujarat and Maharashtra are pro-employer. The volume of investment received by the latter two states also suggests that investors look at the practice more carefully than law.

Yet it is to be recognized that in the absence of a legal reform people are relegated to a second best environment. Flexible practice requires additional investment, and disputes can be harder to resolve. An efficient framework reduces collective wastes from industrial disputes that are colossal, by the international standard. It is observed that though there is a declining trend of the incidence of industrial disputes (strikes and lockouts) after the liberalization, the number of disputes is still 500 per year (2001–07) with an average loss of 25.20 man days per dispute, with bulk of the disputes being lockouts – 48.60 per cent of all disputes. Before 1991, the share of lockouts in the total disputes was merely 20.39 per cent (1981–90); for more see Pal and Saha (2013).

8.4 Unions and the segmentation of the labour market

Economists largely accept that labour unions play many positive roles. First, they reduce the employer's cost of negotiating with a large number of workers, simply by coordinating with all workers. They also facilitate collective actions (such as a strike), and thereby internalize externalities and eliminate potentially destructive free riding by individual workers. Second, labour welfare should be a desirable objective in itself. In countries like India where the government is less capable of redistributing resources via targeted taxes and subsidies unions directly help to transfer income to the working class. Third, contrary to popular perceptions unions are not necessarily detrimental to firm efficiency. The efficient bargaining protocol, if properly followed, will convert the union's role to a partner in the efficient selection of inputs, without sacrificing its interest in rent-sharing (McDonald and Solow, 1981). Some economists have even argued that unions would boost efficiency by encouraging firms to undertake socially optimal training (Booth and Chatterji, 1998).

While the above arguments are not disputed, one may raise concerns about dynamic implication of unions, and the institutional framework for collective bargaining. Over time unions tend to evolve more as firm-specific or industry-specific rent-sharers acting exclusively on behalf of their members, i.e., the currently employed workers of that firm or industry. They do not represent the wider working class; nor do they even take into account the interests of future employees; essentially they are dictated by the interest of the insiders (Lindbeck and Snower, 1986). The institutional protocols of collective bargaining in the real world rarely emulate the efficient bargaining model. In most countries wage alone is subjected to negotiation with employment largely left to the discretion of the employers. In other words, the real life protocols are some variants of the 'right-to-manage' model of bargaining or monopoly union model (Oswald, 1982), which are known to be notoriously inefficient. Union's ability to hold up and inflict significant exit cost on the firm can also cause inefficiency of capital choice (Grout, 1984). The long history of employers' exploitation and natural mistrust between them and their workers are partly responsible for the choice of such inefficient bargaining mechanisms that influence the unions' behaviours and the image they create in public's mind.

At another level, unions respond to incentives just as any economic agents would do. Seeing their firm earning economic rents due to temporary or long-term market protection, the workers would try to claim a share of that. It is a natural response. One difficulty, however, is ascertaining the size of the rent. Financial data (such as sales, profit and loss) are something that management is unlikely to share with the union, except what is furnished with the government after (possibly creative) tax calculations. Therefore, dispute is unavoidable not only regarding what should be the fair share of the surplus, but also with the size of the surplus itself. The theoretical literature on strike (Hart, 1989; Sanchez-Pages, 2009) revolves around asymmetric information and divergent beliefs among the workers and employers. So when the unions go on strike, it is not unjustified, but there is a consequence to it; the whole industry may suffer, and when the unions (again driven by severity of information asymmetry) go too far, the employers may resort to other alternatives, such as avoiding the unions altogether, which is the 'flexible' employment practice that has been noted earlier.

In one sense, informal workers are to be seen as competitors by the unions, and therefore they have reason to campaign for banning informal employment. In fact, in Western economies prohibition of informal employment, child labour and similar practices have all been banned at the behest of organized labour. In developing countries, organized labour knows that they are a minority and therefore they have held a sympathetic view about their poor cousin in the informal sector; but they also think that the protection of workers' welfare and job security in the formal sector is a priority. The same benefits should be eventually extended to all workers once the economy becomes developed. Here lies a problem. It is known from the literature of dual economy that formal-informal dualism is not a transitory one; it may stubbornly persist, and it can segment the labour market on both the demand and the supply sides.

In a recent paper, Saha *et al.*, (2013) have tried to study such dualism in the context of India's recent trade liberalization. The Indian industry can be characterized by three types of dualism. In terms of the exposure to the government regulations there are two sectors – formal and informal. In terms of technology, some are modern and others are backward, finally in terms of the skills of the workers, some employ skilled workers and others are just happy with the unskilled workers. In sum, dualism can be presented in terms of regulation, technology and workers' skills. It is plausible to expect that the informal sector firms will be small, dependent on backward technology and largely will employ unskilled workers. But the formal sector firms can be large or small, and could be technologically modern or backward and then depending on its technology it can employ skilled or unskilled workers.

Regardless of its technology, a formal sector firm is most likely to see its workforce forming a union and can negotiate wage, or both wage and employment. The fact that the unions can engage in industrial disputes has some additional implications for firms that use modern technology. During a prolonged dispute, its capital is to suffer a loss in value much more than a backward technology dependent firm. This would make a modern firm to some extent more vulnerable, and its employer may try to reduce its vulnerability by hiring some workers on contract, if they are unskilled. Hiring them gives the firm leverage against a strong union, simply by reducing the employment of some skilled workers.

Now imagine that the economy is exposed to trade liberalization. If the industry was primarily export oriented, it gets a boost in export. But only the formal sector firms can export, because the informal firms are not registered. Therefore the informal firms do not benefit much from the export opportunities, even though they might have stronger comparative advantage. They might still indirectly benefit from the substitution of the formal firms as they will supply less to the domestic market to meet the increased export demand.

This can be graphically explained. Consider Figure 8.1 where it is demonstrated how the industry equilibrium and its distribution of labour are affected, when there is a positive export shock. Assuming that there is no import, and all of its output are either consumed at home or exported overseas, the aggregate supply consists of the informal and the formal firms' output, given by the curve $S_I + S_F$. On the demand side, there are both the domestic demand denoted by D and the export demand denoted by X. The inverse aggregate demand curve is given by the line $D+X$. I first show the equilibrium before the export shock occurs. The equilibrium output and price are Q_0 and p_0. Out of Q_0, the informal sector's supply is Q_I; the rest is supplied by the formal firms out of which $(Q_F - Q_I)$ is supplied to the domestic market and $(Q_0 - Q_F)$ is exported abroad. As a positive export shock occurs, the aggregate demand curve shifts rightward as given by the $D+X'$ curve. The equilibrium output and price both rise to Q_1 and p_1 respectively. The formal sector firms raise their exports and overall production, but also cut down their domestic supply. Their overseas supply increases to $(Q_I - Q_F^*)$ and domestic supply falls to $(Q_F^* - Q_I^*)$, making room for the informal sector to increase their supply to overseas supply increases to Q_I^*. This is the indirect benefit of the informal sector.

Figure 8.1: Effects of an increase in export demand

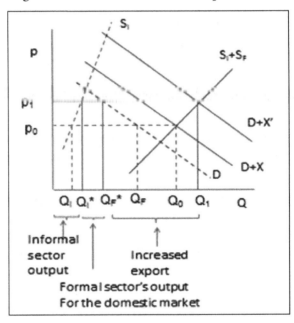

Now consider another industry that does not export, and instead receives some import. Before liberalization, the equilibrium price is higher than the international price, as shown in Figure 8.2. The inverse demand curve (which represents only domestic demand) is given by the line D. On the other hand, the supply comes from three sources: the informal sector (denoted by the inverse supply curve S_I), the formal sector (denoted by S_F), and import denoted by M. The initial equilibrium output and price are Q_0 and p_0 respectively. The informal sector's supply is Q_I and the formal sector's supply is $(Q_F - Q_I)$, and the total import is $(Q_0 - Q_F)$. Now if there is full trade liberalization leading to greater import, the equilibrium price will fall and the equilibrium quantity will rise. Due to a fall in the price, the supply of both the informal and formal firms will fall to Q_I^* and to $(Q_F^* - Q_I^*)$ respectively. But the total import will rise to $(Q_1 - Q_F^*)$. The economy as a whole consumes more output as the import overwhelms the domestic suppliers.

Figure 8.2: Effects of an import shock

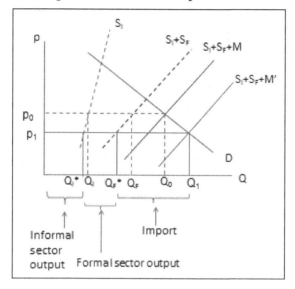

Industries that are vulnerable to import competition are aware of the fact that any unexpected wave of imports will force them to cut production and lay off workers. So it will be wise to have more contract workers in their workforce than permanent workers, even if that means taking some low skilled workers and take a hit on productivity. The contract workers can be laid off, whenever there is a time of increased competition from imports. So, one should expect a positive relationship between import penetration of an industry and the share of contract workers. But this is not the only reason to hire contract workers. Even if the firms are not exposed to foreign competition, as argued above, to hedge against a militant union, the firm can choose to hire some contract workers. Thus, there are two motives for hiring contract workers, to deal with militant trade unions and to protect against import competition. But contract workers are likely to have lower productivity, particularly in modern firms, and that is a price firms have to pay to resort to this type of flexible employment practices.

One may ask: what type of firms is most likely to go for mixed mode of employment? Clearly, the answer depends on how powerful the union is. In Figure 8.3, I provide a graphical analysis. For more details see Saha *et al.* (2013). On the horizontal axis I have measured the union's bargaining power denoted by *a*, which can vary from 0 to 1. The firm's bargaining power is 1-a. The firm's profit is measured along the vertical axis. There are two profit curves corresponding to two options the firm has. It can hire only skilled workers as permanent workers in which case its profit is given by the π_R curve. Alternatively, it can mix some skilled workers (as permanent) with some unskilled workers as contract workers; the profit then is represented by the π_M curve.[5] At low values of a, profit from hiring the skilled workers (as permanent workers) dominates, because the firm does not lose much to a weak union and because of the skills of the workers output is also high. On the other hand, at high values of a, much of the surplus is taken away by the union due to their high bargaining power; the firm would be better off hiring non-unionized contract workers despite their low skills. Thus, as Figure 8.3 shows, there is a critical value of a, above which one will see firms would prefer a flexible workforce.

Figure 8.3: Flexible workforce

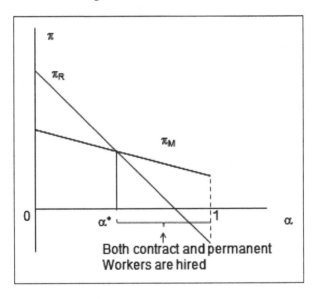

In reality measuring the workers' bargaining power is a much more complex task. It depends on the legal and regulatory structure of the state in which the firm is located, and it also depends on the size of the firm, technology and the type of product it is making. In particular how much it is exposed to trade is critically important. So, as the workers' bargaining power varies between industry and state, so will firms' practice of hiring.

Saha *et al.* (2013) have studied the contract labour problem for the Indian organized sector by using a three dimensional panel of 58 industries over the period of 1998 to 2004 for 15 major Indian states. They show that the share of contract workers in formal firm's employment goes up with union's bargaining power (as captured by the union density or strike-lockout ratio). The same response is seen vis-a-vis import penetration, as the above theoretical discussion suggests. Moreover, they also find that the positive effect of import penetration and the negative effect of export promotion on the share of contract labour are both stronger in those states which have pro-worker labour laws. In sum they conclude that stricter labour regulations as well as trade liberalization have both led to increased contract labour usages.

8.5 Conclusion

There is now considerable evidence that labour regulations in India are hurting formal sector employment and encouraging subversive practices. But whether these regulations have been induced by political pressure groups, or institutional specificities or the legal tradition inherited from the British are yet to be understood. The research on this question is far more limited. Only recently some work has begun in this area with the contribution of Besley and Burgess (2004). If the source of the problem is in the political process, then the problem needs to be corrected there, rather than trying to experiment with different economic policies. On the other hand, if these institutions are trying to address economic inefficiencies (either with the markets or property rights) then it is imperative to identify the source of inefficiencies. This however, may take time, as more research is needed.

Meanwhile, it is important to recognize that no matter how undesirable if one finds the use of contract labour, subcontracting and similarly subversive employment practices, they are in part employers' response to some over-restrictive regulations. The challenge is to strike a compromise between the workers' interests and the firms' investment incentives. This does not necessarily mean that the union's power needs to be curbed; rather both unions and employers need to be held accountable for their actions, and an environment should be created to discourage opportunism and enforce cooperation. Reforming labour regulations in this direction is more imperative now than ever before, because postponing that will only prolong industrial dualism and increase its spread to all sectors.

Endnotes

1   See also Nickell (1997) for an in-depth analysis of this approach.

2   The magnitude of the decline in potential employment as claimed by Fallon and Lucas was contradicted by Bhalotra (1998) and Dutta Roy (2003). Both argued that the estimated loss of employment was exaggerated due to the inclusion of those industries for which the results were not statistically significant.

3   Aghion *et al.*, (2005) find that in comparison to the neutral states the relative effects of industrial deregulation has been significantly positive for the pro-employer states, and significantly negative for the pro-worker states. Hasan *et al.*, (2007) show that after trade reform the elasticity of labour demand has increased in all industries, but they are larger in pro-employer states. Adhvaryu *et al.*, (2013) showed that industrial employment is more sensitive to shocks in areas where labour regulations are less restrictive or more pro-employer. Finally, Saha *et al.*, (2013) captures another effect of rigidity, substitution of permanent workers for contract labour. This is significant in pro-labour states.

4   See also Mazumdar and Sarkar (2013) for a more detailed discussion of wage and productivity growth in the Indian manufacturing sector. Autor (2003) is another important contribution on this topic.

5   There are two other possibilities: hire some skilled workers also as contract workers, and hire some unskilled workers as permanent workers. In Saha *et al.*, (2013) we show that with a mild assumption on the nature of contracting we can rule out these two options as never being chosen.

References

Adhvaryu, A., A. V. Chari and S. Sharma. 2013. 'Firing Costs and Flexibility: Evidence from Firms' Employment Responses to Shocks in India', *Review of Economics and Statistics* 95(3): 727–40.

Aghion P., R. Burgess, S. Redding and F. Zilibotti. 2008. 'The Unequal Effects of Liberalization: Evidence from Dismantling the License Raj in India', *American Economic Review* 98(4): 1397–412.

Ahsan, A. and C. Pagés. 2009. 'Are All Labor Regulations Equal? Evidence from Indian Manufacturing', *Journal of Comparative Economics* 37(1): 62–75.

Autor, D. 2003. 'Outsourcing at Will: The Contribution of Unjust Dismissal Doctrine to the Growth of Employment Outsourcing', *Journal of Labour Economics* 23(1): 1–42.

Becker, G., 1983. 'A Theory of Competition among Pressure Groups for Political Influence', *The Quarterly Journal of Economics* 98(3): 371–400.

Besley, T. and R. Burgess. 2004. 'Can Labour Regulation Hinder Economic Performance? Evidence from India', *The Quarterly Journal of Economics* 119(1): 91–134.

Bhalotra, S. 1998. 'The Puzzle of Jobless Growth in Indian Manufacturing', *Oxford Bulletin of Economics and Statistics* 60(1): 5–32.

Bhattacharjea, A. 2006. 'Labour Market Regulation and Industrial Performance in India: A Critical Review of the Empirical Evidence', *Indian Journal of Labour Economics* 49(2): 211–32.

Booth, A. and M. Chatterji. 1998. 'Unions and Efficient Training', *Economic Journal* 108(447): 328–43.

Botero, J., S. Djankov, R. L. Porta, F. Lopez-De-Silanes and A. Shleifer. 2004. 'The Regulation of Labour', *The Quarterly Journal of Economics* 119(4):1339–82

Chan, A. 2000. 'Chinese Trade Unions and Workplace Relations in State-owned and Joint-venture Enterprises'. In *Changing Workplace Relations in the Chinese Economy*, edited by Malcolm Warner. London: Macmillan Press.

Djankov, S, R. La Porta, F. Lopez-de-Silanes and A. Shleifer. 2003. 'Courts', *Quarterly Journal of Economics* 118(2): 453–517.

Djankov, S. and R. Ramalho. 2009. 'Employment Laws in Developing Countries', *Journal of Comparative Economics* 37(1): 3–13.

Dutta Roy, S. 2003. 'Employment Dynamics in Indian Industry: Adjustment Lags and the Impact of Job Security Regulations', *Journal of Development Economics* 73(1): 233–56.

Fallon, P. and R. Lucas. 1991. 'The Impact of Job-security Regulations in India and Zimbabwe', *The World Bank Economic Review* 5(3): 395–413.

———. 1993. 'Job-security Regulations and the Dynamic Demand for Labour in India and Zimbabwe', *Journal of Development Economics* 40(2): 241–75.

Grout, P. 1984. 'Investment and Wages in the Absence of Binding Contracts: A Nash Bargaining Approach', *Econometrica* 42(2): 449–60.

Hart, O. 1989. 'Bargaining and Strikes', *Quarterly Journal of Economics* 104(1): 25–43.

Hasan, R., D. Mitra, and K. V. Ramaswamy. 2007. 'Trade Reforms, Labor Regulations and Labour-Demand Elasticities: Empirical Evidence from India', *The Review of Economics and Statistics* 119(3): 466–81.

Lindbeck, A. and D. Snower. 1986. 'Wage Setting, Unemployment and Insider-Outsider Relations', *American Economic Review, Papers and Proceedings* 76: 235–39.

Mazumdar, D. and S. Sarkar. 2013. *Manufacturing Enterprise in Asia*. London: Routledge.

McDonald, I. M. and R. M. Solow. 1981. 'Wage Bargaining and Employment', *American Economic Review* 71(5): 896–908.

Nickell, S. 1986. 'Dynamic Models of Labour Demand'. In *Handbook of Labour Economics*, edited by O. Ashenfelter and R. Layard. Amsterdam, North-Holland: Elsevier.

———. 1997. 'Unemployment and Labor Market Rigidities: Europe versus North America', *Journal of Economic Perspectives* 11(3): 55–74.

North, D. C. 1990. *Institutions, Institutional Change, and Economic Performance*. New York: Cambridge University Press.

Olson, M. 1965. *The Logic of Collective Action*. Cambridge, MA: Harvard University Press.

Oswald, A. 1982. 'The Microeconomic Theory of the Trade Union', *Economic Journal* 92(367): 576–95.

Pal, R. and B. Saha. 2013. 'Labour Markets: Balancing Freedom and Protection'. In *Handbook of the Dynamic Indian Economy*, edited by A. Goyal. UK and New Delhi: Oxford University Press.

Ramaswamy, K. V. 1999. 'The Search for Flexibility in Indian Manufacturing', *Economic and Political Weekly* 34(6); 363–68.

Saha, B., K. Sen, and D. Maiti. 2013. 'Trade Openness, Labour Institutions and Flexibilization: Evidence from India', *Labour Economics* 24(October): 180–95.

Saha, B. 2006. 'Labour Institutions in India and China: A Tale of Two Nations', *Journal of South Asian Development* 1(2): 179–205.

Sanchez-Pages, S. 2009. 'Conflict as a Part of the Bargaining Process', *Economic Journal* 119 (539): 1189–1207.

Solinger, D. J. 2002. 'Labor Market Reform and Plight of the Laid-off Proletariat', *China Quarterly* 170(June): 304–26.

Stigler, G. 1971. 'The Theory of Economic Regulation', *Bell Journal of Economics and Management Science* 2 (1): 3–21.

9

Employment Protection Legislation and Threshold Effects
How Firms are Staying below the Legal Size Threshold in Indian Manufacturing

K. V. Ramaswamy

9.1 Introduction and context

India is well known for its extensive set of labour laws providing job security to regular industrial workers in the formal sector. Studying the response of firms to labour regulations constitutes a key component of one's understanding of the impact of labour laws on employment growth and access to good jobs in India. How have firms in India responded to Employment Protection Legislation (EPL) in terms of their hiring strategies, entry and size expansion decisions? Has EPL affected the upward mobility of firms? These are admittedly difficult empirical questions. In this chapter I provide preliminary econometric evidence that manufacturing firms in India employ non-permanent workers (contract workers) to avoid coming under EPL. Even in advanced country contexts, EPL and other related labour regulations are widely perceived to raise the expected cost of employment adjustment in firms covered by legislation, causing discontinuity in firm growth behaviour and employment policies. Labour regulations apply rules with respect to conditions of service, lay-off, retrenchment and closure to firms above a specified employment size. This is argued to raise labour adjustment costs and create pressures on firms to stay below the legal threshold size. Note that the regulations take effect as firm size grows and it generates an implicit tax. As the regulations are defined with reference to few finite employment size levels the literature refers to them as 'threshold effects' (see Gourio and Roys, 2012). The analytical idea of threshold effect is that if labour legislation (or any other economic policy like tax rates) changes discontinuously at the threshold employment size (or it could be asset size or output level) then it should result in discontinuous change in firms' behaviour. This change in behaviour of firms is directly proportional to the costs of compliance above the threshold. The discontinuous regulation can have two effects. First it could influence the propensity of the firm to expand employment above the threshold size impacting firm size distribution. Second it could change the employment policy of firms that cross the threshold size in favour of fixed term or short-term contracts in order to circumvent costs of regulation. In France, firms with 50 employees or more face substantially more regulation than firms with less than 50 and that has been observed to have resulted in many firms with exactly 49 employees (Gourio and Roys 2012). In Italy, stringent regulations apply to firms with above 15 employees and it is shown to have affected the propensity to grow of firms close to the threshold level and resulted in flexible labour contracts and greater separations in firms with greater than 15 employees (Schivardi and Torrini, 2008). In brief, labour regulations impose compliance costs once firms reach the specified employment size and act as disincentive for natural growth of firms. Tybout (2000) observed that for many developing countries, '… the size distribution exhibits a 'missing middle' because it never pays to be just large enough to attract enforcement'. Firms are often observed to use contract workers (secondary workers and labour outsourcing) to stay below the legal threshold size to escape labour regulations. Size-dependent regulations that reduce the average firm size have been shown to have output and productivity effects using calibrated growth models (Guner, et al., 2008; Gourio and Roys, 2012). Econometric evidence for threshold effects that is an outcome of change of behaviour firms with employment size close to the legal threshold has been very little in developing country contexts. The objective of this chapter is to fill this gap in the literature. It makes two contributions. First, I provide evidence of threshold effect in terms of changing workforce composition within firms that has created a two-tier workforce consisting of regular and non-permanent workers. The possibility of labour market outcomes contrary to the intension of size based EPL that is, increasing access to job security or good jobs, is explored using establishment level data. India is well-known for its EPL whose coverage was widened through a reduction of the employment size threshold from 300 workers to 100 workers in 1982. Second, I will examine the issue of threshold effects using firm-level panel data in the context of geographic variations in labour regulations within a single developing country that avoids the problems associated with cross-country regressions.

It may be useful to summarize the key features of size distribution of manufacturing employment in India. Dhar and Lydall (1961) were the first to observe the missing middle in the data, the thin share of employment size class 50 to 499 in Indian manufacturing employment.[1] A recent comparative study of manufacturing enterprises in Asia observes that the size group of 6–49 workers accounts for more than 55 per cent of total non-household manufacturing in 2005 (Mazumdar and Sarkar, 2013). The share of large factories with more than 500 workers was close to 20 per cent and the remaining 25 per cent is the share of size group with 50–499 workers in the same year. Another study estimates that in 2005 nearly 85 per cent are employed in enterprises with less than 50 workers if own-account/household enterprises in total manufacturing employment are included (Hasan and Jandoc, 2013). This dualistic size structure in manufacturing employment has remained unchanged over the last two decades. More importantly, within the formal sector employment of contract workers (not subjected to labour regulations) has substantially increased in recent years. The share of contract workers in total workers employed in manufacturing has gone up to 32 per cent in 2009–10 from little less than 20 per cent in 1999–00. In Figure 9.1 the trend of contract intensity in Indian manufacturing since 1986 is shown.

Figure 9.1: Contract-worker intensity in manufacturing

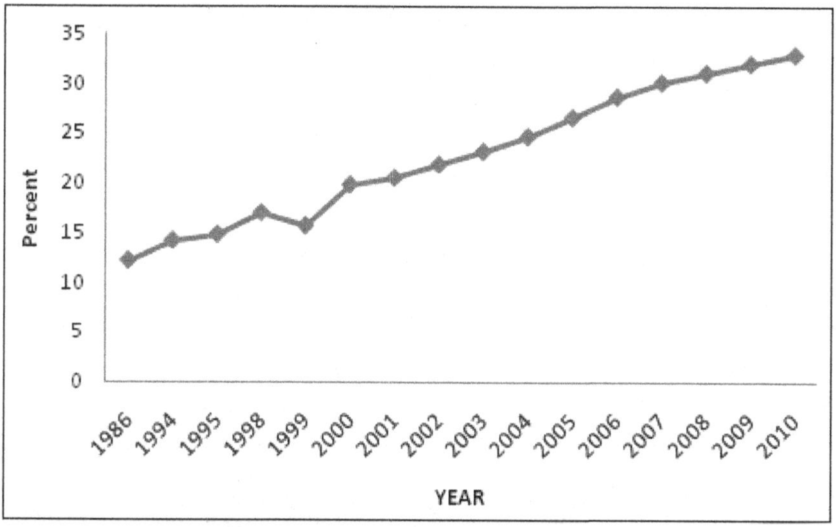

Source: ASI Summary Results, various years

In this background the present chapter asks how firms have responded to size-dependent labour regulations. Has it led to greater relative intensity of contract-workers use in firms falling below the specified employment/workforce size? Is this behaviour more significant in labour intensive industries and in those States of India with more rigid rules? My study is based on panel data of factories in the manufacturing sector over a period of 10 years between 1998–99 and 2007–08. I employ a definition of firm size consistent with labour laws. The key findings are (1) contract-worker intensity is higher in the size class 50–99 relative to other employment size groups; (2) average contract-worker intensity is relatively higher in labour intensive industries and in inflexible states; and (3) the relationship between contract-worker intensity and firm size is non-linear. Contract-worker intensity first declines, reaches a peak and then declines again.

9.1.1 Review of earlier studies

In this brief review studies of Indian manufacturing that have taken into account firm size or used the data on both large and small factories will be covered. Studies investigating the impact of labour regulations in manufacturing have been severely constrained by their lack of access to firm level data. Firm level data was not disclosed due to confidentiality clauses in the collection of statistics act. Only very recently such data with firm identification numbers have been made available to researchers in India. Fallon and Lucas (1993) were the first to study the impact of labour regulations on large firms in India. Their study used annual observations on 36 industries for the period 1959–82 on census sector that covered factories with more than 50 workers. Their results showed that the amendment to the IDA in 1976 which imposed government permission for firms employing more than 300 workers negatively affected employment. The decline in employment was shown to be higher in sectors where the fraction of employees in private sector enterprises with more than 300 workers was higher.

Hasan and Jandoc (2013) have assembled three large establishment level data sets that encompass formal and informal manufacturing to study size distribution over time. They compare firm size distribution across Indian states for three selected years, namely, 1994–95, 2000–01, and 2004–05. They partition Indian states into 'rigid' and 'flexible' labour regulation states after making some modification to the approach of Besley and Burgess (2004). They distinguish five size groups 1–9, 10–49, 50–99,100–199 and firms with more than 200 workers. They do not find a significant difference in how employment shares vary across the different size groups for the two sets of states. In the subgroup of labour-intensive industries greater prevalence of larger enterprises in flexible states was observed. In all the three years contract intensity peaked in the size class 50–99 in both labour intensive as well as all industries taken together. However, the size classes are measured by all production workers (regular plus contract), which deviated from the definition used in the context of labour regulations. The difference in mean contract intensity was not subjected to statistical tests.

Adhvaryu *et al.* (2013) used establishment data from ASI for 1987, 1990 and 1994 to test the prediction that the degree of employment response to shocks vary inversely with the degree of employment protection. Their study found that firms adjust to demand fluctuations by making adjustment to labour in flexible states than in inflexible states. In restrictive states firms are found to make adjustments to non-labour inputs in response to shocks measured by variation in agricultural incomes at the district level. However, they do not touch upon the mode of adjustment of labour in terms of work-force composition. Dougherty *et al.* (2011) study the impact of employment protection legislation on total factor productivity (TFP) and labour productivity using plant level panel data. TFP estimation is carried out using a restricted sample of plants with more than 200 workers and a classification of states based on labour reforms based on Dougherty (2008). TFP gains are found to be more for labour-intensive plants in states with lax regulations.

Including this introduction this chapter is divided into five sections. Section 9.2 presents the set of propositions that would be tested. Section 9.3 discusses the data base, measurement problems and issues related to classification of states and industry groups. Results are discussed in section 9.4. Conclusions of the study are presented in section 9.5.

9.2 Testable propositions

In India firms graduating into the formal sector face different regulatory costs of formality at different employment size levels. First, the Factory Act that contains rules to regulate occupational health and safety of workers if the firm has employed above 10 workers and if they are using electricity or 20 workers if they are not. Second, Chapter V-A of the IDA requires notice and compensation for lay-off, retrenchment and closure if the firm employs not less than 50 workers. Third, Chapter V-B requires notice, compensation and permission from government for lay-off, retrenchment and closure, if it employs more than 100 workers. Others like the Industrial Employment (Standing Orders) Act that lays down terms and conditions of work come into force if the firm employs more than 100 workers or less depending on the state law in which the firm is located. The Chapter V-B of IDA that requires permission from government authority for lay-off, termination and closure has been the most contentious provision in the context of Indian labour market rigidity debate. The size threshold is defined in terms of number of permanent workers in a given factory whose names appear in its muster roll. In other words, non-permanent workers could be employed to stay below the legal cut-off size. The dominant category of non-permanent workers is the contract workers or workers employed through a contractor. IDA is not applicable to contract workers hence their lay-off or termination does not require notice, compensation or permission. In addition firms are widely observed to pay contract-workers wages that are less than that is paid to regular workers and constitute additional cost savings for firms close to legal threshold employment size.

Compliance capability of firms will vary with firm size and it depends on their marginal profitability relative to marginal adjustment costs. As compliance costs start biting after a legally defined workforce size is attained one can expect greater effort on the part of firms to search for flexibility or ways to reduce potential adjustment costs. This aspect can be captured by the concept of contract-worker intensity. Contract-worker intensity is the share of contract workers in total number of workers in a firm.

Given this framework, I look for threshold effects in the following ways:

(1) Whether average contract-worker intensity is higher in the employment size group 50–99. This is expected if the objective of the firm is to stay below the size threshold of 100 workers. Here the employment size class is measured by number of permanent or regular workers in order to be consistent with the definition of IDA and other labour laws.

(2) Is there a non-linear relationship between contract-worker intensity and firm size? In other words, non-linearity could occur because the productivity advantage of size could outweigh compliance costs thus reducing the incentive to hire non-permanent workers. In order to capture the economies of scale effect, I measure factory size by total number of employees, a widely accepted measure of plant size.

(3) Is the average contract-worker intensity higher in labour-intensive industries? It may be argued that adjustment costs imposed by labour regulations would be greater in industries with high ratio of labour to capital. In addition if labour-intensive industries are export market-oriented industries and exporting firms are subject to greater demand uncertainty and seasonal fluctuations in demand or market order size then they are relatively adversely affected by rigid labour laws.

(4) Is contract-worker intensity higher in labour intensive industries located in inflexible states? Compliance costs can be expected to have greater bite in states within India that are supposed to be relatively inflexible in terms of their approach as revealed in the state-level amendments as argued in the literature (Besley and Burgess, 2004).

9.3 Data and measurement issues

The source of data is the ASI conducted by the MOSPI of the Government of India. I utilize unit level panel data spanning the period 1998–99 to 2007–08. The advantage is that ASI has recently made available factory identifiers such that an unbalanced panel of manufacturing factories can be set up as the data base.[2]

I started with raw data that contained 358,036 observations on open factories.[3] All observations (15,080) on non-manufacturing activities are dropped. They are: cotton-ginning and agriculture, recycling, electricity generation and distribution, water, construction, repair of motor vehicles and personal goods, and other business services. Two manufacturing industries – aircraft and nuclear plants – are dropped as they are government-owned business with little exposure to market competition. Production of fur is dropped as there were very few observations. For the remaining observations the following criteria was applied after dropping duplicate observations (observations recorded twice for the same factory in the same year). Observations are dropped if data on total output, fixed capital, total employment, total basic inputs and total non-basic inputs are found to be missing. Further those observations with negative fixed capital, zero values for total output, total employment, total basic and non-basic inputs; wrong or missing codes for rural or urban areas, type of organization, type of ownership, state identification and those with initial year of production greater than 2008 have been dropped. This data cleaning has left one with a total of 251,856 observations in the panel (Table 9.1).

The data set contains data on 25 states and 5 union territories (UT hereafter). In India, labour law is a concurrent list, where both the central and the state government formulate and enforce different labour laws. Firms in union territories are also subject to central government laws administered by their respective labour departments. The cleaned data set contains no observation on the following states and UTs: Arunachal Pradesh, Lakshadweep, Sikkim, and Mizoram. Observations from Andaman and Nicobar Islands have been dropped because of dominance of handicraft activities. The frequency distribution in terms of the number of years that a factory appears in the panel is shown in the appendix Table A9.1. There are 102,076 factories in the panel.

The ASI frame is based on the lists of registered factories/units maintained by the Chief Inspector of Factories (CIF) in each state/union territory. It includes all factories employing 10 or more workers if using power and if not using power the criterion is 20 or more workers on any day of the preceding 12 months. The ASI frame is revised once in three years and further divides the sampling frame into two components, called census sector and the sample sector. All factories with 100 or more workers were fully enumerated and covered under the census sector and the remaining factories were covered on a sampling basis using an efficient sampling design (Saluja and Yadav, 2008).

Table 9.1: Sample size and per cent lost after data cleaning

Year	Original sample	Used sample	Deleted	Per cent lost
1999	23693	15864	7829	33.0
2000	24733	17060	7673	31.0
2001	31121	21950	9171	29.5
2002	33461	23925	9536	28.5
2003	33854	24397	9457	27.9
2004	45494	31951	13543	29.8
2005	39760	27965	11795	29.7
2006	43738	30411	13327	30.5
2007	43381	30597	12784	29.5
2008	38801	27736	11065	28.5
	358036	251856	106180	29.7

Source: ASI Unit level panel data 1998–99 to 2007–08

It is important to note that once a factory is categorized as belonging to census or sample, it remains in the same category unless warranted by change in the number of workers. The definition of census sector changed later as follows. For the period 1997–98 to 1999–2000 the census sector included (1) all factories with 200 or more workers; (2) selected 'significant units' with fewer than 200 workers which 'contributed significantly to the value of output' in ASI between 1993–94 and 1995–96; and (3) all plants in 12 industrially backward districts and all public sector undertakings. Effective from 2000–01, the definition of census sector was modified to include all factories with more than 100 workers and all factories in the following five industrially backward states/union territories; Manipur, Meghalaya, Nagaland, Tripura and Andaman and Nicobar Islands. As a consequence one could observe entry and exit consistently only for factories with at least 200 workers in the data set. This is not a limitation as analysis of plant entry and exit is not the objective of the present chapter. The employment size distribution of sample units over the time period of the panel 1998–99 to 2007–08 is presented in the appendix Table A9.2.

Factory size is often measured by number of workers employed. Workers are divided into two categories, regular and contract. Regular workers are those directly employed by the factory and enjoy job-security benefits. Contract workers are those employed by the factory through an intermediary, that is a labour contractor or agent and they are not on the muster roll of the factory. Total workers in a factory refer to the sum of regular and contract workers. The threshold limit of 100 workers stipulated by the IDA refers to total number of regular workers. The ASI publishes size distribution of factories that uses total workers employed as the definition of employment size. There is a need to use total number of regular workers as the definition of firm size as my objective is to measure the impact of labour regulations. In my data set I found that a large proportion of firms has reported only regular workers and have not reported the number of contract workers. The data entered under the category total workers is often found to contain only the figures on regular workers. I have estimated the number of contract workers in each factory in the following way. The time-series data on mean ratio of contract workers to regular workers for the period 1998–9 to 2007–08 for all the three three-digit NIC industries is reported by the Labour Bureau (Labour Bureau, 2011). I have estimated the number of contract workers in each factory (factory with a missing observation on contract workers) by applying the mean ratio of contract to regular workers. Wherever both contract and regular workers have been reported I have used the original figures. The total number of workers is re-estimated by adding the estimated number of contract workers to the reported number of regular workers in each factory. Further 13,000 factories have not reported the number of regular workers. They were considered as having only contract workers and zero direct workers. Following this estimation I carried out the estimation of size distribution of factories using regular workers employed as the size criterion. The key focus variable in my analysis is the ratio of contract to total workers called contract-worker intensity of production. The basic descriptive statistics of the main sample of factories is presented in two parts in Table 9.2. Part A is based on all observations with estimates for missing data on contract workers and regular workers. Part-B is based on all observations but excluding observations with missing data. Notice that the average number of all three types of workers per factory is lower in Part-A compared to Part-B. However the average number of direct and total workers per factory is very similar.

All observations have a five-digit NIC-2004 code to identify the industry of the sample factory. For the sake of convenience I have collapsed these five-digit industry codes into manageable three-digit industry codes. I relied upon the classification used in Hasan and Jandoc (2013) to select the set of labour intensive industries. They have used the criterion of ratio of total employment to net total assets excluding land and buildings as a measure of capital intensity and classified industries into labour intensive and capital intensive industries. Industries not falling into either of the two categories are classified as others. The labour intensive industries are: beverages, tobacco, wearing apparel, leather, footwear, saw-milling, wood products including furniture, glass and glass-products, non-metallic mineral products and others that include watches and sports goods.[4] The distribution of sample observations by the states and UTs is shown in Table A3 in the appendix.

9.3.1 State groups by index of labour regulation

One important approach to measure the impact of labour regulations is to take advantage of inter-state variations in labour regulations first suggested by Besley and Burgess (2004). Under the Indian constitution both state and central (federal) government can legislate over subjects under the concurrent list. Labour laws

Table 9.2: Descriptive statistics: All years and all plants

A: using all observations with estimates for missing observations*					
Variable	Observations	Mean	Std. dev	Min	Max
Contract workers	251856	56.1	499.5	0	44641
Regular workers	251856	113.4	492.5	0	49692
Total workers	251856	169.4	800.7	1	70059
Ratio of contract to total workers	251856	0.30	0.26	0	1
B: using all observations after excluding missing observation					
Variable	Observations	Mean	Std. dev	Min	Max
Contract workers	74341	133.8	864.9	0	44641
Regular workers	238553	119.7	505.3	1	49692
Total workers	251856	152.8	714.4	1	49692
Ratio of contract to total workers	NE	NE	NE	NE	NE

Note: * See text for explanation
NE: Not estimated

Source: ASI unit level panel data 1998–99 to 2007–08

like IDA, Factories Act etc. are central acts but each state can make amendments to them. Besley and Burgess (BB hereafter) used inter-state variations in IDA to capture inter-state differences in labour regulation. BB classified each state-level amendment to IDA in 15 major states of India during 1949 to 1992. They assigned each amendment in these states a value of -1 (pro-employer), +1 (pro-worker) and zero (neutral). BB used net direction of change if a state was found to have passed multiple amendments in a given year. An index of labour regulation for each state is estimated as cumulated value of its annual scores up to the year 1992. This method yielded an index of labour regulation for each state that indicated the extent of strictness in the stance of a state towards labour regulations (inflexible or flexible). The BB approach has been criticized and evaluated in detail by Bhattacharjea (2006 and 2009) and other studies have attempted to make corrections to the original BB index based on his criticism (Ahsan and Pages, 2009; Gupta, Hasan and Kumar, 2009). Two important examples are Gujarat and Uttar Pradesh. Gujarat was designated as pro-worker (inflexible) by BB on the basis of a solitary amendment in 1973 that imposed a penalty on employers for not nominating representatives to firm level joint management councils (Bhattacharjea, 2006). Uttar Pradesh was also classified as pro-worker state by BB as 'they found that Uttar Pradesh had made no amendments to the central IDA over the entire 35 year period of their study…' (Bhattacharjea, 2006). It was pointed out by Bhattacharjea (2006) that Uttar Pradesh had amended its own 1947 IDA in 1983 and had set the threshold for permission for lay-offs, retrenchment and closure at 300 workers in contradistinction to threshold limit of 100 workers set by the central IDA amendment of 1982. This clearly suggested that a modification of the original BB classification is necessary.

After 1992, there has been very limited state-level amendment activity except in three cases, namely, Gujarat, Uttar Pradesh and Andhra Pradesh. Gujarat in March 2004 amended the IDA as applied to Gujarat by amending section V-D that said chapters V-A and V-B are not applicable to establishments declared to be in SEZ (special economic zones) by the Government of India. This amendment takes worker termination in an SEZ out of the purview of industrial dispute definition as defined by IDA. However such establishments are required to give one month notice and a compensation of 45 days' pay for every year of continuous service. Andhra Pradesh in August 2003 amended the Contract Labour Regulation and Abolition (CLRA) Act of 1970 by permitting employment of contract labour in a host of activities that are not considered to be core activity of an establishment. Uttar Pradesh amended the IDA in 2002 by changing the threshold for retrenchment from 300 workers to 100 workers thereby bringing the Uttar Pradesh IDA in line with the central amendment of 1982. By this amendment Uttar Pradesh can be said to have tightened the labour regulations after having maintained the threshold at 300 workers since 1983.

Given this background, I have classified the following six states as flexible states. They are Andhra Pradesh, Gujarat, Karnataka, Tamil Nadu, Rajasthan and Uttar Pradesh. Of this Andhra Pradesh, Karnataka, Tamil Nadu and Rajasthan have been classified as pro-employer by BB and as flexible by Gupta, Kumar and Hasan (2009). Gujarat by the most recent amendment of 2004 can be classified as pro-employer or flexible. Only Uttar Pradesh is somewhat ambiguous as noted above due to its raising threshold amendment of 2002. However, given its record of maintaining higher threshold for 19 years I have classified Uttar Pradesh as flexible. In other words, I have a set of six flexible states that have been by and large unambiguous. Of the remaining 24 states and UTs, I classify 14 of them as 'inflexible' and the remaining have been grouped as 'Others'. This classification is shown in the appendix Table A4 and the corresponding distribution of sample observations is shown in Table A4.1.

Econometric analysis is based on observations belonging only to two groups, namely, flexible and inflexible states.

9.4 Results

9.4.1 Descriptive statistics

As has been noted earlier, it is important to measure firm size by the number of regular workers to be consistent with IDA definition. Table 9.3 shows the distribution of median total-worker size by firm size groups defined in terms of regular workers. Nine employment size groups have been created. The two size groups of interest to one are 10–49 and 50–99. The median total-worker size in the size class 50–99 is closer to the upper limit of the size class that clearly suggests existence of large number of firms with above 100 workers in this size class. In other words firms are employing contract workers to stay below the threshold size of 100 as per IDA V-B. Similarly inference can be drawn that the size-class 10–49 has number of firms above 50 even though the median total-worker size is closer to the mid-point of the size class.

Table 9.3: Median firm by employment size group

Size-class*	Median firm size measured by total workers**	No. of observations
0–9	7	54,831
10–49	23	91,814
50–99	78	30,274
100–199	154	31,795
200–499	325	28,391
500–999	705	9,423
1000–1999	1422	3,348
2000–4999	3051	1,626
5000+	11124	354
All	37	251,856

*Size classes defined by regular workers
** Total workers= regular + contract-workers

Source: ASI unit level panel data 1998–99 to 2007–08

Figure 9.2: Mean contract-worker intensity by firm size

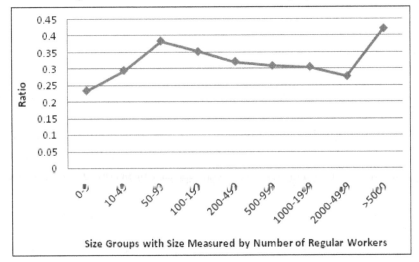

Source: Author's estimates based on ASI unit level panel data 1998–99 to 2007–08

In Figure 9.2, average contract intensity by employment size groups is graphed. Contract intensity peaks in the size group 50–99 underlining the importance of threshold effect. This threshold size is required to be tested separately using econometric methods. In addition the impact of differences in factor intensity (labour intensity of the industry) and regulatory stance of the state (flexible versus inflexible) can be tested after controlling for year-specific effects in the panel data. The size group 100–199, which is just above the legal cut-off size of 100 workers, has a mean contract intensity of 0.35 that is higher than the sample average of 0.30. Simple mean contract-worker intensity is found to be higher in labour intensive industries (0.38) but similar in two industry groups, namely, flexible (0.29) and inflexible (0.30).

9.4.2 Contract-worker intensity: Role of firm size, industry-labour-intensity and inflexible-states

A simple dummy variable regression model is estimated for the pooled data with logarithm of contract–worker intensity as the dependent variable. The econometric model takes the form:

$$\ln\left(CW_{eist}\right) = \alpha + \beta_1\left(S_{eist}\right) + \beta_2\left(LI_i\right) + \beta_3\left(Flex_s\right) + \beta_4\left(S_{eist} \times LI_i\right) + \beta_5\left(S_{eist} \times Flex_s\right) + \beta_6$$
$$\left(LI_i \times Flex_s\right) + \beta_7\left(S_{eist} \times LI_i \times Flex_s\right) + \lambda T + \varepsilon_{eist} \qquad \text{(Equation 9.1)}$$

Wherein (CW_{eist}) is the log of contract-worker intensity of establishment e in i^{th} industry and in s^{th} state in year t. (S_{eist}) are establishment size dummies that take the value 1 if the establishment falls in the size group 50–99 and zero otherwise. Note that S_{eist} captures an establishment characteristic, which is size of workforce. (IL_i) are labour-intensity dummies that takes the value 1 if the industry belongs to the category labour-intensive industry and zero otherwise, $(Flex_s)$ are the state specific labour flexibility indicators that takes the value 1 for states in the group inflexible-states and zero otherwise. $(S_{eist} \times LI_i)$, $(S_{eist} \times Flex_s)$, $(LI_i \times Flex_s)$ and $(S_{eist} \times LI_i \times Flex_s)$ are the four interaction dummies that capture the interaction of size and labour-intensive industry, size and flexibility indicator, labour-intensity and flexibility indicator and finally the interaction of size, labour-intensive industry and flexibility indicator. T denotes year fixed effects and ε_{eist} is an error term that is assumed to satisfy the standard properties. In actual estimation of equation (9.1) year dummy is interacted with industry and state dummies to control for industry-year and state-year fixed effects. A positive coefficient of the four dummy variables would indicate that mean contract-worker intensity is higher in their respective groups relative to other excluded groups after controlling for year-specific effects.

In Table 9.4, the results of estimating equation (9.1) is presented.[5] The coefficients of establishment size, industry labour intensity and state-specific flexibility indicators are positive and highly significant. The significance of threshold effects of labour regulations is indicated by the positive coefficient of size group 50–99. Similarly the average contract-worker intensity is significantly higher in labour intensive industries and in inflexible states relative to the omitted group. Three interaction dummies are significant. The interaction dummy for size group 50–99 and industry labour intensity is positive but insignificant. Observe that the interaction term (size x industry-labour-intensity x state-specific flexibility) is positive and significant that clearly indicates that firms in the size-group 50–99 in labour-intensive industries located in inflexible-states have higher contract-worker intensity. This result is consistent with the threshold effects of labour regulations.

Table 9.4: Regression of contract intensity on employment size-group, industry labour-intensity and state-specific flexibility indicators

Dependent variable: $\log(CW_{eist})$	
S_{eist} (Size-group 50–99)	0.092*** (11.4)
IL_i (Industry-labour-intensity)	0.188*** (30.8)
$Flex_s$ (State-specific-flexibility)	0.021*** (6.1)
$S_{eist} \times LI_i$ (Size x Industry-labour-intensity)	0.013 (0.68)
$S_{eist} \times Flex_s$ (Size x State-specific-flexibility)	0.076*** (6.7)
$LI_i \times Flex_s$ (Industry-labour-intensity x State-specific-flexibility)	0.082*** (9.9)
$S_{eist} \times IL_i \times Flex_s$ (Size x Industry-labour-intensity x State-specific-flexibility)	0.128*** (4.9)
State-Year FE	YES
Industry-Year FE	YES
Constant	–0.840*** (–265.3)
Observations	225572
R^2	0.08
F(25,225546)	831.9***

*Significant at 10 per cent, **Significant at 5 per cent, ***Significant at 1 per cent
Note: Robust 't' statistics in brackets

The relationship between contract-worker intensity and firm size could be non–linear as compliance capability varies with firm size. Large establishments could have lower average costs due to economies of scale and this could enable them to meet higher compliance costs of labour legislation. In this context, how contract-worker intensity varies with the size of total employment (regular + contract + managerial staff) is important. There would be firm specific time-invariant unobserved factors that affect the dependent variable that is contractorker intensity in their case. This requires a fixed effect model. With unit level panel data it is possible to test this hypothesis in a fixed effect (FE) model with state-year and industry-year specific effects. It is perhaps reasonable to postulate that contract-worker intensity and firm size takes the form of a cubic function. I estimate the following fixed effect model.

$$\ln(CW_{eist}) = \alpha_{eis} + \beta_1 \ln(ES_{eist}) + \beta_2 (\ln ES_{eist})^2 + \beta_3 (\ln ES_{eist})^3 + \mu_{st} + \eta_{it} + \varepsilon_{eist}$$

(Equation 9.2)

where, $\ln(CW_{eist})$ is the log contract-worker intensity of establishment e in i^{th} industry and in s^{th} state in year t. $\ln(ES_{eist})$ is log total employment, followed by the square of the log total employment and cube of the log employment. The signs of the three slope coefficients $\beta_1, \beta_2, \beta_3$ will indicate the curvature of the non-linear relationship between contract-worker intensity and firm size. α_{eis} are firm specific fixed effects that capture time-invariant unobserved heterogeneity that affect the dependent variable. In addition there would be time-variant unobserved factors common to all firms within a state like population growth or urbanization. Similarly, there would be time-variant unobserved factors common to all firms within industries like technological change or access to raw material. μ_{st} and η_{it} are the state-year and industry-year fixed effects introduced to account for such factors that may impact contract-worker intensity. ε_{eist} is the error term with standard properties. Firm size is assumed to be exogenously determined by technology and is not influenced by measured contract-worker intensity that is a behavioural outcome variable.

In Table 9.5, the estimates of equation (9.2) are shown. The coefficient of size is negative, size-squared is positive and size-cubed is negative and all the three coefficients are highly significant. This suggests that contract-worker intensity first declines, reaches a maximum and then declines again. This finding is consistent with the expectation that after reaching some level of establishment size the benefits of size expansion outweighs costs of regulatory compliance decreasing the incentive to hire contract workers.

In order to assess the robustness of the findings an OLS regression has been estimated with the union of the regressors in Table 9.4 and Table 9.5. The resulting estimates are presented in Table 9.6. The coefficients of all the 10 regressors have the same sign and similar statistical significance compared to their corresponding estimates in Table 9.4 and Table 9.5 respectively. This suggests that my estimates are reasonably robust.

Table 9.5: Regression of contract intensity on employment size, size-squared and size-cubed: FE model

Dependent variable: $\log(CW_{eist})$	
$\ln(ES_{eist})$	-0.476*** (-11.6)
$\ln(ES_{eist})^2$	0.137*** (13.7)
$\ln(ES_{eist})^3$	-0.008*** (-11.7)
State-Year FE	Yes
Industry-year FE	Yes
Constant	-1.485*** (-28.1)
Observations	245484
R^2	0.13
$F(21,99466)$	447.9***

*Significant at 10 per cent, **Significant at 5 per cent, ***Significant at 1 per cent
Note: Robust 't' statistics in brackets

Table 9.6: Regression of contract intensity on employment size-group, industry labour-intensity, state-specific flexibility indicators and employment size, size-squared and size-cubed

Dependent variable: $\log(CW_{eist})$	
S_{eist} (Size-group 50–99)	0.085*** (10.3)
IL_i (Industry-labour-intensity)	0.190*** (31.1)
$Flex_s$ (State-specific-flexibility)	0.023*** (6.7)
$S_{eist} \times LI_i$ (Size x Industry-labour-intensity)	0.011 (0.58)
$S_{eist} \times Flex_s$ (Size x State-specific-flexibility)	0.074*** (6.5)
$LI_i \times Flex_s$ (Industry-labour-intensity x State-specific-flexibility)	0.078*** (9.3)
$S_{eist} \times IL_i \times Flex_s$ (Size x Industry-labour-intensity x State-specific-flexibility)	0.134*** (5.1)

$\ln(\text{ES}_{eist})$	-0.194***
	(-10.2)
$\ln(\text{ES}_{eist})^2$	0.049***
	(10.8)
$\ln(\text{ES}_{eist})^3$	-0.003***
	(-11.3)
State-year FE	YES
Industry-year FE	YES
Constant	-1.605***
	(-63.9)
Observations	225572
R^2	0.09
$F(28,225543)$	750.7***

*Significant at 10 per cent, **Significant at 5 per cent, ***Significant at 1 per cent
Note: Robust 't' statistics in brackets

9.5 Conclusion

This chapter perhaps for the first time in the literature on Indian manufacturing tested the hypothesis of threshold effects using establishment level panel data. Labour regulations are size-dependent rules and therefore constitute a basis for threshold effects. Firms could use non-permanent workers to escape from higher adjustment costs of larger firm size. I have measured this outcome by contract-worker intensity. Contract-worker intensity is found to be higher in size class 50–99 relative to others supporting the conjecture that firms use non-permanent workers to stay below the size threshold of 100. The average contract-worker intensity of factories in size group 50–99 is found to be higher in labour intensive industries located in states categorized as inflexible. This supports the hypothesis that size dependent regulations will cause discontinuous change in firm behaviour in the sense that firms will employ contract-workers to stay below the threshold size. In other words EPL changes the workforce composition and hiring practices of Indian manufacturing firms.

My results have two implications. First, the presence of significant threshold effect suggest loss of potential output gains. Size-dependent labour regulation perhaps restricts the emergence of large firms in labour intensive industries in Indian manufacturing. Second, they do not necessarily improve access to good jobs. Contrary to the job security enhancing intension of EPL the employment status of average workers in establishments close to or just above the employment size of 100 workers appears to be worse and more vulnerable because of stricter size-dependent regulations.

This chapter can be extended in several directions for further verification and analysis. First, one would like to know what proportion of new entrants in manufacturing belongs to employment size below the legal threshold and what proportion graduate into larger size? Second, one may examine the relationship between initial employment size and employment growth of firms over time in flexible states relative to inflexible states. The idea of threshold effects of regulations is important for policy and can be applied in other areas of economic policy like tax and other fiscal incentives based on asset size of firms.

Appendix

Table A9.1: Sample distribution of factories by number of years of appearance in the data set

Number of years	Frequency	Per cent
1	51,921	50.87
2	17,457	17.1
3	12,017	11.77
4	6,305	6.18
5	3,512	3.44
6	2,551	2.5
7	2,041	2
8	2,235	2.19
9	1,653	1.62
10	2,384	2.34
Total	102,076	100

Source: ASI unit level panel data 1998–99 to 2007–08

Table A9.2: Distribution of sample units by year and employment size*
(Employment size class)

Year	0–9	10–49	50–99	100–199	200–499	500–999	1000–1999	2000–4999	'5000+
1999	3,953	5,640	1,486	1,317	2,219	770	291	142	46
2000	4,421	6,340	1,566	1,240	2,182	832	298	141	40
2001	4,897	7,437	2,690	3,012	2,579	850	295	153	37
2002	4,502	8,610	3,499	3,413	2,617	829	277	143	35
2003	4,317	8,636	3,742	3,659	2,716	853	295	148	31
2004	7,074	12,497	4,102	4,038	2,857	906	304	142	31
2005	6,684	10,034	2,779	3,965	3,017	967	334	155	30
2006	7,050	11,173	3,434	3,892	3,235	1,059	371	167	30
2007	6,708	11,522	3,558	3,632	3,408	1,123	416	197	33
2008	5,225	9,925	3,418	3,627	3,561	1,234	467	238	41
All	54,831	91,814	30,274	31,795	28,391	9,423	3,348	1,626	354

Source: ASI unit level panel data 1998–99 to 2007–08

Note: * Employment size is defined by the number of regular workers in a factory

Table A9.3: Sample distribution by state: All plants and all years

Sr. no.	State	No. of Observations
1	Jammu and Kashmir	2,534
2	Himachal Pradesh	3,509
3	Punjab	14,585
4	Chandigarh (UT)	1,396
5	Uttarakhand	3,354
6	Haryana	11,222
7	Delhi (UT)	6,977
8	Rajasthan	10,805
9	Uttar Pradesh	20,344
10	Bihar	3,909
11	Nagaland	659
12	Manipur	280
13	Tripura	1,899
14	Meghalaya	403
15	Assam	5,838

Sr. no.	State	No. of Observations
16	West Bengal	12,727
17	Jharkhand	4,101
18	Orissa	5,053
19	Chattisgarh	4,176
20	Madhya Pradesh	7,536
21	Gujarat	20,156
22	Daman and Diu (UT)	3,667
23	Dadra and Nagar Haveli (UT)	3,375
24	Maharashtra	28,956
25	Andhra Pradesh	17,397
26	Karnataka	14,330
27	Goa	2,968
28	Kerala	8,680
29	Tamil Nadu	28,162
30	Pondicherry (UT)	2,858
	Total	251,856

Note: UT=Union Territory
Source: ASI unit level panel data 1998–99 to 2007–08

Table A9.4a: Classification of states based on labour regulations

Flexible	Inflexible	Others
Andhra Pradesh	Assam	Chandigarh (UT)
Gujarat	Bihar	Dadar NH (UT)
Karnataka	Jharkhand	Daman (UT)
Rajasthan	Delhi (UT)	Jammu and Kashmir
Uttar Pradesh	Goa	Manipur
Tamil Nadu	Haryana	Meghalaya
	Himachal Pradesh	Nagaland
	Kerala	Tripura
	Madhya Pradesh	Pondicherry (UT)
	Chhattisgarh	Uttara Khand
	Maharashtra	
	Orissa	
	Punjab	
	West Bengal	

Note: UT=Union Territory
Source: Authors' classification, see text

Table A9.4b: Sample distribution by state group

State-group	Frequency	Per cent
Others	20,425	8.1
Flexible states	111,194	44.1
Inflexible states	120,237	47.7
Total	251,856	100

Source: ASI unit level panel data 1998–99 to 2007–08

Table A9.5a: List of labour-intensive industries

Industry	NIC 2004 Code
Beverages	155
Tobacco	160
Wearing apparel	181
Leather	191
Footwear	192
Saw-milling	201
Wood products	202
Glass and glass products	261
Non-metallic mineral products	269
Furniture	361
Others	369

Source: Author's classification, See text

Table A9.5b: Regression of contract intensity on employment size-group, industry-labour intensity and state-specific-flexibility indicators

Dependent variable: CW$_{eist}$	
S$_{eist}$ (Size-group 50–99)	0.454*** (16.3)
IL$_i$ (Industry-labour-intensity)	0.073*** (34.9)
Flex$_s$ (State-specific-flexibility)	–0.001 (–1.1)
S$_{eist}$ x LI$_i$ (Size x Industry-labour-intensity)	0.026*** (3.7)
S$_{eist}$ x Flex$_s$ (Size x State-specific-flexibility)	0.028*** (7.2)
LI$_i$ x Flex$_s$ (Industry-labour-intensity x State-specific-flexibility)	0.020*** (7.1)
S$_{eist}$ x IL$_i$ x Flex$_s$ (Size x Industry-labour-intensity x State-specific-flexibility)	0.083*** (8.5)
State-year FE	YES
Industry-year FE	YES
Constant	0.201*** (100.0)
Observations	231431
R^2	0.07
F(25,231405)	627***

*Significant at 10 per cent, **Significant at 5 per cent, ***Significant at 1 per cent

Note: Robust 't' statistics in brackets

Endnotes

The author is grateful to Professor K. L. Krishna for comments on an earlier draft of this chapter. I take responsibility for all errors and interpretation.

1　A later study by Little, Mazumdar and Page (1982) confirmed the problem of missing middle in Indian manufacturing. See Mazumdar and Sarkar (2008), chapter 9 for a detailed discussion of dualism in Indian manufacturing.

2   Dougherty et al., (2011) is another important study that has used a data set that is identical to that of the present study.

3   I wish to record that confidentiality of the unit level data was maintained and adequate precautions have been taken to avoid disclosing the identity of the units directly or indirectly.

4   The list of labour intensive industries along with their three digit codes is shown in Table A5 in the appendix.

5   It may be noted that firms with zero contract-workers will have zero contract-worker intensity and the log specification forces them to be dropped. This may bias the coefficient estimates. As a robustness check, I have estimated equation (9.1) without using the log specification for the dependent variable. The estimates are presented in Table A9.5b in the appendix. The results are broadly similar with all the interaction variables statistically significant.

References

Adhvaryu, A., A. V. Chari and S. Sharma. 2013. 'Firing Costs and Flexibility: Evidence from Firms' Employment Responses to Shocks in India', *Review of Economics and Statistics* 95(3): 727–40. Earlier version available at: http://www.yale.edu/adhvaryu/research.html. Accessed on 24 January 2013.

Ahsan, A. and C. Pages. 2009. 'Are All Labor Regulations Equal? Evidence from Indian Manufacturing', *Journal of Comparative Economics* 37(1): 62–75.

Besley, T. and R. Burgess. 2004. 'Can Labour Regulation hinder Economic Performance? Evidence from India', *Quarterly Journal of Economics* 119(1): 91–134.

Bhattacharjea, A. 2006. 'Labour Market Regulation and Industrial Performance in India', *Indian Journal of Labour Economics* 49(2): 211–32.

_____. 2009. 'The Effects of Employment Protection Legislation on Indian Manufacturing', *Economic and Political Weekly* 44(22): 55–62.

Dougherty, S. 2008. 'Labour Regulation and Employment Dynamics at the State Level in India'. *OECD Economics Department Working Papers, No. 624*. Paris, France: OECD publishing.

Dougherty, S., C. Veronica, F. Robles and K. Krishna. 2011. 'Employment Protection Legislation and Plant level-Productivity in India'. *Working Paper No.17693*. Available at: http://www.nber.org/papers/w17693. Accessed on 24 January 2013.

Dhar, P. N. and H.F. Lydall. 1961. *The Role of Small Enterprises in Indian Economic Development*. Mumbai: Asia Publishing House.

Fallon, P. R. and R. E. B. Lucas. 1993. 'Job Security Regulations and the Dynamic Demand for Industrial Labor in India and Zimbabwe', *Journal of Development Economics* 40(2): 241–75.

Guner, N., G. Ventura and Y. Xu. 2008. 'Macroeconomic Implications of Size-dependent Policies', *Review of Economic Dynamics* 11(4): 721–44.

Gourio, F. and N. A. Roys. 2012. 'Size-dependent Regulations, Firm Size Distribution and Reallocation'. *Working Paper No.18657*. NBER. Available at: http://www.nber.org/papers/w18657. Accessed on 24 January 2013.

Gupta, P., R. Hasan and U. Kumar. 2009. 'Big Reforms but Small Payoffs: Explaining the Weak Record of Growth in Indian Manufacturing', *India Policy Forum* 5: 59–123. New Delhi: Sage Publications.

Hasan, R. and K. Jandoc. 2013. 'Labor Regulations and the Firm Size Distribution in Indian Manufacturing'. In *Reforms and Economic Transformation in India*, edited by J. Bhagwati and A. Panagariya. New York: Oxford University Press.

Labour Bureau. 2011. *Annual Survey of Industries 2007–08, Vol.II: Report on Absenteeism, Employment, Labour Turnover and Labour Cost.* New Delhi: Ministry of Labour and Employment, Government of India. Available at: http://labourbureau.nic.in/reports.htm. Accessed on 24 January 2013.

Little, I. M. D., D. Mazumdar and J. Page. 1987. *Small Manufacturing Enterprises.* New York: Oxford University Press and the World Bank.

Mazumdar, D. and S. Sarkar. 2008. *Globalization, Labor Markets and Inequality in India.* London and New York: Routledge.

_____, 2013, *Manufacturing Enterprise in Asia: Size Structure and Economic Growth.* London, New York and Canada: Routledge and IDRC.

Saluja, M. R. and B. Yadav. 2008. 'Industrial Statistics in India Sources, Limitations and Data Gaps'. Working Paper available at: http://www.idfresearch.org/working.asp. Accessed on 24 January 2013.

Schivardi, F. and R. Torrini. 2008. 'Identifying the Effects of Firing Restrictions through Size–Contingent Differences in Regulation', *Labour Economics* 15(3): 482–511.

Tybout, J. 2000. 'Manufacturing Firms in Developing Countries: How Well Do They Do, and Why?', *Journal of Economic Literature* 38(1): 11–44.

10

Who is a Worker?

Searching the Theory of the Firm for Answers

Jaivir Singh

10.1 Introduction

There appears to be a persistent paradox that dogs the Indian economy – namely, that in spite of a comparatively high rate of growth of output, the expansion in formal employment is quite small. It is standard practice to attribute this to the constriction in the demand for labour caused by restrictive labour laws.[1] The laws are perceived to inhibit employers from hiring maximal number of workers because employers have to carry 'stocks' of labour even when there are product market downturns, leading employers to constrain hiring and possibly increase capital–labour ratios. However, while this question is central to the contemporary policy imagination, it needs to be realized that the role of labour law and regulation in labour markets is more complex than merely reducing it to a question of the law governing the hiring and firing of workers in response to fluctuations in product demand. A more nuanced understanding of the role of labour market institutions raising questions about the scope and coverage of labour law as the Indian economy sets about transforming itself, is an essential input for the contemporary policymaker.

A recent review article by MacLeod makes one aware of the pitfalls of standard labour market analysis.[2] He reminds one that the traditional study of labour markets is content to work with a competitive model where wages reflect the abilities of workers as well as the efficient allocation of labour, though these outcomes may be inequitable in many ways. Apart from signifying inequitable distribution of income, they represent inadequate insurance for workers in the face of unforeseen labour shocks. The many institutions that surround labour concerns like minimum wages, unions, termination compensation, unemployment insurance, centralized bargaining, are typically viewed as devices that compensate these risks and inequities. If it is believed on faith that the market generates economic efficiency, then these interventions cannot but generate inefficiency. This in turn means that there is an inevitable equity (fairness) – efficiency trade off. The cost imposed in terms of efficiency loss is further said to compound matters because the restriction on the ability of firms to make adjustments in response to exogenous changes harms all workers in the long run. Counter to this standard discourse, MacLeod points to the fact that some form of 'labour law' has been in place since antiquity and that maybe there is a need to approach the question of labour law (and its reform) outside of the obsession with the fairness-efficiency trade off. Drawing on the transaction cost perspective that views institutions as devices that substitute for some market failure, he feels that the labour market institutions can possibly be viewed as a response to some market failure – the institution in question may actually be solving a resource allocation problem. Having said this, MacLeod feels that there is still no clear understanding of how law works or the impact of legal rules on economic performance and that these are matters worth pursing as objects of research. This chapter works in sympathy with this perspective and proceeds to raise some broad concerns regarding labour law reform in India. It does so by profiling the parameters that define the legally recognized worker in India. It is demonstrated that the narrowing of the definition has led to progressive exclusion of workers from being recognized legally, an act that may cause damage to the section of the work force that makes a relationship specific investment in the job it is hired to perform. This hazard is articulated by invoking the theoretical literature that defines the boundaries of the firm, which in turn is conjoined with some legal scholarship to suggest that there may be some economic benefits to allow (at least some categories of) workers to have long-term rights on their jobs.

The first step in this regard is to attempt superimposing the categories of the Indian workforce against the laws that cover them. This is attempted in Section 10.2 of the chapter, at the end of which it is apparent that the legally assured benefits that a worker enjoys is contingent on whether he is legally recognized as a *workman* and justifies our motivation to investigate as to *who is a worker?* How we choose to accept this answer defines one's notions of work and reflects how we value such work. To get help in this task, we turn to the theory of the firm, hoping to gain some insight from the discussion on identifying the boundaries of the firm. This is attempted in Section 10.3 of the chapter, drawing on interdisciplinary work that seeks to engage with both legal and economic understandings of the firm. In the final Section 10.4 of the chapter the contents of the previous two sections are counterposed against each other to suggest some concerns that should be kept in mind in the event of labour law reform in India.

10.2 The law and the 'worker'

There is a standard manner in which the structure of the Indian labour market is described – it is said that the Indian work force is approximately between 430 to 471 million (as per the NSSO 2009–10 survey) with 53 per cent employed in agriculture, about 11 per cent being employed in manufacturing with the rest being situated in the residual services sector. To this one can add another key structural feature of the Indian labour market to sharpen the depiction – it is widely suggested that only about 10 per cent or so of the labour force can be described as being employed by the organized sector (industry and services in public sector, private corporate sector and factory manufacturing), with the rest of the non-agricultural work force more or less situated in the urban informal sector where both wages and conditions of work are inferior to the organized sector.[3] A picture of this structure can be captured in the figure below that shows half the labour force as being involved with agricultural activity, (measured from the left), and with 10 per cent of the labour force situated in the organized sector at the right end of the figure. A picture of this structure can be captured in the figure below which maps the approximately 430 million strong Indian workforce on to a line. The line shows that half the labour force is involved in agricultural activity (mesured from the left) with 10 per cent of the labour force being situated at the right end of the line.

Figure 10.1: Total work force: 430 million

◆ Agriculture	◆ Services/informal	◆ Organized
(50 per cent)	(40 per cent)	(10 per cent)

As suggested by Mehrotra et al. the dynamics behind this picture involve two kinds of transitions – (1) the movement of unskilled labour from agriculture attracted by higher wages to the unorganized/informal sector; and (2) the movement from the informal sector to the formal sector.[4] It is widely decried that the formal/manufacturing sector has not been able to absorb the burgeoning labour force that is both expanding demographically as well as attempting to shift across sectors in search of productive work. While this categorization of the labour force above is made without direct reference to labour laws – the reach of labour laws more or less follows the statistical classification. A complementary institutional description of the Indian labour market would emphasize the fact that while labour laws protect formal sector labour, protective labour laws do not cover the bulk of the labour force – that is the agricultural as well as the informal sector work force. In other words, the many Indian labour laws are operational only for a worker who is employed in a legally recognized category of establishment where law sanctions labour benefits and in addition if she is legally recognized as a labourer; both conditions are fulfilled typically only if the worker is employed in the formal sector.[5]

As a first step it is useful for us to unravel more clearly as to who is the worker as per the law. It is of course very difficult to cover the entire set of criteria used by the many labour laws in existence. However to broadly begin the exercise, the size of the employing establishment, often enough, determines whether laws pertaining to social security or conditions of work are applicable. Thus, safety and health requirements become mandatory only if the Factories Act 1948 covers the unit – applying only to factories using power and employing 10 or more workers, and if not using power, employing 20 or more workers on any day of the preceding 12 months. Other than this, some form of safety and health measures also kick–in if specific sectoral laws such as the Mines Act 1952 or Plantations Labour Act 1951 cover the establishment. Turning to social security, a law such as The Employees' Provident Fund and Miscellaneous Provisions Act 1952 only covers establishments employing more than 20 workers. The size of the establishment becomes even larger for both standard terms of employment and procedures to be followed for disciplinary action to prevail, requiring the establishment to employ 50 or more workers so that it can be covered by the Industrial Employment (Standing Orders) Act, 1946. More famously under the Industrial Disputes Act 1947 only establishments employing more than 100 workers need to get permission from the government before lay-offs, retrenchment or closure is effected.

Apart from the size of the employing establishment, Indian labour law also uses functional and/or remunerative criterion to exclude certain categories of workers from being labelled as workers. It is important to look at this in some detail, beginning by viewing how the Industrial Disputes Act understands the category of the worker. We look at this definition quite centrally because for a worker to raise a dispute obviously requires for him to possess a legal standing as a worker, the details of which are covered by Section 2 (s) of the Act. It may also be noted other labour laws often carry definitions of a worker which are very similar. Section 2(s) of the Industrial Disputes Act defines a 'workman' as:

> any person (including an apprentice) employed in any industry to do any skilled or unskilled manual, supervisory, technical or clerical work for hire or reward, whether the terms of employment be expressed or implied, and for the purposes of any proceeding under this Act, in relation to an industrial dispute, includes any such person who has been dismissed, discharged or retrenched in connection with, or as a consequence of, that dispute or whose dismissal, discharge or retrenchment has led to that dispute but does not include any such person –
>
> i) who is subject to the Army Act 1950 or the Air Force Act 1950 or the Navy Act, 1957; or
>
> ii) who is employed in the police service or as an officer or other employee of a prison; or
>
> iii) who is employed mainly in a managerial or administrative capacity; or
>
> who being employed in a supervisory capacity, draws wages exceeding one thousand six hundred rupees per mensem or exercises, either by the nature of the duties attached to the office or by reason of the powers vested in him, functions of a managerial nature.

The first point to note is that the definition explicitly excludes Army, Navy, Air Force, Police and Prison personnel as well as supervisors earning more than a stipulated amount and all managers/administrators. Over time, additions to such exclusions have also been made by court rulings. One particularly interesting case decided by a constitution bench of the Supreme Court – *H.R Adyanthaya vs. Sandoz (India) Ltd.* – decided on whether 'medical representatives' are workmen as per Section 2 (s) of the Industrial Disputes Act.[6] The Court noted that the legislature has been adding to the definition beginning with work being understood as 'skilled or unskilled manual or clerical work', going on to add 'supervisory' and 'technical' in an amendment 1956 and in a subsequent 1982 amendment defining work as 'any manual, unskilled, skilled, technical, operational, clerical or supervisory work'. The Court went through (sometimes conflicting) case law and felt that for 'a person to be a workman he must be employed to do the work of any of the categories, viz., manual, unskilled, skilled, technical, operational, clerical, or supervisory.' Turning specifically to the medical representatives, the court countered the view that the medical representatives performed duties of a skilled nature since 'the word 'skilled' … will not include the work of a sales promotion employee such as a medical representative' and further stating that '(t)hat word has to construed ejusdem generis[7] and thus construed, would mean skilled work whether manual or non-manual, which is of a genre of the other types of work mentioned in the definition.' A connected contention over the term *skilled* shows up in another case *Ahmedabad Pvt. Primary Teacher's Association vs. Administrative Officer and Ors.*, where gratuity was denied to a teacher because she apparently did not qualify as an employee under the Payment of Gratuity Act 1972 Act.[8] The court confronted the question that given the definition in the Act (which clearly echoes the Industrial Disputes Act definition) 'to do any skilled, semi-skilled, or unskilled, manual, supervisory technical or clerical work', whether teachers could be covered by the definition as employees. In other words the court considered 'the correctness of the view with regard to the applicability of the Act to the teachers as a class.' Invoking the discussion around 2 (s) of Industrial Disputes Act in a number of cases it was said that those involved in education cannot be called workmen as it is not 'skilled or unskilled manual work or supervisory work or technical work or clerical work.'[9] It is said that

> Teachers do not answer description of being employees who are skilled, semi-skilled or unskilled. These three words used in association with each other intend to convey that a person who is 'unskilled' is one who is not skilled and a person who is semi skilled may be one who falls between two categories meaning he is neither fully skilled or unskilled.

The court goes on to say that it aims to achieve meaning by taking the three words and applying the rule of construction *noscitur a sociis*.[10] The argument is that since 'trained or untrained teachers are not 'skilled', 'semi-skilled', 'unskilled', 'manual', 'supervisory', 'technical' or 'clerical' employees they are also not employed in 'managerial' or 'administrative' capacity. Occasionally, even if they do some administrative work as part of their duty with teaching, since their main job is imparting education, they cannot be held employed in 'managerial' or 'administrative' capacity. Teachers are clearly not intended to be covered by the definition of 'employee.' In a similar vein in the case of *Sonepat*

Co-Op Sugar Mill vs. Ajit Singh[11] it was held that since the H. R. Adyanthaya judgment – teachers, advertising managers, chemists, gate sergeants, welfare officers were not allowed to be 'workman' and so for similar reasons legal assistants cannot be considered 'workmen'.

Apart from the set of exclusions pointed out above, Section 2(s) of the Industrial Disputes Act further constructs the legal figure of the worker using phrases such as 'work for hire and reward', 'terms of employment be expressed and implied' and by explicitly referring to the circumstance of 'dismissal, discharge or retrenchment'. Thus the worker comes to be defined as being employed with reference to disputes against employers, particularly in relation to the category of termination disputes. In this regard the interpretation of the courts has played an important role in defining what it means for a person to be 'employed in any industry' – one important early case being *Dharangadhara Chemical Works Ltd. vs. State of Saurashtra*[12]. Among other things the judgment overtly states that

> (t)he essential condition of a person being a workman … is that he should be employed to do the work in that industry, that there should be, in other words, an employment of his by the employer and that there should be the relationship between the employer and him as between employer and employee or master and servant.

Thus the problem raised in the case as to who can be classified as a worker is resolved using the master-servant rubric.

Turning to the details, the case involved an establishment that manufactured salt by allotting a plot of land to an *agaria* (a jobber of sorts) who was paid ₹ 400 as initial expense to level the land and sink a well on it. The salt superintendent tested the density of the water and the brine was brought up and stored in reservoirs. The superintendent tested the manufactured crystals and if they were of right quality the *agaria* was paid for the salt. The company owned both the salt that was accepted as well as that which was rejected – the *agarias* could not move the salt or sell it and were paid at the end of the season against salt crystals that conformed to a certain level of quality. The *agarias* worked seasonally manufacturing salt, resorting to agricultural work over the monsoon period and typically used family labour but were free to hire in labour as well. The salt company did not prescribe hours of work or exercise control over hours of work, nor were holidays specified and furthermore no muster roll was maintained.

A dispute emerged between the *agarias* and the company regarding conditions under which the company employed them. The dispute was referred to a tribunal and the company reacted by arguing that *agarias* were not 'workmen' – a point which they argued all the way up to the Supreme Court. The Supreme Court emphasized the point that a workman should be 'employed' and that to be employed 'there should be the relationship between employer and employee or master and servant.' The 'test' for this relationship 'is the existence of a right of control in respect of the manner in which the work is to be done.' The judgment also points to the distinction between *contract for services* and a *contract of service*. This distinction is articulated invoking a British judgment – 'In the one case the master can order or require what is to be done while in the other case he can not only order or require what is to be done but how it shall be done.' Yet another British judgment is invoked – this judgment raises the instance of contracts of service where the master cannot control the manner in which the work is to be done. (Case of a captain of a ship) A ship's master, a chauffer and a reporter of a newspaper are under a contract of service but a ship's pilot, a taxi-man and a newspaper contributor are employed under a contract for services. Under a contract of service 'a man is employed as a part of a business and his work is an integral part of the business; whereas, under a contract for services, his work, although done of the business, is not integrated into it but is only accessory to it'. Yet another British judgment invoked speaks of 'four indicia of a contract of service' (1) master's power of selection; (2) the payment of wages; (3) master's right of control of the method of doing work; and (4) master's right of suspension or dismissal. Yet further British cases are invoked including Halsbury's Laws of England, ending up with the view 'that the prima facie test for determination of the relationship between master and servant is the existence of the right of the master to supervise and control the work done by the servant not only in the matter of directing what work the servant is to do but also the manner in which he shall do his work…' Thus, the Court argued that though others may have assisted the agarias and their wages worked out on a piece–rate basis, since 'supervision and control' was exercised at all stages of the operation by the company, they were indeed 'workmen within the definition of the term contained in s. 2 (s) of the Act'.

Down the line, while some socialist jurisprudence attempted to expand the meaning of control to 'economic control'[13] this more expansive approach to understanding the employer-employee relationship has not stuck. Thus, more recently when called upon to define the rights of contract labour, the courts continue to base their analytical thinking in line with the orthodox 'master and servant' tradition. In the influential (but in some senses a somewhat odd case) of *Steel Authority of India*,[14] clarification was sought from a Constitution Bench as to whether the act of 'abolishing' contract labour under the *Contract Labour (Regulation and Abolition) Act* necessarily means the absorption of the labour as regular employees by the principal employer. In this case the Supreme Court (overruling a previous judgement that said that abolition of contract labour required the erstwhile principal employer to employ the workers in regular jobs[15]) stated quite categorically that there was no obligation on the employer to employ the contract labour that may have been abolished by the government. Among the reasons provided for this stance it is said that 'the contract labour is not rendered unemployed as is generally assumed but continues in the employment of the contractor as the notification does not sever the relationship of master and servant between contractor and contract labour.' This reasoning is at odds with the fact that the 'notification made under Section 10 (2) of the *Contract Labour (Regulation and Abolition) Act* is presumably notified because the appropriate government has information that the activity for which contract labour has been hired through a contractor is either necessary for the industry, perennial in nature, is/can be performed by regular workmen or work sufficient to employ full time workers. If this is indeed the case then there is a clear and direct link with employer, but the court makes it clear that whether the relationship is real or sham is an independent issue to be litigated as an industrial dispute separately. A more recent case[16] creates a test to discern whether the contract labour agreement is 'sham, nominal and is a mere camouflage', by pointing out that if the contract is for the supply of labour then the labour will work under the 'directions, supervision and control of the principal employer' but since the salary is paid by the contractor the 'ultimate supervision and control lies with a contractor'. The facts of this case involved a very protracted tussle between a set of unskilled labourers at the Madras airport, who had been used as loaders for decades without gaining the benefits of being in a direct employment relationship with the employer. The innovation of the judgment is to label the contractor's control as *primary* and the principal employer's control as *secondary*. This test is clearly designed to make it harder for workers hired as contract labour to establish an employment relationship with the principal employer.

Outside the world of large gangs of unskilled contract workers, the argument of a lack of an employer-employee or master and servant relationship has also been used by the courts to counter job claims by 'retainers' who had entered into a fixed term contract to service TVs with the employing firm.[17]In fact recent labour jurisprudence and even statutory law has been re-orienting itself to privileging fixed-term contracts as a distinct category. While there has been no large scale legislated change as such, the rules governing Industrial Employment (Standing Orders) Act[18] were amended in 2003 by inserting the term 'fixed term employment' where 'a fixed term employment of workman' is defined to carve out the figure of a worker who is engaged on the basis of a contract of employment for a fixed period. While ostensibly covered by the same conditions as more permanent workers, the rules make it clear that no temporary workman – whether monthly, weekly or piece-rated, no probationer, badli or fixed term employment workman can be entitled to any notice or pay in lieu thereof if her services are terminated.[19] Though the changes in the rules governing standing orders were appealed by the UPA government in 2007, the spirit of the fixed term contract understanding of the contract of employment has been encouraged by the supreme court to signal support to employers who counter compensation claims due to workers upon termination of the employment relationship.[20] The *Industrial Disputes Act* requires establishments employing more than 50 workmen to pay compensation upon retrenchment if the worker has been in employment for more than 240 days. Over the years judicial interpretation of the definition of retrenchment[21] came to expand the meaning of the term well beyond the termination of services of surplus labour – culminating with a constitution bench of the Supreme Court associating retrenchment with 'the termination by the employer of the service of a workman for any reason whatsoever except those expressly excluded in the section.'[22] More recently the definition has been interpreted not to be inclusive but to exclude, a point that can be illustrated by the case of *Municipal Council, Samarala vs. Raj Kumar*, where a worker had been repeatedly hired using a series of fixed term contracts[23]. In this case the court interpreted the exception to recognizing a termination of employment in the definition of retrenchment (Section 2(oo) (bb) of the Industrial Disputes Act which says 'termination of the service of the workman as a result of the non-renewal of the contract of employment between the employer and the workman concerned on its expiry or such contract being terminated under a stipulation in that behalf contained therein') by emphasizing not the first part of the exception, which did not apply in the case because renewal of the fixed term contract was taking place repeatedly, but the second part of the exception by privileging the fact that the employing establishment had on hand some written rules and stipulations which allowed for fixed term contracts.

Yet other new employment relationships have also recently come to be set by the Supreme Court – particularly and forcefully affecting the categories of daily wage, casual workers and ad hoc workers employed by the government. An older jurisprudence was sympathetic enough to such workers, awarding them permanent employment if they had been employed for a long time in the establishment[24]. However a recent five judge judgment – *Secretary, State of Karnataka and Ors vs. Umadevi and Ors*, makes it clear that that daily wage, casual workers, ad-hoc workers working for the government (Central, State and instrumentalities of the State) cannot have the legitimate expectation that they will gain permanent jobs even if they have been working in the establishment for a while.[25] In this judgment it is stated that while courts are often 'swayed' by the fact that people have been working for some time, on the grounds of that they may be in a weak bargaining position – however this generates another kind unfairness because by gaining employment in this manner the worker circumvents being employed by due procedure (with the Court emphasizing the violation of Article 14 and 16 of the Constitution).In fact it goes on further to say that no court should insist on regularization of temporarily hired labour – the fate of such affected workers is to depend on government policy, which the Court encourages the government to formulate.[26] In this context it is argued that the worker was 'aware of the nature of the employment when he first took it up' and presumably therefore must not have any expectation of any automatic change in her status.

Such awareness of their position is of course also very important for the so called white collar worker as no labour law covers rights in the job other than the Indian Contract Act 1872. Here the importance of termination clauses written into the contract of employment becomes very important, with very few default legal rules to fall back on if such clauses are poorly specified. The standard form contract has a termination clause associated with employment contracts at will – a period of notification before termination or some compensation in lieu, which is the maximum that courts uphold if cases are litigated. By and large litigation in white-collar cases is thin, with courts oriented to upholding the contract when cases appear before them.[27]

This is of course not to interpret the above description to say that all labour cases that have appeared before the Supreme Court recently are necessarily unsympathetic to worker interest. In fact a series of recent cases – *Harjinder Singh vs. Punjab State Warehousing Corporation*[28] and *Bhilwara Dugdh Utpadak Sahakari S. Ltd.vs. Vinod Kumar Sharma Dead by L.Rs. and Ors.*[29] – invoke the notions of the rights of workers and award litigating workers rights over their 'contractual' jobs. Rather the central point of the description is to point to the contents of the contemporary jurisprudence that constructs the figure of work and the worker in opposition to an earlier more 'socialist' oriented labour jurisprudence. The description basically throws up two broad points – one that the worker is understood in a very narrow sense – a sense that works with some idea of an industrial work force and wants only notions and words around this category to be acceptable as a worker, leaving, as we saw, work such as teaching, sales representatives, legal assistants and so on out of the judicially recognized category of the worker. Secondly while there may be a core of protected workers all those at the edge and even some in the core are being employed following terms of what is typically labelled in common law jurisdictions as 'employment contracts at will', sometimes the terms are in fact more stringent because termination benefits are often enough entirely absent.

This is indeed the outcome sought by the rhetoric of labour law reform, which bemoans the stringency of Indian labour law with the traditional emphasis on rights of workers – so to speak laws that will encourage flexibility.[30] While fairness arguments are often counterpoised to this, some concern needs to be voiced regarding the economic loss that may accompany intemperate orientation towards very narrow categorization of workers and insistence on common law doctrines such as 'master and servant' and 'employment at will' type definitions of the employment relation. Though the term 'employment at will' or 'contract at will' is not found in Indian labour law and is characteristically indigenous to American labour jurisprudence, the substance of the doctrine typifies employer – labour relations over the 'flexible' segment of the Indian labour market. The 'at will' doctrine developed in the United States in the nineteenth century urges that there should be no legal interference in both the employer's act of hiring and discharge of workers as well the act of a worker terminating the relationship at will.[31] The historical origin of the doctrine is associated with liberating the servitude of workers from their master-employers and in a sense suggests an equality of employers and workers. However, today this means that employers can discharge workers without any obligation and it is precisely this type of regime that governs the ostensibly 'reformed' segment of the Indian labour market.

10.3 The 'worker' and the boundaries of the firm

Richard Epstien, a natural votary for 'contracts at will' doctrine in employment, has written expansively on the many virtues of using this legal framework to regulate employment relations.[32] The listed merits include fairness, efficiency and even the possible generation of favourable distributional consequences but for our purpose we do not dwell on the rhetoric of these arguments, which follow a standard trajectory; rather it is useful to highlight a set of points raised by him as to when exceptions to the contract at will are economically justified. Richard Epstein tells us that contract at will works best when performances on both sides follow each other closely – the mechanisms of fire or quit takes care of transgressions on either side. However, if one party has to perform in full, then 'this bonding mechanism will break down because there are no longer two unperformed promises of roughly equal value to stand as security for each other.'[33] Such 'imperfect bonding' includes instances when employers refuse to pay wages or when there are job related personal injuries and more generally when work itself covers an extended period of time. Apart from these qualifications, Epstien insists that the benefits of contracts at will are enormous because they permit 'the ceaseless marginal adjustments that are necessary in any ongoing productive activity conducted, as all activities are, in conditions of technological and business change.'[34]

The 'contract at will' understanding of employment, sits easily within the economics textbook version of the firm where well-defined inputs flow into the firm and come out at the other end as well defined outputs. Labour as a factor of production is understood as numbers that are subject to 'ceaseless marginal adjustments'. However, if one thinks of a world where the caveats mentioned by Epstien are important and not mere exceptions, where labour is not ahistorical and work is spread out over a period of time, then the simple domain of fire or quit as devices to govern the employment relation appear to be quite a bit more complicated.

To approach the matter requires us, in the first instance to move away from the black box theory of the firm and follow Coase in his classic 1937 paper, where he approached the firm somewhat differently by demanding an explanation for the existence of the firm.[35] He suggested that the firm comes into being as a structure of hierarchical commands replacing the market because the 'costs of the price mechanism' make the organization of every economic activity in the market excessively costly. The limits of the firm are reached when the marginal benefit of functioning within the firm equals the marginal cost of administrative mistakes. While Coase emphasized the 'costs of the price mechanism' (the term that metamorphosed into transaction costs) as negotiation costs, subsequent work by Williamson[36] and Klien *et al.*[37] has gone on to link transaction costs with opportunism associated with relationship-specific investment, which leads to hold up problems. This work demonstrates that vertical integration can prevent such opportunism, but, because it emphasizes only the benefits of integration, the limits to the firm remain undefined.

The limits to the firm have come to be more rigorously delineated by Grossman and Hart by invoking the notion of residual rights of ownership[38]. Briefly speaking, the model they suggest is driven by the idea that economic activity can be thought of in two stages where the first, ex-ante stage involves making relationship specific investments, followed by a second ex-post stage when production decisions are made. While ex-post contracts are assumed to be efficient, the ex-ante contracts are said to be typically incomplete on account of transactions costs associated with hold ups. Thus, ownership defined by residual rights (property rights that remain with a party in relation to non-human assets after she has contracted out whatever she wants to) becomes an important determinant of the ex-post surplus, which in turn affects incentives to make ex-ante investments. Thus a merger does not yield unambiguous benefits since the owner-manager looses incentives to invest in the ex-ante relationship specific investment. Hence if what determines the size of the firm is the most favourable level of ex-ante investment, then highly complementary assets should be owned in common but as the firm grows and the relation of one asset to the other diminishes then separation is better (though integration prevents hold ups, such gains do not adequately compensate incentive losses).

The Grossman and Hart model looks at costs and benefits of integration only in terms of incentives for top management – in work that extends the model, Hart and Moore look at the implications of changes in ownership on incentives of not only owner-managers but also non-owners of assets (employees).[39] The typical scenario investigated in this work involves an asset worked on by several people where employers have ownership rights though employees do not and involves analysing how the incentives of employees change as integration occurs or, to phrase it differently, when asset ownership becomes more or less concentrated. In this model agents take action today – say make an asset-specific investment in developing a skill – which will pay off tomorrow as the fruits of increased productivity. However such a pay-off will accrue to the agent only if she has access to the particular asset in question. Since writing complete contracts today to cover such situations is not possible (returns tomorrow being un-contractible today) the agent's marketability/bargaining position tomorrow will depend on her access to assets and is hence sensitive to allocation of asset ownership. Therefore agent's action of investment today is related to whether she owns the asset and if she does not own it, then who owns it. The broad propositions to emerge from the model are that (1) for efficient investment, ownership of assets should lie with agents who are indispensible to the economic activity in question even though they do not necessarily make the ex ante investment decisions; and (2) for efficient investment assets that are complementary should be owned together.

The creativity of the Grossman-Hart and Hart-Moore model has been to incorporate an incident from the multidimensional legal definitions that construct property in law, residuarity, and use it to gain an understanding of the contours of the firm. There are perhaps yet other dimensions of property law, which can be invoked to supplement and extend the model, and one of these directions is to look to the notion of *property in work*. As a first step in this direction, it is important to discern the institutional assumptions regarding labour made in these property rights models of the firm. To begin it is important to go back to the understanding of labour with which Coase formulated his idea of the firm. The role of labour is quite central to this construction – he says that costs of negotiating and concluding a separate contract for each exchange transaction are bound to be very high, in particular a factor of production does not typically sign a series of contracts with those he is cooperating in a firm. Instead of a series of short contracts there is one longer contract – thus for a certain remuneration a factor agrees to obey directions of the entrepreneur within certain limits. To quote him in this context, he says

> The details of what the supplier is expected to do is not stated in the contract but is decided by the purchaser. When the direction of recourses (within the limits of the contract) becomes dependent on the buyer in this way, that relationship which I term a 'firm' is obtained. A firm is likely therefore to emerge in those cases where a very short-term contract would be unsatisfactory. It is obviously of more importance in the case of services – labor than it is in the case of the buying of commodities. In the case of commodities the main items can be stated in advance and the details which will be decided later will be of minor significance. (Coase, 1937, 392)

A particularly striking feature of this conceptualization is that it engages explicitly with the legal understanding of labour (albeit a very specific set of labour law doctrines) with Coase going on to state that in approaching the firm there is a need to consider the legal relationship of 'master and servant'. He particularly identifies the essentials of the relationship using a quote from a law text that emphasizes the point that the law of master and servant is distinguished by 'personal services to the master' – 'otherwise the contract is a contract for sale of goods or the like'. Drawing on the legal text, he quotes as saying that, the 'master must have the right to control the servant's work', so as to make the relationship definitive. This is in contrast to relations with an independent contractor where 'the contractor or performer is not under the employer's control in doing the work or effecting the service: he has to shape and manage his work so as to give the result he has contracted to effect'. Thus, Coase clearly feels that it is this *direction* and *control* of work that sets an important boundary on economic activity – defining what is internal and external to the firm.

It is possibly because they were not able to appreciate the nuance of the legal – institutional context that Alchian and Demstetz were able to come up with their visceral reaction to Coase's theory of the firm[40]. They famously quip that they see no difference between what the employer can do – fire or sue the worker, and what can be done to a grocer – stop purchasing from him and/or sue him for faulty products. With the belief that employers as well as independent contractors face the same transactional frictions, it is suggested that the authority model of the firm should be replaced by viewing the firm as a 'nexus of contracts'. There have been a number of counters to this view, for instance Masten's constructive view[41] of the firm, particularly takes cognisance of the fact that that there are multiple uses of the term *contract* that gain meaning contextually in different institutional settings.[42]. It is pointed out that one can observe that the law treats commercial and employment relations very differently – apart from different information disclosure regimes governing the two categories of contracts, the obligation of obedience demanded of an employee (given effect judicially by requiring the employment relationship to be characterized by the employer exercising control over the tasks of the employee), contrasts with a contract with an independent contractor that typically stipulates results but does not stipulate control as to how these results are to be obtained. While firing the worker or the grocer as an act of exercising sanctions appears similar, the fact that the burden of proof lies on the worker in common law to contest the firing reinforces the point that the degree of control exercised by an employer is more stringent than over an independent contractor. This view of the law as a device that sets up standard terms, so that differences in legal defaults, sanctions and procedures governing commercial and employment transactions provides one an impetus to turn to a legal theory of the firm, possibly to fix an economic understanding of the firm.

Orts suggests this explicitly, exhorting one to reorient themselves by doing the obverse of the typical *law and economics* agenda of solving legal problems by applying economic analysis and instead think of resolving conflicts regarding the economic theory of the firm by using legal analysis to surmount conceptual difficulties.[43] The 'legal theory of the firm' he offers poses the firm as a nexus of agency relationships rather than as the mythical nexus of contracts – he feels that

> agency principles expressed in law are needed to account for firms because the essential feature of the firm is not agreement of individuals through contracts – which also characterize transactions in the market – but the creation of legal authority and power, often in a hierarchical form[44]

Among other things this formulation allows one to grasp agency costs as not being confined to *shirking* by agents (so ubiquitously emphasized by economists) but *sharking* by principals as well (i.e., abusing their position of authority and power to act self-servingly). However Orts's legal theory of the firm also prominently acts as a complement to the economic theory of the firm to help outline the boundaries of the firm. He says that 'If the motivation for creating firms is economic, however the mechanisms by which firms are established is legal'.[45] These legal mechanisms draw lines 'lines of control, ownership and employment', which are not rigidly fixed but 'fluctuate according to size and firm structure'.[46] In relation to employment, as has been pointed out, the notion of employer control is an essential component of the legal employer–employee relationship, with an employee subject to the authority of an employer *inside* the firm and an independent contractor is *outside* the firm.[47] However when we look at some legal analysis, there is some cause to question the large-scale acceptance of characterizing the employment relation as the employer necessarily exercising control over the tasks of the employee.

In a particularly insightful note Otto Kahn-Fruend observed that the usual 'control test' used to distinguish between a servant and an independent contractor or between a contract of employment and a contract for work or stated in yet another way, the contract of service and a contract for services needs to be analytically questioned.[48] He pointed out that the traditional control test grew around the idea that the master tells the servant 'how' to do the work and not just 'what' to do. The source of this distinction lies in methods of production where the employer was able to instruct the labourer because he had superior knowledge, skill and experience in 'choice and handling' of tools and typically covered relationships such as those between farmers and agricultural labour, householders and domestic servants, craftsmen and journeymen and could even be stretched to those between 'a factory owner and an unskilled 'hand''. In these relationships, it is further pointed out, knowledge and skill was handed down over generations and not imparted in universities and technical schools. In other words the control test imagines both technical and managerial skills to reside in the person of the employer. In more contemporary times, Kahn-Fruend notes that to believe that the employer 'controls' is 'unrealistic and almost grotesque' because the technical knowledge with the employee can be vastly superior to the employer.[49] The control test therefore needs to be transformed according to him by shifting away from an obsession with orders towards an organization test where the question is 'did the alleged servant form a part of the alleged master's organization?'[50]

If one is to take this reasonably seriously then it needs to be understood what it means for a worker to be a part of the master's organization – surely a worker is a part of the organization variously. However, notwithstanding the profundity of his central insight, Coase thought of the employment relation quite narrowly – as it has been seen, largely in terms of the law of master and servant. While later work has gone on to give more substance to the idea of transaction costs, sourcing it in the vagaries associated with relationship specific investment, the conception of employment relation continues being contained within the master and servant rubric and furthermore largely in terms of contract at will.[51] This is possibly appropriate frame to approach labour, if the incentives for ex-ante asset specific skill (also person-specific) residing in labour are not of central concern and the incentives for labour dwell sufficiently in the acts of firing and quitting. It is precisely because skill of this kind and any associated legal doctrines were not voiced by Coase, later work on the firm also continues to function with an institutional/legal base that consists of a common law understanding of the employment relation – master and servant largely within the confines of the contract at will doctrine.

However, it is not at all necessary to look at the relations between an employer and employee only as one of contract and thwart the impulse to look at the relation in terms of property, or more explicitly as property in work. Njoya suggests there is a good case to be made for using ownership or property as analytical tools to examine the employment relationship – in fact she shows that practice of Anglo-American law includes the use of a series of doctrines such as reliance, estoppel, legitimate expectations and probable expectation in employment disputes that definitely have a more property-like orientation than doctrines concentrating purely on contract.[52] The term property is construed here as not as the usually perceived absolute property rights but rather as a relative entitlement, an entitlement that requires law to interpret 'fairness in dismissal' not as just adherence to procedure but as assurance of substantive job security. Njoya associates the demise of job security in America and the United Kingdom with the increasing emphasis on short-term share value and proceeds to focus her work towards arguing that greater job security will improve overall 'efficiency' from a multiple stakeholder perspective of the firm.

The central idea here – property in work – is of obvious interest if one is to think of relation specific investment made by workers. To appreciate the significance of the idea, there is a need to begin by thinking of 'property in work' in terms of a continuum similar to the manner in which Heller uses degrees of exclusion to conceptually approach private property – he points to the range of rights associated with the idea of property, starting with the absence of exclusion associated with the open access of the commons at one end, leading to the excessive exclusion of the anti-commons at the other end, placing conventional private property somewhere in the middle of the continuum.[53] Analogously in the case of property in work, one can think of one end of the continuum as the rights or rather lack of rights that govern spot labour contracts with the other end being typified by an instance when the law disallows the worker from being fired for any reason whatsoever and placing varying degrees of job security in between. Thus every worker can be mapped as being given a degree of property rights in work by law and every such worker is also placed relationally to the *master's organization* or using another parlance *the firm*. The varieties of a workers' relation with the firm could cause one to think of a more integrated firm as one where labour is employed with the guarantee of greater job security and to associate a less integrated firm with the act of employing labour with lower guarantees of job security. This is not as distant from the property rights understanding of the firm as may appear at first glance. The property rights version of the firm, which as we noted identifies the firm with the non-human assets it owns, non-human assets because of the presence of anti-slavery laws disallow one from owning another human being. While accepting that a firm cannot own workers as assets, if workers are a part of the firm with strong rights on their jobs then they have a degree of assimilation into the organization which can be thought of as akin to a management-labour 'joint-ownership' of the firm – of course such ownership is quite removed from the standard definitions of ownership but it is *property* and *ownership* in so much so property rights on jobs are relational manifestations of contract. On the other hand workers with weaker property rights on their jobs are less assimilated into the firm because they are relatively less constituent of the organization. Clearly a firm uses a wide variety of labour services and if one were to think along conventional lines, it could be argued that the firm can contract tenure as it sees fit – the freedom to contract as per mutual need is a sufficient basis for the variety of labour needs of a firm. It is precisely here that a counter argument can be made while contracts work well enough with unskilled workers things may not be so easy when it comes to skilled workers. The contract, as has been widely recognized, provides sufficient incentives to perform work – the threat of firing the worker is a good enough incentive to solicit the needed work but if the effort put in by the work is not immediate and easily substituted by another worker then the incentive lives elsewhere. Such effort on part of the worker is clearly an ex-ante effort and invoking one of the central points of the property rights theory of the firm, this effort is going to be hard for the firm to contract with potential workers and must therefore be thought of as not contractible or in terms of an incomplete contract. It is in the 'completion' of such contracts that the property in work awarded by law plays a vital role – by taking into account rights of property in work either by judicial invocation of doctrine or through the statute, workers can calculate their chances of retaining a job and on this basis make a variety of relationship specific investments such as gaining skills, choosing to settle in a location, committing to a firm/person etc. This is clearly of value if ex–ante relationship specific investment by workers is important to production and would be less valuable in a setting where production requires little or no skill. Where there is little specific skill requirement a worker substitutes for another and if law forces property as work, this would impose a burden on the firm which it would shake off by getting such unskilled labour through a contractor having signed a contract for services. In a manner what is being suggested is very much in consonance with the property rights theory of the firm where it is said that if assets are sufficiently complementary and ex-ante contracts incomplete it is optimal for the firm to be more integrated but as activity gets to be less specific to the manager at the centre non-integration is better. The additional feature being suggested here is that the contents of labour law in so much so as it defines property rights in work affects a variety of incentives and is thus a crucial determinant of the boundary of the firm. As Orts says that it is important to work with the legal theory of the firm as a supplement to economics so that one can better enter normative worlds to engender 'norms of social trust for economic stability and progress'.[54]

10.4 Directions for labour law reform

This interaction between the law and the theory of the firm is important for making suggestions on the broad direction that labour law reform in India should take. As noted initially, the call for labour law reform has been so overwhelmingly placed against a background where it is believed that the law – both the statue and its legal interpretation by courts and governments, has given workers too many rights. The apocryphal invocations include statues that disallow large employers from retrenching workers without executive government permission, state governments who are pro-worker and of course a Supreme Court jurisprudence which has traditionally attempted to give tenure to workers very widely. However notwithstanding the fact that there has been little or no change in the statute, as has been shown that the judicial interpretation of the law has pushed towards a legal regime which encourages the use of both contract labour and fixed term contracts. This transpires largely by ensuring that the worker is kept out of the category of being a 'workman' – a worker who cannot thus claim rights on the job as well as other rights. It is thus of no surprise that the largest expansion in employment has been in the informal/casual/contract workers categories.

This perhaps indicates as and when more reform of the labour law is attempted, it will be to increasingly create a work force without rights. It will definitely ease the concerns voiced so often in the literature, expanding output and employment, but what might it do relationship specific investment and the value that might generate for the economy? Since the incentive effects of property in work typically affect ex ante decisions – it is harder to measure this loss empirically, since the loss lies in what may have happened but for a different legal regime. Nevertheless such a legal regime needs to be imagined, which is sensitive to the value encapsulated in the investment made by a worker in a skill specific to a relation of employment. It is of course beyond the scope of this chapter to detail such a regime and only a set of very tentative and preliminary concerns can be raised.

An incorporation of the concerns requires that it will have to be acknowledged that rights of workers are not just concerns of fairness that have to be traded off against efficiency. That too, but rights also have to be correctly formulated provide economic incentives. Such a legal regime will have to imagine the worker in a manner very different from the current regime that seeks to exclude workers from being categorized as workers. In this context following at least one among the many suggestions made by the Second Labour Commission can be a beginning.

> The Commission is of the view that their coverage as well as the definition of the term 'worker' should be the same in all groups of laws, subject to the stipulation that social security benefits must be available to all employees including administrative, managerial, supervisory and others excluded from the category of workmen and others not treated as workmen or excluded from the category of workmen... We propose that instead of having separate laws, it may be advantageous to incorporate all the provisions relating to employment relations, wages, social security, safety and working conditions etc. into a single law with separate parts in respect of establishments employing less than 20 persons.[55]

After giving all workers more or less the same rights described by the *Second Labour Commission* as a first step, issues of tenure can be differentially built into the law. To recall what is at stake here is the fact that the law needs to provide a defence against opportunistic treatment of workers who may have invested in the relationship by providing them with some security of tenure. While this is not an easy task, as it requires a sensitive engagement with building discerning legal boundaries, the broad strategy would perhaps be to keep in mind certain ideas expressed by Collins with respect to law and employment protection in the United Kingdom.[56] He feels to put into effect any kind of meaningful protection – it is very difficult to legislate details that will pertain to all cases and places faith in creatively constructing judicial tests of the employment relation. Indeed there may be a chance that the Indian judiciary could think with a suitably expanded categorization of a worker that a core worker (integrated with the firm) ends up being judicially recognized as fulfilling not only the control test covering a spectrum of tasks but also understand how the worker is placed in relation to the organization of the firm through a carefully conceived organization test. An integral part of this, of course, would be a reasonable system of severance compensation to take care of concerns of in-period flexibility of labour.[57]

Endnotes

1 This concern was initially voiced in Fallon and Lucas (1993) and more recently, among others, in the much-cited work of Besley and Burgess (2004). While the rhetoric of the ills of restrictive labour laws is very much a part of Indian Government documents such as the Economic Surveys and Planning Commission Reports (See Ministry of Finance, 2006 and 2012; Planning Commission, 2006, 2011, and 2012); Bhattacharjea (2006) has shown that the Besley and Burgess methodology of capturing labour laws as an indexed variable is extremely flawed.

2 See Macleod (2011).

3 See Anant *et al.* (2006).

4 See Mehrotra *et al.* (2012).

5 See Sankaran (2007) who summarizes details of the law in this regard. It also needs to be noted in this context that a number of workers employed within 'formal' enterprises could still fall outside the capacity of the law due to the nature of the work they perform which can act as exclusionary criteria – criteria which is characteristically juridical. See also Sankaran (2006).

6 H. R. Adyanthaya vs. Sandoz (India) Ltd. AIR, 1994 SC 2608.

7 The term is Latin for 'of the same kind' and is a judicial technique to interpret loosely written statutes, aiming to gain specificity out of general statements by joining associative words.

8 Ahmedabad Pvt. Primary Teachers' Association vs. Administrative Officer and Ors., (2004) 1SCC755.

9 Particularly quoting the case of A. Sundarambal vs. Govt. of Goa, Daman and Diu, among many others. MANU/SC/0282/1988: (1989)ILLJ61SC.

10 Comprehended from accompanying words

11 Sonepat Co-Op Sugar Mill vs. Ajit Singh, (2005) 3 SCC 1. In fact in yet another case legal assistant was called a professional and not a 'workman' – see Muir Mills Unit of NTC(UP) Ltd. Vs. Swayam Prakash Srivastava, (2007) 1 SCC 491.

12 A1R1957SC264, (1957) ILLJ477SC, [1957]1SCR152.

13 Hussainbhai vs. Alath Factory Employees' Union, (1978) 2 LLJ 397 (SC). The judgment says 'Where a worker or group of workers labours to produce goods or services and these goods or services are for the business of another, that other is, in fact, the employer. He has economic control over the workers' subsistence, skill, and continued employment. If he, for any reason, chokes off, the worker is, virtually, laid off. The presence of intermediate contractors with whom alone the workers have immediate or direct relationship *ex contractu* is of no consequence when, on lifting the veil or looking at the conspectus of factors governing employment, we discern the naked truth, though draped in different perfect paper arrangement, that the real employer is the Management, not the immediate contractor.'

14 Steel Authority of India vs. National Union Water Front Workers AIR, (20010 SC 3527.

15 Air India Statutory Corporation vs. United Labour Union, (1997) (9) SCC 377.

16 International Airport Authority of India vs. International Air Cargo Workers Union and another, (2009) 13 SCC 374.

17 Electronics Corporation of India Ltd. vs. Electronics Corporation of India Service Employees Union, (2006) 7 SCC 330.

18 *The Industrial Employment (Standing Orders) Act* 1946 requires that in all industrial establishments employing more than 100 workmen, the terms and conditions of service be framed in accordance with a stipulated model.

19 See Srivastava (2003).

20 See Kaul (2006) where a number of relevant cases are listed.

21 Retrenchment is defined in Section 2(oo) of the Industrial Disputes Act as 'The termination by the employer of the service of a workman for any reason whatsoever, otherwise than as punishment inflicted by way of disciplinary action, but does not include –

(a) voluntary retirement of the workman; or

(b) retirement of the workman on reaching the age of superannuation if the contract of employment between the employer and workman concerned contains a stipulation in that behalf; or

(bb) termination of the service of the workman as a result of the non-renewal of the contract of employment between the employer and the workman concerned on its expiry or such contract being terminated under a stipulation in that behalf contained therein; or

(c) termination of the service of a workman on the grounds of continued ill health.'

22 Punjab Land Development and Reclamation Corporation Ltd. Chandigarh v. Presiding Officer Labour Court Chandigarh and others, (1990) 3 SCC 682.

23 Municipal Council, Samarala vs. Raj Kumar, (2006) 3 SCC 81.

24 Among many cases the following can be mentioned as a sample where the Supreme Court was happy to award regularization – Dharwad District Public Works Department vs. State of Karnataka, (1990) IILLJ 318SC; Daily Rated Casual Labour vs. Union of India and Ors., (1988) ILLJ370SC; Bhagwati Prasad vs. Delhi State Mineral Development Corporation, (1990) ILLJ 320SC.

25 Secretary, State of Karnataka and Ors vs. Umadevi and Ors AIR 2006 SC 1806, (2006) 4 SCC1.

26 This point is repeated in subsequent judgments – for instance in the case of Union of India and Ors vs. Vartak Labour Union, (2011) 4 SCC 200, workers in service for the past thirty to forty years, of course with short breaks, were refused regularization, though the Court exhorted the Union of India to enact 'an appropriate regulation/scheme for absorption and regularization of the services of the casual workers.'

27 For example in A. N. Shukul vs. Phillips India and Others, given the employment contract and the terms written in the Delhi High Court accepted the contested termination as legally sound since it was for a process of reorganization and reconstruction – following Y. K. Sethi vs. BASF India (CS908) 1761/2006).

28 (210) IILJ 277SC, (2010) 3SCC 192.

29 AIR 2011 SC 3546.

30 For instance Dougherty (2008) says that India affords some of the strictest protection in the world to workers and that comprehensive reforms allowing employer flexibility in firing workers need to replace the second best changes evident.

31 See Tomlins (1993).

32 See Epstien (1984).

33 Epstien (1984), 979.

34 Epstien (1984), 982.

35 Coase (1937).

36 See Williamson (1975) and Williamson (1985.)

37 See Klien *et al.* (1978).

38 See Grossman and Hart (1986) .

39 Hart and Moore (1990). A more general non-specialist account can be found in Hart (1989).

40 Alchian and Demsetz (1972).

41 This refers to the idea that the firm serves a useful purpose.

42 Masten (1988).

43 Orts (1998).

44 Orts (1998), 272.

45 Orts (1998), 294.

46 Orts (1998), 314.

47 Orts (1998), 304–05.

48 Kahn-Fruend (1951).

49 Kahn-Fruend (1951), 506.

50 Kahn-Fruend (1951), 507.

51 In Hart and Moore (1990) the implicit assumptions suggest a typical master and servant relationship coupled clearly with some form of employment contracts at will. The relation between the owner of an asset and a worker, by virtue of his ownership over the asset, allows the owner to exclude some or all workers from the asset, which in turn causes workers to work in the interest of the asset owner. This situation is contrasted with the case when such an owner contracts for a service from someone else who owns the asset, where workers work in the interest of this other owner of the asset. The former case is described as a person having more control over an asset and its associated workers since they are employed by the person than if such a person had an arms-length contract with another who employs workers.

52 Njoya (2007).

53 Heller (1999).

54 Orts (1998), 328.

55 Ministry of Labour and Employment, *Report of the Second Commission on Labour*, Vol. II, 37, (Government of India, 2002).

56 Collins (1990).

57 I would like to acknowledge The Humphrey Institute of Public Affairs, University of Minnesota, where I visited as a Visiting Scholar in 2008 and was able to do much of the research for this chapter.

References

Alchian, A. and H. Demsetz. 1972. 'Production, Information Costs and Economic Organization', *American Economic Review* 62(5): 777–95.

Anant, T. C. A., R. Hasan, P. Mohapatra, R. Nagaraj and S. K. Sasikumar. 2006. 'Labor Markets in India: Issues and Perspectives'. In *Labor Markets in Asia: Issues and Perspectives*, edited by J. Felipe and R. Hasan, 205–300. Basingstoke: Palgrave Macmillan.

Besley, T. and R. Burgess. 2004. 'Can Regulation Hinder Economic Performance? Evidence from India', *Quarterly Journal of Economics* 119(1): 91–134.

Bhattacharjea, A. 2006. 'Labour Market Regulation and Industrial Performance in India: A Critical Review of the Empirical Evidence', *Indian Journal of Labour Economics* 49(2): 211–232.

Coase, R. H. 1937. 'The Nature of the Firm', *Economica* New Series 4(16): 386–405.

Collins, H. 1990. 'Independent Contractors and the Challenge of Vertical Disintegration to Employment Protection Laws', *Oxford Journal of Legal Studies* 10(3): 353–80.

Dougherty, S. 2009. 'Labour Regulation and Employment Dynamics at the State Level in India'. *OECD Economics Department Working Paper No. 624*. OECD Publishing.

Epstien, R. A. 1984. 'In Defence of the Contract at Will', *University of Chicago Law Review* 51(4): 947–82.

Fallon, P. R. and R. E. B. Lucas. 1993. 'Job Security Regulation and Dynamic Demand for Industrial Labor in India and Zimbabwe', *Journal of Development Economics* 40(2): 241–75.

Grossman, S. and O. Hart. 1986. 'The Costs and Benefits of Ownership: A Theory of Vertical and Lateral Integration', *Journal of Political Economy* 94(4): 691–719.

Hart, O. 1989. 'An Economist's Perspective on the Theory of the Firm', *Columbia Law Review* 89(7): 1757–74.

Hart, O. and J. Moore. 1990. 'Property Rights and the Nature of the Firm', *The Journal of Political Economy* 98(6): 1119–58.

Heller, M. A. 1999. 'The Boundaries of Private Property', *Yale Law Journal* 108(6): 1163–223.

Kahn-Fruend, O. 1951. 'Servants and Independent Contractors', *Modern Law Review* 14(4): 504–09.

Kaul, B. T. 2006. 'Labour Law – I', *Annual Survey of Indian Law* XLII: 494.

Klien, B., R. Crawford and A. Alchian. 1978. 'Vertical Integration, Appropriable Rents and the Competitive Contracting Process', *Journal of Law and Economics* 21(2): 297–326.

Masten, S. E. 1988. 'A Legal Basis for the Firm', *Journal of Law, Economics, & Organization* 4(1):181–98.

Macleod, W. B. 2011. 'Great Expectations: Law, Employment Contracts, and Labor Market Performance'. In *Handbook of Labor Economics*, edited by O. Ashenfelter and D. Card, 1591–696, vol. 4, part B. Amsterdam: Elsevier.

Mehrotra, S., A. Gandhi, P. Saha and B. K. Sahoo. 2012. 'Creating Employment in the Twelfth Five-Year Plan', *Economic and Political Weekly* 47(19): 63–73.

Ministry of Finance. 2006. *Economic Survey 2005-06*. New Delhi: Government of India.

_____. 2012. *Economic Survey 2012-13*. New Delhi: Government of India.

_____. 2002. *Second National Commission on Labour, Report*. New Delhi: Government of India.

Njoya, W. 2007. *Property in Work: The Employment Relationship in the Anglo-American Firm*. Ashgate, Hampshire: Aldershot.

Orts, E. W. 1998. 'Shirking and Sharking: A Legal Theory of the Firm', *Yale Law & Policy Review* 16(2): 265–329.

Planning Commission. 2006. *Towards Faster and More Inclusive Growth: An Approach to the 11th Five Year Plan*. New Delhi: Government of India.

_____, 2012. *Faster, More Inclusive and Sustainable Growth, 12th Five Year Plan*. New Delhi: Government of India.

_____, 2011. *Report of the Working Group on Employment, Planning and Policy for the Twelfth Five year Plan (2012–17)*. New Delhi: Government of India.

Sankaran, K. 2006. 'Protecting the Worker in the Informal Economy: The Role of Labour law'. In *Boundaries and Frontiers of Labour Law: Goals and Means in the Regulation of Work*, edited by Guy Davidov and Brian Laugille. Oxford and Portland: Hart Publishing.

_____, 2007. 'Labour Laws in South Asia: The Need for an Inclusive Approach'. *Discussion paper No.176*. Geneva: International Institute for Labour Studies.

Srivastava, S. C. 2003.' Labour Law – I', *Annual Survey of Indian Law* XXXIX: 511.

Tomlins, C. L. 1993. *Law, Labour and Ideology in the Early American Republic*. Cambridge: Cambridge University Press.

Williamson, O. 1975. *Markets and Hierarchies: Analysis and Antitrust Implications*. New York: Free Press.

_____, 1985. *The Economic Institutions of Capitalism*. New York: Free Press.

11

Labour Jurisprudence of the Supreme Court
Recent Trends

Ramapriya Gopalakrishnan

11.1 Introduction

Following the adoption of the new economic policy by the Government of India in 1991, there have been significant changes in the employment pattern in industrial establishments in the country on account of the array of low cost flexible labour practices adopted by employers. There has been a steep increase in the employment of precarious workers while the share of the permanent workforce has considerably declined.[1] Contract workers and other kinds of non-regular workers are engaged in large numbers to perform work of a regular or permanent nature.[2] They are however paid substantially lower wages than permanent workers doing work of the same or similar kind.[3] Disguised employment is rampant and workers are often engaged under sham contracting arrangements and in the guise of trainees and probationers to keep labour costs low and also to circumvent the law.[4] Other practices adopted by employers to cut labour costs and circumvent the law include sub-contracting, outsourcing jobs and keeping the number of workers below the threshold level prescribed under the law.[5] The designation of workers as managers, supervisors, engineers etc. is yet another strategy adopted by employers to circumvent the law.[6] The weak enforcement of labour laws by the state machinery has facilitated the adoption of such practices.[7]

Alongside the adoption of such practices, employers have been pressing for labour law reforms in order to give them greater flexibility in hiring and firing workers. Two of their main demands are the removal of provisions in the Industrial Disputes Act, 1947 relating to prior governmental provisions for effecting closures, and the lay-off and retrenchment of workers in industries employing a 100 or more workers and the removal of the restrictions on the use of contract labour under the Contract Labour (Regulation and Abolition) Act, 1970.[8]

The increasing informalization of labour in the formal sector has disadvantaged workers in the sector in more ways than one. It has led to denial of permanency, fair wages and other benefits to a large section of workers. It has also resulted in greater fragmentation of the workforce which in turn negatively impacts the freedom of association and collective bargaining rights of workers in the sector.[9] The increasing use of unfair methods by employers to dissuade workers from joining trade unions has also adversely affected the organizational and bargaining rights of workers.[10]

At a time when labour rights have been weakened as a result of government policies, employer practices and executive indifference, the manner in which the judiciary, particularly, the higher judiciary addresses labour rights issues is of critical importance. The rulings of the Supreme Court of India, the apex court are part of the law of the land and are binding on all courts in the country. The Supreme Court of India is credited with having built a strong edifice for the protection of labour rights.[11] It has expansively interpreted the fundamental rights protected under the Constitution of India so as to encompass the right to dignity, right to livelihood and right to health that are important labour rights. It has been lauded for its interpretation of labour enactments in the light of the social philosophy of the Constitution embodied in the Directive Principles of State Policy. It has been commended for pioneering public interest litigation procedures where it has made a radical departure from the procedural rigours that traditional litigation is associated with to afford access to justice to disadvantaged and marginalized groups including bonded labourers, child labourers and construction workers.[12] Given this rich history, the Supreme Court would have held out a lot of hope for the working class in the country that has faced several challenges following the adoption of the policies of globalization, liberalization and privatizations by the government.

Unfortunately, going by the barrage of criticism of the labour jurisprudence of the Supreme Court in recent times, it appears that the Court has not lived up its promise.[13] Comparing and contrasting the response of the Court to labour rights issues in the new millennium with its earlier rulings, labour activists and scholars have rued that there has been a 'paradigm shift in the approach of the Court'[14] on account of its 'being influenced by the values fostered by globalization'[15] and that it had adopted an 'anti-worker stance.'[16]

Is this criticism justified? Has there indeed been a blanket shift in the approach of the Court to all kinds of labour issues in the new millennium or has it been confined to certain kinds of issues? What has been the rationale behind the shift in approach? This chapter sets out to examine these issues. It analyses the approach of the Court over the last decade and a half to collective as well as individual labour rights issues concerning workers in the formal and informal sectors.

11.2 Significant rulings

This section discusses the approach of the Supreme Court to labour rights issues in the period from 2000 to 2010 on the basis of some examples. It examines judgments related to contract workers, temporary workers, the right to strike, privatization of state-run industries and industrial discipline among other issues.

11.2.1 Rulings related to contract workers

11.2.1.1 Entitlement of contract workers to permanent absorption

Section 10(1) of the Contract Labour (Regulation and Abolition) Act, 1970 permits the central as well as state governments to abolish the engagement of contract labour for work of a permanent nature in any establishment covered by the Act by the issue of a notification. The Act however does not spell out the implications of the issue of such a notification on the contract labour employed in the establishment. It is silent on the aspect of whether or not the concerned contract workers would be entitled to be absorbed as direct permanent workers in the user enterprise following the issue of such a notification. In *Steel Authority of India Ltd. vs. National Union Waterfront Workers*[17] (SAIL case), the Supreme Court considered the issue of entitlement of contract labour to permanent absorption in an industrial establishment upon the issue of a notification under section 10(1) of the Act.

The same issue had earlier arisen for the consideration of the Court in *Air India Statutory Corporation vs. United Labour Union*.[18] In the *Air India* case decided on 6 December 1996, interpreting the provisions of the Act in the light of the directive principles enshrined in Part IV of the Constitution of India, the Court observed that the Act did not intend to denude contract labourers of their livelihood and that they would be entitled to absorption on a regular basis in the establishment upon the issue of an abolition notification under the Act. In the *SAIL* case however, decided on 30 August 2001, the Court overruled the judgment in the *Air India* case holding that it could not read into the Act some remedy not specified in the Act. The Court observed:

> The principle that a beneficial legislation needs to be construed liberally in favour of the class for whose benefit it is intended does not extend to reading in the provisions of the Act what the legislature has not provided whether expressly or by necessary implication or substituting remedy or benefits for that provided by the legislature.

On this basis, the Court held that contract labour employed in a establishment have no right to automatic absorption when a notification for abolition of contract labour in the establishment is issued by the government under section 10 of the Act.

11.2.1.2 *Wage parity for contract workers*

As per the rules framed by the central government as well as some state governments under the Contract Labour (Regulation and Abolition) Act, 1970, when contract labour engaged through an intermediary contractor in an establishment perform the same or similar kind of work as the workers directly employed by the principal employer of the establishment, they would be entitled to the same wages, holidays and hours of work as the direct workers in that establishment. In *Uttar Pradesh Rajya Vidyut Utpadan Board vs. Uttar Pradesh Vidyut Mazdoor Sangh*,[19] the Supreme Court considered the correctness of the order issued by the Labour Commissioner, Uttar Pradesh holding that the contract labour working in a filtration plant in a thermal power project should be paid the same wages as that paid by the Uttar Pradesh RajyaVidyut Utpadan Board to its employees in the main filtration plant.

Holding that the manner in which the Labour Commissioner had arrived at a conclusion about the similarity of work was highly unsatisfactory, the Court observed as follows:

> Nature of work, duties and responsibilities attached thereto are relevant in comparing and evaluating as to whether the workmen employed through the contractor perform the same or similar kind of work as workmen directly employed by the principal employer. Degree of skill and various dimensions of a given job have to be gone

into to reach a conclusion that the nature of duties of the staff in two categories are on a par or otherwise. Often the difference may be of a degree. It is well settled that nature of work cannot be judged by mere volume of work; there may be qualitative difference as regards reliability and responsibility.

11.2.2 Rulings related to temporary/casual workers

11.2.2.1 Entitlement of temporary/casual workers to regularization and permanency

In *Secretary, State of Karnataka vs. Umadevi,*[20] the Supreme Court considered the claim of temporary workers employed by the state to regularization and permanency based on the fact that they had continued in employment for a number of years. Even while noting that the state and its instrumentalities at times resort to employing people on a temporary basis without following the prescribed procedure, in order to perform the duties attendant to sanctioned posts and the fact that such people could be employed on a temporary basis for a considerable length of time, the Court rejected the claim of the workers. The Court's approach to the issue in the *Umadevi* case stands out in stark contrast to its earlier approach in cases such as *Dharwad District PWD Literate Daily Wage Employees Association vs. State of Karnataka*[21] and *Daily Rated Casual Labour vs. Union of India.*[22] While earlier in similar cases, the court issued directions for the grant of permanency to such workers taking into consideration the nature of their work and the length of their continuous service, in *Umadevi,* the Court gave greater importance to the mode of their entry into employment. Emphasizing the need for adherence to the constitutional scheme of public employment, the Court held that unless the appointment was in terms of the relevant rules after a proper competition among duly qualified people, it would not confer any right on them for regularization and permanent absorption. Criticizing its earlier approach, the Court observed:

> While directing that appointments, temporary or casual, be regularised or made permanent, the courts are swayed by the fact that the person concerned has worked for some time and in some cases for a considerable length of time. It is not as if the person who accepts an engagement either temporary or casual in nature, is not aware of the nature of his employment. He accepts the employment with open eyes. It may be true that he is not in a position to bargain— not at arm's length—since he might have been searching for some

employment so as to eke out his livelihood and accepts whatever he gets. But on that ground alone, it would not be appropriate to jettison the constitutional scheme of appointment and to take the view that a person who has temporarily or casually got employed should be directed to be continued permanently.

The Court also justified its new approach on the basis of financial considerations. It observed:

Obviously, the State is also controlled by economic considerations and financial implications of any public employment. The viability of the department or the instrumentality of the project is also of equal concern for the State. The State works out the scheme taking into consideration the financial implications and the economic aspects. Can the court impose on the State a financial burden of this nature by insisting on regularisation or permanence in employment, when those employed temporarily are not needed permanently or regularly? As an example, we can envisage a direction to give permanent employment to all those who are being temporarily or casually employed in a public sector undertaking. The burden may become so heavy by such a direction that the undertaking itself may collapse under its own weight. It is not as if this had not happened. So, the court ought not to impose a financial burden on the State by such directions, as such directions may turn counterproductive.

11.2.2.2 Wrongful termination of temporary/causal workers

As per Section 25-F of the Industrial Disputes Act, 1947, no worker employed in any industry who has been in continuous service for a year or more shall be terminated from service unless he or she has been given one month's notice in writing indicating the reasons for the termination or has been paid one month's wages in lieu of such notice. The provision also requires the employer to pay the worker compensation at the rate of 15 days average pay for every completed year of service. Section 25-B of the Act provides that a worker shall be deemed to be in continuous service for one year if he or she has worked for a minimum of 240 days. The Supreme Court had held that an employer cannot terminate the service of even a casual worker, seasonal worker or daily rated worker without complying with the mandatory requirements of section 25-F of the Act and that any termination of service effected in violation of the mandatory requirements of section 25-F would be illegal and void.[23] The Court had also held that any worker wrongfully terminated from service in violation of section 25-F would be entitled to the relief of reinstatement and back wages.[24]

However, in recent times, the Court has held that a distinction should be drawn between daily wager who does not hold a post and a permanent worker for the purpose of grant of consequential relief when his or her termination from service is held to be invalid in law. In cases such as *Haryana State Electronics Corporation vs. Mamni*[25] and *Madhya Pradesh Administration vs. Tribhuban*[26] concerning temporary workers and Jagbir Singh vs. Haryana State Agricultural Marketing Board[27]concerning a daily wage worker, the Court has taken the view that that monetary compensation would meet the ends of justice and that a direction for reinstatement of the worker with back wages would not be the proper relief.

11.2.3 Privatization: Scope of judicial review and right of workers to be heard

In *BALCO Employees Union vs. Union of India,*[28] trade unions of workers of a government-run aluminium manufacturing company challenged the decision of the central government to disinvest the majority of the shares in the company in favour of a private company on the ground that it was arbitrary. They also contended that the decision being one that adversely affected the interest of the company's workers, they ought to have been heard prior to and at different stages of the process of disinvestment. The Court held that no case had been made out by the unions that the decision of the government was in any way arbitrary or capricious. More generally, the Court held that it is not for the courts to consider whether a particular public policy is wise or whether a better policy can be evolved and that such an economic policy decision could not be interfered with unless it was against any law or was established to be mala fide. The Court ruled that workers are not entitled to a right of hearing or consultation prior to the making of such decisions and cannot claim a right of continuous consultation at various stages of the disinvestment process. This seems to be contrary to the spirit of the ruling in *National Textile Workers Union vs. P. R. Ramakrishnan*[29] where the Court considered the issue of whether the affected workers have a right to be heard during legal proceedings to wind up a company. The Court in that case had ruled that the concerned workers have the right to be heard in the determination of the question whether the enterprise should continue to run or be shut down.

11.2.4 Right to strike

In July 2003, the Government of Tamil Nadu dismissed 170,241 employees and teachers invoking the provisions of the Tamil Nadu Essential Services Maintenance Act (TESMA) that prohibited strikes in services declared as 'essential' under the Act and Tamil Nadu Ordinance 3 of 2003 that allowed for the summary dismissal of employees on strike. Rule 22 of the Tamil Nadu Government Servants Conduct Rules also prohibited government employees from engaging in strikes. They were dismissed for participating in a strike protesting against the withdrawal of pensionary and other benefits. The employees filed cases challenging the validity of TESMA, the Ordinance, Rule 22 of the Government Service Conduct Rules and their dismissals and this led to the Supreme Court pronouncing a judgement in *T. K. Rangarajan vs. Government of Tamil Nadu*[30]centred on the issue of government employees' right to strike. Following the earlier rulings of the Court in *All India Bank Employees Association vs. The National Industrial Tribunal (Bank Disputes),*[31]*Radhey Shyam Sharma vs. Post Master General,*[32] the Court held that government employees have no fundamental right to strike. It also went on to hold that they have no legal right to strike and that there was no moral or equitable justification for them to go on strike. While the Court did not make any pronouncement in respect of the constitutional validity of the laws under challenge, it made some observations of a general nature regarding strikes. It observed as follows:

> Strike as a weapon is mostly misused which results in chaos and total maladministration. Strike affects the society as a whole and particularly when two lakh employees go on strike en masse, the entire administration comes to a grinding halt. In the case of strike by a teacher, the entire educational system suffers; many students are prevented from appearing in their exams which ultimately affects their whole career. In case of strike by doctors, innocent patients suffer; in case of strike by employees of transport services, entire movement of the society comes to a standstill: business is adversely affected and number of persons find it difficult to attend to their work, to move from one place to another or one city to another. On occasions, public properties are destroyed or damaged and finally this creates bitterness among the public against those who are on strike.

The Court also went on to make the following observation:

> In the prevailing situation, apart from being conscious of rights, we have to be fully aware of our duties, responsibilities and effective

methods for discharging the same. For redressing their grievances, instead of going on strike, if employees do some more work honestly, diligently and efficiently, such gesture would not only be appreciated by the authority but also by people at large. The reason being, in a democracy even though they are government employees, they are part and parcel of the governing body and owe duty to the society.

While the Court in the above mentioned judgment has made observations condemning strikes by workers, earlier in judgments such as that in *B. R. Singh vs. Union of India*,[33] it had recognized that 'the right to strike is an important weapon in the armoury of workers.'

11.2.5.Industrial discipline

The Supreme Court has in recent years stressed on the need for industrial discipline in cases where workers have questioned the imposition of the punishment of dismissal by employers pursuant to disciplinary proceedings. It has cautioned the courts below against being swayed by misplaced sympathy for workers and interfering with penalties imposed by employers.[34] In some cases, the Court has upheld the imposition of dismissal although the misconduct alleged to have been committed by the concerned worker does not seem to be so grave as to warrant an extreme punishment. For instance, in a case where a bus conductor was found to have charged some passengers higher fare but issued tickets for lower fare on just one occasion, the Court upheld the punishment of dismissal.[35] Similarly, in another case where a bus conductor was found to have not issued tickets to some passengers on one occasion which resulted in a loss of ₹ 16 to the concerned transport corporation, the court upheld the punishment of dismissal.[36] In *Hombe Gowda Educational Trust vs. State of Karnataka*,[37] *(2006) 1 SCC 430*, the Court made the following observation:

> This Court has come a long way from its earlier viewpoints. The recent trend in the decisions of this Court seek to strike a balance between the earlier approach to industrial relations wherein only the interest of the workmen was sought to be protected, with the avowed object of fast industrial growth of the country. In several decisions of this Court it has been noticed how discipline at the workplace/ industrial undertakings received a setback. In view of the change in economic policy of the country, it may not now be proper to allow employees to break discipline with impunity.

11.2.6 Coverage of the IDA

In the 70s and 80s, the Supreme Court had interpreted the terms 'workman' and 'industry' in a wide manner so as to extend the reach of the Industrial Disputes Act, 1947. The Court had held that it is the nature of work and not the designation of the employee that would determine whether he is a 'workman' or not.[38] Even workers engaged through intermediary contractors were in some cases held to be 'workmen' under the Act based on the nature of their work and the tests of supervision and control.[39] However, from 2000 onwards, the Court has taken a narrower view while determining whether an employee is a 'workman' covered by the Act. In cases such as *National Small Industries Corporation Ltd. vs. V. Lakshminarayan*,[40] the Court placed greater emphasis on the designation mentioned in the letter of appointment than on the nature of work of the employee and his past history of employment with the company in question. The Court also held that three landmark judgments of the 80s regarding the determination of whether an employee is a 'workman' were no longer good law.[41] In *State of U.P. vs. Jai Bir Singh*,[42] a five-judge Bench of the Supreme Court decided that the landmark judgment of the Court in *Bangalore Water Supply and Sewerage Board vs. A. Rajappa*[43] regarding the interpretation of the term 'industry' needs to be reconsidered. In the judgment in *Jai Bir Singh*, the Court observed as follows:

> It is experienced by all dealing in industrial law that overemphasis on the rights of the workers and undue curtailment of the rights of the employers to organize their business, through employment and non-employment, has given rise to a large number of industrial and labour claims resulting in awards granting huge amounts of back wages for past years, allegedly as legitimate dues of the workers, who are found to have been illegally terminated or retrenched. Industrial awards granting heavy packages of back wages, sometimes result in taking away the very substratum of the industry. Such burdensome awards in many cases compel the employer having moderate assets to close down industries causing harm to interests of not only the employer and the workers but also the general public who is the ultimate beneficiary of material goods and services from the industry.

The Court also observed, 'An overexpansive interpretation of the definition of 'industry' might be a deterrent to private enterprize in India where public employment opportunities are scarce.'

11.3 Shift in approach

The above mentioned examples would indicate that there is a discernible shift in the approach of the Supreme Court to labour rights issues in recent times. A change in approach is clearly evident in the manner in which the Court has dealt with issues concerning the rights of both informal workers and formal workers in the formal sector. It is also evident in the manner in which the Court has dealt with issues concerning the collective rights of workers such as the right to strike and the right of workers to be heard during the making of economic policy decisions affecting them and issues related to industrial discipline concerning workers in formal employment. A change in approach is again evident in the manner in which the Court has interpreted labour enactments.

11.3.1 Economic rationale

The observations of the Court in several judgments indicate that economic considerations have played a role in its decision-making. The Court has adopted a narrower, restrictive approach while dealing with issues having significant financial implications for the state, state-run industries and institutions as well as private employers. This is particularly evident from its own observations in the *Umadevi* case[44] referred to above where it has indicated that the courts should not impose any undue financial burden on the state and its observations in *State of U.P. vs. Jai Bir Singh*[45] where it has indicated that awards directing the payment of back-wages at times threaten the very continuance of the enterprise in question. The Court's observations in *Hombe Gowda Educational Trust vs. State of Karnataka*,[46] indicate that the Court has been concerned about the need for fast industrial growth of the country. Similarly, its observations in *State of U.P. vs. Jai Bir Singh*[47] where the Court has indicated that the manner in which the courts interpret labour enactments should not be a deterrent to private enterprise in the country again show concern for the growth of private enterprise.

In a few judgments where there is a marked departure from its earlier approach, notably, in *Hombe Gowda Educational Trust vs. State of Karnataka*,[48] the Court has explicitly referred to the 'changed economic policy' or the 'changed economic scenario' or the 'prevailing situation' in the country. This would seem to indicate a concern on the part of the Court that its judgments be in tandem with and further the prevailing economic policies of the government and not be contrary to it. It clearly appears from a few of the judgments referred to above that the Court fears that focussing on workers' rights and interests would be detrimental to the economic policies in place today.

11.3.2 Implications of shift in approach

Scholars and activists have criticized the shift in approach. They allege that the Court has abandoned the compassionate, humane and equitable approach that it earlier had towards labour rights issues and become insensitive to the concerns of workers.[49] Instead, it has shown great concern for the industry.[50] They have also alleged that the Court has failed to maintain a balance between the interests of capital and labour[51] and been biased towards employers.[52]

The judgments in *SAIL* and *Umadevi* have been criticized on the ground of encouraging the hire and fire policies increasingly adopted by employers in the country[53] and keeping workers in a permanent state of insecurity.[54] As it is, the number of cases in which the use of contract labour is actually prohibited is very small in number[55] and even in the rare case when it is prohibited, pursuant to the judgment in the *SAIL* case, the concerned contract workers stand little chance of being absorbed as permanent workers of the user enterprise. The judgment in *SAIL* is therefore alleged to have contributed to the increasing use of contract labour for work of a permanent nature.[56] The judgment in *Umadevi* is alleged to stand in the way of justice for casual or temporary workers who have a genuine case for being made permanent. The *Umadevi* judgment is also faulted on the ground that it has the effect of punishing the victim instead of the officials who wilfully hired people in violation of the recruitment rules.[57] The judgment in the *BALCO* case on privatization has been criticized on the ground that it has limited the scope of judicial review in such cases. It also permits the process of disinvestment to be carried on in a non-transparent manner without any participation from the concerned workers at any stage. It is alleged that by permitting the process to be carried without any transparency, the judgment did a great disservice not just to workers but also to the nation.[58] The judgment in the *T. K. Rangarajan* case related to the right of strike has been criticized on the ground that its ramifications go beyond the public sector as it not just negates the rights of government employees but clearly indicates that the judiciary is not in favour of strikes by workers at all.[59] It has been alleged that the judgment would boost aggressive behaviour on the part of private employers as well as governments.[60] The judgments of the Court relating to denial of full back-wages to temporary workers found to have been wrongfully terminated from service have been criticized on the ground of overlooking the plight of the workers.[61]

All in all, the labour jurisprudence of the Supreme Court in the first decade of the new millennium is said to have diluted and undermined labour rights.[62] This in turn is alleged to have led to the working class losing faith in the judiciary and no longer viewing it as their last bastion of hope.[63]

11.4 Judgement in Harjinder Singh – a turning point?

The widespread criticism of the shift in approach of the Court soon found echoes in the Court itself. In an introspective vein, in the case of *Harjinder Singh vs. Punjab State Warehousing* Corporation,[64] where an order of reinstatement with backwages for a temporary worker illegally terminated from service was upheld, a Division Bench of the Court acknowledged that there had indeed been a shift in the approach of the Court in labour cases and that it had been brought about by the policies of globalization and liberation. In the court's words:

> Of late, there has been a visible shift in the courts' approach in dealing with cases involving the interpretation of social welfare legislations. The attractive mantras of globalisation and liberalisation are fast becoming the raison d'être of the judicial process and an impression has been created that the constitutional courts are no longer sympathetic towards the plight of industrial and unorganised workers.

One of the judges on the Bench in his supplementing judgment stated that 'At this critical juncture the Judges' duty, to my mind, is to uphold the constitutional focus on social justice without being in any way misled by the glitz and glare of globalization.'

The judgment in said to have raised the hopes of the trade union movement in the country.[65] Observers however wondered whether it would mark a real shift in the approach of the court to labour related issues or just remain a flash in the pan.[66]

11.4.1 Exceptional cases that had bucked the trend even earlier

The question that would obviously arise at this point is whether the observations of the Court in *Harjinder Singh* have led to any course correction or decisive change. Put in other words, is there any significant difference in the labour jurisprudence of the Court in the decade leading up to *Harjinder Singh* and thereafter. Before taking a look at the post-*Harjinder Singh* labour jurisprudence of the Court, it would be important to point out that there are cases even prior to the judgment in *Harjinder Singh* where the Court had adopted a different approach. These include cases where different Benches of the Court had departed from the leading judgments referred to above on the basis that the facts of the case at hand were different. Some such examples are discussed below.

In *Trambak Rubber Industries Ltd. vs. Nashik Workers Union*[67] taking note of the fact that all the workers in a factory had been designated as trainees, the Court observed as follows:

> It would be impossible to believe that the entire production activity was being carried on with none other than the so-called trainees. If there were trainees, there should have been trainers too. The management evidently came forward with a false plea dubbing the employees/workmen as trainees so as to resort to summary termination and deny the legitimate benefits. On the facts and evidence brought on record, the conclusion was inescapable that the appellant employer resorted to unfair labour practice.

The Court therefore upheld the order of the High Court directing reinstatement of the concerned workers.

In *U.P. State Electricity Board vs. Pooran Chandra Pandey*,[68] a Division Bench of the Court observed that the *Umadevi* judgment could not be mechanically applied without considering the particular facts of each case. It held that the judgment in *Umadevi* would have no application when regularization was sought on the basis of the principles of equality and non-discrimination. However, a larger Bench of the Court in *Official Liquidator vs. Dayanand*[69] held that the judgment in *U.P. State Electricity Board vs. Pooran Chandra Pandey* should not be treated as binding and should be read as obiter. The Court also stressed on the need for judicial discipline by way of adherence to binding precedents. In *ONGC vs. ONGC Contractual Workers Union*,[70] the Court upheld the order of the Industrial Tribunal lifting the veil and holding that the workers in question were workers of ONGC and directing their regularization in the service of ONGC.

In *Maharashtra State Road Transport Corporation and another vs. Casteribe Rajya Parivahan Karamchari Sangthatan*,[71] the Court held that the judgment in the *Umadevi case* does not denude the industrial and labour courts of their statutory power to order permanency of the workers who have been victims of unfair labour practice. Industrial courts can therefore order permanency of workers in public employment affected by unfair labour practices, irrespective of the *Umadevi* judgment. The judgment has thus 'greatly softened the *Umadevi* blow.'[72]

In *Divisional Manager, New India Assurance Co. Ltd. vs. A. Sankaralingam*,[73] (2008) 10 SCC 698, the Court upheld an award for reinstatement with backwages of a worker alleged to be a part time worker who was terminated from service in violation of section 25-F of the IDA. In *Novartis India Ltd. vs. State of West Bengal*[74] (2009) 3 SCC 124, the Court upheld the award of the Industrial Tribunal directing payment of full back-wages to two workers who had been unlawfully dismissed from service and also indicated that payment of back-wages should be calculated on the basis of revised wages and not last drawn wages.

The aforesaid examples would make it clear that the entire labour jurisprudence of the court related to workers in the formal sector in the decade leading up to *Harjinder Singh* cannot be blanketly categorized as 'anti-worker" or as being against the interests of workers.

11.4.2 Labour jurisprudence of the Court post-Harjinder Singh

This section now goes on to examine whether or not the judgment in *Harjinder Singh* has signalled a new era. Following the *Harjinder Singh* judgment, there are cases where the Court has upheld workers' rights or made observations in favour of workers. Some such examples are discussed below:

11.4.2.1 Examples of cases where court upheld workers' rights or made observations in favour of workers

In *Bhilwara Dugdh Utpadak Sahakaris Ltd. vs. Vinod Kumar Sharma*,[75] where the employer denied any employer-employee relationship with the concerned workers, the Court made the following observation:

> In order to avoid their liability under various labour statutes, employers are often resorting to subterfuge by trying to show that their employees are that of a contractor. It is high time that this subterfuge must come to an end. Labour Statutes were meant to protect the employees/workmen because it was realized that the employers and the employees are not in an equal bargaining position. Hence, protection of employees was required so that they may not be exploited. However, this new technique of subterfuge has been

adopted by some employers in recent years in order to deny the rights of the workmen under various labour statutes by showing that the concerned workmen are not their employees but are the employees/ workmen of a contractor, or that they are merely daily wage or short term or casual employees when in fact they are doing the work of regular employees. This Court cannot countenance such practices anymore. Globalization/liberalization in the name of growth cannot be at the human cost of exploitation of workers.

The Court in that case upheld the order of the finding of the Labour Court that the concerned workers were the workers of the principal employer and not the contractor.

In *Bajaj Auto Ltd. vs. Rajendra Kumar Jagannatha Kathari*,[76] the Court held that the practice of the company in adopting a rotational system whereby workers were employed for only seven months a year and then terminated from service so that they could not complete 240 days of continuous service and be entitled to protection under the IDA was held to be an unfair labour practice. Consequently, the High Court's order awarding compensation to the affected workers was upheld. In *Sunil Kumar Ghosh and others vs. K. Ram Chandran and others*,[77] a case where the ownership of a factory was transferred from one company to another without the consent of the concerned workers, the Court held that the workers could not be forced to work under another employer unless they had consented to that. On that basis, it upheld the order of the High Court directing the payment of all retirement benefits to the workers. In *Delhi International Airport (P) Ltd. vs. Union of India*,[78] (2011) 12 SCC 449, the Court held that Delhi International Airport (P) Ltd. (DIAL), a private entity that took over the Delhi Airport under an Operation, Management and Development Agreement would be bound by a central government notification issued under the Contract Labour Act prohibiting the employment of contract labour by the Airport Authority of India (AAI) in the Delhi Airport for the work of trolley retrieval, and that therefore DIAL could not engage contract labour for trolley retrieval work.

In *Deepali Gundu Surwase vs. Kranti Junior Adhyapak Mahavidyalaya*[79] concerning the termination from service of a school teacher, the Supreme Court restored the order of the School Tribunal directing payment of full back-wages along with reinstatement. It observed:

The courts must keep in mind that in cases of wrongful or illegal termination, the wrongdoer is the employer and the sufferer is the employee/workman and there is no justification to give a premium to the employer of his wrongdoing by relieving him of the burden to pay to the employee/workman his dues in the form of full backwages.

In *Anoop Sharma vs. Executive Engineer, Public Health Division No.1, Panipat (Haryana)*,[80] a case where a casual worker had been terminated from service in violation of section 25-F of the Industrial Disputes Act, the Court upheld the award of the Labour Court for reinstatement with payment of back-wages and held that the High Court was not justified in relying upon the alleged illegality of employment of the appellant for upsetting the award of reinstatement.

In *U. S. Rajasekaran vs. State Bank of Mysore*,[81] holding that *Umadevi* would have no application to the peculiar facts of the case of the petitioner as it was founded on the right to equality and non-discrimination, the Court directed the respondent bank to grant him permanency on the basis that he had put in a service of 240 days in a block of 12 calendar months. In *Union of India vs. Vartak Labour Union*,[82] even while a Division Bench of the Court followed the ruling in *Umadevi*, it observed that the conduct of Border Roads Organization, the employer in engaging casual workers for long periods with artificial breaks does not behove the Union of India and its instrumentalities, which are supposed to be model employers. The Court also expressed the hope that the government would consider enacting a scheme for absorption and regularization of the casual workers engaged by the Border Roads Organization.

11.4.2.2 Per contra

On the other hand, the leading judgments on labour rights issues in the first decade of the new millennium, that is, the judgments in *SAIL, Umadevi, BALCO* and *T.K. Rangarajan* still continue to hold the field and are followed while deciding cases of a similar nature.[83] Other judgments of that period, in respect of issues such as that of grant of relief to casual and temporary workers in cases of unlawful termination, also continue to be followed.[84] Besides, there are some rulings where the Court does not appear to have been sympathetic to workers and their concerns. A couple of such rulings are discussed below:

Designation of workers as officers: In the process of reorganizing its work pattern, the management of Siemens Limited had invited applications from the workers of a unit in the company to undergo training for a two year period as Officer Trainees and thereafter be designated as Junior Executive Officers.

According to the Siemens Employees Union, although the designation of Junior Executive Officer belonged to the managerial cadre, the job description of the post was largely that of a worker. It would therefore result in a reduction of job opportunities for workers. The union also alleged that the introduction of the scheme was contrary to the terms of a settlement of 1982 as per which officers or managerial staff shall not be asked to normal production work. The Siemens Employees Union therefore filed a case alleging that the introduction of the promotional scheme amounted to an unfair labour practice under the Maharashtra Recognition of Trade Unions and Prevention of Unfair Labour Practices Act, 1971. The case went up to the Supreme Court and in *Siemens Ltd. vs. Siemens Employees Union*,[85] the Court examined the issue of whether the introduction of the promotional scheme amounted to an unfair labour practice.

The Court held that when by way of rearrangement of work, the management gives promotional opportunities to the existing workers, merely because some of the work of the executive officers would be the same as that of existing workers, it would not amount to an unfair labour practice. The Court made the following observation in its judgment:

> It is also to be kept in mind that in the changed economic scenario, the concept of unfair labour practice is also required to be understood in the changed context. Today every State, which has to don the mantle of a welfare State, must keep in mind that twin objectives of industrial peace and economic justice and the courts and statutory bodies while deciding what unfair labour practice is must also be cognizant of the aforesaid twin objects.

Proportionality of punishment: The case of *Manoj H. Mishra vs. Union of India*[86] concerned the General Secretary of the union of Class III and IV employees at the Kakarapar Atomic Power Project in Surat, Gujarat, who was also a worker in the plant. He had written a letter to the editor of a newspaper about an incident in 1994 when flood water had entered the plant. In the letter, he suggested that officials in the plant had been negligent. He also stated that no proper arrangements were in place for meeting such natural calamities. Disciplinary proceedings were initiated against him on the grounds of unauthorized communication with the press, criticizing the project management and causing embarrassment to the project authorities and he was dismissed from service. The Supreme Court rejected the contention of the worker that he had acted as a whistleblower opining that he was educated only up to the twelfth standard and

310 | Ramapriya Gopalakrishnan

not an expert on the functioning of atomic energy plants. The Court also took the view that the worker had failed to maintain the level of confidentiality and discretion that was required to be maintained by an employee of the plant. On that basis, the Court upheld his dismissal from service rejecting the contention that the punishment was unjustified and disproportionate to the gravity of the charges levelled against him.

11.4.3 Court's approach post-Harjinder Singh

Summing up, following the judgment in *Harjinder Singh*, there have been several cases in which the Court has interpreted and applied the law so as to further workers' interests. At the same time, there are rulings where the court has not been sympathetic to the interests of workers that labour activists may categorize as 'anti-worker.' Moreover, the leading rulings in the period between 2000 and 2010 still continue to hold the field. In the circumstances, it appears that there is no one uniform approach post-*Harjinder Singh* nor has that been the case prior to the ruling in *Harjinder Singh*. Given these facts, it cannot be categorically said that post-*Harjinder Singh*, the dominant trend evident in the period from 2000–10 does not hold sway today.

11.5 Court's approach in cases concerning particularly disadvantaged groups of workers

The cases discussed up to this point in the chapter largely relate to informal as well as formal workers in the formal sector. It would now be of interest to examine the approach of the court to workers in the informal sector.

Over the last three decades, a number of public interest litigation (PIL) actions have been instituted before the Supreme Court to protect the rights of marginalized groups of workers such as bonded labourers, child labourers, construction workers etc. This section discusses the Court's approach to such cases during the period under review on the basis of some examples.

In *National Campaign Committee for Central Legislation on Construction Labour vs. Union of India*,[87] a PIL seeking effective implementation of the Building and Other Construction Workers (Regulation of Employment and Conditions of Service) Act, 1996, the Court issued directions for the establishment of welfare boards and registration centres in each district. It also directed that regular meetings of the Board be held and that programmes be conducted to bring about awareness of the provisions of the Act.

In *Centre for Environment and Food Security vs. Union of India*,[88] a PIL filed against the central and state governments for formulation of appropriate schemes and proper utilization of funds allocated under the National Rural Employment Guarantee Act, finding that the government of Orissa had failed to effectively implement the provisions of the Act, the Court directed compliance report to be filed by state of Orissa in respect of the funds allocated, utilization of funds, number of persons employed and paid allowances under the Act. The Court also directed the CBI directed to conduct a comprehensive investigation into the implementation of the Act in 6 districts in Orissa.

In *Delhi Jal Board vs. National Campaign for Dignity & Rights of Sewerage and Allied Workers*[89] where a direction for payment of compensation to the families of deceased sewage workers was questioned by the Board, the Court issued directions for payment of enhanced compensation. It also upheld the directions of the High Court for provision of medical treatment free of charge; compensation to workers who suffer on account of occupational illness or accident, provision of protective equipment, issue of employment cards etc. In *Gainda Ram vs. Municipal Corporation of Delhi*,[90] the Court recognized the fundamental right of hawkers to carry on their business and the need for a law to regulate this right. Noting that a Model Street Vendors (Protection of Livelihood and Regulation of Street Vending) Bill had been framed, it directed the government to bring out a law to regulate hawking.

In *Public Union for Civil Liberties vs. State of Tamil Nadu*,[91] the Court directed the government to have periodical surveys with a view to eradicate bonded labour conducted by District Vigilance Committees, to submit reports to the National Human Rights Commission (NHRC), to ensure effective implementation of the Minimum Wages Act, the Inter-State Migrant Workers Act and the Child Labour (Prohibition and Regulation) Act. It also directed the NHRC to effectively monitor the implementation of the provisions of the Act. In *Bachpan Bachao Andolan vs. Union of India*,[92] a case highlighting the plight of children employed in circuses, the Court directed the central government to issue the necessary notifications to prohibit the employment of children in circuses within a period of two months. It also directed the government to conduct simultaneous raids on circuses to rescue children employed there, and to prepare a proper scheme for the rehabilitation of rescued children.

11.5.1 Cases concerning women workers

While attempting to assess the Court's approach, it is important to take a look at the manner in which the Court has dealt with cases concerning only women workers as well. A few such cases are discussed below:

In *Air India Cabin Crew Association and others vs. Union of India and others*,[93] the Court upheld the policy decision of Air India to bring about parity in the conditions of air hostesses and flight pursers, their male counterparts by permitting air hostesses to perform flying duties up to the age of 58 years and allowing them to be designated as in-flight supervisors, on the basis that it was the prerogative of the management to place an employee in a position where he or she would be able to contribute the most to the company. The judgment has been hailed as an important milestone in the fight against discrimination by Air India's female employees (Kalpana Sharma in a The Hindu article on 26 November 2011, 'The Other Half – Another Battle Won'). However, earlier in July 2003, in the judgment in *Air India Cabin Crew Association vs. Yashaswinee Merchant*,[94] the Court rejected the contention that the early age retirement policy for air hostesses in Air India whereby unlike their male counterparts, they could perform flying duties only up to the age of 50 years and thereafter have the option of accepting ground duties amounted to discrimination on the basis of sex. In that case, the Court proceeded on the basis that the terms and conditions of the workers of Air India were governed by settlements and awards and no decision could be taken contrary to that.

In *Medha Kotwal Lele vs. Union of India*,[95] taking note of the fact that the guidelines issued earlier in *Vishaka vs. State of Rajasthan*[96] to prevent the sexual harassment of women at the workplace and address complaints of sexual harassment of women had not been effectively complied with although it was 15 years since the guidelines had been issued, the Court directed the governments of various states to ensure that complaints committees were duly constituted and that necessary instructions were issued to statutory bodies to comply with the guidelines. It also directed the state governments that were yet to effect appropriate amendments to the government servants conduct rules and the Industrial Employment (Standing Orders) Act to do so. In *Seema Lepcha vs. State of* Sikkim,[97] the Court directed the government of Sikkim to give wide publicity to the measures taken for implementation of the *Vishaka* guidelines.

In *Municipal Corporation of Delhi vs. Female Workers* (Muster Roll),[98] the Court considered the issue of entitlement of daily wage women workers of the

Municipal Corporation of Delhi to maternity benefit. The Corporation took the stand that the Maternity Benefits Act, 1961 would not be applicable to daily wage workers. It also contended that the Corporation was not an establishment covered by the Act. The Court held that daily wage workers would also be entitled to the benefits under the Act. Furthermore, it held that the principles contained in Art.11 of the Convention on Elimination of All Forms of Discrimination Against Women (CEDAW) must be read into the contract of service between the Municipal Corporation and the workers so that they immediately become entitled to the benefits under the Act.

11.6 Conclusion

Undoubtedly, there has been a shift in the approach of the Supreme Court to labour related issues in the first decade of the new millennium. There has been a significant change in the manner in which the Court has interpreted and applied labour legislation during the period. This has been acknowledged by the Court itself in its rulings in a few cases. The Court has also indicted that it is the prevailing economic policies that have led to the change in approach. As stated earlier in this chapter, the shift in approach in particularly apparent in cases having a bearing on the policies of flexibilization and privatization; cases involving the collective rights of workers, cases relating to industrial discipline and cases concerning the unlawful termination of workers from service. It is obvious from some of its rulings that the Court has been wary of imposing any 'undue financial burden' on the employer and impeding the growth of industry.

However, there are cases during that period where the Court had departed from the dominant trend, taken a different perspective and ruled to protect workers' interests. These include cases where management strategies to disguise employment relationships and evade labour laws have been questioned, cases relating to permanency for temporary workers and the grant of the relief of reinstatement and/or back-wages to unlawfully terminated workers.

Following the 2010 ruling of the Court in *Harjinder Singh vs. Punjab State Warehousing Corporation* had stressed on the need to decide labour related cases keeping in mind constitutional principles, there are several cases where the Court has interpreted and applied the law so as to uphold the rights of workers. At the same time, there are cases where the Court has adopted an approach that may be viewed as unsympathetic to workers.

While there has been a shift in approach to cases relating to the rights of informal workers as well as formal workers in the formal sector, in respect of cases concerning workers in the informal sector seeking the implementation of labour welfare laws where there is no sharp conflict between the interests of employers and workers, the approach of the Court seems to have been no different than what it was in earlier decades. The Court has adopted a progressive approach in cases concerning marginalized workers such as street vendors and sewage workers.

In cases concerning women workers in particular, the Court had adopted a progressive approach in respect of the grant of maternity benefits to workers on daily wages. In the case relating to women employees of Air India decided in 2011 that has been referred to above, even while affirming the judgment of the High Court founded on the principles of equality and non-discrimination, the Court appears to have given greater importance to the 'prerogative of the management' to decide on work-related policies and the service conditions of workers rather than the right of women to equality and non-discrimination.[99]

On an overall analysis, it may be concluded that from between 2000 and 2010, the Court had departed from precedent and adopted a new approach in respect of some important issues concerning workers in the formal sector in the light of the change in the economic climate in the country. However, at the same time, there were cases where the court had upheld the rights of workers and protected their interests. The last three years have seen a mix of cases where the Court has upheld workers' rights as well as cases where the Court does not appears to have been sensitive to workers' concerns. Furthermore, the landmark judgments of the Court on labour rights issues during that period continue to hold sway to this day. In other words, the Supreme Court's judgments on labour related issues at present are a mixed bag.

Endnotes

1   K. R. Shyam Sundar, *Non-regular Workers in India: Social Dialogue and Organizational and Bargaining Strategies*, 4,8, 11,12 (Geneva: ILO, 2011).

2   Ibid, 11–12, also see *Society for Labour and Development, A Study of the Contract Labour System in the Garment Industry in Gurgaon*, 18 (New Delhi, 2012).

3   Rajeev, Meenakshi, Contract Labour in India: A Pragmatic View, IGIDR Proceedings/Project Report Series, August 2009, online at www.igidr.ac.in/pdf/publication/PP-062-33.pdf (last accessed on 17 February 2014); K.R. Shyam Sundar, 'The Contract Labour in India, The Battle between Flexibility and Fairness', in Contract Labour in India, Issues and Perspectives, edited by K. R. Shyam Sundar, 60–61 (Daanish Books, 2012); 'A Study of the Contract Labour

System in the Garment Industry in Gurgaon', ibid, 18; ILO, *Towards an Employment Strategy for India*, 25–26 (Geneva: ILO, 2009).

4   For example, see J. C. B. Annavajhula and Surenedra Pratap, 'Worker Voices in an Auto Production Chain', *Economic and Political Weekly* XLVII(33): 46, 56 (18 August 2012). Also see K. R. Shyam Sundar, *Non-regular Workers in India*, supra n. 1: 4, 42, 43.

5   *Towards an Employment Strategy for India*, supra 3:44; 'A Study of the Contract Labour System in the Garment Industry in Gurgaon', supra n. 2:15, 44.

6   Shyam Sundar, supra n.1:19.

7   Shyam Sundar, supra n.3:37–40.

8   Government of India, Ministry of Labour and Employment, *Report of the Second National Commission on Labour*, 363, 348–49 (paras.6.84, 6.85 and 6.109) (New Delhi, 2002).

9   A. N. Sharma, *Flexibility, Employment and Labour Market Reforms*, XLI(21): 2078 at 2083 (27 May 2006).

10   G. Singh, 'Judiciary Jettisons Working Class', *Combat Law* 7(6) (Nov-Dec 2008): 24 at 29

11   Ibid, 24

12   See R. Gopalakrishnan, 'Enforcing Labour Rights through Human Rights Norms: The Approach of the Supreme Court of India', in *Human Rights at Work: Perspectives on Law and Regulation*, edited by Fenwick and Novitz, 195 (Oxford: Hart Publlshing, 2010).

13   For example, see P. Jha, 'State's Growing Intolerance towards Labour in India: A Note Based on Some Recent Developments', *The Indian Journal of Labour Economics* 48(4) (2005): 897 at 907.

14   V. Kumar, 'Co-opted by Globalization', *Combat Law* 7(6) (Nov–Dec 2008): 114; N. G. R. Prasad, 'Protect Thy Worker', *Combat Law* 7(6) (Nov–Dec 2008): 86.

15   P. Karat, 'Supreme Court in Liberalized Times', 9 August 2003, available at: http://www.countercurrents.org/hr-karat090803.htm, last accessed on 17 February 2014. Also see P. Bhushan, 'Supreme Court and PIL: Changing Perspectives under Liberalization', *Economic and Political Weekly* (XXXIX(18) (2004): 1772.

16   A. N. Sharma, supra n. 9: 2083.

17   Steel Authority of India Limited vs. National Union Waterfront Workers, (2001) 7 SCC 1.

18   Air India Statutory Corporation vs. United Labour Union, (1997) 9 SCC 377.

19   Uttar Pradesh Rajya Vidyut Utpadan Board vs. Uttar Pradesh Vidyut Mazdoor Sangh, (2009) 17 SCC 318.

20   Umadevi vs. State of Karnataka, (2006) 4 SCC 1.

21   Dharwad District Literate PWD Daily Wage Employees Association vs. State of Karnataka, (1990) 2 SCC 396.

22   Daily Rated Casual Labour vs. Union of India, (1988) 1 SCC 122.

23   State Bank of India vs. N. Sundara Money, (1976) 1 SCC 822s

24   L. Robert d'Souza vs. Executive Engineer, Southern Railway and Another, (1982) 1 SCC 645.

25   Haryana State Electronics Corporation Ltd. vs. Mamni, (2006) 9 SCC 434,

26   Madhya Pradesh State Administration vs. Tribhuban, (2007) 9 SCC 748.

27   Jagbir Singh vs. Haryana State Agricultural Marketing Board, (2009) 15 SCC 327.

28 BALCO Employees Union vs. Union of India, (2002) 2 SCC 333.

29 National Textile Workers Union vs. P. R. Ramakrishnan, (1983) 1 SCC 228.

30 T.K. Rangarajan vs. Government of Tamil Nadu, (2003) 6 SCC 581.

31 All India Bank Employees Association vs. The National Industrial Tribunal (Bank Disputes) AIR, 1962 SC 171.

32 Radhey Shyam Sharma vs. Post Master General AIR, 1965 SC 311.

33 B. R. Singh vs. Union of India, (1989) 4 SCC 710.

34 UPSRTC vs. Vinod Kumar, (2008) 1 SCC 115; LIC of India vs. R. Dhandapani, (2006) 13 SCC 613.

35 Deputy Manager, APSRTC vs. B. Swamy, (2007) 12 SCC 40.

36 UPSRTC vs. Motilal, (2003) 3 SCC 605.

37 Hombe Gowda Educational Trust vs. State of Karnataka, (2006) 1 SCC 430.

38 Arkal Govind Raj Rao vs. Ciba Geigy of India Limited, (1985) 3 SCC 371.

39 Hussainbhai vs. Alath Factory Thezhilali Union, (1978) 4 SCC 357.

40 National Small Industries Corporation Ltd. vs. V. Lakshminarayanan, (2007) 1 SCC 214.

41 The judgment in Mukesh Tripathi vs. LIC, (2004) 8 SCC 387 that overruled the judgment in Arkal Govind Raj Rao vs. Ciba Geigy of India Limited, (1985) 3 SCC 371, S. K. Verma, (1983) 4 SCC 213 and Ved Prakash Gupta vs. Delton Cable, (1984) 2 SCC 569.

42 State of U.P. vs. Jai Bir Singh, (2005) 5 SCC 1.

43 Bangalore Water Supply and Sewerage Board vs. A. Rajappa, (1978) 2 SCC 213.

44 Umadevi vs. State of Karnataka, (2006) 4 SCC 1.

45 State of U.P. vs. Jai Bir Singh, (2005) 5 SCC 1.

46 Hombe Gowda Educational Trust vs. State of Karnataka, (2006) 1 SCC 430.

47 State of U.P. vs. Jai Bir Singh, (2005) 5 SCC 1.

48 Hombe Gowda Educational Trust vs. State of Karnataka, (2006) 1 SCC 430.

49 L. Sharath Babu and R. Shetty, *Social Justice and Labour Jurisprudence*, 45 (New Delhi: Sage Publications, 2007).

50 Ibid, 47.

51 Singh, supra n.10: 33.

52 Kumar, supra n.14: 114 at p.117.

53 Babu and Shetty, supra n.46: 47; Prasad, supra n.14: 88.

54 Singh, supra n.10: 25.

55 T. S. Papola, 'Contract Labour: An Academic Perspective', in *Contract Labour in India*, edited by Shyam Sundar supra n.3: 77 at p.81.

56 Singh, supra n.10: 25.

57 Singh, supra n.10: 26.

58 Singh, supra n.10: 31.

59 P. Bidwai, 'A Blow to Citizenship Rights', *Frontline* 20(17) (16–29 August 2003), available at: www.frontline.in/static/html/fl2017/stories/20030829006912700.htm, last accessed on 17 February 2014.

60 Ibid.

61 Ibid.

62 Supra n. 10.

63 S. Singhvi, 'Supreme Court: Friend No More', *Combat Law* 7(6) (November-December 2008): 126, 129.

64 Harjinder Singh vs. Punjab State Warehousing Corporation, (2010) 3 SCC 192.

65 S. Viswanathan, 'Time for Judges to Revisit Directive Principles', *The Hindu*, Chennai edition, (1 March 2010).

66 V. Venkatesan, 'Introspection Time', *Frontline* 27(4), (13–26 February 2010); M. J. Antony, 'Labour Law Muddle', *Business Standard* (3 February 2010).

67 Trambak Rubber Industries Limited vs. Nashik Workers' Union, (2003) 6 SCC 416.

68 U.P. State Electricity Board vs. Pooran Chandra Pandey, (2007) 11 SCC 92.

69 Official Liquidator vs. Dayanand, (2008) 10 SCC 1.

70 ONGC vs. ONGC Contractual Workers Union, (2008) 12 SCC 275.

71 Maharashtra State Road Transport Corporation vs. Casteribe Rajya Parivahan Karamchari Sanghatan, (2009) 8 SCC 556.

72 J. Cox, 'With Eyes Wide Open: Recent Trends in Supreme Court Labour and Industrial Judgments', in *Contract Labour in India*, edited by Shyam Sundar, supra n.3: 109 at 121.

73 Divisional Manager, New India Assurance Company Limited vs. A. Sankaralingam, (2008) 10 SCC 698.

74 Novartis India Limited vs. State of West Bengal, (2009) 3 SCC 124.

75 Bhilwara Dugdh Utpadak Sahakaris Ltd. vs. Vinod Kumar Sharma, (2011) 10 SCR 819.

76 Bajaj Auto Ltd. vs. Rajendra Kumar Jagannatha Kattar, (2013) 5 SCC 691.

77 Sunil Kumar Ghosh and Others vs. K. Ram Chandran and Others, (2011) 14 SCC 320.

78 Delhi International Airport Private Limited vs. Union of India, (2011) 12 SCC 449.

79 Deepali Gundu Surwase vs. Kranti Junior Adhyapak Mahavidyalaya, (2013) 3 SCC 780.

80 Anoop Sharma vs. Executive Engineer, Public Health Division No. 1, Panipat (Haryana), (2010) 5 SCC 497.

81 H.S. Rajashekara vs. State Bank of Mysore, (2012) 1 SCC 285.

82 Union of India vs. Vartak Labour Union, (2011) 4 SCC 200.

83 For example, the judgment in Umadevi was followed in Union of India vs. ArulmozhiInaiarasu, (2011) 7 SCC 397 and State of U.P. vs. Rekha Rani, (2011) 11 SCC 441.

84 For example, in BSNL vs. Man Singh, (2012) 1 SCC 558 and Rajasthan Development Corporation vs. Gitam Singh, (2013) 5 SCC 136, the Court held that in the case of unlawful termination of a daily wage worker, monetary compensation would meet the ends of justice.

85 Siemens Ltd. vs. Siemens Employees Union, (2011) 9 SCC 775.

86 Manoj H. Mishra vs. Union of India, (2013) 6 SCC 213.

87 National Campaign Committee for Central Legislation on Construction Labour vs. Union of India, (2009) 3 SCC 269, (2011) 4 SCC 653, (2011) 4 SCC 655, (2012) 3 SCC 336.

88 Centre for Environment and Food Security vs. Union of India, (2011) 5 SCC 676, (2011) 5 SCC 668.

89 Delhi Jal Board vs. National Campaign for Dignity & Rights of Sewerage and Allied Workers, (2011) 8 SCC 568.

90 Gainda Ram vs. Municipal Corporation of Delhi, (2010) 10 SCC 715.

91 Public Union for Civil Liberties vs. State of Tamil Nadu and others, (2013) 1 SCC 285.

92 Bachpan Bachao Andolan vs. Union of India, (2011) 5 SCC 1.

93 Air India Cabin Crew Association and others vs. Union of India and others, (2012) 1 SCC 619.

94 Air India Cabin Crew Association vs. Yeshaswinee Merchant, (2003) 6 SCC 277.

95 Medha Kotwal Lele vs. Union of India, (2013) 1 SCC 297.

96 Vishaka vs. State of Rajasthan, (1997) 6 SCC 241.

97 Seema Lepcha vs. State of Sikkim ,(2011) 13 SCC 641.

98 Municipal Corporation of Delhi vs. Female Workers (Muster Roll), (2000) 3 SCC 224.

99 supra n. 87.

Contributors

K. V. Ramaswamy is Professor at Indira Gandhi Institute of Development Research, Mumbai.

Jayan Jose Thomas is Assistant Professor at the Department of Humanities and Social Sciences at the Indian Institute of Technology, New Delhi.

Ajit K. Ghose is Professor at the Institute for Human Development, New Delhi.

Rana Hasan, Sneha Lamba and **Abhijit Sen Gupta** are part of the India Resident Mission of the Asian Development Bank, New Delhi.

M. R. Narayana is Professor of Economics at the Institute for Social and Economic Change, Bangalore.

Deb Kusum Das is Associate Professor in Economics at Ramjas College, University of Delhi. He is also associated with ICRIER, New Delhi as an external consultant.

Kunal Sen is Professor of Development Economics and Policy, The University of Manchester, UK.

Pilu Chandra Das is Lecturer in Economics at Dayal Singh Evening College, University of Delhi.

Bishwanath Goldar is Professor at the Institute of Economic Growth, Delhi.

Suresh Chand Aggarwal is Professor, Department of Business Economics, University of Delhi.

Bibhas Saha is Senior Lecturer at the Department of Economics, University of East Anglia, Norwich, UK.

Jaivir Singh is Associate Professor at the Centre for the Study of Law and Governance, Jawaharlal Nehru University, New Delhi.

Ramapriya Gopalakrishnan is a lawyer in Madras High court, Chennai.

Index

Printed in the United States
by Baker & Taylor Publisher Services